LEARNING AND YOUR LIFE

Essentials of Student Success

Robert S. Feldman
Danica Lavoie

Canadian Edition

McGraw-Hill Ryerson
Connect. Learn. Succeed.

P.O.W.E.R. LEARNING AND YOUR LIFE: ESSENTIALS FOR STUDENT SUCCESS
CANADIAN EDITION

ISBN-13: 978-0-07-092351-5
ISBN-10: 0-07-092351-5

1 2 3 4 5 6 7 8 9 10 QDB 1 9 8 7 6 5 4 3 2

Printed and bound in the United States of America

Care has been taken to trace ownership of copyright material contained in this text; however, the publisher will welcome any information that enables them to rectify any reference or credit for subsequent editions.

Publisher: *Cara Yarzab*
Sponsoring Editor: *Karen Krahn*
Marketing Manager: *Margaret Janzen*
Developmental Editor: *Sara Braithwaite*
Senior Editorial Associate: *Marina Seguin*
iLearning Slaes Specialist: *Lisa Gillman*
Photo/Permissions Editor: *Indu Arora*
Supervising Editor: *Graeme Powell*
Copy Editor: *Elspeth McFadden*
Production Coordinator: *Sheryl MacAdam*
Cover and Interior Design: *Laserwords Private Limited*
Cover Credit: *Back cover (left to right): Cultura RF/Getty Images; © Stockbyte/PunchStock; PBNJ Productions/ age fotostock; © Flying Colours Ltd/Getty Images. Front cover (left to right): BananaStock/Jupiter Images; © Creatas Images/Jupiter Images; Terry Vine/Blend Images/Punchstock; Blend Images/Getty Images*
Page Layout: *Laserwords Private Limited*
Printer: *Quad/Graphics*

Library and Archives Canada Cataloguing in Publication

Feldman, Robert S. (Robert Stephen), 1947-
    P.O.W.E.R. learning and your life : essentials for student success / Robert S. Feldman, Danica Lavoie.
    — Canadian ed.
    Includes bibliographical references and index.
    ISBN 978-0-07-092351-5

    1. College student orientation. 2. Study skills. 3. College students—Life skills guides. I. Lavoie, Danica
    II. Title. III. Title: POWER learning and your life.
LB2343.3.F443 2012
378.1'98   C2011-905897-9

ROBERT S. FELDMAN

Professor Feldman is a Fellow of both the American Psychological Association and the Association for Psychological Science. He is a winner of a Fulbright Senior Research Scholar and Lecturer award and has written some 100 scientific articles, book chapters, and books. His books include *Improving the First Year of College: Research and Practice; Understanding Psychology*, 9/e; and *Development Across the Life Span*, 5/e. One of his most recent publications, *Psychology and Your Life*, afforded Professor Feldman an opportunity to work closely with returning and commuter students. It was through that experience that he devoted research and development to applying the P.O.W.E.R. Plan.

Professor Feldman's research interests encompass the study of honesty and truthfulness in everyday life, development of non-verbal behaviour in children, and the social psychology of education. His research has been supported by grants from the National Institute of Mental Health and the National Institute on Disabilities and Rehabilitation Research.

Professor Feldman occupies his spare time with serious cooking and earnest, but admittedly unpolished, piano playing. He also loves to travel. He lives with his wife, who is an educational psychologist, in a home overlooking the Holyoke mountain range in western Massachusetts.

DANICA LAVOIE

At the tender age of 17, Danica Lavoie left Dalhousie, a town in northern New Brunswick (population 3600), to attend Humber College in Toronto (population 2 million). It was there that she encountered some remarkable professors—Michael Hatton, Pam Hanft, and Wayson Choy—who inspired her and encouraged her to continue her studies. She went on to complete an Honours Bachelor of Arts in Psychology from the University of Waterloo; a Master of Business Administration from York University's Faculty of Administrative Studies, now known as the Schulich School of Business; and later on, a Teacher of Adults Certificate from Ryerson University.

While studying for her MBA, Danica was offered the opportunity by one of her former professors to teach part-time at Humber College. Only 22 at the time, it was this teaching experience that many years later motivated her to return to the classroom after a successful career in banking and as an entrepreneur. Currently, Professor Lavoie teaches marketing and business courses at Centennial College in Toronto, at both the undergraduate and graduate level. She has never regretted moving from her lucrative business career into teaching, noting that "every semester is different, and every day brings a chance to make a difference in a student's life."

Professor Lavoie lives just outside Toronto with her husband Martin and her German Munsterlander dog, Marley. When she isn't teaching or writing, she enjoys cooking, travelling, and playing Scrabble on Facebook.

Brief Table of Contents

1 Becoming an Expert Student

2 Making the Most of Your Time

3 Reading and Remembering

4 Taking Notes

5 Taking Tests

6 Leveraging Technology and Doing Research

7 Writing and Presenting

8 Making Decisions and Solving Problems

9 Collaborating with Others

10 Managing Stress and Money

11 Planning Your Career (online)

Table of Contents

1 P.O.W.E.R. Learning: Becoming an Expert Student

Looking Ahead 2

The Benefits of a Post-secondary Education 2

    Try It! 1: Why Are You Going to College or University? 3

What Canadian Employers Value 5

P.O.W.E.R. Learning: Five Key Steps to Achieving Success 5

    Prepare 7

    Try It! 2: What Are Your Goals? 9

    Organize 10

    Course Connections
    Looking at the Big Picture 11

    Work 12

    Evaluate 13

    Try It! 3: Examining the Causes of Success and Failure
    WORKING IN A GROUP 14

    Rethink 15

    Career Connections
    P.O.W.E.R. Learning and the World of Work 16

Learning More about Yourself 17

    Try It! 4: What's Your Learning Style?
    ●●●●● PERSONAL STYLES 20

    Try It! 5: What Is Your Striving Style?
    ●●●●● PERSONAL STYLES 22

    Time to Reflect 29

    Looking Back 30

    Key Terms and Concepts 31

    Resources 31

    Taking It to the Net 32

    The Case of . . .
    Vexed in Vancouver 33

2 Making the Most of Your Time 34

Looking Ahead 35

Managing Your Time Effectively 35

    Try It! 1: Find Your Time Style
    ●●●●● PERSONAL STYLES 36

    Prepare: Learn Where Your Time is Going 36

Handling Competing Priorities 37

    Try It! 2: Create a Time Log 38

    Course Connections
    Study Time: How Much Is Enough? 40

    Try It! 3: Set Priorities 41

    Try It! 4: Urgent? Important? 42

Organize: Master the Moment   43

Work: Dealing with Surprises and Distractions   49

Try It! 5: Find Your Procrastination Quotient   53

Career Connections
On-the-job Time Management   55

Evaluate: Check Your Use of Time   56

Rethink: Reflect on Your Personal Style of Time Management   56

Time to Reflect   58

Looking Back   59

Key Terms and Concepts   59

Resources   59

Taking It to the Net   60

The Case of . . .
Time Crunched   61

3 Reading and Remembering   62

Looking Ahead   63

Sharpening Your Reading Skills   63

Prepare: Plan Your Approach   64

Try It! 1: Discover How Advance Organizers Help   65

Try It! 2: Create an Advance Organizer   67

Organize: Gather the Tools of the Trade   67

Try It! 3: Discover Your Attention Span
PERSONAL STYLES   69

Work: Get the Most out of Your Reading   70

Course Connections
Textbook Tips: Starting Off on the Right Page   71

Try It! 4: Mark Up a Book Page
WORKING IN A GROUP   74

Memorizing Key Material   76

Try It! 5: Do-it-yourself Acronyms and Acrostics   78

Evaluate: Evaluating What You Have Read   80

Career Connections
The Job of Reading   81

Rethink: Getting It the Second Time   82

Time to Reflect   83

Looking Back   84

Key Terms and Concepts   84

Resources   84

Taking it to the Net   85

The Case of . . .
The Five-pound Reading Packet   86

4 Taking Notes   87

Looking Ahead   88

Taking Notes in Class   88

Prepare: Consider Your Goals   88

Organize: Get the Tools of Note-taking Together   89

Work: Process—Don't Just Copy—Information   90

Try It! 1: Determine Your Listening Style
PERSONAL STYLES   91

Note-taking Methods to Use in Class 93

Try It! 2: Outline a Lecture
WORKING IN A GROUP 95

Evaluate: Think Critically about Your Notes 100

Try It! 3: Evaluate Your Class Notes 101

Course Connections
Note-taking: A Collaborative Approach 102

Rethink: Activate Your Memory 102

Try It! 4: Practise Your Note-taking Skills 103

Creating Study Notes 103

Career Connections
Taking Notes on the Job:
Meetings of the Minds 105

Time to Reflect 106

Looking Back 107

Key Terms and Concepts 107

Resources 107

Taking It to the Net 108

The Case of . . .
Not Missing a Thing 109

5 Taking Tests

Looking Ahead 111

What Tests Measure 111

Prepare: Preparing to Be Tested 112

Try It! 1: Complete a Test Preparation Checklist 116

Try It! 2: Form a Study Group
WORKING IN A GROUP 117

Try It! 3: Measure Your Test-taking Style
●●●●● PERSONAL STYLES 118

Course Connections
Special Techniques for Dealing with Math Anxiety 119

Organize: Reducing Anxiety on the Day of the Test 120

Work: Test-taking Strategies 121

Try It! 4: Understand Action Verbs in Essay Questions 125

Evaluate: Check Your Work 126

Career Connections
Tests for a Lifetime 127

Rethink: Post-test Analysis 128

Try It! 5: Take a Test on Taking Tests 130

Time to Reflect 132

Looking Back 133

Key Terms and Concepts 133

Resources 134

Taking It to the Net 135

The Case of . . .
That Sinking Feeling 136

6 Leveraging Technology and Doing Research

Looking Ahead   138

You and Technology   138

Course Connections
Getting the Most out of Instructors'
PowerPoint Presentations   144

Using Technology to Learn
at a Distance   145

Try It! 1: Assess Your Course-taking Style
●●●●● PERSONAL STYLES   146

**Prepare: Identify Distance Learning
Course Possibilities**   147

Try It! 2: Get Some Distance
on the Problem   148

Organize: Obtain Access to Technology   148

**Work: Participate in a Distance
Learning Class**   149

**Evaluate: Consider Your "Classroom"
Performance**   149

**Rethink: Reflect on What and
How You Learned**   149

Using Netiquette as You
Connect and Collaborate
with Others   150

Try It! 3: Using Email Netiquette   152

Developing Information
Competency   153

Try It! 4: Work the Web:
Information, Please!   157

Career Connections
Using the Web at Work   162

Plagiarism: What It Is
and How to Avoid It   162

A Final Word   164

Time to Reflect   165

Looking Back   166

Key Terms and Concepts   167

Resources   167

Taking It to the Net   168

The Case of . . .
The Empty Page   169

7 Writing and Presenting

Looking Ahead   171

Writing at the Post-
secondary Level   171

The Process of Writing   172

Prepare: Explore Your Topic   172

Try It! 1: Create a Mind Map   173

Organize: Create an Outline   173

Work: Write the Initial Draft   *173*

Try It! 2: Overcoming Writer's Block   *174*

Evaluate: Rest, Reread, Revise—
then Rest, Reread, and Revise Again   *174*

Rethink: Reflect on Instructor
Feedback   *175*

Creating and Delivering Effective Presentations   *178*

Try It! 3: Measuring Your Anxiety
about Speaking in Public   *179*

Course Connections
The 10 Dos and Don'ts of Making
Effective Presentations   *184*

A Final Word   *184*

Try It! 4: Getting Feedback
on Your Presentation   *185*

Career Connections
Presenting Yourself in a Job Interview   *185*

Time to Reflect   *187*

Looking Back   *188*

Key Terms and Concepts   *188*

Resources   *189*

Taking It to the Net   *189*

The Case of . . .
The "Creative" Presenter   *190*

8 Making Decisions and Solving Problems   *191*

Looking Ahead   *192*

Making Better Decisions: A Framework   *192*

Prepare: Examine Your Goals   *192*

**Organize: Consider and Assess
Your Alternatives**   *193*

Try It! 1: Use Freewriting   *194*

**Work: Make Your Decision
and Carry It Out**   *195*

Career Connections
Weighing Options   *197*

Evaluate: Consider the Outcome   *198*

**Rethink: Reconsider Your Goals
and Options**   *199*

Problem-Solving: Applying Critical Thinking to Find Solutions   *199*

Try It! 2: Exercise Your Problem-
Solving Skills

WORKING IN A GROUP   *202*

Applying Critical Thinking to Everyday Problems   *204*

Try It! 3: Distinguish Fact from Opinion   *206*

Course Connections
Using Critical Thinking in Your Classes   *207*

Try It! 4: What's the Real Explanation?   *208*

Time to Reflect   *210*

Looking Back   *211*

Key Terms and Concepts   *211*

Resources   *211*

Taking It to the Net   *213*

The Case of . . .
The Missing Roommate   *214*

9 Collaborating with Others

Looking Ahead 216

Working Productively
in Groups 216

**Prepare: Choose Group Members
Thoughtfully** 216

**Organize: Select a Topic for
a Group Project Creatively** 217

**Work: Determine How the Group
Will Function** 217

Try It! 1: Organize a Brainstorming
Session 218

**Evaluate: React Positively When
Things Don't Go as Planned** 219

Rethink: A Post-mortem Meeting 219

Communicating Well
with Others 220

Living in a Diverse World 221

Try It! 2: Determine the Diversity
of Your Community 224

Career Connections
Diversity in the Workplace 226

Course Connections
Diversity in the Classroom 229

Managing and Resolving
Conflicts 229

Try It! 3: Switch "You" to "I"
WORKING IN A GROUP 231

Time to Reflect 234

Looking Back 235

Key Terms and Concepts 235

Resources 236

Taking It to the Net 236

The Case of . . .
Keeping Your Mouth Shut 237

10 Managing Stress and Money

Looking Ahead 239

Living with Stress 239

Managing Stress 241

Try It! 1: Assess Your Level of
Mental Health 242

Try It! 2: Look for the Silver Lining 246

Managing Your Money 250

Try It! 3: Test Your Knowledge
of Personal Finance 251

Course Connections
Staying Alert in Class ... 252

**Prepare: Track the Money Coming
In and Going Out** ... 253

Organize: Prepare a Budget ... 254

Career Connections
Budgeting on the Job ... 257

Work: Balance Your Budget ... 257

**Evaluate: Review Your Budget
Regularly** ... 258

Try It! 4: Determine Your Saving Style
●●●●● PERSONAL STYLES ... 259

**Rethink: Revisit Your Budget When
Circumstances Change** ... 260

Using Credit Wisely ... 260

Time to Reflect ... 264

Looking Back ... 265

Key Terms and Concepts ... 266

Resources ... 266

Taking It to the Net ... 267

The Case of . . .
The Breaking Point ... 268

11 Planning Your Career Available online at McGraw-Hill Connect

Looking Ahead ... 2

Career Planning ... 2

Prepare: Identify Your Career Goals ... 2

Try It! 1: Identifying Your Long-term ... 3

Organize: Find Career Opportunities ... 4

Career Goals ... 3

Creating a Career Portfolio ... 5

Course Connections
Career Guides ... 6

Try It! 2: Cataloguing Your
Personal History ... 8

Try It! 3: Creating a Resume ... 12

**Evaluate: Career Portfolio, Part III:
Get Feedback on Your Resume
and Cover Letter** ... 15

Rethink: Rethink Your Initial Career Choice ... 17

Other Job Search Strategies ... 18

Career Connections:
Starting Over: Once You Have
a Job You Want ... 20

Job Interviews ... 20

Try It! 4: Interviewing ... 24

Moving Your Career Forward
and Striving Styles ... 25

Time to Reflect ... 27

Looking Back ... 28

Key Terms and Concept ... 28

Resources ... 29

Taking It to the Net ... 30

The Case of . . .
Interviewophobia ... 31

What makes this textbook different from many others?

Like many students in their first year of post-secondary education, you are probably feeling overwhelmed. You may be on your own for the first time, going back to school after a few years in the working world, or juggling the needs of a family while you further your education. Whether your parents are paying your way, you've saved your own money, or you have a large student loan hanging over your head, the pressure to succeed is always present. That's where this textbook comes in. While the content of most textbooks used in college and university programs is designed with a *specific* course in mind, this textbook contains content that you will be able to apply to *all* of your courses. It is a handbook designed to teach you how to be successful—in college, in university, and as a lifelong learner.

I know all about that pressure, because I felt it, too. I only wish back then that I'd been able to take a course on how to be a successful student. So decades later, when as a Professor at Centennial College, I was given the chance to design such a course, I jumped at the opportunity. And a few years after that, when McGraw-Hill came knocking at my door to see if I'd be interested in developing the Canadian edition of a textbook on student success, I jumped at that, too.

You see, it's one thing to learn about nursing or marketing or aviation technology; it's quite another to learn how to be a successful student in any of those disciplines.

Being a successful student means recognizing how you learn, what you value, and what you are striving for. It means knowing how to manage your time and your money. It means learning how to take notes, how to write tests, and how to make good decisions. Being a successful student requires you to learn how to research, how to write, and how to present. It involves collaborating with others and using technology to make your life more effective and efficient. And *that's* what this textbook is all about.

What's special about the Canadian edition?

The Canadian edition of *POWER Learning and Your Life: Essentials of Student Success* has been designed specifically to meet the needs and wants of Canadian educators and their students, while addressing the skills most sought after by Canadian employers. I've drawn on feedback from reviewers, discussions with colleagues, and comments from my own students in developing a text that draws on sound andragogy, while emphasizing interactivity, critical thinking, and cooperative learning.

Each chapter begins with learning outcomes based on Bloom's taxonomy, and the material within the chapter has been developed and organized around these specific outcomes. Hands-on exercises, labelled "Try It!", Course and Career Connections, and end-of-chapter cases are included in every chapter. All of these features are designed to promote active learning by encouraging students to get involved with the material.

The benefits of recently introduced technologies such as collaboration software, desktop organization tools, and citation software have been included in a redesigned chapter on technology, where the emphasis has shifted to how technology can be leveraged to make students' lives more effective and efficient. Indeed, references to new technologies are woven throughout the text, where students will find helpful information on a wide range of topics, including what to expect from a distance learning course, how to take advantage of the features of e-readers and online note-taking software, and how to use citation software to avoid plagiarism.

The most notable difference from the American edition is a new chapter on Writing and Speaking, which addresses some of the fundamental skills in the Conference Board of Canada's Employability Skills 2000+, which is introduced at the beginning of the book. In this chapter, students are introduced to the concept of writing as a process, and are provided with a framework for case analysis and a format for developing a business report. They are also introduced to how to create and deliver an effective presentation, as well as how to use presentation slides to complement a presentation.

Other additions to the Canadian edition include the Striving Styles assessment developed by Canadian psychotherapist Dr. Anne Dranitsaris, the SMART approach to goal-setting, Stephen Covey's importance/urgency quadrant, the Cornell method of note-taking, and the SQ3R approach to reading. The chapter on collaborating with others has been expanded to include much-needed information on group formation and how to make group work more effective. Finally, the last chapter has been refocused on finances, with a much greater emphasis placed on the uses and abuses of credit, a major issue for today's students. The Career chapter has been moved to an online environment, and addresses the use of Linked In as a powerful networking tool.

I hope you will enjoy not only *reading* this book, but also *using* this book, much as you would a workbook. Complete the surveys in it, highlight it, make notes in the margins, and refer back to it throughout your time as a student. Use it as a *resource* when you find yourself in later years struggling with a course, or studying for a test, or trying to get a group to collaborate on a project. Review it when you have to analyze a case, or write a report, or prepare a presentation. Apply what you've learned in this text to all of the other courses you take, and it will go a long way towards ensuring that you become the very best student you can be.

Features

Student-Friendly Design and Layout: The book has been designed to capture students' attention and enhance student engagement. Students will find images, charts, and photos throughout this innovative learning tool, illustrations of the diversity of students as well as the latest in technological aids and devices.

Systematic Framework for Success: Each chapter utilizes the principles of the P.O.W.E.R. system (Prepare, Organize, Work, Evaluate, and Rethink) so students can clearly see how easy it is to incorporate this effective process into their everyday routine. The P.O.W.E.R. plan illustration in each chapter highlights the key steps for the corresponding chapter material.

Reinforced Learning across Chapters: Following their introduction in the first chapter, concepts like multiple intelligences, learning styles, and striving styles are reinforced throughout the book.

Skill-Building Opportunities: Each chapter offers numerous exercises and activities to reinforce key concepts and relate the material to students' other courses.

Connection of Academic and Career Success: Each chapter links the text material to the world of work and demonstrates how the chapter strategies are related to career choices and success.

Development of Critical Thinking Skills: Throughout the text, students are encouraged to assess their skills, reflect on their progress, and think critically about related experiences. Cases in each chapter provide an opportunity for students to consider what they have learned and use critical thinking skills to respond to related questions.

Additional Resources: At the end of each chapter, students are directed to on-campus, text, and Web-based resources to advance their learning.

Instructor Resources

McGraw-Hill Connect™ is a web-based assignment and assessment platform that gives students the means to better connect with their coursework, with their instructors, and with the important concepts that they will need to know for success now and in the future.

Connect can help instructors to perform these aspects of their teaching:

- Deliver assignments, quizzes, and tests online.
- Edit existing questions and author entirely new problems.
- Track individual student performance—by question, assignment, or in relation to the class overall—with detailed grade reports.
- Integrate grade reports easily with Learning Management Systems (LMS) such as WebCT and Blackboard.

By choosing Connect, instructors are providing their students with a powerful tool for improving academic performance and truly mastering course material. Connect also provides 24/7 online access to an eBook—an online edition of the text—to aid instructors in successfully completing their work, wherever and whenever they choose.

Additional resources for the Instructor, available within Connect, include the following:

- An **Instructor's Manual** with teaching strategies and tips, sample syllabi, and creative classroom activities.
- **PowerPoint slides** for each chapter offering instructional support and providing a visual complement to lectures. The slides are comprehensive and can be adapted to meet the needs of any course.
- A **Test Bank** for each chapter offering a variety of multiple choice, true or false, and short answer questions.

Student Resources

Connect provides students with a powerful tool for improving academic performance and truly mastering course material, plus 24/7 online access to an interactive and searchable eBook. Connect allows students to practise important skills at their own pace and on their own schedule. Importantly, students' assessment results and instructors' feedback are all saved online—so students can continually review their progress and plot their course to success. Additional resources available within Connect include Flashcards, Try It! activities, Cases, and a Glossary.

Achieving the Goals of POWER Learning

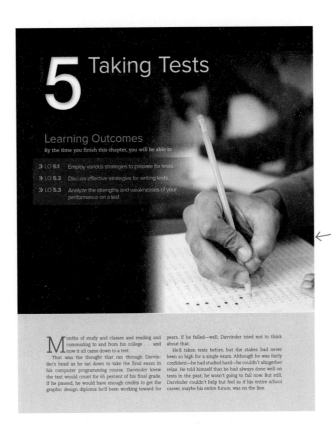

Chapter-opening scenarios describe an individual grappling with a situation that is relevant to the subject matter of the chapter. Readers will be able to relate to these vignettes, which feature students running behind schedule, figuring out a way to keep up with reading assignments, or making decisions about what to do after graduation.

The **Career Connections** feature links the material in the chapter to the world of work, demonstrating how the strategies discussed in the chapter are related to career choices and success in the workplace.

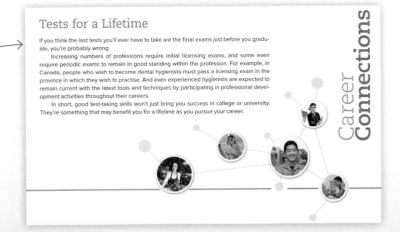

Tests for a Lifetime

If you think the last tests you'll ever have to take are the final exams just before you graduate, you're probably wrong.

Increasing numbers of professions require initial licensing exams, and some even require periodic exams to remain in good standing within the profession. For example, in Canada, people who wish to become dental hygienists must pass a licensing exam in the province in which they wish to practise. And even experienced hygienists are expected to remain current with the latest tools and techniques by participating in professional development activities throughout their careers.

In short, good test-taking skills won't just bring you success in college or university. They're something that may benefit you for a lifetime as you pursue your career.

Career
Connections

Every chapter includes a **Course Connections** box that shows students how to use the chapter's content to maximize their success in particular classes.

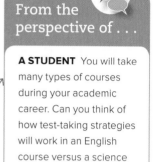

From the Perspective of . . . . These features highlight career-specific situations and answer the question of why this course matters and how it will impact student growth long after graduation.

Special Techniques for Dealing with Math Anxiety

For many students, the greatest test anxiety comes when they're taking a test involving math. Math seems to bring out the worst fears in some people, perhaps because it's seen as a discipline in which answers are either totally right or totally wrong, or perhaps because they've felt they've "hit the wall" and they'll never be able to understand a new concept, no matter how hard they try.

Such feelings about math can be devastating, because they can prevent you from doing well even if you know the material. If you suffer from math anxiety, keep these things in mind:

- Math is like any other subject: The greatest component of success is the effort you put in, not whether you have a "math gene" that makes you naturally good at math. It's not true that you are either born "good at math" or not, or that there's some "secret" about math that some people know and others don't.
- It's also not true that there's only one way to solve a math problem. Sometimes there are a variety of routes to coming up with a solution. And keep in mind that the solution to math problems often calls for creativity, not just sheer logic.
- It's a false stereotype that women are not as good at math as men, but it's a stereotype that many women accept. Research has shown that when men do badly on a math test, they're most likely to think that they haven't put in enough effort; but when women don't do well on a math test, they're three times more likely than men to feel that they don't have enough ability to be successful.[1] That's an erroneous view of the world. Don't become a prisoner of stereotypes.

Use these special strategies to deal with math problems on exams:

BEFORE TESTS:

1. Math is cumulative, building on prior concepts and knowledge. Make sure you review math fundamentals before moving on to more advanced topics.
2. Ask questions in class. Don't be afraid that you'll ask the wrong question in the wrong way. Instructors want you to understand their subject.
3. Make use of review sessions and other study resources.
4. Practise, practise, practise. The more experience you have completing math problems under pressure, the better you'll do. Practise math problems using a timer in order to simulate an actual test.

DURING TESTS:

1. Analyze math problems carefully. What are the known quantities or constants, and what pieces of information are missing? What formula(s) or theorem(s) apply?
2. Consider drawing a diagram, graph, or probability tree.
3. Break down calculations into their component parts.
4. Check your math carefully.
5. Be neat and logical in your presentation, and show every step as you solve problems. Your instructor may give you partial credit if you lay out every step you're going through. In addition, some instructors may require you to show your work.

Try It! activities in each chapter provide opportunities for gaining hands-on experience with the material covered in the chapter. These include questionnaires, self-assessments, and group exercises to do with classmates. The Try It! activities, along with other assessment opportunities, are also available on Connect.

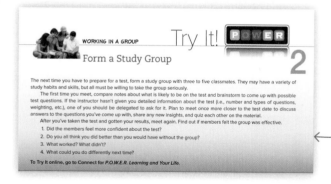

WORKING IN A GROUP

Try It! **POWER**

Form a Study Group

2

The next time you have to prepare for a test, form a study group with three to five classmates. They may have a variety of study habits and skills, but all must be willing to take the group seriously.

The first time you meet, compare notes about what is likely to be on the test and brainstorm to come up with possible test questions. If the instructor hasn't given you detailed information about the test (i.e., number and types of questions, weighting, etc.), one of you should be delegated to ask for it. Plan to meet once more closer to the test date to discuss answers to the questions you've come up with, share any new insights, and quiz each other on the material.

After you've taken the test and gotten your results, meet again. Find out if members felt the group was effective.

1. Did the members feel more confident about the test?
2. Do you all think you did better than you would have without the group?
3. What worked? What didn't?
4. What could you do differently next time?

To Try It online, go to Connect for *P.O.W.E.R. Learning and Your Life.*

Time to Reflect feature encourages students to reflect back on what they learned in the chapter and how they will use that information going forward.

Time to Reflect: What Did I Learn?

1. Generally speaking, how does being tested make you feel?

2. What factors seem to contribute to your success or failure on a particular test or exam? Which of these factors are under your control?

3. What strategies do you plan to use in the future to improve your performance on tests?

Resources feature in each chapter includes an updated list of the three types of resources that are useful in finding and utilizing information relevant to the chapter: a list of on-campus resources, books, and websites.

[RESOURCES]

ON CAMPUS

Colleges and universities provide a variety of resources for students having difficulties with test-taking. Some offer general workshops reviewing test-taking strategies. As well, if you are planning to take a specific standardized test, you may be able to sign up for a course offered through your college or university (or through such commercial organizations as Princeton Review or Kaplan).

If you are experiencing difficulties in a specific course, you may be able to find a tutor to help you. Some institutions have tutoring centres or campus learning centres that can provide one-to-one assistance. It's also important to speak to your instructor, who has likely encountered many students with similar problems and may have some useful test-taking strategies.

If you find that you are experiencing significant test anxiety when taking a test or in the days leading up to it, talk to one of the professionals at your campus counselling centre or health centre. They can help you learn relaxation techniques and can provide counselling to help make your anxiety manageable.

IN PRINT

If you have difficulty with test anxiety, you'll want to check out *Insider's Guide to Beating Test Anxiety* (Bedford, 2010).

In *How to Ace Any Test* (Wiley, 2004), Beverley Chin provides a variety of techniques designed to improve your performance on any kind of test.

Eileen Tracy's *The Student's Guide to Exam Success* (Open University Press, 2006) gives an overview of strategies for test-taking success.

Key terms appear in boldface in the text and are defined in the margins. In addition, they are listed in a Key Terms and Concepts section at the end of the chapter, with accompanying page references.

[KEY TERMS AND CONCEPTS]

Academic honesty (p. 126)
Cramming (p. 118)

Educated guessing (p. 124)
Plagiarism (p. 126)

Study group (p. 115)
Test anxiety (p. 117)

Taking It to the Net exercises encourage students to use the Internet to build on their understanding of the concepts presented in the chapter and to explore other perspectives.

TAKING IT TO THE NET

1 Seeing exams from other classes can help you get an idea of the kinds of questions that are often asked on exams. Use an Internet search engine to locate examples of exams from other colleges and universities. One strategy would be to use the Google search engine at **www.google.ca**, and type "examples of exams" (including the quotation marks) at the search prompt. Look at several exams. How many of the questions on these exams were true–false? How many were multiple-choice? How many were essays?

2 Practise answering essay questions by comparing and contrasting the information different Web pages offer about the same topic. For example, go to Yahoo! (**http://ca.yahoo.com**) and enter the phrase "essay exams" (using quotation marks). Read the strategies for essay exams offered in two different websites. Then write a paragraph describing the information both sites had in common, and another paragraph describing the information that was unique to each site.

The Case of . . .
That Sinking Feeling

This is going to be easy, Janelle Ross said to herself as she sat down to take her test, a midterm exam covering the basics of restaurant management. She had spent a few hours the previous night and an hour right before class studying key terms and concepts. She felt she knew the material. She felt ready.

Janelle was surprised to see, though, that the exam had two parts: a multiple-choice section and an essay section. Janelle hadn't really thought about what she might say in an essay. But she figured working on the multiple-choice questions might help give her some ideas.

The first two multiple-choice questions Janelle answered easily, but she got stuck on the third one. She went back and forth over two possible answers and

finally decided just to leave that question blank. The pattern was the same for the rest of the multiple-choice questions: A few questions Janelle would answer easily, then she'd get stuck on a hard one.

Finally, Janelle finished the multiple-choice questions and came to the essay. Only then did she notice the instructions that indicated the essay was worth 50 marks, and the multiple-choice questions 25 marks. Then Janelle got another shock: She had only ten minutes left to write her essay! Her mind froze—and Janelle had the horrible feeling that she didn't have enough time to complete the test. Even though she had studied, Janelle now felt certain she would fail.

1. What mistakes did Janelle make in her test preparation that probably harmed her performance?

2. What mistakes did Janelle make during the test that hurt her?

3. What was right about Janelle's initial approach to the test?

4. What should Janelle have done differently in calculating the amount of time to devote to each portion of the test? Why?

5. What specific strategies would have helped Janelle with the multiple-choice questions? What strategies could she have used on the essay?

6. If you were in Janelle's shoes, what would you do with only ten minutes left in the test?

Each chapter ends with a case (**The Case of . . .**) to which the principles described in the chapter can be applied. Cases are based on situations that students might themselves encounter. Each case provides a series of questions that encourage students to consider what they've learned and to use critical thinking skills in responding to these questions.

With Gratitude

I want to begin by thanking the mentors whose sage advice helped me forge my life's path: Michael Hatton, Helen K. Sinclair, and Perrin Lewis. Each of you played an important role in making me understand what I could do and who I could become. I also want to thank my husband, Martin Durand, who supported me in so many ways throughout the two years it took to complete work on this book. A special thank you also goes out to Dr. Anne Dranitsaris for developing a student version of her Striving Styles framework specifically for this textbook.

I would also like to thank the many people in Higher Education at McGraw-Hill Ryerson who helped make this text possible. They include former Sponsoring Editor Lisa Rahn, who first proposed that I get involved with the project; Sponsoring Editor Karen Krahn; Developmental Editor Sara Braithwaite, who worked closely with me every step of the way; Publisher Cara Yarzab; Permissions Editor Indu Arora; Supervising Editor Graeme Powell; Copyeditor Elspeth McFadden; and publishing representatives Lisa Gillman and Jordan Johnston.

And last, but certainly not least, I owe a debt of gratitude to the reviewers who provided feedback on early drafts of the 1st Canadian edition of *P.O.W.E.R. Learning and Your Life*. Their carefully considered comments and suggestions are reflected in the final version of the text.

Natalie Atkin, *U of Windsor*

Ingrid Bajewsky, *Nipissing University*

Anne Bartlett, *UPEI*

Michael Boulay, *Stratford Career Institute*

Hedy Chase-Rattner, *Seneca College of A A &T*

Debbie Cox, *Conestoga College*

Gillian Fowler, *Eastern College*

Jillian Hull, *Douglas College*

John Jennings, *Mount St. Vincent U*

Mikal Radford, *Sheridan College*

Kristen Rosen, *Seneca College of A A &T*

Rajeev Sachdev, *Trios College*

Beth Shewkenek, *Saskatoon Business College*

Susan Slessor, *Georgian College*

Mickey Sloot, *Lambton College*

Drew Smylie, *Centennial College*

Kirsten Somers, *Mount St. Vincent U*

Michael Sullivan, *Centennial College*

Kerry Surman, *Algonquin College*

Bill Thompson, *Trillium College (Oshawa)*

Virginia Vranckx, *Trillium College (Oshawa)*

Danica Lavoie

1

P.O.W.E.R. Learning: Becoming an Expert Student

Learning Outcomes

By the time you finish this chapter, you will be able to

》 LO 1.1   Discuss the benefits of a post-secondary education.

》 LO 1.2   List the skills, attitudes, and behaviours valued by Canadian employers.

》 LO 1.3   Identify the basic principles of P.O.W.E.R. Learning and the ways in which expert students use P.O.W.E.R. Learning to set goals and achieve academic success.

》 LO 1.4   Compare and contrast learning styles, striving styles, and multiple intelligences. Identify your own styles, and reflect on how they relate to your academic success.

The day has started off with a bang. Literally. As Nandini Singh reaches sleepily to turn off her clock radio's continual buzzing at 6:35 A.M., she knocks the clock off the table next to her bed. The loud bang it makes as it hits the floor wakes her fully, and it rouses her daughters sleeping in the next room, who grumble resentfully.

Struggling out of bed, Nandini reflects on the day ahead. It's one of her most intense days—two shifts at two different part-time jobs on different sides of town. She also must get her children ready for school and then take them to swimming lessons in the afternoon. And on top of all that, she has an exam that morning at the college she attends.

After a quick shower, Nandini manages to get her daughters off to school, and then joins her fellow paralegal students on campus. She glances at her paralegal textbook and feels a wave of anxiety flood over her: Will I do well enough on my exam? How will I manage to hold down two jobs, take care of my family, and have enough time to study? Will I find a job as a paralegal after graduation? Will I make my children proud? . . . And underlying them all is a single challenge: Will I be successful in college and in my career?

Looking Ahead

Whether academic pursuits are a struggle or come easily to you . . . whether you are returning to post-secondary education or attending for the first time . . . whether you are gaining new skills for your current job or have been at home caring for your children and are now starting on a whole new career path . . . whether you are attending college or university in your own hometown or have travelled from another country to be here—whatever your situation, pursuing post-secondary education is a challenge. Every one of us has concerns about our own capabilities and motivation; and new situations—like starting college or university—make us wonder how well we'll succeed.

That's where this book comes in. It is designed to help you learn the most effective ways to approach the challenges you encounter, not just in college or university, but in your career, too. It will teach you practical strategies, and it will provide hints and tips that can lead you to success, all centred on an approach to achieving classroom and career success. That approach is called P.O.W.E.R. Learning.

This book is designed to be useful in a way that is different from other texts. It presents information in a hands-on format. It's meant to be used, not just read. Write on it, underline words and sentences, use a highlighter, circle key points, and complete the questionnaires right in the book. The more exercises you do, the more benefit you'll get from the book. The ideas in this book will help you throughout your post-secondary education and throughout your career, so it's a good idea to invest your time here and now. If the learning techniques you master here become second nature, the payoff will be enormous.

In the first part of this chapter, you'll read about the benefits of post-secondary education and examine the skills, attitudes, and behaviours valued by Canadian employers. After that, you'll be introduced to the basics of the P.O.W.E.R. Learning process, a process that is used throughout the book and is a fundamental building block in achieving academic and career success. Finally, in the last half of the chapter, you'll discover a number of interactive tools that will help you uncover the ways in which you learn best, what you truly value, and how you can use your learning style, striving style, and multiple intelligences to become an expert student.

figure 1.1

Canada is one of the most multicultural countries in the world. (Wordle created at **www.wordle.net**.)

≫ LO 1.1 The Benefits of a Post-secondary Education

Congratulations. You are enrolled in an institution of higher learning. Clearly, you agree with Canadians who, when surveyed by the Canadian Council on Learning in 2008, overwhelmingly agreed that adult learning is critical to success

Why Are You Going to College or University?

Place a 1, a 2, and a 3 by the three most important reasons that you have for attending college/university:

_____ I want to get a good job when I graduate.

_____ I want to make my family proud.

_____ I couldn't find a job.

_____ I want to try something new.

_____ I want to get ahead at my current job.

_____ I want to pursue my dream job.

_____ I want to improve my reading and critical thinking skills.

_____ I want to become a more cultured person.

_____ I want to make more money.

_____ I want to learn more about things that interest me.

_____ A mentor or role model encouraged me to go.

_____ I want to prove to others that I can succeed.

Now consider the following:

1. What do your answers tell you about yourself?
2. What reasons besides these did you think about when you were applying to college or university?
3. How do you think your reasons compare with those of your fellow students?

To Try It online, go to Connect for *P.O.W.E.R. Learning and Your Life*.

in life and to satisfaction with one's life. The reasons that people go to college or university vary from the practical ("I need new skills for my job"), to the noble ("I want to build a better life for my family"), to the vague ("Why not? I don't have anything better to do"). Consider your own reasons for enrolling, as you complete **Try It! 1**, "Why Are You Going to College or University?"

It's likely that one of your primary motivations for pursuing post-secondary education is to further your career. In fact, a survey of first-year college students found that almost three-quarters of them want to learn about things that interest them, get training for a specific career, land a better job, and make more money (see **Figure 1.2** on page 4). Statistics clearly demonstrate that a post-secondary education helps people find better jobs. On average, college and university graduates earn about 75 percent more than high school graduates over their working lifetime.[1] That difference adds up: Over the course of their working lifetimes, college graduates earn close to a million dollars more than those with only a high school diploma. Furthermore, as jobs become increasingly complex and technologically sophisticated, a post-secondary education is becoming an entry-level requirement for many jobs.

There are many reasons for pursuing a college or university education:

> **You'll learn to think critically.** Here's what one student said about his college experience after he graduated: "It's not about what you major in or which classes you take. . . . It's really about learning to think. Wherever you end up, you'll need to be able to analyze and solve problems—to figure out what needs to be done and do it."[2] Education improves your ability to understand the world—to understand it as it now is, and to prepare to understand it as it will be.

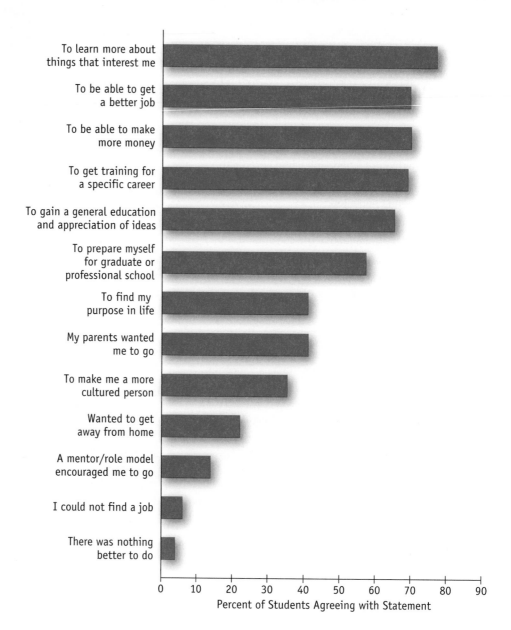

figure 1.2

Choosing College

These are the most frequently cited reasons that first-year college students gave when asked in a U.S. survey why they had enrolled in college.[2]

To learn more about things that interest me

To be able to get a better job

To be able to make more money

To get training for a specific career

To gain a general education and appreciation of ideas

To prepare myself for graduate or professional school

To find my purpose in life

My parents wanted me to go

To make me a more cultured person

Wanted to get away from home

A mentor/role model encouraged me to go

I could not find a job

There was nothing better to do

Percent of Students Agreeing with Statement

0 10 20 30 40 50 60 70 80 90

> **You'll learn how to communicate better.** Post-secondary institutions provide you with the opportunity to communicate your thoughts and ideas orally and in writing; teachers provide important feedback on how to do this well. As you learn in the next section of this chapter, communication is a skill that is highly valued by Canadian employers.

> **You'll be able to better deal with advances in knowledge and technology that are changing the world.** Genetic engineering . . . drugs to reduce forgetfulness . . . foods that make us smarter—no one knows what the future will hold. But you can prepare for it through a post-secondary education. Education can provide you with intellectual tools that you can apply regardless of the specific situation in which you find yourself.

> **You'll learn to adapt to new situations.** College and university are different worlds from high school or the workplace. They present new experiences and new challenges. Your adjustment to the culture of your college or university will prepare you for future encounters with new situations.

> **You'll be better prepared to live in a world of diversity.** The ethnic composition of Canada is changing rapidly. Whatever your ethnicity, chances are

you'll be working and living with people whose backgrounds, lifestyles, and ways of thinking may be entirely different from your own.

You won't be prepared for the future unless you understand others and their cultural backgrounds, as well as how your own cultural background affects you.

> **You'll make learning a lifelong habit.** Higher education isn't the end of your education. Education will build upon your natural curiosity about the world, and it will make you aware that learning is a rewarding and never-ending journey.

> And finally, the obvious: **You will boost your career prospects.** You will acquire skills, attitudes, and behaviours that Canadian employers value; and you will earn more money over the course of your lifetime than someone who has not obtained a diploma or degree.

»LO **1.2** What Canadian Employers Value

Forging a successful career depends, as much as anything else, on the "fit" between what employers are looking for and what you have to offer. In this section, we focus on uncovering the main skills, attitudes, and behaviours sought by Canadian employers. Later, we will provide you with an opportunity to examine how you can best harness your talents to offer employers what they are seeking.

Canadian employers are a diverse lot. They span the public and private sectors, large and small businesses, and every industry imaginable. Is it really possible that they can come to an agreement on the qualities they look for in an employee? They can, and they have. The result is the Employability Skills 2000+, a publication of the Conference Board of Canada, which can be found in **Figure 1.3** on page 6. It divides the skills desired by employers into three main categories: fundamental skills, personal management skills, and teamwork skills.

To accompany the Employability Skills 2000+, the Conference Board has developed a Skills Assessment and Portfolio Building Tool (SCT) for students, employees, and job-seekers. The SCT allows you to assess your own essential skills and employability attitudes and behaviours and to create a printout that you can share with your professor. To access the Skills Assessment and Portfolio Building Tool, go to **http://conferenceboard.checkboxonline.com/Survey.aspx?s=b5cfd4 c7ef204b5cb3e6a6c1f7e07628.**

To help you develop the skills, attitudes, and behaviours valued by Canadian employers, it's time to introduce you to a fundamental process that will help you achieve success, both in school and in life beyond: P.O.W.E.R. Learning.

»LO **1.3** P.O.W.E.R. Learning: Five Key Steps to Achieving Success

P.O.W.E.R. Learning
A system designed to help people achieve their goals, based on five steps: **P**repare, **O**rganize, **W**ork, **E**valuate, and **R**ethink

The term **P.O.W.E.R. Learning** is an acronym—a word formed from the first letters of a series of steps—for an approach to learning that will help you take in, process, and make use of the information you'll acquire in college or university. It will help you to achieve your goals, both while you are in school and after you graduate.

Employability Skills 2000+

The skills you need to enter, stay in, and progress in the world of work—whether you work on your own or as a part of a team.

These skills can also be applied and used beyond the workplace in a range of daily activities

Fundamental Skills	Personal Management Skills	Teamwork Skills
The skills needed as a base for further development	The personal skills, attitudes and behaviours that drive one's potential for growth	The skills and attributes needed to contribute productively

Fundamental Skills

You will be better prepared to progress in the world of work when you can:

Communicate

- read and understand information presented in a variety of forms (e.g., words, graphs, charts, diagrams)
- write and speak so others pay attention and understand
- listen and ask questions to understand and appreciate the points of view of others
- share information using a range of information and communications technologies (eg., voice, e-mail, computers)
- use relevant scientific, technological and mathematical knowledge and skills to explain or clarify ideas.

Manage Information

- locate, gather and organize information using appropriate technology and information systems
- access, analyze and apply knowledge and skills from various disciplines(e.g.,arts, languages, science, technology, mathematics, social sciences and the humanities)

Use Numbers

- decide what needs to be measured or calculated
- observe and record data using appropriate methods, tools and technology
- make estimates and verify calculations

Think & Solve Problems

- assess situations and identify problems
- seek different points of view and evaluate them based on facts
- recognize the human, interpersonal, technical, scientific and mathematical dimensions of a problem
- identify the roof cause of a problem
- be creative and innovative in exploring possible solutions
- readily use science, technology and mathematics as ways to think, gain and share knowledge, solve problems and make decisions
- evaluate solutions to make recommendations or decisions
- implement solution
- check to see if a solution works, and act an opportunities for improvement

Personal Management Skills

You will be able to offer yourself greater possibilities for achievement when you can:

Demonstrate Positive Attitudes & Behaviours

- feel good about yourself and be confident
- deal with people, problems and situations with honesty, integrity and personal ethics
- recognize your own and other people's good efforts
- take care of your personal health
- show interest, initiative and effort

Be Responsible

- set goals and priorities balancing work and personal life
- plan and manage time, money and other resources to achieve goals
- assess, weigh and manage risk
- be accountable your actions and the actions of your group
- be socially responsible and contribute to your community

Be Adaptable

- work independently or as a part of a team
- carry out multiple tasks or projects
- be innovative and resourceful: identify and suggest alternative ways to achieve goals and get the job done
- be open and respond constructively to charge
- learn from your mistakes and accept feedback
- cope with uncertainty

Learn Continuously

- be willing to continuously learn and grow
- assess personal strengths and areas for development
- set your own learning goals
- identify and access learning sources and opportunities
- plan for and achieve your learning goals

Work Safely

- be aware of personal and group health and safety practices and procedures, and act in accordance with these

Teamwork Skills

You will be better prepared to add value to the outcomes of a task, project or team when you can:

Work with Others

- understand and work within the dynamics of a group
- ensure that a team's purpose and objectives are clear
- be flexible: respect, be open to and supportive of the thoughts, opinions and contributions of other in a group
- recognize and respect people's diversity, individual differences and perspectives
- accept and provide feedback in a constructive and considerate manner
- contribute to a team by sharing information and expertise
- lead or support when appropriate, motivating a group for high performance
- Understand the role of conflict in a group to reach solutions.
- manage and resolve conflict when appropriate

Participate in Projects & Tasks

- plan, design or carry out a project or task from start to finish with well-defined objectives and outcomes
- develop-a plan, seek feedback, test, revise and implement
- work to agreed quality standards and specifications
- select and use appropriate tools and techonology for a task or project
- adapt to changing requirements and information
- continuously monitor the success of a project or task and identify ways to improve

The Conference Board of Canada

255 Smyth Road, Ottawa
ON K1H 8M7 Canada
Tel. (613) 526-3280
Fax (613) 526-4857

Internet: www.conferenceboard.ca/education

figure 1.3

Conference Board of Canada's Employability Skills 2000+

The Conference Board's Employability Skills 2000+ tells you what most Canadian employers are looking for, and it is also a great resource when you are writing your resumé!

Students go to school for their own individual reasons. Gwen recently visited a friend in the hospital and was struck by how much she wanted to be a part of the health-care community. John has survived several rounds of layoffs at his job and wants to make himself more marketable.

Prepare, **O**rganize, **W**ork, **E**valuate, and **R**ethink. That's it. It's a simple framework, but an effective one. Using the systematic framework that P.O.W.E.R. Learning provides (illustrated in the P.O.W.E.R. Plan diagram in the margin) will increase your chances of success at any task, from writing a paper to buying the weekly groceries to filling out a purchase order.

Keep this in mind: P.O.W.E.R. Learning isn't a product that you can simply pull down off the shelf and use without thinking. P.O.W.E.R. Learning is a process, and you are the only one who can make it succeed. Without your personal investment in the process, P.O.W.E.R. Learning consists of just words on paper.

Relax, though. You already know each of the elements of P.O.W.E.R. Learning; and you may discover that you are already putting this process, or parts of it, to work for you. You've applied and been accepted at an institution of higher learning. You may have also held down a job, started a family, and paid your monthly bills. Each of these accomplishments required that you use P.O.W.E.R. Learning. What you'll be doing throughout this book is becoming more aware of these methods and how they can be used to help you in situations you will encounter in school and your career.

P.O.W.E.R. Plan

P Prepare

Chinese philosopher Lao Tzu said that travellers taking a long journey must begin with a single step. But even before they take that first step, travellers need to know several things: what their destination is, how they're going to get there, how they'll know when they reach the destination, and what they'll do if they have trouble along the way. In the same way, you need to know where you're headed as you embark on the academic journeys involved in pursuing a post-secondary education. Whether you are performing a major, long-term task, such as landing a new and better job, or a more limited activity, such as getting ready to complete a paper due in the near future, you'll need to prepare for the journey.

Setting Goals

From the perspective of . . .

A STUDENT What goals did you set when you decided to go school? What can you do to ensure that you meet these goals?

Long-term goals
Aims relating to major accomplishments that take some time to achieve

Short-term goals
Relatively limited steps toward the accomplishment of long-term goals

SMART approach to goal setting
A framework for goal setting that emphasizes that goals should be specific, measurable, achievable, realistic, time-bound

Before we seek to accomplish any task, all of us do some form of planning. The trouble is that most of the time such planning is done without conscious thinking, as if we are on autopilot. However, the key to success is to make sure that planning is systematic.

The best way to plan systematically is to use goal-setting strategies. In many cases, goals are clear and direct. It's obvious that our goal in washing dishes is to have the dishes end up clean. We know that our goal at the gas station is to fill the car's tank with gas. We go to the post office to buy stamps and mail letters.

Other goals are not so clear-cut. In fact, often the more important the task—such as going to college or university—the more complicated our goals may be.

What's the best way to set appropriate goals? Here are some guidelines:

> **Set both long-term and short-term goals. Long-term goals** are aims relating to major accomplishments that take some time to achieve. **Short-term goals** are relatively limited steps you would take on the road to accomplishing your long-term goals. For example, one of the primary reasons you're enrolled in a post-secondary institution is to achieve the long-term goal of helping your career. But in order to reach that goal, you have to accomplish a series of short-term goals, such as completing a set of required courses and earning your diploma or degree. Even these short-term goals can be broken down into shorter-term goals. In order to complete a required course, for instance, you have to accomplish a series of short-term goals, such as completing a paper, taking several tests, and so on. For practice in setting long- and short-term goals, complete **Try It! 2**, "What Are Your Goals?", on page 9, "What Are Your Goals?"

The **SMART approach to goal setting** has been around for a long time. The acronym SMART reminds us that goals must be Specific, Measurable, Achievable, Realistic, and Time-Bound. Let's look at each of these in turn.

> **Set goals that are Specific.** Saying that "some day I'll learn a new language" is not specific enough. When you are setting a goal, make it as specific as possible. Which language? Where will you learn it? How will you learn it? Online? In a classroom setting? When will you learn it? The more specific and vivid the goal, the easier it is to achieve it.

> **Set goals that are Measurable.** Goals should represent some measurable change from a current set of circumstances. Your behaviour ought to change in some way that can be expressed in terms of numbers—to show an increase ("raise my grade point average 10 percent"), a decrease ("reduce wasted time by two hours each week"), or a level to be maintained ("keep in touch with my out-of-town friends by writing four email messages each month"), developed ("participate in one workshop on critical thinking"), or restricted ("reduce my phone expenses 10 percent by speaking and texting less").

"If I had one hour to chop down a tree, I'd spend the first thirty minutes sharpening the saw."
Abraham Lincoln

What Are Your Goals?

Before you begin any journey, you need to know where you are going. To plan your academic journey—and your later career—you first need to set goals. *Short-term goals* are relatively limited objectives that bring you closer to your ultimate goal. *Long-term goals* are aims relating to major accomplishments that take more time to achieve.

In this **Try It!**, think about your short- and long-term academic and career goals for a few minutes, and then list them, using the SMART approach to goal setting. Because short-term goals are based on what you want to accomplish in the long term, first identify your long-term goals. Then list the short-term goals that will help you reach your long-term goals. An example is provided of both a long-term and a short-term goal:

Long-Term Goal #1 *Get a nursing diploma or degree* _____
   Related Short-Term Goals:
   - *Complete four courses with a grade of B or above each term*
   - _____
   - _____
   - _____

Long-Term Goal #2: _____
   Related Short-Term Goals:
   - _____
   - _____
   - _____
   - _____

Long-Term Goal #3: _____
   Related Short-Term Goals:
   - _____
   - _____
   - _____
   - _____

Long-Term Goal #4: _____
   Related Short-Term Goals:
   - _____
   - _____
   - _____
   - _____

Long-Term Goal #5: _____
   Related Short-Term Goals:
   - _____
   - _____
   - _____
   - _____

After you complete the lists, consider how easy or difficult it was to identify your long-term goals.

1. How many of your long-term goals relate to your education, and how many to your future career?
2. Do any of your short-term goals relate to more than one long-term goal?
3. In what ways will using the SMART approach to goal setting help you achieve your goals?

To Try It online, go to Connect for *P.O.W.E.R. Learning and Your Life.*

> **Set goals that are <u>A</u>chievable.** Someone once said, "A goal without a plan is but a dream." Everyone would like to win gold medals at the Olympics or star in videos or write best-selling novels. Unfortunately, you are unlikely to achieve such goals. It isn't enough to have a goal. Depending on the goal, you may also need the physical, emotional, or intellectual capacity, *and* the motivation and determination required to achieve it.

> **Set goals that are <u>R</u>ealistic.** We all want world peace and an end to poverty. Few of us have the resources or capabilities to bring either about. On the other hand, it is realistic to want to work in small ways to help others, such as by becoming a Big Brother or Big Sister or by volunteering at a local food bank. Be honest with yourself. There is nothing wrong with having big dreams. But it is important to be realistically aware of all that it takes to achieve them. If your long-term goals are unrealistic and you don't achieve them, the big danger is that you may incorrectly conclude that you are inept and lack ability, and you may then use this as an excuse for giving up. If goals are realistic, you can develop a plan to attain them, spurring you on to attain more.

> **Set goals that are <u>T</u>ime-bound.** As mentioned earlier, the more specific the goal, the better. This also applies to timing. When setting a goal, you should have a specific time frame in mind for achieving it. Procrastination is all too easy; before you know it, that goal you set five years ago is pushed far down your priority list, overtaken by more pressing matters and new responsibilities.

Finally, recognize that your goals should not be independent of one another. Instead, they should fit together into a larger dream of who you want to be. Every once in a while, step back and consider how what you're doing today relates to the kind of career and life that you would ultimately want to have.

Organize

By determining where you want to go and expressing your goals in terms that can be measured, you have already made a lot of progress.

The next step in P.O.W.E.R. Learning is to organize the tools you'll need to accomplish your goals. Building upon the goal-setting work you've undertaken in the preparation stage, it's time to determine the best way to accomplish the goals you've identified.

How do you do this? Suppose you've decided to build a set of bookshelves for one room in your house. Let's say that you've already determined the kind of bookshelves you like and you've figured out the basic characteristics of the ones you will build (the preparation step in P.O.W.E.R. Learning). The next stage involves gathering the necessary tools, buying the wood and other building materials, sorting the construction supplies, and preparing the room for your building project—all aspects of organizing for the task.

Similarly, your academic success will hinge to a large degree on the thoroughness of your organization for each academic task that you face. In fact, one of the biggest mistakes that students make is plunging into an academic project—studying for a test, writing a paper, completing an in-class assignment—without being organized.

Looking at the Big Picture

It's natural to view college or university as a series of small tasks—classes to attend, a certain number of pages to read each week, a few papers due during the term, quizzes and final exams to study for, and so on.

But such a perspective may lead you to miss what college and university, as a whole, are all about. Using the P.O.W.E.R. Learning framework can help you to take the long view of your education, considering how it helps you achieve your long- and short-term goals for your professional and personal life (the *Prepare* step) and what you'll need to do to maximize your success (the *Organize* step). By preparing and organizing even before you set foot in the classroom for the first time, you'll be able to consider what it is that you want to get out of your post-secondary experience and how it fits into your life as a whole.

Two Kinds of Organization: Physical and Mental

Physical organization involves the mechanical aspects of task completion. For instance, you need to ask yourself if you have the appropriate tools, such as pens, paper, and a calculator. If you're using a computer, do you have access to a printer? Do you have a way to back up your files? Do you have the books and other materials you'll need to complete the assignment? Will the campus bookstore be open if you need anything else? Will the library be open when you need it? Do you have a comfortable place to work?

Mental organization is even more critical. Mental organization is accomplished by considering and reviewing the academic skills that you'll need to complete the task at hand successfully. You are an academic general in command of considerable forces—the basic skills, knowledge, and resources that you have at your command. You will need to make sure your forces are at their peak of readiness. For example, if you're working on a math assignment, you'll want to consider the basic math skills that you'll need and brush up on them. Thinking about these skills actively will help you organize mentally. Similarly, you'll want to mentally review your knowledge of engine parts before beginning car repair work (either for a class project class or at the side of the road!).

Why does producing mental organization matter? The answer is that it provides a context for when you actually begin to work. Organizing paves the way for better subsequent performance.

Too often, students or workers on the job are in a hurry to meet a deadline and figure they had better just dive in and get it done. Organizing can actually save you time, because you're less likely to be anxious and end up losing your way as you work to complete your task.

Much of this book is devoted to strategies for determining—*before* you begin work on a task—how to develop the mental tools for completing an assignment. However, as you'll see, all of these strategies share a common theme: that success comes not from a trial-and-error approach, but from following a systematic plan for achievement. Of course, this does not mean that there will be no surprises along the way, nor that simple luck is never a factor in great accomplishments. But it does mean that we often can make our own luck through careful preparation and organization.

You're ready. The preliminaries are out of the way. You've prepared and you've organized. Now it's time to start actually doing the work.

In some ways, work is the easy part, because—if you have conscientiously carried out the preparation and organization stage—you should know exactly where you're headed and what you need to do to get there.

It's not quite so easy, of course. How effectively you'll get down to the business at hand depends on many factors. Some may be out of your control. There may be a power outage that closes down the library or a massive traffic jam that delays you getting to the office. But most factors should be under your control. Instead of getting down to work, however, you may find yourself thinking up "useful" things to do—like finally cleaning underneath the couch—or simply sitting captive in front of the TV. This kind of obstacle to work relates to motivation.

Finding the Motivation to Work

"If only I could get more motivated, I'd do so much better with my _____" (*school-work, job, diet, exercising*—you fill in the blank).

All of us have said something like this at one time or another. We use the concept of **motivation**—or its lack—to explain why we just don't work hard at a task. But when we do that, we're fooling ourselves. We all have some motivation, that inner power and psychological energy that directs and fuels our behaviour. Without any motivation, we'd never get out of bed in the morning.

We've also seen evidence of how strong our motivation can be. Perhaps you're an avid runner and you love to jog in the morning and compete in weekend races. Or maybe your love of music helped you learn to play the guitar, making practising for hours a pleasure rather than a chore. Or perhaps you're a single parent, juggling work, school, and family; and you get up early every morning to make breakfast for your kids before they go off to school.

All of us are motivated. The key to success in the classroom and on the job is to tap into, harness, and direct that motivation.

If we assume that we already have all the motivation we need, P.O.W.E.R. Learning becomes a matter of turning the skills we already possess into a habit. It becomes a matter of redirecting our psychological energies toward the work we wish to accomplish.

In a sense, everything you'll encounter in this book will help you to improve your use of the motivation that you already have. But there's a key concept that underlies the control of motivation: you have to view success as a consequence of effort. In Canadian writer Malcolm Gladwell's book *Outliers,* for example, Gladwell notes that to become a true master in a field—the Sidney Crosby of hockey or the Measha Brueggergosman of opera, for example—requires about 10 000 hours of concentrated effort.

Effort produces success.

Suppose, for example, you've gotten a good performance review from your new supervisor. The boss beams at you as she discusses your results. How do you feel?

You will be pleased, of course. But at the same time you might think to yourself, "Better not get a swollen head about it. It was just luck." Or perhaps you explain your success by thinking, "The new boss just doesn't know me very well."

If you often think this way, you're cheating yourself. Using this kind of reasoning when you succeed, instead of patting yourself on the back and thinking with satisfaction, "All my hard work really paid off," is sure to undermine your future success.

Motivation
The inner power and psychological energy that directs and fuels behaviour

A great deal of psychological research has shown that thinking you have no control over what happens to you sends a powerful and damaging message to your self-esteem—that you are powerless to change things. Just think of how different it feels to say to yourself, "Wow, I worked at it and I did it," as compared with "I lucked out" or "It was so easy that anybody could have done it."

In the same way, we can delude ourselves when we try to explain our failures. People who see themselves as the victims of circumstance may tell themselves, "I'm just not smart enough," when they don't do well on an academic task. Or they might give an excuse: "My co-workers don't have children to take care of."

The way in which we view the causes of success and failure is, in fact, directly related to our success. Students who generally see effort and hard work as the reason behind their performance usually do better in college and university. Workers who see their job performance in this way usually do better in their careers. It's not hard to see why: When such individuals are working on a task, they feel that the greater the effort they put forth, the greater their chances of success. So they work harder. They believe that they have control over their success; and if they fail, they believe they can do better in the future.

The great golfer Gary Player said it best: "The harder I work, the luckier I get." Here are some tips for keeping your motivation alive, so you can work with your full energy behind you:

> **Take responsibility for your failures—and successes.** When you do poorly on a test, don't blame the teacher, the textbook, or a job that kept you from studying. When you miss a work deadline, don't blame your boss or your incompetent co-workers. Analyze the situation, and see how you could have changed what you did to be more successful in the future. At the same time, when you're successful, think of the things you did to bring about that success.

> **Think positively.** Assume that the strengths that you have will allow you to succeed and that, if you have difficulty, you can figure out what to do.

> **Accept that you can't control everything.** Seek to understand which things can be changed and which cannot. You might be able to get an extension on a paper due date, but you are probably not going to be excused from an institution-wide requirement.

To further explore the causes of academic success, consider the questions in **Try It! 3**, "Examining the Causes of Success and Failure," discussing them with your classmates.

> ## E Evaluate

"Great! I'm done with the work. Now I can move on."

It's natural to feel relief when you've finished the work necessary to fulfill the basic requirements of a task. After all, if you've written the five double-spaced pages required for an assignment or balanced a complicated office budget, why shouldn't you heave a sigh of relief and just hand in your work?

The answer is that if you stop at this point, you'll almost be guaranteed a mediocre result. Did Shakespeare dash off the first draft of *Hamlet* and, without another glance, send it off to the Globe Theatre for production? Do professional athletes just put in the bare minimum of practice to get ready for a big game? Think of one of your favourite songs. Do you think the composer wrote it in one sitting and then performed it in a concert?

It's all too easy to make excuses for our own failures. Can you think of a time when you shifted blame away from yourself for a failure? Was it a reasonable course of action? Why or why not?

3

Examining the Causes of Success and Failure

Complete this Try It! while working in a group. First, consider the following situations:

1. Although he researched his report thoroughly, Farrukh is told by his professor that he has not referenced it properly. Farrukh is disgusted with himself and says, "I'll never be good at writing research reports. I might as well give up trying."

2. Yuqi's English professor suggested that she apply for a scholarship offered to first-year students. She wins the scholarship but later finds out that only five people applied for it. She decides she only succeeded because she had no real competition.

3. Usually an A student, Alicia's grades this semester are lower than she expected. Her financial circumstances have forced her to take a part-time job, and while she no longer worries about money, she is disappointed with her performance at school. Distressed, she considers quitting school entirely, because she thinks that she'll never be able to achieve the high marks she is accustomed to.

Now consider the following questions about each of the situations:

1. What did each person conclude was the main cause of his or her performance?
2. What effect does this conclusion seem to have on the person?
3. Taking an outsider's point of view, what would *you* think was probably the main cause of each person's performance?
4. What advice would you give to each?

Now consider these broader questions:

1. What are the most important reasons why some people are more successful than others?
2. How much does ability determine success? How much does luck determine success? How much do circumstances determine success?
3. If someone performs poorly at a job, what are the possible reasons for his or her performance? If someone performs well, what are the possible reasons for his or her performance? Is it harder to find reasons for good performance or for poor performance? Why?

To Try It online, go to Connect for *P.O.W.E.R. Learning and Your Life*.

Evaluation
An assessment of the match between a product or activity and the goals it was intended to meet

In every case, the answer is no. Even the greatest creation does not emerge in perfect form, immediately meeting all the goals of its producer. Consequently, the fourth step in the P.O.W.E.R. process is **evaluation**, which consists of determining how well the product or activity we have created matches our goals for it. Let's consider some steps to follow in evaluating what you've accomplished:

> **Take a moment to congratulate yourself and feel some satisfaction.** Whether studying for a test, writing a paper, completing a report, or drafting a memo, you've done something important. You've moved from ground zero to a spot that's closer to your goal.

> **Compare what you've accomplished with the goals you're seeking to achieve.** Think back to the goals, both short-term and long-term, that you're seeking to achieve. How closely does what you've done match what you're aiming to do? For instance, if your short-term goal is to complete a math problem set with no errors, you'll need to check over the work carefully to make sure you've made no mistakes.

- **Evaluate your accomplishments as if you were a respected mentor from your past.** If you've written a paper, reread it from the perspective of a favourite teacher. If you've prepared a report, imagine you're presenting it to a boss who taught you a lot. Think about the comments you'd give if you were this person.

- **Evaluate what you've done as if you were your current instructor or supervisor.** This time, consider what you're doing from the perspective of the person who gave you the assignment. How would he or she react to what you've done? Have you followed the assignment to the letter? Is there anything you've missed?

- **Based on your evaluation, revise your work.** If you're honest with yourself, it's unlikely that your first work will satisfy you. So go back to the Work stage and revise what you've done. But don't think of it as a step back: Revisions you make as a consequence of your evaluation bring you closer to your final goal. This is a case where going back moves you forward.

R Rethink

They thought they had it perfect. But they were wrong.

In fact, it was a $1.5 billion mistake—a blunder on a grand scale. The finely ground mirror of the Hubble space telescope, designed to provide an unprecedented glimpse into the vast reaches of the universe, was not so finely ground after all.

Despite an elaborate system of evaluation designed to catch any flaws, there was a tiny blemish in the mirror that was not detected until the telescope had been launched into space and started to send back blurry photographs. By then, it seemed too late to fix the mirror.

Or was it? NASA engineers pondered the problem for months, devising and discarding one potential fix after another. Finally, after bringing a fresh eye to the situation, they formulated a daring solution that involved sending a team of astronauts into space. Once there, a space-walking Mr. Goodwrench would install several new mirrors in the telescope, which could refocus the light and compensate for the original flawed mirror.

Although the engineers could not be certain that the $629 million plan would work, it seemed like a good solution, at least on paper. It was not until the first photos were beamed back to Earth, though, that NASA knew their solution was A-OK. These photos were spectacular.

It took months of reconsideration before NASA scientists could figure out what had gone wrong and devise a solution to the problem they faced. Their approach exemplifies—on a grand scale—the final step in P.O.W.E.R. Learning: rethinking.

Rethinking what you've accomplished earlier means bringing a fresh—and clear—eye to what you've done. It involves using **critical thinking**, thinking that involves reanalyzing, questioning, and challenging our underlying assumptions. While evaluation means considering how well what we have done matches our initial goals, rethinking means reconsidering not only the outcome of our efforts, but also our goals and the ideas and process we've used to reach them. Critically rethinking what you've done involves analyzing and synthesizing ideas, and seeing the connections between different concepts.

Rethinking involves considering whether our initial goals are practical and realistic or if they require modification. It also requires asking yourself what you would do differently if you could do it over again.

Critical thinking

A process involving reanalysis, questioning, and challenge of underlying assumptions

Prepare

Organize

Work

Rethink

Evaluate

P.O.W.E.R. Learning and the World of Work

As we've discussed, the P.O.W.E.R. Learning process has applications both in the classroom and on the job. In **Career Connections** boxes, we'll highlight ways in which the principles we're discussing can help you excel in the workplace. Take a look at these "help wanted" advertisements and online postings. They illustrate the importance of the components of P.O.W.E.R. Learning in a wide variety of fields.

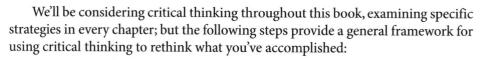

We'll be considering critical thinking throughout this book, examining specific strategies in every chapter; but the following steps provide a general framework for using critical thinking to rethink what you've accomplished:

> **Reanalyze, reviewing how you've accomplished the task.** Consider the approach and strategies you've used. What seemed to work best? Do they suggest any alternatives that might work better the next time?

> **Question the outcome.** Take a "big picture" look at what you have accomplished. Are you pleased and satisfied? Is there something you've somehow missed?

> **Identify your underlying assumptions; then challenge them.** Consider the assumptions you made in initially approaching the task. Are these underlying assumptions reasonable? If you had used different assumptions, would the result have been similar or different?

> **Consider alternatives rejected earlier.** You've likely discarded possible strategies and approaches prior to completing your task. Now's the time to think about those approaches once more and determine if they might have been more appropriate than the road you've followed.

> **What would you do differently if you had the opportunity to try things again?** It's not too late to change course.

> **Finally, reconsider your initial goals.** Are they achievable and realistic? Do your goals, and the strategies you used to attain them, need to be modified? Critically rethinking the objectives and goals that underlie your efforts is often the most effective route to success.

Completing the Process

The rethinking step of P.O.W.E.R. Learning is meant to help you understand your process of work and to improve the final product if necessary. But mostly it is meant to help you grow, to become better at whatever it is you've been doing. Like a painter looking at his or her finished work, you may see a spot here or there to touch up; but don't destroy the canvas. Perfectionism can be as paralyzing as laziness. Keep in mind these key points:

> **Know that there's always another day.** Your future success does not depend on any single assignment, paper, or test. Don't fall victim to self-defeating thoughts such as "If I don't do well on this particular assignment, I'll never graduate" or "Everything is riding on this one project." Nonsense. In school, on the job, and in life, there is almost always an opportunity to recover from a failure.

> **Realize that deciding when to stop work is often as hard as getting started.** Knowing when you have put in enough time studying for a test, revising a paper, or reviewing your figures on an estimate is as much a key to success as preparation. If you've carefully evaluated what you've done and if you've seen that there's a close fit between your goals and your work, it's time to stop work and move on.

> **Use the strategies that already work for you.** Although the P.O.W.E.R. Learning framework provides a proven approach to attaining success, employing it does not mean that you should abandon strategies that have brought you success in the past. Using multiple approaches, and personalizing them, is the surest road to success.

» LO 1.4 Learning More about Yourself

Consider what it would be like to be a member of the Trukese people, a small group of islanders in the South Pacific. Trukese sailors often sail hundreds of miles on the open sea. They manage this feat with none of the navigational equipment used by Western sailors. No compass. No chronometer. No sextant. They don't even sail in a straight line. Instead, they zigzag back and forth, at the mercy of the winds and tides. Yet they make few mistakes. Almost always they are able to reach their destination with precision. How do they do it?

They can't really explain it. They say it has to do with following the rising and setting of the stars at night. During the day, they take in the appearance, sound, and feel of the waves against the side of the boat. But they don't really have any idea of where they are at any given moment, nor do they care. They just know that ultimately they'll reach their final destination.

It would be foolhardy to suggest that the Trukese don't have what it takes to be successful sailors. The fact that they don't use traditional Western navigational equipment when they're sailing does not mean that they are any less able than Western navigators.

What about academic or career success? Isn't it reasonable to assume that there are different ways to reach academic goals and professional goals? Wouldn't it be surprising if everyone learned in exactly the same way?

Doing well in college or university and, ultimately, on the job, depends on an awareness of yourself. How do you learn? What are your strengths? What are your weaknesses? What do you value? What do you do better than most people, and what are your areas for improvement? If you can answer such questions, you'll be able to harness the best of your talents and anticipate challenges you might face. The interactive tools provided in this section of the chapter will go a long way towards helping you better understand what makes you unique and how to make the most of your potential.

Each of us has preferred ways of learning, approaches that work best for us either in the classroom or on the job. And our success is not just dependent on how well we learn, but on how we learn.

A **learning style** reflects a person's preferred manner of acquiring, using, and thinking about knowledge. We don't have just one learning style, but a variety of styles. Some involve our preferences regarding the way information is presented to us, some relate to how we think and learn most readily, and some relate to how our personality traits affect our performance. An awareness of your learning styles will help you in college by allowing you to study and learn course material more effectively. On the job, knowing your learning styles will help you master new skills and techniques, ensuring you can keep up with changing office practices or an evolving industry.

We'll start by considering the preferences we have for how we initially perceive information.

What Is Your Preferred Learning Style?

One of the most basic aspects of learning styles concerns the way in which we initially receive information from our sense organs. People have different strengths in terms of how they process information and which of their senses they prefer to use in learning. Specifically, there are four different types of learning styles:

Read/write learning style. If you have a **read/write learning style,** you prefer information that is presented visually in a written format. You feel most comfortable reading, and you may recall the spelling of a word by thinking of how the word looks. You probably learn best when you have the opportunity to read about a concept rather than listening to a teacher explain it.

> **Visual/graphic learning style.** Those with a **visual/graphic learning style** learn most effectively when material is presented visually in a diagram or picture. You might recall the structure of an engine or a part of the human body by reviewing a picture in your mind, and you might benefit from instructors who make frequent use of visual aids in class such as videos, maps, and models. Students with visual learning styles find it easier to see things in their mind's eye—to visualize a task or concept—than to be lectured about them.

> **Auditory/verbal learning style.** Have you ever asked a friend to help you put something together by having her read the directions to you while you worked? If you did, you may have an **auditory/verbal learning style.** People with auditory/verbal learning

Glossary (margin)

Learning style
One's preferred manner of acquiring, using, and thinking about knowledge

Read/write learning style
A style that involves a preference for written material, favouring reading over hearing and touching

Visual/graphic learning style
A style that favours material presented visually in a diagram or picture

Auditory/verbal learning style
A style that favours listening as the best approach to learning

Steven Spielberg, an award-winning filmmaker, is a self-admitted visual learner. How can you use your own learning style to influence your career decisions?

styles prefer listening to explanations rather than reading them. They love class lectures and discussions, because they can easily take in the information that is being talked about.

> **Tactile/kinesthetic learning style.** Those with a **tactile/kinesthetic learning style** prefer to learn by doing—touching, manipulating objects, and doing things. For instance, some people enjoy the act of writing because of the feel of a pencil or a computer keyboard—the tactile equivalent of thinking out loud. Or they may find that it helps them to make a three-dimensional model to understand a new idea.

Learning styles have implications for effective studying or for learning new skills on the job:

> If you have a **read/write style,** consider writing out summaries of information, highlighting and underlining written material, and using flash cards. Transform diagrams and math formulas into words.

> If you have a **visual/graphic style,** devise diagrams and charts. Translate words into symbols and figures.

> If you have an **auditory/verbal style,** recite material out loud when trying to learn it. Work with others in a group, talking through the material, and consider recording lectures, with your professor's approval, of course.

> If you have a **tactile/kinesthetic style,** incorporate movement into your study. Trace diagrams, build models, arrange flash cards and move them around. Keep yourself active when learning, taking notes, drawing charts, and jotting down key concepts.

Table 1.1 presents a summary of the features of these learning styles, and **Try It! 4,** "What's Your Learning Style?" will help you figure out which of the four is your preferred learning style.

Tactile/kinesthetic learning style

A style that involves learning by touching, manipulating objects, and doing things

From the perspective of . . .

A NURSING ASSISTANT
You shouldn't see your learning style as a limitation. Repeating instructions aloud is one way for nursing assistants who are auditory learners to ensure they are comprehending instructions. How can you adapt your learning style in multiple career settings?

table 1.1	The Four Learning Styles		
Category	Type	Description	Using the Style
Learning Styles	Read/write	A style that involves a preference for material in a written format, favouring reading over hearing and touching.	Read and rewrite material, take notes and rewrite them; organize material into tables; transform diagrams and math formulas into words.
	Visual/graphic	A style that favours material presented visually in a diagram or picture.	Use figures and drawings; replay classes and discussions in your mind's eye; visualize material; translate words into symbols and figures.
	Auditory/verbal	A style in which the learner favours listening as the best approach.	Recite material out loud; consider how words sound; study different languages; record lectures or training sessions; work with others, talking through the material.
	Tactile/kinesthetic	A style that involves learning by touching, manipulating objects, and doing things.	Incorporate movement into studying; trace figures and drawings with your finger; create models; make flash cards and move them around; keep active during class and meetings, taking notes, drawing charts, jotting down key concepts.

4

What's Your Learning Style?

Read each of the following statements and rank them in terms of their usefulness to you as learning approaches. Base your ratings on your personal experiences and preferences, using the following scale:

1 = Not at all useful

2 = Not very useful

3 = Neutral

4 = Somewhat useful

5 = Very useful

	1	2	3	4	5
1. Studying alone					
2. Studying pictures and diagrams to understand complex ideas					
3. Listening to class lectures					
4. Performing a process myself rather than reading or hearing about it					
5. Learning a complex procedure by reading written directions					
6. Watching and listening to film, computer, or video presentations					
7. Listening to a book or lecture on tape					
8. Doing lab work					
9. Studying teachers' handouts and lecture notes					
10. Studying in a quiet room					
11. Taking part in group discussions					
12. Taking part in hands-on demonstrations					
13. Taking notes and studying them later					
14. Creating flash cards and using them as a study and review tool					
15. Memorizing how words are spelled by spelling them "out loud" in my head					
16. Writing down key facts and important points as a tool for remembering them					
17. Recalling how to spell a word by seeing it in my head					
18. Underlining or highlighting important facts or passages in my reading					
19. Saying things out loud when I'm studying					
20. Recalling how to spell a word by "writing" it invisibly in the air or on a surface					
21. Learning new information by reading about it in a book					
22. Using a map to find an unknown place					
23. Working in a study group					
24. Finding a place I've been to once by just going there without directions					

(continued)

Scoring: The statements cycle through the four learning styles in this order: (1) read/write; (2) visual/graphic; (3) auditory/verbal; and (4) tactile/kinesthetic.

To find your primary learning style, disregard your 1, 2, and 3 ratings. Add up your 4 and 5 ratings for each learning style (i.e., a "4" equals 4 points and a "5" equals 5 points). Use the following chart to link the statements to the learning styles and to write down your summed ratings:

Learning Style	Statements	Total (Sum) of Rating Points
Read/write	1, 5, 9, 13, 17, and 21	
Visual/graphic	2, 6, 10, 14, 18, and 22	
Auditory/verbal	3, 7, 11, 15, 19, and 23	
Tactile/kinesthetic	4, 8, 12, 16, 20, and 24	

The total of your rating points for any given style will range from a low of 0 to a high of 30. The highest total indicates your main learning style. Don't be surprised if you have a mixed style, in which two or more styles receive similar ratings.

To Try It online, go to Connect for *P.O.W.E.R. Learning and Your Life.*

What Is Your Striving Style™?

Figuring out how best to leverage your college or university education begins with understanding who you are meant to be. Investing several years of your life in study only to find out that the work you have studied for does not align with your needs and values is a depressing thought. No matter which diploma or degree you want to pursue, what you strive to be influences how you learn and achieve. The Striving Styles™ Personality Assessment, developed by Canadian psychotherapist Dr. Anne Dranitsaris, helps you understand how to best approach learning by identifying what Dranitsaris calls your striving style and the predominant need that must be met for you to feel confident and secure. In **Try It! 5**, "What Is Your Striving Style?" you can determine your striving style. For a more in-depth report on your striving style, visit the Connect site for *P.O.W.E.R. Learning and Your Life* or **www.striving-styles.com**. **Table 1.2** on page 25 contains a summary of each striving style along with a description of how people of each style learn best.

Striving Style

A mode of thought and behaviour driven by a predominant need that directs the way in which we seek satisfaction from our lives.

5 Try It!

What Is Your Striving Style?

STRIVING STYLES™ SELF-ASSESSMENT–Student Version*

Rate how *often* the description in each of the following sentences applies to you	
Section A Never = 0; Rarely = 1; Infrequently = 2; Frequently = 4; Always = 5	
1. I prefer to have the choice and responsibility for making my own decisions.	
2. Others turn to me to know what to do in most situations.	
3. I look for chances to be in charge of people and activities.	
4. I usually know what is best for my friends and expect them to listen to my advice.	
5. I find it hard to see the point of people getting emotional or creating drama.	
6. I like to have goals for myself for school and my future.	
7. For me, doing my school work and projects is more important than my social life.	
8. I am uncomfortable when I have to let others be in charge.	
Section A Total	
Section B Never = 0; Rarely = 1; Infrequently = 2; Frequently = 4; Always = 5	
1. I like being with people and easily make friends with others.	
2. I have many friends and I enjoy introducing people to each other.	
3. When I am involved in group activities, I tend to talk a lot and get others involved.	
4. I have a hard time saying no to invitations from friends. My social calendar is usually pretty full.	
5. I like to see the positive in people and have a hard time understanding when they hurt my feelings.	
6. I can sometimes get so involved with my friends and their problems that I forget about my own chores or homework.	
7. I like giving compliments to people and letting my friends know how special they are to me.	
8. I see everyone I meet as a potential friend.	
Section B Total	
Section C Never = 0; Rarely = 1; Infrequently = 2; Frequently = 4; Always = 5	
1. I enjoy being the center of attention and look for chances to be there.	
2. I have many talents and do lots of things well.	
3. I am very conscious of how I look and work hard to make sure I look good.	
4. I often try to act like other people tell me I should act.	
5. I believe I am meant to do something important.	
6. I like to let people know what I can do and special things I have done.	
7. When I'm having fun, I will lose track of time and force myself to stay awake even if I'm tired so I don't miss anything.	
8. I often end up doing things that make others notice me.	
Section C Total	
Section D Never = 0; Rarely = 1; Infrequently = 2; Frequently = 4; Always = 5	
1. I like to be involved in a lot of activities most of the time.	
2. I have a strong need for adventure, excitement, and new and different experiences.	
3. I don't like having to do the same thing the same way twice.	

4. I tend to be outgoing, friendly, and sociable with many friends and acquaintances.	
5. I like to be where the action is.	
6. I am good when a problem needs to be solved or when there is trouble happening.	
7. I don't really think about how what I do might make other people feel.	
8. I need a lot of freedom and don't like it when people try to make me follow rules.	
Section D Total	

Section E — Never = 0; Rarely = 1; Infrequently = 2; Frequently = 4; Always = 5	
1. I seek beauty, originality, and creativity in all I do.	
2. Others describe me as being moody and emotional.	
3. I tend to have only a few friends, but I am very close with them.	
4. I don't feel it is important to conform to what others or society thinks I should do.	
5. I tend to be a perfectionist and am self-critical.	
6. I feel that most people do not understand me.	
7. I look calm on the outside even though there is a lot going on inside of me.	
8. I enjoy spending time alone in nature.	
Section E Total	

Section F — Never = 0; Rarely = 1; Infrequently = 2; Frequently = 4; Always = 5	
1. I get absorbed in things that interest me, spending hours alone with them.	
2. I like to know as much as I can about how things work. I also like to do things well	
3. When I am tired or feel pressure, I tend to withdraw from others and spend a lot of time alone.	
4. I believe I'm different than others and I don't like it when others try to make me conform.	
5. I will challenge people in authority (such as teachers or parents) by disagreeing or questioning them.	
6. I don't like to talk about myself and others find me difficult to know.	
7. I am not naturally curious about what I feel or how others feel.	
8. I say what's on my mind and sometimes people think I'm being critical, even when I'm not.	
Section F Total	

Section G — Never = 0; Rarely = 1; Infrequently = 2; Frequently = 4; Always = 5	
1. My friends often come to me for my opinions on things.	
2. I enjoy schoolwork where I can independently research, investigate, or create new ideas about how things might be in the future.	
3. I try to understand the deeper meaning of things.	
4. I prefer to figure out how something works than to ask for help.	
5. I sometimes know things are going to happen before they do.	
6. I am talented at solving problems and dealing with things that are complicated.	
7. I sometimes focus too much on little, unimportant things and avoid what I really need to do.	
8. When I am tired or stressed I tend to overindulge in food, alcohol, or other things that aren't really good for me.	
Section G Total	

(continued)

5 (concluded)

Section H	Never = 0; Rarely = 1; Infrequently = 2; Frequently = 4; Always = 5	
1. Others would describe me as loyal, hardworking, and predictable.		
2. I don't like change because it's more comfortable when things stay the same.		
3. I try to do what is expected of me and am respectful of authority.		
4. I tend to say no when asked to try new things, preferring to stay with what I am familiar with.		
5. I have a hard time saying no when people ask me to do important things for them.		
6. I prefer to be with the friends I know well rather than meeting new people.		
7. I sometimes worry and can imagine terrible things when I think about the future.		
8. I tend to focus more on doing things with people and less on getting to know who those people are (what they like, what they think about things, etc.)		
	Section H Total	

Overall Totals

Once you have answered the questions in each of the sections, place your scores in the <u>first column below.</u> Your striving style is the style in which you have scored highest. If you have two similar scores, read the descriptions of each of the striving styles and determine which most accurately describes how you see yourself.

Total Scores	Striving Style	Predominant Need	Key Characteristics
Section A Total _____	Leader	To be in Control	Analytical, driven, goal oriented, implements, organizes others
Section B Total _____	Socializer	To be Connected	Sociable, outgoing, sentimental, seeks personal and social success
Section C Total _____	Performer	To be Recognized	Extro verted, innovative, seeks novelty, goal and achievement driven
Section D Total _____	Adventurer	To be Spontaneous	Adventurous, hands-on, impulsive, pleasure-seeking, straightforward
Section E Total _____	Artist	To be Creative	Inaccessible, holistic, enigmatic, self-contained, seeks inner intensity
Section F Total _____	Intellectual	To be Knowledgeable	Solitary, introspective, seeks knowledge, expert, aloof
Section G Total _____	Visionary	To be Perceptive	Idealistic, creative thinker, futuristic revolutionary, discovering
Section H Total _____	Stabilizer	To be Secure	Intense, obsessive, detached, authoritarian, dutiful

*Based on the Striving Styles™ Personality System © Sage, Kahuna Enterprises 2010

To Try It online, go to Connect for *P.O.W.E.R. Learning and Your Life.*

table 1.2 The Eight Striving Styles

Category	Type	Description	How this Style Learns
Striving Styles	Leader	Self-directed, can experience difficulty accepting opinions of others.	Enjoy logical discussions in study groups, but dislike tangents. Have high expectations of self and others, including the teacher.
	Socializer	Skilful communicators, tend to take criticism personally.	Learn best in structured settings where you can discuss with your peers.
	Performer	Success-oriented, enthusiastic learners, like recognition.	Engage in learning through discussions with teacher and other students.
	Adventurer	Spontaneous, enjoy constant activity, enjoy group work.	Learn by doing, like to challenge teachers.
	Artist	Diligent, motivated to learn mainly about subjects that interest them.	Struggle to assess quality of your own work; learn best when you get to know and can consult with the teacher.
	Intellectual	Enjoy the learning process.	Need to have respect for the teacher, prefer to learn at your own pace.
	Visionary	Strong work ethic, dislike memorization.	Learn though interaction with others, whether in person or through reading.
	Stabilizer	Tenacious and persistent with their studies, need to master fundamentals before moving on.	Learn best in well-structured environment with clear, precise assignments.

Multiple Intelligences: Showing Strength in Different Domains

Do you feel much more comfortable walking through the woods than navigating city streets? Are you an especially talented musician? Is reading and using a complicated map second nature to you?

If so, in each case you may be demonstrating a special and specific kind of intelligence. According to psychologist Howard Gardner, rather than asking "How smart are you?", we should be asking "How are you smart?" To answer the latter question, Gardner has developed a theory of multiple intelligences that offers a unique approach to understanding learning styles and preferences.

The multiple intelligences view says that we have eight different forms of intelligence, each relatively independent of the others and linked to a specific kind of information processing in our brains:

> ▸ **Logical-mathematical intelligence** involves skills in problem solving and scientific thinking.

> ▸ **Linguistic intelligence** is linked to the production and use of language.

> ▸ **Spatial intelligence** relates to skills involving spatial configurations, such as those used by artists and architects.

> ▸ **Interpersonal intelligence** is found in learners with particularly strong skills involving interacting with others, such as sensitivity to the moods, temperaments, motivations, and intentions of others.

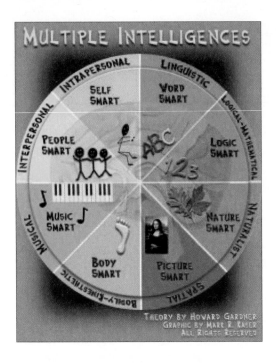

> **Intrapersonal intelligence** relates to a particularly strong understanding of the internal aspects of oneself and having access to one's own feelings and emotions.

> **Musical intelligence** involves skills relating to music.

> **Bodily kinesthetic intelligence** relates to skills in using the whole body or portions of it in the solution of problems or in the construction of products or displays, exemplified by dancers, athletes, actors, and surgeons.

> **Naturalist intelligence** involves exceptional abilities in identifying and classifying patterns in nature.

All of us have the same eight kinds of intelligence, although to varying degrees; and they form the core of our learning styles and preferences. While relatively independent of one other, these separate intelligences do not operate in isolation. Instead, any activity involves several kinds of intelligence working together. **Table 1.3** describes each of the types of intelligence and shows how each is used. Later on in this book, we'll also introduce you to the notion of "emotional intelligence" which, while not part of Howard Gardner's model, is a valuable addition to the work done in this area.

table 1.3 Multiple Intelligences

Category	Type	Description	Using the Intelligence
Multiple Intelligences	Logical-mathematical	Strengths in problem solving and scientific thinking.	Express information mathematically or in formulas.
	Linguistic	Strengths in the production and use of language.	Write out notes and summarize information in words; construct stories about material.
	Spatial	Strengths involving spatial configurations, such as those used by artists and architects.	Build charts, graphs, and flowcharts.
	Interpersonal	Found in learners with particularly strong skills involving interacting with others, such as sensitivity to the moods, temperaments, motivations, and intentions of others.	Work with others in groups.
	Intrapersonal	Strengths in understanding the internal aspects of oneself and having access to one's own feelings and emotions.	Build on your prior experiences and feelings about the world; use your originality.
	Musical	Strengths relating to music.	Write a song or lyrics to help remember material.
	Bodily kinesthetic	Strengths in using the body or parts of it in the solution of problems or in the construction of products or displays, exemplified by dancers, athletes, actors, and surgeons.	Use movement in studying; build models.
	Naturalist	Exceptional strengths in identifying and classifying patterns in nature.	Use analogies based on nature.

Put It All Together

Here are some key facts to remember about learning styles, striving styles, and multiple intelligences:

> **You have a variety of styles.** As you can see in the summaries in **Tables 1.1** (page 19), **1.2** (page 25), and **1.3** (page 26), there are several types of learning styles, striving styles, and intelligences. For any given task or challenge, some types may be more relevant than others. Furthermore, success is possible even when there is a mismatch between what you need to accomplish and your own pattern of preferred styles. It may take more work, but learning to deal with situations that require you to use less-preferred styles is important for college or university and for your career.

> **Your style reflects your preferences regarding which abilities you *like* to use—not the abilities themselves.** Styles are related to our preferences and the mental approaches we like to use. You may prefer to learn in a tactile way, but that in itself doesn't guarantee that the products that you create in that way will be good. You still have to put in work! Conversely, you can produce very good results using approaches that are difficult and uncomfortable for you.

> **Your style may change over the course of your life.** You can learn new styles and expand the range of learning experiences in which you feel perfectly comfortable. In fact, you can conceive of this book as one long lesson in learning styles because it provides you with strategies for learning more effectively in a variety of ways.

> **You should work on improving your less-preferred styles.** Although it may be tempting, don't always make choices that increase your exposure to preferred styles and decrease your practice with less-preferred styles. The more you use approaches for which you have less of a preference, the better you'll be at developing the skills associated with those styles.

> **Work cooperatively with others who have different styles.** If your instructor or supervisor asks you to work cooperatively, seek out classmates or co-workers who have styles that are different from yours. Working with people with differing styles will help you to achieve collective success, and you can also learn from observing others' approaches to tackling tasks.

Deal with Learning Disabilities

If you, like millions of people in North America, have a learning disability of any kind, the process of becoming an expert student will present additional challenges. **Learning disabilities** are defined as difficulties in processing information when listening, speaking, reading, or writing; in most cases, learning disabilities are diagnosed when there is a discrepancy between learning potential and actual academic achievement.

One of the most common kinds of learning disabilities is *dyslexia,* a reading disability that produces the misperception of letters during reading and writing, unusual difficulty in sounding out letters, spelling difficulties, and confusion between right and left. Although its causes are not yet completely understood, one likely explanation is a problem in the part of the brain responsible for breaking words into the sound elements that make up language.

Another common disability is *attention deficit hyperactivity disorder* (or *ADHD*), which is marked by inattention, an inability to concentrate, and a low

Learning disabilities
Difficulties in processing information when listening, speaking, reading, or writing, characterized by a discrepancy between learning potential and actual academic achievement

tolerance for frustration. For the 1 to 3 percent of adults who have ADHD, planning, staying on task, and maintaining interest present unusual challenges. Not only are these challenges present in college or university, but they also affect job performance.

People with learning disabilities are sometimes viewed as unintelligent. Nothing could be further from the truth: There is no relationship between learning disabilities and IQ. For instance, dozens of well-known and highly accomplished individuals suffered from dyslexia, including physicist Albert Einstein, Virgin Group founder Richard Branson, Apple founder Steve Jobs, and actors Will Smith, Orlando Bloom, and Keanu Reeves.

By the time they reach a post-secondary institution, most people with learning disabilities have already been diagnosed. If you have a diagnosed learning disability and you need special services, it is important to disclose your situation to your instructors and counsellors and to take advantage of the support they can offer.

In some cases, students with learning disabilities have not been appropriately evaluated prior to college or university. If you have difficulties such as mixing up and reversing letters frequently and suspect that you have a learning disability, there will likely be an office on campus that can provide you with guidance. One place to start is your campus counselling or health centre.

Many sorts of treatments, ranging from learning specific study strategies and the use of specially designed computer software to the use of medication, can be effective in dealing with learning disabilities. However, just because you are having trouble with reading assignments doesn't automatically mean that you have a learning disability. The kind of reading you do in college or university is more difficult than in other contexts, and there's also more of it; so you can expect to find academic reading challenging. It's only when reading represents a persistent, long-term problem—one that won't go away no matter how much work you do—that a learning disability becomes a possible explanation. An excellent Canadian website for post-secondary students with learning disabilities can be found at **www.youth2youth.ca**.

A learning disability in no way dictates what you are able to accomplish.

Time to Reflect: What Did I Learn?

1. Look back at the Employability Skills 2000+ list (Figure 1.3 on page 6), which describes the skills valued by Canadian employers. Which of these skills do you already possess? Which need more work?

2. Before reading this chapter, had you ever considered the fact that there are many different kinds of intelligence? How can knowing this have an impact on how you see other people?

3. Canadian writer Malcolm Gladwell has put forth the notion that to be a true master in any field requires about 10 000 hours of concentrated effort, which translates into about 3 hours a day, every day, for 10 years. What do you enjoy doing that would make you want to put in that kind of effort? Could you see yourself committing to that amount of time and effort? Why or why not?

Looking Back

What are the benefits of a post-secondary education?

> The reason first-year college students most often cite for attending college is to get a better job, and college graduates do earn more on average than non-graduates.

> A post-secondary education provides many benefits in addition to improved career prospects. These include becoming well educated, learning to think critically and communicate effectively, understanding the interconnections among different areas of knowledge and our place in history and the world, and understanding diversity.

What do Canadian Employers value in a potential employee?

> Canadian employers are seeking a set of skills, attitudes, and behaviours relating to three main categories: fundamental skills, personal management skills, and teamwork skills.

What are the basic principles of P.O.W.E.R. Learning?

> P.O.W.E.R. Learning is a systematic approach people can easily learn, using abilities they already possess, to acquire successful habits for learning and achieving personal goals.

> P.O.W.E.R. Learning involves **p**reparation, **o**rganization, **w**ork, **e**valuation, and **r**ethinking.

How do expert students use P.O.W.E.R. Learning?

> To *prepare*, learners set both long-term and short-term goals, making sure that their goals are realistic, measurable, and under their control—and will lead them toward their final destination.

> They *organize* the tools they will need to accomplish those goals.

> They get down to *work* on the task at hand. Using their goals as motivation, expert learners also understand that success depends on effort.

> They *evaluate* the work they've done, considering what they have accomplished in comparison with the goals they set for themselves during the preparation stage.

> Finally, they *rethink,* reflecting on the process they've used, taking a fresh look at what they have done, and critically reassessing their goals.

How can I use knowledge about my learning and striving styles and multiple intelligences to be more successful?

> People have patterns of diverse learning styles—characteristic ways of acquiring and using knowledge.

> Learning styles include read/write, visual/graphic, auditory/verbal, and tactile/kinesthetic styles.

> Striving styles include leader, socializer, performer, adventurer, artist, intellectual, visionary, and stabilizer.

> The multiple intelligences view suggests that we have eight different forms of intelligence, each relatively independent of the others.

> Knowing more about how you learn, how you are smart, and how you like to interact with the world around you can help you identify the specific techniques that will allow you to master material in class and on the job more effectively.

KEY TERMS AND CONCEPTS

Auditory/verbal learning style (p. 18)

Bodily-kinesthetic intelligence (p. 26)

Critical thinking (p. 15)

Evaluation (p. 14)

Interpersonal intelligence (p. 25)

Intrapersonal intelligence (p. 26)

Learning disabilities (p. 27)

Learning style (p. 18)

Linguistic intelligence (p. 25)

Logical-mathematical intelligence (p. 25)

Long-term goals (p. 18)

Motivation (p. 12)

Musical intelligence (p. 26)

Naturalist intelligence (p. 26)

P.O.W.E.R. Learning (p. 5)

Read/write learning style (p. 18)

Short-term goals (p. 8)

SMART approach to goal setting (p. 8)

Spatial intelligence (p. 25)

Striving style™ (p. 21)

Tactile/kinesthetic learning style (p. 19)

Visual/graphic learning style (p. 18)

RESOURCES

ON CAMPUS

Every college and university provides a significant number of resources to help its students succeed and thrive, ranging from the activities coordination office to a multicultural centre to writing labs to career centres. You can check them out on your institution's website, or in the calendar or phone directory.

Here's a list of some typical campus resources, many of which we'll be discussing in future chapters:

- Activities/clubs office
- Adult and re-entry centre
- Advising centre
- Alumni office
- Art gallery
- Bookstore
- Career centre
- Chaplain/religious services
- Child care centre
- Cinema/theatre
- Computing centre/ computer labs
- Continuing education
- Disability centre (learning or physical disabilities)

- Financial aid office
- Fitness centre/ gymnasium
- Health centre
- Honours program
- Housing centre
- Information centre
- Intramural sports
- Language lab
- Lost and found
- Math lab
- Multicultural centre
- Museum
- Online education (distance learning) office
- Off-campus housing and services
- Ombudsperson/ conflict resolution

- Photography lab
- Police/campus security
- Post office
- Printing centre
- Registration office
- Residential life office
- School newspaper
- Student government office
- Student affairs office
- Study abroad/ exchange programs
- Testing centre
- Volunteer services
- Work-study centre
- Writing lab

If you are commuting to school, your first "official" encounters on campus are likely to be with representatives of the college or university's Student Affairs Office or its equivalent. The Student Affairs Office has the goal of maintaining the quality of student life, helping to ensure that students receive the support they need. Student Affairs personnel are often in charge of student orientation programs that help new students familiarize themselves with their new institution.

Whatever representatives you deal with during your first days on campus, remember that their job is to help you. Don't be shy about asking questions about what you may expect, how to find things, and what you should be doing.

Above all, if you are experiencing any difficulties, be certain to make use of your institution's resources. Success in post-secondary education does not come easily for anyone, particularly when it demands juggling responsibilities of work and family. You should make use of whatever support your college or university offers.

IN PRINT

To learn more about Canadian writer Malcolm Gladwell's 10 000 hour theory, take a look at his fascinating book *Outliers: The Story of Success* (Little, Brown and Company, 2008).

For a practical guide on surviving your first year, check out *Off to College: Now What? A Practical Guide to Surviving and Succeeding Your First Year of College,* a paperback book authored by Jessica Linnell (Atlantic Publishing Company, 2009).

Are you an international student who is new to the Canadian education system? You'll want to examine *Succeeding as an International Student in the United States and Canada* by author Charles Lipson (University of Chicago Press, 2008).

Gail Wood's book *How to Study: Use Your Personal Learning Style to Help You Succeed When It Counts* (Learning Express Press, 2000) provides an introduction to learning styles, offering tips and suggestions for making use of the way that you learn.

ON THE WEB

The following websites provide the opportunity to extend your learning about the material in this chapter.

> Macleans.ca's on-campus website (**http://oncampus.macleans.ca/education/**) offers students up-to-the-minute news, advice, blogs, information on student finance, scholarships, and co-op. It serves as the companion site to *Maclean's* magazine's annual University Ranking issue.

> *Campus Life* magazine's online site (**www.campuslifemagazine.ca**) is 100% student driven, from the writing to the cover models. The site offers a broad selection of articles of interest to post-secondary students.

> GlobeCampus (**www.globecampus.ca/**) is *The Globe and Mail*'s site dedicated to undergraduate education in Canada, and is a companion site to *The Globe and Mail*'s annual Canadian University Report, a survey of over 40 000 students across Canada.

> To examine each of the Striving Styles in more depth, visit **www.annedranitsaris.com**.

> If you haven't yet done so, be sure to visit the Conference Board of Canada's free "Skills Credentialing Tool for Individuals" at **www.conferenceboard.ca/topics/ education/default.aspx**.

TAKING IT TO THE NET

1. Find out what percentage of the Canadian population of has received a college diploma or undergraduate degree, by visiting the Education, Training and Learning section of Statistics Canada's website at **www.statcan.gc.ca**. The site provides information about the Canadian population based on the Canadian census, which is conducted every five years in Canada (the latest one was conducted in 2011). How many men have received a post-secondary diploma or certificate? How many women?

2. Do you control your destiny, or are you controlled by it? This *Psychology Today* "Locus of Control" test assesses how you view the relative impact of hard work versus luck on achieving success. (**http://psychologytoday.tests.psychtests. com/take_test.php?idRegTest=1317**)

The Case of . . .
Vexed in Vancouver

It was during the second week of classes that the questioning started. Until then, Jian had been fairly confident in his decision to enrol at a college in the Vancouver suburbs to gain training to be a medical technician. He had been excited to try something new and to start a new career, but more and more he was wondering if he'd made the right choice.

To get to campus, Jian had to take a 45-minute bus ride, because his wife needed the car to get to her office in downtown Vancouver. Jian was also keeping his part-time job as an executive assistant at a doctor's office, a job that meant another long commute. And on top of that, Jian needed to find time among work, classes, and studying to help care for his five-year-old son.

Maybe, Jian was beginning to think, college hadn't been such a good idea. True, he could earn more money as a medical technician and begin a more promising career. But was it really worth all this added time and stress? Plus, Jian had never done very well academically. Why would college be any different? If he wanted to make more money, he could just add more shifts at his current job.

Why bother with college? Jian thought to himself. What an expense, and what a hassle. For what?

1. What arguments could you provide Jian as to the value of a college education?

2. Do you think that Jian's doubts are common?

3. What might you suggest that Jian do to help deal with his doubts about the value of college?

4. Why might a student's doubts about the value of college be especially strong during the beginning weeks of college?

5. Do you share any of Jian's concerns about the value of a college education? Do you have additional ones?

2 Making the Most of Your Time

Learning Outcomes

By the time you finish this chapter, you will be able to

》 LO 2.1   Explain why it is important to manage time more effectively and discuss techniques that can help you better manage your time.

》 LO 2.2   Analyze how to handle competing priorities.

》 LO 2.3   Identify strategies for dealing with surprises and distractions.

As Jen Wong waits in line for her morning cup of coffee, she mentally goes over the things she needs to get done during the day: *Get to the gym at 8:00 A.M. for her morning yoga class . . . study for her anatomy quiz over lunch at 12:30 . . . from 1:30 to 4:30, go to classes at the college where she's studying for her massage therapist diploma . . . meet her boyfriend at 5:00 to watch his son's soccer game . . . go home, make dinner, finish an assignment, and spend some time catching up with her friends on Facebook.* She has the nagging feeling that there's something else she needs to do, but she can't put her finger on it.

Jen finally gets to the head of the line to pay for her double-double, which she starts drinking even before she pays for it. Glancing at a clock as she leaves the Tim Hortons, she gives up the thought of getting in some last-minute studying for her anatomy quiz before her yoga class. It will be a minor miracle if she even makes it to the gym on time.

Jen has been up less than an hour, and already she is running behind schedule.

Looking Ahead

Are your days like Jen's? Are you constantly trying to cram more activities into less time? Do you feel as if you never have enough time?

You're not alone: Most of us wish we had more time to accomplish the things we need to do. However, some people are a lot better at juggling their time than others. What's their secret?

There is no secret. No one has more than 24 hours a day and 168 hours a week. The key to success lies in figuring out our priorities and better using the time we do have.

Time management is like juggling a bunch of tennis balls: For most of us, juggling doesn't come naturally; but it is a skill that can be learned. Not all of us will end up perfect jugglers (whether we are juggling tennis balls or time); but, with practice, we can become a lot better at it.

The P.O.W.E.R Plan in this chapter starts where every P.O.W.E.R. Plan starts—with Preparation—where you learn to account for the ways you currently use—and misuse—time. Then, it helps you Organize, by providing you with tools that help you track your time and strategies that help you manage your priorities and competing goals. After that comes Work—where you implement the tools and give the strategies a try. Then it's time to Evaluate— how are the tools and strategies working for you? How are you dealing with the inevitable interruptions and counterproductive personal habits that can sabotage your best intentions? And finally, it's time to Rethink—to reflect on how your personal style of time management affects you and others in your life, and to examine some of the special challenges involved in juggling the priorities of school and work with other aspects of life, such as child rearing or hobbies. The P.O.W.E.R. Plan in this chapter will provide you with skills that are important not only for success in post-secondary education and on the job, but in your personal life as well.

» LO 2.1 Managing Your Time Effectively

Without looking up from the page, answer this question: What time is it?

Most people are pretty accurate in their answer. And if you don't know for sure, it's very likely that you can find out. Your cellphone may display the time; there may be a clock on the wall, desk, or computer screen; or maybe you're riding in a car that shows the time in the instrument panel. Time is something from which we can't escape. Even if we ignore it, it's still going by, ticking away, second by second, minute by minute, hour by hour. So the main issue in using your time well is this: Who's in charge? We can allow time to slip by and let it be our enemy. Or we can take control of it and make it our ally.

By taking control of how you spend your time, you'll increase your chances of becoming more successful in your post-secondary education and in your career. Here's another way to look at it: The better you are at managing the time you devote to your studies and your job, the more time you will have to spend on your outside interests. How you approach time and time management will undoubtedly be a reflection of the learning style, striving style, and multiple intelligences you uncovered in Chapter 1. You can get a sense of your own personal "time style" by completing **Try It! 1**, "Find Your Time Style," on the next page.

The goal of time management is not to schedule every moment so we become pawns of a timetable that governs every waking moment of the day. Instead, the goal is to permit us to make informed choices as to how we use our time. Rather than letting the day slip by, largely without our awareness, the time management procedures we'll discuss can make us better able to harness time for our own ends. In short, time management doesn't confine us. On the contrary, it frees us to do the things we want and need to do.

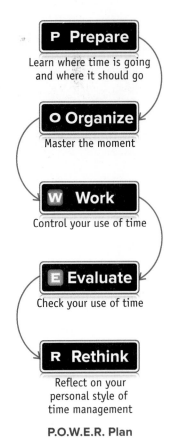

P Prepare
Learn where time is going and where it should go

O Organize
Master the moment

W Work
Control your use of time

E Evaluate
Check your use of time

R Rethink
Reflect on your personal style of time management

P.O.W.E.R. Plan

1

Find Your Time Style

Rate how well each of the statements below describes you.   Use this rating scale:

1 = Doesn't describe me at all

2 = Describes me only slightly

3 = Describes me fairly well

4 = Describes me very well

	1	2	3	4
1. I often wake up later than I should.				
2. I am usually late for classes and appointments.				
3. I am always in a rush getting places.				
4. I put off big tasks and assignments until the last minute.				
5. My friends often comment on my lateness.				
6. I am easily interrupted, putting aside what I'm doing for something new.				
7. When I look at a clock, I'm often surprised at how late it is.				
8. I often forget appointments and have to reschedule them.				
9. When faced with a big task, I feel overwhelmed and turn my mind away from it until later.				
10. At the end of the day, I have no idea where the time went.				

Rate yourself by adding up the points you assigned. Use this scale to assess your time style:

10–15 = Very efficient time user

16–20 = Efficient time user

21–30 = Time use needs work

31–40 = Victim of time

To Try It online, go to Connect for *P.O.W.E.R. Learning and Your Life.*

 **Prepare**

Learn Where Your Time Is Going

Before you get somewhere, you need to know where you're starting from and where you want to go. So the first step in improving your time management skills is figuring out how you're managing your time *now*.

"Where did the day go?" If you've ever said this to yourself, one way of figuring out where you've spent your time is

[
"You may delay, but time will not."

Benjamin Franklin
]

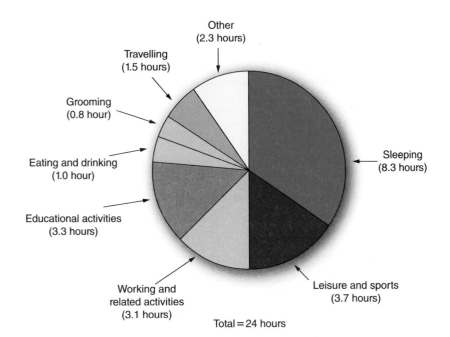

figure 2.1
Time Use of Full-Time University and College Students on an Average Weekday
Source: Courtesy of U.S. Bureau of Labor Statistics

to create a time log. A time log is the most essential tool for improving your use of time.

A **time log** is simply a record of how you actually have spent your time—including interruptions. It doesn't have to be a second-by-second record of every waking moment. But it should account for blocks of time in increments as short as 15 minutes. By looking at how much time you spend doing various activities, you now know where your time goes. How does it match with your perceptions of how you spend your time? Be prepared to be surprised, because most people find that they're spending time on a lot of activities that just don't matter very much.

Let's take a look at the results of a study of time use for full-time university and college students. As you can see from **Figure 2.1**, surprisingly little time—about 3.3 hours of every day—is actually spent on activities related to education. Perhaps it's not so surprising when you consider that, according to a study done in 2009 by Nielsen Online, the total number of minutes spent worldwide on Facebook alone increased by 566% over a one-year period; and involvement with social networking sites is only expected to increase. How does the pie chart in Figure 2.1 compare to how *you* spend your time?

Look at the blank time log in **Try It! 2**, Create a Time Log." As you fill out the log, be specific, indicating not only what you were doing at a given time (for example, "studying for economics quiz") but also the interruptions that occurred (such as "answered cellphone twice" or "switched to Internet for 10 minutes").

Time log
A record of how one spends one's time

> **From the perspective of . . .**
>
> **A STUDENT** Time logs can be helpful tools when determining how you spend your time; they can also help you find more time for the activities you enjoy doing. In what areas of your life do you wish you had more time to spend?

» LO 2.2 Handling Competing Priorities

By this point you should have a good idea of what's taking up your time. But you may not know what you should be doing instead.

To figure out the best use of your time, you need to determine your priorities. **Priorities** are the tasks and activities you need and want to do, rank-ordered from most important to least important. Your priorities should be rooted in your

Priorities
The tasks and activities that one needs and wants to do, rank-ordered from most important to least important

Try It!

Create a Time Log

		Eating &		Educational	Work &	Leisure &		
	Grooming	Drinking	Travelling	Activities	Related	Sports	Sleep	Other
6–7 a.m.								
7–8 a.m.								
8–9 a.m.								
9–10 a.m.								
10–11 a.m.								
11 a.m.–Noon								
Noon–1 p.m.								
1–2 p.m.								
2–3 p.m.								
3–4 p.m.								
4–5 p.m.								
5–6 p.m.								
6–7 p.m.								
7–8 p.m.								
8–9 p.m.								
9–10 p.m.								
10–11 p.m.								
11 p.m.–Midnight								
Midnight–6 a.m.								
Total hours spent per category								

Time Log

Day: _____   Date: _____

Keep track of the way you spend your time across seven days on time logs. Insert the amount of time you spend on each activity during each one-hour period for a single day. Do the same thing for every day of the week on separate time logs. Be sure to make copies of this log before you fill it in for the first day, or you can print out copies at the *P.O.W.E.R. Learning* website.

   Analyze your log: After you complete your log for a week, the next step is to analyze how you spend your time according to the major categories on the log, a task that will appeal particularly to those of you with strong logical-mathematical intelligence. Add up the number of hours you spend on each category, and divide the number of hours for each category by 168, which is the number of hours you have in a week. This will give you a percentage for the week for each category. Those of you who are visual/graphic learners will probably want to go one step further and transform these percentages into a pie chart like the one shown in **Figure 2.1.**

Now consider the following:

1. What do you spend most of your time on?

2. Are you satisfied with the way that you are using your time? Are there any areas that seem to use up excessive amounts of time?

3. Do you see some simple fixes that will allow you to use time more effectively?

My Weekly Time Use Pie Chart

 WORKING IN A GROUP

Compare your use of time during an average week with those of your classmates and the students who were surveyed in Figure 2.1. What are the major similarities and differences in the use of time?

To Try It online, go to Connect for *P.O.W.E.R. Learning and Your Life*.

values and your goals. There are no right or wrong priorities; you have to decide for yourself what you wish to accomplish. Maybe spending time on your studies is most important to you, or working to earn more money, or maybe your top priority is spending time with your family. Only you can decide. Furthermore, what's important to you at this moment may be less of a priority to you next month, next year, or five years from now. Revisiting your priorities, and assessing whether they still fit with your values and goals, is something that should be done on a regular basis.

For the purpose of effective time management in college or university, the best procedure is to start off by identifying priorities for an entire term. What do you need to accomplish? Don't just choose obvious, general goals, such as "passing all my classes." Instead, think about your priorities in terms of the SMART approach to goal setting introduced in Chapter 1: specific, measurable activities, such as "studying ten hours before each exam"—not "studying harder," a goal which is too vague. (Look at the example of a priority list in **Figure 2.2** and also the **Course Connections** feature on page 40.)

Write your priorities on the chart in **Try It! 3,** "Set Priorities," on page 41. After you've filled out the chart, organize it by giving each priority a ranking from 1 to 3. A "1" represents a priority that absolutely must be done; without it, you'll suffer a major setback. For instance, showing up for work should receive a "1" for a priority

Priority	Ranking
Study for each class at least 30 minutes/day	1
Start each major paper 1 week in advance of due date	2
Hand in each paper on time	1
Review for test starting a week before test date	2
Be on time for job	1
Check in with Mom once a week	3
Work out 3x/week	3

figure 2.2
Sample List of Priorities

ranking; carving out time to take those guitar lessons you always wanted to take might be ranked a "3" in terms of priority. The important point is to rank-order your priorities to reveal what is and is not important to accomplish during the term.

Setting priorities will help you to determine how to make the best use of your time. No one has enough time to complete everything; prioritizing will help you make informed decisions about what you can do to maximize your success.

Recognize What Is Important and What Is Urgent

Every priority is not as important as every other, and all priorities are not equally urgent. For example, suppose an economics assignment worth 2% of your final mark is due Wednesday morning and you also have a marketing test scheduled

Course **Connections**

Study Time: How Much Is Enough?

What would you guess is the average number of hours instructors think you should be studying each week? In the view of instructors queried in a national survey, students should spend, on average, six hours per week preparing for each class in which they're enrolled. And if they're taking courses in the sciences and engineering, instructors expect their students to put in even more hours.[1]

Keep in mind that study time does *not* include actual class time. If you add that in, someone taking four classes would need 24 hours of outside class preparation and would be in class for 16 hours—for a total of 40 hours, or the equivalent of full-time employment. If you are enrolled in a fast-track program or career college, where the training is even more intense and fast-paced, you may find yourself working the equivalent of two full-time jobs!

If you've underestimated the amount of time instructors believe is necessary to devote to class preparation, you may need to rethink the amount of time you'll need to allocate to studying. You might also speak to your individual instructors to see what they believe is an appropriate amount of preparation. Although they may not be able to give exact figures, their estimates will help you to prioritize what you need to do to be a successful student.

Set Priorities

Set your priorities for the term. They may include getting to class on time, finishing papers and assignments by their due dates, maintaining a good reputation with your boss, or spending time with your family. To get started, list your priorities in any order. Be sure to consider priorities relating to your classes, work, family, social obligations, and health. After you list them, assign a number to each one indicating its level—giving a "1" to the highest priority items, a "2" to medium priority items, and a "3" to the items with the lowest priority.

List of Priorities	
Priority	**Priority Ranking**

Now redo your list, putting your number 1s first, followed by as many of your number 2s and 3s as you feel you can reasonably commit to.

Final List of Priorities
Priority
1.
2.
3.
4.
5.
6.
7.
8.
9.
10.

1. What does this list tell you about your greatest priorities? Are they centred around school, career, friends and family, or some other aspect of your life?
2. Do you have so many "1" priorities that they will be difficult or impossible to accomplish successfully? How could you go back to your list and trim it down even more?
3. What does this listing of priorities suggest about how successful you'll be during the upcoming term?

To Try It online, go to Connect for *P.O.W.E.R. Learning and Your Life.*

Try It!

Urgent? Important?

Fill in the quadrants in **Figure 2.3** to help you figure out what is truly urgent and what is really important. Revisit the priorities you identified in **Try It! 3**, but this time distinguish the important priorities from the less important and the urgent from the not-so-urgent, taking into account *what* <u>and</u> *who* will be impacted if a priority is not addressed in time.

figure 2.3
Priority Setting: The Importance of Distinguishing What is Important and What Is Urgent
(adapted from Covey, Stephen [2004]. *The Seven Habits of Highly Successful People* [Fireside])

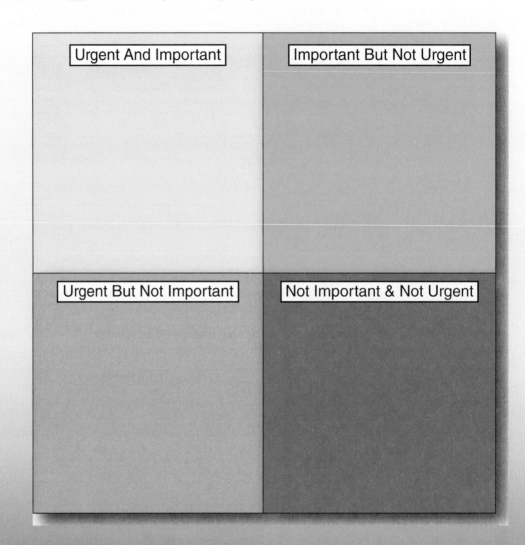

Urgent And Important

Important But Not Urgent

Urgent But Not Important

Not Important & Not Urgent

To Try It online, go to Connect for *P.O.W.E.R. Learning and Your Life.*

Wednesday afternoon, worth 25% of your final mark. While both may be urgent, they should not receive the same amount of attention. How much time you spend on each should reflect its relative impact on your grades.

Similarly, if you are working on a group project and everyone is supposed to submit a draft of his or her part by a specific date, not meeting this deadline will have an impact not only on you, but also on everyone else in your group. With even one section missing, the entire project could be delayed. Tasks of this nature, where a missed deadline has a detrimental impact on a lot of other people, should take on greater importance and urgency than those that affect only you.

With these ideas in mind, work through **Try It! 4**, "Urgent? Important?"

⊙ Organize | Master the Moment

Having completed the first step of your time management P.O.W.E.R. Plan, preparation, you now know where you've lost time in the past; and your new list of priorities is telling you where you need to head in the future.

It's time to move to step 2: Organize. This is a major step.

Being organized is key to taking control of your time; to do it well requires a few tools.

> A **master calendar** that shows all the weeks of the term in one place. Those of you who have a tactile/kinesthetic learning style should probably purchase a large, inexpensive erasable/wipe-off calendar from your local office supply store and place it above your workspace. Another alternative is to create an electronic master calendar using templates you can find readily on the Internet or by using programs like Microsoft Outlook or Google Calendar. Whether you choose an erasable or electronic calendar, you can use different colours to indicate different types of activities; i.e., red for school due dates, blue for social activities, and so on. Storing your calendar electronically is a particularly efficient approach to time management, because you can access it from anywhere and download it to your iPod, Blackberry, or other electronic organizer.

> The important point about your master calendar is that it should include every week of the term and seven days per week. In other words, it should capture your entire life for the next few months, at a glance. You should put assignment due dates and quiz and test dates into this calendar; and you should also include statutory holidays, medical and dental appointments, important birthdays and anniversaries, upcoming trips, and social activities. In this way, you can readily identify the bottlenecks, those times when you have too much going on at once and will need to consider getting something done ahead of schedule. (See the example of a master calendar in **Figure 2.4** on page 44.)

> A **weekly timetable** is a master grid with the days of the week across the top and the hours along the side. It will permit you to write in all your regularly scheduled activities, as well as one-time appointments when they arise. (A blank weekly timetable is provided in **Figure 2.5** on page 45. You can also find it online at Connect for *P.O.W.E.R. Learning and Your Life,* or use the one that comes with your calendar software.)

> A **daily to-do list** can be integrated into your online calendar program; it can be written on a small, portable calendar that includes a separate page for each day of the week; or it can simply be a small notebook, with a separate sheet of paper for every day of the week. Whatever form your daily to-do list takes, make sure it's portable, because you'll need to keep it with you all the time.

Master calendar
A schedule showing the weeks of a longer time period, such as a term or semester, with all assignments and important activities noted on it

Weekly timetable
A schedule showing all regular, prescheduled activities due to occur in the week, together with one-time events and commitments

Daily to-do list
A schedule showing the tasks, activities, and appointments due to occur during the day

figure 2.4
A Sample Master Calendar

September 2012

Sun	Mon	Tue	Wed	Thu	Fri	Sat
						1 Camping
2	3 Labour Day	4 Classes start	5	6	7	8
9	10	11 English Quiz 5%	12 Psych Quiz 10%	13	14	15
16	17	18	19	20 Acctg Quiz 5%	21	22 8 p.m. Tiff's birthday party
23	24 Math test 20%	25 English quiz 5%	26 Mktg Report due, 15%	27	28 9 a.m. Dentist	29 Study Group Mtg
30						

October 2012

Sun	Mon	Tue	Wed	Thu	Fri	Sat
	1	2	3	4 English quiz 5%	5	6
7	8 Thanksgiving	9 English midterm 20%	10 Mktg midterm 25%	11 Acctg midterm 20%	12 Psych midterm 20%	13
14 Brunch with Maria	15	16	17	18 Acctg quiz 5%	19	20 Study Group Mtg
21	22	23 English quiz 5%	24 Mkting Report Due 15%	25	26	27 Halloween party at pierre's
28	29	30	31			

November 2012

Sun	Mon	Tue	Wed	Thu	Fri	Sat
				1 Acctg Quiz 5%	2	3 Weekend in montreal
4 Montreal	5	6 English quiz 5%	7 Mktg Test 25%	8	9	10 Study Group Mtg
11	12	13	14	15 Acctg quiz 5%	16 Psych quiz 10%	17
18	19	20	21	22	23	24
25	26	27	28 Mktg Report due, 15%	29 Acctg Quiz 5%	30 Psych quiz 10%	

December 2012

Sun	Mon	Tue	Wed	Thu	Fri	Sat
						1 Study Group Mtg
2	3 Martin's Birthday	4	5 Group Report Due, 30%	6	7	8
9	10 Final Exam Week	11	12	13	14	15 Xmas Shopping
16	17	18	19	20	21	22
23	24	25 Christmas	26 Boxing Day	27	28	29
30	31					

The basic organizational task you face is filling in these three schedules. You'll need at least an hour to do this, so set the time aside. In addition, there will be some repetition across the three schedules, and the task may seem a bit tedious. But every minute you invest now in organizing your time will pay off in hours that you will save in the future.

Follow these steps in completing your schedule. The steps are similar, whether you track your appointments on paper or electronically:

> **Start with the master calendar, which shows all the weeks of the term on one page.** Write on the master calendar every class assignment, quiz, or test you have for the entire term, noting it on the date that it is due. Use your course outline or syllabus as your guide. Where due dates are not provided, ask your professor for guidance. Also include major events at work, such as days when you might need to work overtime. In addition, include important activities from your personal life and student activities, drawn from your list of priorities. For instance, if your spouse or child has a performance or your college or university has a sporting event you want to attend, be sure to mark it down.

Finally, schedule some free time—time when you promise yourself you will do something that is just plain fun. Consider these days to be written in stone, and promise yourself that you won't use them for anything else except for something enjoyable. Just knowing that you have some down time planned will help you to throw yourself into more demanding tasks. In addition, getting into the habit of allowing yourself time to relax and reflect on your life is as important as any other time management skill you may learn.

You now have a good idea of what the next few weeks have in store for you. You can identify just by looking at your master calendar the periods when you are going to be especially busy. You can also note the periods when you will have less to do.

Use the off-peak periods to get a head start on future assignments! In this way, your master schedule can help you head off disaster before it occurs.

▶ **Now move to the blank weekly timetable provided in Figure 2.5** on page 46. Fill in the times of all your fixed, prescheduled activities—the times when your classes are scheduled, when your study groups meet, when you have to be at work, or when you have to pick up your child at daycare, as well as any other regularly recurring appointments. In electronic calendars like Microsoft Outlook, it is very easy to schedule any type of recurring appointment—whether it occurs weekly, biweekly, monthly, or even annually—the latter being particularly useful for remembering birthdays, anniversaries, or your annual medical checkup.

Short- and long-term priorities may not always match. What would you do if a test scheduled in a class you needed to graduate conflicted with your daughter's weekly soccer game?

Once you've filled in the weekly timetable, as in the sample version provided in **Figure 2.6**, you get a bare-bones picture of the average week. You will still need to take into account the specific activities that are required to complete the assignments on the master calendar.

To move from your "average" week to specific weeks, make photocopies of the weekly timetable that now contains your fixed appointments. Make enough copies for every week of the term. On each copy, write the week number of the term and the specific dates it covers.

Using your master calendar, add assignment due dates, tests, and any other activities on the appropriate days of the week. Then pencil in blocks of time necessary to prepare for those events.

How much time should you allocate for schoolwork? One very rough rule of thumb holds that every one hour that you spend in class requires, on average, two hours of study outside of class to earn a B and three hours of study outside of class to earn an A. Do the arithmetic: If you are taking five 3-hour courses weekly or 15 credits (with each credit equivalent to an hour of class per week), you'll need to plan for 30 hours of studying each week to earn a B average—an intimidating amount of time. Of course, the amount of time you must allocate to a specific class will vary from week to week, depending on what is happening in the class.

If you estimate that you'll need five hours of study for a midterm exam in a certain class, pencil in those hours. Don't set up a single block of five hours. People remember best when their studying is spread out over shorter periods

Week

	14 Sunday	15 Monday	16 Tuesday	17 Wednesday	18 Thursday	19 Friday	20 Saturday
7 am							
8 00							
9 00							
10 00							
11 00							
12 pm							
1 00							
2 00							
3 00							
4 00							
5 00							
6 00							
7 00							
8 00							
9 00							
10 00							
11 00							

figure 2.5
A Weekly Timetable Template

Week

	14 Sunday	15 Monday	16 Tuesday	17 Wednesday	18 Thursday	19 Friday	20 Saturday
7 am							
8 00							
9 00		Economics Room D3-02		Economics Room D3-02	Study Group Meeting MKTG Library	Work Tim Hortons	
10 00							
11 00			Statistics Room B1-02		Statistics Room B1-02		
12 pm				Study Group Meeting ECON Library			
1 00		Lunch	Lunch with Drew	Lunch	Lunch		Yoga Class Hot Yoga Centre
2 00		Human Resources D3-06	Marketing C3-26	Human Resources D3-06	Marketing C3-26		
3 00							
4 00							
5 00			Soccer Practice Recreating				
6 00		Supper		Supper			
7 00		Work Tim Hortons	Supper	Work Tim Hortons	Supper	Supper out with friends Restaurant	
8 00			Volunteer Work Community Centre		Finance-Night course A2-15		
9 00							
10 00							
11 00							

figure 2.6
A Sample Weekly Timetable

Sometimes it is okay (and even necessary) just to relax. Make sure that you make time to unwind!

rather than attempted in one long block of time. Besides, it will probably be hard to find a block of five straight hours on your weekly calendar.

Has your professor assigned a major project that isn't due until the end of the term? Unfortunately, many students assume that they can pull off a major project by turning their attention to it a few days before it is due. This is *not* the best way to approach a major project. Like anything else that takes a lot of effort, time for a major project should be planned out and inserted into your weekly timetable.

Whether it's a group or individual project, you should begin by breaking up any major project into its component parts and identifying a reasonable amount of time required for completion of each task. A major group research project might involve, for example, 4 group meetings of 1 hour each, 10 hours of research, 5 hours of writing, 3 hours of editing, 1 hour of proofreading, and 1 hour to put together an integrated bibliography. Once you've identified the tasks and the time they require, put the tasks into the logical order in which they must be accomplished, noting which tasks involve time overlap. If it's a group project, allocate the tasks by putting a group member's name beside each one.

Now, starting with the LAST task, and taking into account how long each task takes, work your way *backwards* from the project due date. Do this with the next-to-last task, and so on, until you've worked your way back to the very first task. You will now know the very latest date on which work on the project must begin. You have just created a "**workback**" from the project's due date, and can transfer these tasks into your weekly timetable.

Keep in mind that estimates are just that: estimates. Don't think of them as set in stone, but don't deliberately under- or over-estimate the amount of work required either. And remember: It's crucial not to over-schedule yourself. You'll still need time to eat, to talk with your friends, to spend time with your family, and to enjoy yourself in general. If you find that your life is completely filled with things that you feel you must do in order to survive and that there is no room for fun, then take a step back and cut out something to make some time for yourself in your daily schedule. Finding time for yourself is as important as carving out time for what others want you to do. Besides, if you are overworked, you're likely to "find" the time by guiltily goofing off without really setting aside the time and enjoying it.

Workback

Planning when to start a project by working your way back from its due date.

To-Do List for
_____

Mon 17/10/2011

☐ ! ⬤ Task Subject	Status	Due Date	Priority	% Complete	Done
☑ Call Navendra about quiz	Not Started	Mon 17/10/2011	■ 2	0 %	
☑ Finish Marketing Assignment	In Progress	Mon 17/10/2011	1	60 %	
☑ Call dentist for appt	Not Started	Mon 17/10/2011	■ 3	0 %	
☑ Meet with Prof. Lavoie	Done	Mon 17/10/2011	1	100 %	✔
☑ Pick up Megan at school	Done	Mon 17/10/2011	1	100 %	✔
☑ Bring book to library	Done	Mon 17/10/2011	■ 2	100 %	✔
☑ Do laundry	Not Started	Mon 17/10/2011	■ 3	0 %	
☑ Work on outline Economics	In Progress	Mon 17/10/2011	■ 2	30 %	

figure 2.7
Sample Daily To-Do List

> **If you've taken each of the previous steps, you're now in a position to work on the final step of organization for successful time management: completing your daily to-do list.** Unlike the master calendar and weekly timetable—both of which you develop weeks or even months in advance—complete your daily to-do list just one day ahead of time, preferably at the end of the day.

List all the things that you intend to do the next day, and their level of priority. Start with the things you know you *must* do and which have fixed times, such as classes, work schedules, and appointments. These are your first priority items. Then add in the other things that you *should* accomplish, such as an hour of study for an upcoming test or a trip to the garage to have the oil changed in your car. Finally, list things that are lower priority but still desirable—setting aside time for a run or a walk, for example. If you use an electronic to-do list, like the one in Microsoft Outlook, turn on the auditory reminder function to remind you when a task is scheduled to begin.

Don't schedule every single minute of the day. That would be counterproductive, and you'd end up feeling as if you'd failed if you deviated from your schedule. Instead, think of your daily to-do list as a path through a forest. If you were hiking, you would allow yourself to deviate from the path, occasionally venturing onto side tracks when they looked interesting. But you'd also be keeping tabs on your direction so you would end up where you needed to be at the end of the hike, rather than miles away from your car or home.

Like the sample daily to-do list in **Figure 2.7** above, include a column to check or cross off after you've completed an activity. There's something very satisfying in acknowledging what you have accomplished.

From the perspective of . . .

A WORKING PARENT
The balancing act between work and family can be a challenge. How can a weekly timetable help you ensure all areas of your life are getting the attention they deserve?

>> LO2.3  ## Dealing with Surprises and Distractions

We've now reached Step 3 of the P.O.W.E.R. Plan for managing your time: Work. The good news is that you've already done a lot of the work, because much of work in time management is in the preparation and organization. The work involved in time management is to follow the schedules and to-do lists that you've prepared and organized. But it won't be easy. Our lives are filled with surprises. Things take longer than we've planned. A friend we haven't spoken to in a while calls to chat, and it seems rude to say that we don't have time to talk. Crises occur; buses are late; computers break down; kids get sick.

The difference between effective and ineffective time management lies in 1) how well you take control of your environment, 2) how efficiently you work, 3) how well you deal with procrastination, and 4) how well you balance competing responsibilities.

Take Control of Your Environment

It is up to you to take active control of your environment and not let it take control of you. Here are a few suggestions to help you do just that:

> **Just say no.** You don't have to agree to every request and every favour that others ask of you. You're not a bad person if you refuse to do something that will eat up your time and prevent you from accomplishing your goals. And if you do decide to do someone else a time-consuming favour, try to come up with the most efficient way of accomplishing it. Don't let all your time get taken up by the priorities of others. This advice is especially important for those of you with strong interpersonal intelligence, who tend to put the needs of others ahead of your own.

> **Get away from it all.** Go to the library. Lock yourself into your bedroom. Find a quiet, out-of-the-way coffee shop. Any of these places can serve to isolate you from everyday distractions and thereby permit you to work on the tasks that you wish to complete. Try to adopt a particular spot as your own, such as a corner desk in a secluded nook in the library. If you use it enough, your body and mind will automatically get into study mode as soon as you seat yourself there.

> **Enjoy the sounds of silence.** Although many people insist they accomplish most while a television, radio, or CD is playing, scientific studies suggest otherwise: We are able to concentrate best when our environment is silent. So even if you're sure you work best with a soundtrack playing, experiment and work in silence for a few days. Even those of you with strong musical intelligence may be surprised to find out that you get more done in less time than you would in a more distracting environment.

> **Take a break from e-distractions.** Text messages, phone calls, Facebook status updates, instant messages, email. Who doesn't love to hear from others? We may not control when communications arrive, but we can make the message wait until we are ready to receive it. Take a break and shut down your communication distractions for a period of time. When it comes to emails and social networking sites like Facebook, set aside a specific time each day to deal with them, rather than turning your attention to the computer every time an email is received or a friend's status is updated. Consider turning off audible or visual notifications entirely, so you won't be distracted by them.

> **Expect the unexpected.** Interruptions and crises, minor and major, can't be eliminated. However, they can be prepared for.

How is it possible to plan for surprises? Though it may still be too early in the term to get a clear picture of what sorts of unanticipated events you'll encounter, you should keep an eye out for patterns. Perhaps one instructor routinely gives surprise assignments. Maybe you're asked to work extra hours on the weekends because a certain co-worker doesn't show up for his or her shift.

You'll never be able to escape the interruptions and surprises that will require your attention. But by trying to anticipate them, and by thinking about how you'll react to them, you'll be positioning yourself to react more effectively when they do occur. Another way to prepare for the unexpected is to stick to your to-do list as best you can; that way, the time that you need to deal with the unexpected will be available to you.

Work Smarter, Not Harder

Thanks to smart phones, computers, and the Internet, you are never more than a click away from a massive encyclopedia of the world's knowledge. Learning to leverage this knowledge is one of the most important investments you can make. Here are some additional strategies for working smarter rather than harder:

> **Accomplish the task in the most efficient way possible.** We tend to do things the way we've always done them, without considering whether there might be a more efficient way to accomplish what we've set out to do. For example, you may consider heading out to your local bookstore to see whether they have a particular book. Why not check online first or phone ahead? You'll save time and gas, and you'll also avoid the possibility of wasting even more time browsing once you reach the bookstore!

> **Match the amount of effort you expend to the importance of the task.** You probably wouldn't spend just ten minutes deciding which car to buy, but you might spend ten minutes selecting a pair of shoes. The same goes for school work. The amount of time you put into a report worth 25% of your mark should differ significantly from the time you spend studying for a weekly 1% quiz.

> **Develop a consistent approach to tasks you do regularly.** Whether it's folding towels or developing a business presentation, there are efficiencies to be gained by approaching tasks that you do regularly in the same way each time. When it comes to your school work, reuse presentation or report templates that have worked well for you in the past. Examine some of the templates available in Microsoft Word or PowerPoint to get ideas. Why reinvent the wheel if someone has already put time and effort into developing something that you can use as a foundation?

> **Use electronic devices to help you manage your time—and your life—more effectively.** Use your smart phone or computer calendar's "reminder" functions whenever it makes sense to do so. Input due dates for upcoming assignments, then ask to be reminded about the task a few days and/or hours in advance. Invest an hour of your life putting important birthdays and anniversaries into your electronic calendar; use the "recurring annually" function with no end date, and you will never forget these dates again. Add in a reminder a week in advance of the date to prepare an e-card and purchase a gift online, a timesaver if ever there was one. And if you are an auditory/verbal learner, go one step further by making that reminder an auditory one.

Deal with Procrastination

Procrastination, the habit of putting off tasks that need to be accomplished, is like a microscopic parasite. It is invisible to the naked eye, but it eats up your time nonetheless.

Procrastination
The habit of putting off tasks that need to be accomplished

You can't control interruptions and crises that are imposed upon you by others. But even when no one else is throwing interruptions at us, we make up our own. Ever wonder how much time the average Canadian spends on social networking sites? A study by Ipsos Reid revealed that the average Facebook user, for instance, spends 5.9 hours per week on the site. How do you compare? Check out **Figure 2.8** to find out.

figure 2.8
Ipsos Reid Poll on Time Spent on Social Networking Sites[2]

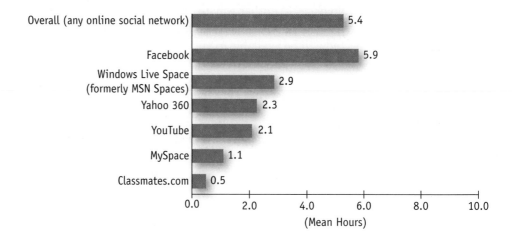

Overall (any online social network)	5.4
Facebook	5.9
Windows Live Space (formerly MSN Spaces)	2.9
Yahoo 360	2.3
YouTube	2.1
MySpace	1.1
Classmates.com	0.5

(Mean Hours)

The problem with procrastinating is that you are merely delaying the inevitable. Eventually, the task *must* get done, and you *know* it must get done. The longer you delay, the more stressed you get, and the more you open yourself up to any number of potential problems: not finding the information you are looking for, running out of printer ink, not having time to ask the professor for clarification, and so forth. Procrastinating when working on a group project is even more stressful—perhaps not for you, but certainly for the people you are working with. Professors usually expect group projects to have a unified look and to read as though they were written by one person. To accomplish this requires careful editing and proofreading—tasks which take time, and which cannot wait for procrastinators to get their act together!

To identify whether you are a procrastinator, find your "Procrastination Quotient" in **Try It! 5**, "Find Your Procrastination Quotient," on page 53.

If you find yourself procrastinating, several strategies can help you:

> **Break large tasks into small ones.** People often procrastinate because a task they're seeking to accomplish appears overwhelming. If writing a 15-page paper seems nearly impossible, think about writing a series of five 3-page papers. If reading a 750-page book seems impossible, think of it as reading several 250-page books.

> **Start with the simplest part of a task, and then do the harder parts.** Succeeding initially on the easy parts can make the harder parts of a task less daunting, and make you less apt to procrastinate in completing the task.

> **Just begin!** Sometimes the hardest part of an activity is simply getting started. So take the leap and begin the task, and the rest may follow easily.

> **Work with others.** Just being in the same physical location with others can motivate you sufficiently to accomplish tasks that you consider unpleasant and on which you might be tempted to procrastinate. For instance, filling out tedious order forms can be made easier if you collaborate with co-workers. Beware, though: If you spend too much time socializing, you lower the likelihood of success.

> **Keep the costs of procrastination in mind.** Procrastination doesn't just result in delay; it may also make the task harder than it would have been if you hadn't procrastinated. Not only will you ultimately have less time to complete the task, but you also may have to do it so quickly that its quality may be diminished. In the worst case scenario, you won't be able to finish it at all. And if others are involved in the task, you will be making their lives difficult as well, something they will remember the next time you are looking to work in their group.

Find Your Procrastination Quotient

Do you procrastinate? To find out, circle the number that best applies for each question:

1. I invent reasons and look for excuses for not acting on a problem.

Strongly agree   4   3   2   1   **Strongly disagree**

2. It takes pressure to get me to work on difficult assignments.

Strongly agree   4   3   2   1   **Strongly disagree**

3. I take half measures that will avoid or delay unpleasant or difficult tasks.

Strongly agree   4   3   2   1   **Strongly disagree**

4. I face too many interruptions and crises that interfere with accomplishing my major goals.

Strongly agree   4   3   2   1   **Strongly disagree**

5. I sometimes neglect to carry out important tasks.

Strongly agree   4   3   2   1   **Strongly disagree**

6. I schedule big assignments too late to get them done as well as I know I could.

Strongly agree   4   3   2   1   **Strongly disagree**

7. I'm sometimes too tired to do the work I need to do.

Strongly agree   4   3   2   1   **Strongly disagree**

8. I start new tasks before I finish old ones.

Strongly agree   4   3   2   1   **Strongly disagree**

9. When I work in groups, I try to get other people to finish what I don't.

Strongly agree   4   3   2   1   **Strongly disagree**

10. I put off tasks that I really don't want to do but know that I must do.

Strongly agree   4   3   2   1   **Strongly disagree**

Scoring: Total the numbers you have circled. If the score is below 15, you are not a chronic procrastinator and you probably have only an occasional problem. If your score is 16–25, you have a minor problem with procrastination. If your score is above 25, you procrastinate quite often and should work on breaking the habit.

Now, consider the following:

- If you do procrastinate often, why do you think you do it?
- Are there particular kinds of assignments that you are more likely to procrastinate on?
- Is there something that you are putting off doing right now? How might you get started on it?

 WORKING IN A GROUP

Think about the last time you procrastinated. Describe it as completely as you can. What was the task? What did you do rather than doing what needed to be done? What could you have done to avoid procrastinating in this situation? Ask others what strategy they might suggest for avoiding procrastinating.

To Try It online, go to Connect for *P.O.W.E.R. Learning and Your Life.*

Balance Competing Responsibilities

Balance school and work demands

Juggling school and a job can be a real challenge. Not only must you manage your time to complete your schoolwork, but in many cases you'll also face time management demands while you are on the job. Here are some tips to help you keep everything in balance:

> "I had a friend who was taking classes to become a paralegal. He always complained about how he didn't have enough time between taking classes and holding down his job. But he was always inviting me and his other friends out to movies, insisting we stay at the bar for one more round. It wasn't a surprise when he eventually dropped out of school. It wasn't that he didn't have enough time. It was that he spent it on all the wrong things."
>
> **Bell Hansom, restaurant manager**

▸ **If you have slack time on the job, get some studying done**. Try to keep at least some of your textbooks, class notes, or notecards always with you so you can refer to them. Of course, you should never do school work without your employer's prior agreement. If you don't get permission, you may jeopardize your job.

▸ **Use your lunch hour effectively**. Although it's important to eat a nutritious lunch and not to wolf your food down, you may be able to use some of the time allotted to you for lunch to fit in some studying.

▸ **Ask your employer about flextime**. If your job allows it, you may be able to set your own hours, within reason, as long as the work gets done. If this is an option for you, use it. Although it may create more time management challenges for you than would a job with set hours, it also provides you with some flexibility.

▸ **Accept new responsibilities carefully**. If you've barely been keeping up with the demands of work and school, don't automatically accept new job responsibilities without carefully evaluating how they fit with your long-term priorities. If your job is temporary and you're not planning to stay, you might want to respectfully decline substantial new duties or an increase in the number of hours you work. On the other hand, if you plan to continue in the job once you're done with school, accepting new responsibilities may be more reasonable.

Balance School and Work Obligations with Family Demands

If you have a job and are a student and you also have caregiver responsibilities for children or other family members, time management is especially challenging. Your family demands—and deserves—substantial quantities of your time, and juggling school and work along with family obligations can prove to be exhausting. However, there are some specific strategies that can help.

▸ **Dealing with child-care demands:**

Provide activities for your children. Kids enjoy doing things on their own for part of the day. Plan activities that will keep them happily occupied while you're doing school work.

Make spending time with your children a priority. Carve out "free play" time for your kids. Even 20 minutes of good time devoted to your children will give all of you—you *and* them—a lift. No matter how busy you are, you owe it to your children, and to yourself, to spend time as a family.

Enlist your child's help. Children love to play adult and, if they're old enough, you can ask them to help you study. Maybe they can help you clear a space to study. Perhaps you can give them "assignments" that they can work on while you're working on your assignments.

Encourage your child to invite friends over to play. Some children can remain occupied for hours if they have a playmate.

On-the-Job Time Management

In the business world, schedules are unpredictable. Crises occur, perhaps due to manufacturing problems or client demands, which require sudden flurries of work. Perhaps you have a demanding boss who may, without warning, give you an urgent assignment due the next morning. Time is always at a premium. You may be forced to drop everything you normally work on and pitch in on a sudden new task. As a result, your plans to complete your everyday work may be disrupted completely.

Simply put, time management is an essential survival skill when developing your career. Learning the basic principles of time management now will help you well beyond your years in college or university, throughout your later career. You'll also want to learn new time-management strategies specific to the working world. For instance, if you supervise other employees, it may be possible to delegate some work to them, allowing them to help you complete assignments on time. Or sometimes it may be possible to deflect assignments brought to you by a boss to some other unit or department. Always keep in mind what you can do alone and what you cannot complete without the aid of co-workers. Don't be afraid to ask for help. In the working world, the end result is what counts above all.

Use television appropriately. Television viewing is not all bad; and some shows and DVDs can be not just engaging, but educational. The trick is to pick and choose what your children watch.

Find the best child care or babysitters that you can. The better the care your children are getting, the better you'll be able to concentrate on your classes or your job. You may still feel guilty that you're not with your children as much as you'd like, but accept that guilt. Remember, your attendance in class and good performance at work builds a better future for your children.

Use your children's "downtime" effectively. If your children are young, use their nap time as a chance to catch up on work or chores. Or consider getting up early, before your children wake up, for a period in which you will have fewer interruptions than later in the day.

▸ **Dealing with the elder-care demands:**

Encourage as much independence as possible on the part of older adults for whom you are responsible. Not only will it take some of the pressure off you, but it will be helpful to the older adult.

Ask for support from your siblings and other family members. Caring for an ill or aging parent should be a family affair, not a burden that falls on any one individual.

Determine what community resources are available. Local centres for the aged may provide assistance not only to the elderly but also to their caregivers.

Respect your own needs. Remember that your own priorities are important. Elders for whom you are responsible will understand that you will sometimes need to put yourself first.

 ## Check Your Use of Time

Your time management P.O.W.E.R. Plan is on track. Now it's time to Evaluate your progress. Evaluating how you use your time is pretty straightforward: You either accomplished what you intended to do in a given period, or you didn't. Did you check off all the items on your daily to-do list? If you go over your list at the end of every day, you will know how successful your time management efforts have been, and you will be able to incorporate any activities you missed into the next day's to-do list.

Checking off the completed items on your to-do list is important because it provides an objective record of what you have accomplished on a given day. Just as important, it provides you with concrete reinforcement for completing the task. There are few things more satisfying than gazing at a to-do list with a significant number of check marks.

Of course, you won't always accomplish every item on your to-do list. That's not surprising, nor even particularly bad, especially if you've included some second- and third-level priorities that you don't absolutely have to accomplish anyway.

Give yourself a pat on the back for completing the things that you've accomplished. Successful time management is not easy, and if you've improved at all, you deserve to feel some personal satisfaction.

Reflect on Your Personal Style of Time Management

At the end of the day, after you've evaluated how well you've followed your time management plan and how much you've accomplished, it's time to Rethink where you are. Maybe you've accomplished everything you set out to do. Every task for the day is completed, and every item on your to-do list has a check mark next to it.

Or maybe you have the opposite result. Your day has been a mess, and you feel as if nothing has been accomplished. Because of a constant series of interruptions and chance events, you've been unable to make headway on your list.

Or—most likely—you find yourself somewhere in between these two extremes. Some tasks got done, while others are still hanging over you. Now is the time to rethink in a broad sense how you manage your time by doing the following:

> **Reassess your priorities.** Are your long- and short-term goals appropriate? Are you expecting too much of yourself, given the constraints in your life? Reassess your priorities in order to be sure you're attempting to do what is most important to you.

> **Reconsider your personal style of time management.** We've outlined one method of time management. Although it works well for most people, it isn't for everyone. Some people just can't bring themselves to be so structured and scheduled. They feel hemmed in by to-do lists.

  If you're one of those people, fine. You don't need to follow the suggestions presented in this chapter exactly. In fact, if you go to your campus bookstore or any office supply store, you'll find lots of other aids to manage your time. Publishing companies produce elaborate planners, such as Daytimers. In addition, software companies produce computerized time management software, such as Microsoft's Outlook or Novell's GroupWise, that reside on computers and on wireless handheld devices such as the BlackBerry or iPhone. Many cellphones contain a calendar system and alarm, and they can be set to provide periodic reminders.

However you choose to manage your time, the important thing is to do so consistently. And remember that whatever approach to time management you take, it will work best if it is compatible with your own personal values and strengths. Keep experimenting until you find an approach that works for you.

> **Consider doing less.** If you keep falling behind, do less. There are only 24 hours in the day, and we need to sleep for about a third of the time. In the remaining hours, it is impossible to carry a full load of classes and work full-time and care for a child and still have some time left to have a normal life.

Consequently, if you consistently fall behind in your work, it may be that you are just trying to do too much. Reassess your goals and your priorities, and make choices. Determine what is most important to you. It's better to accomplish less, if it is accomplished well, than to accomplish more, but poorly.

> **Use your free time well.** Although it is a problem that many of us would envy, some people have too much time on their hands. Their classes may not be too demanding, or work demands may suddenly slacken off. If this happens to you, take advantage of it. For example, you might use the extra time to simply relax and enjoy your more unhurried existence. There is a lot to be said for having time to let your thoughts wander. We need to take time out to enjoy our friends, admire the flowers in the park, exercise, and consider the spiritual side of our lives.

> "Our costliest expenditure is time."
> **Theophrastus, quoted in Diogenes Laertius's *Lives and Opinions of Eminent Philosophers*, tr. R. D. Hicks**

On the other hand, if you consistently have more time than you know what to do with, reflect on what you want to accomplish and add some activities that help you reach your goals. For example, consider becoming involved in an organization on campus. Volunteer your time to the community. Think about taking an extra course during the next term.

But whatever you decide to do, make a real decision. Don't let the time slip away. Once it's gone, it's gone forever.

Time to Reflect: What Did I Learn?

1. Generally speaking, how would you characterize your time management skills?

2. What would be the benefit to you personally if you could manage time more effectively; i.e., what goals might you accomplish if you had more time at your disposal?

3. Based on what you learned about time management in this chapter, what do you plan to do differently in the future? Be specific.

Looking Back

How can I manage my time most effectively?

> Decide to take control of your time.

> Become aware of the way you use your time now.

> Set clear priorities.

> Distinguish the important priorities from the not-so-important and the urgent from the not-so-urgent.

> Use time management tools such as a master calendar, a weekly timetable, and a daily to-do list.

How can I control my environment?

> Control your environment by saying no, getting away from it all, working in silence, taking control of communications, and leaving some slack in your schedule to accommodate the unexpected.

How can I work smarter, instead of harder?

> Accomplish tasks in the most efficient way possible, match the amount of effort you expend to the importance of the task, develop a consistent approach to tasks you do regularly, and use electronic devices to help you manage your time.

How can I avoid procrastination?

> Avoid procrastination by breaking large tasks into smaller ones, starting with the easiest parts of a task first; working with other people; and calculating the true costs of procrastination.

How can I balance competing priorities?

> Consider how your competing priorities relate to one another.

> Manage work time carefully, use slack time on the job to perform school assignments, use flextime, accept new responsibilities thoughtfully, and assign the proper priority to work.

[KEY TERMS AND CONCEPTS]

Daily to-do list (p. 43)

Master calendar (p. 43)

Priorities (p. 37)

Procrastination (p. 51)

Time log (p. 37)

Weekly timetable (p. 43)

Workback (p. 48)

[RESOURCES]

ON CAMPUS

The person who determines when classes meet is usually known as the registrar. If you are having difficulty in scheduling your classes, the registrar's office may be helpful. In addition, your academic adviser can help you work out problems in enrolling in the classes you want.

For help with such issues as planning a study schedule for the upcoming term, dealing with multiple assignments and obligations on the same date, or tips on dealing with competing academic and work demands, consult with your campus learning centre. The staff can help you sort out the various options you may have.

IN PRINT

Stephen Covey's *The Seven Habits of Highly Successful People* (Fireside, 2004) and Alan Axelrod and Brian Tracy's *Eat That Frog! 21 Great Ways to Stop Procrastinating and Get More Done in Less Time* (Berrett-Kohler, 2007) offer practical, hands-on guides to time management.

How to Do Everything with Microsoft Outlook (Osborne-McGraw-Hill, 2007), by Bill Mann, provides a quick, hands-on introduction to Microsoft's Outlook software, a popular time management program that is part of the Microsoft Office Suite.

Finally, Veronique Vienne and Erica Lennard's *The Art of the Moment: Simple Ways to Get the Most Out of Life* (Clarkson Potter, 2002) is an antidote to the impulse to schedule every minute of our days. The book celebrates taking time out and devoting it to oneself, providing a practical guide to rest and relaxation.

ON THE WEB

Connect for P.O.W.E.R. Learning and Your Life provides online versions of all the time management forms present in this chapter. You can complete the forms online or download them and print out as many copies as you need. The following websites provide the opportunity to extend your learning about the material in this chapter.

> The University of Victoria's Office of Counselling Services provides two useful sites:

  • Effective hints on how to plan study time, ideas about when to study, as well as tips on how to study (**www.coun.uvic.ca/learning/time-management/**).

  • A handy self-management checklist that allows visitors to the site to better achieve their goals with the time that they have (**www.coun.uvic.ca/learning/motivation/self-management.html**). It also provides effective techniques for avoiding procrastination and distractions, two major obstacles to effective time management.

> From Penn State University, try this nifty online interactive time management exercise (**http://pennstatelearning.psu.edu/resources/study-tips/time-mgt/exercise**). This site also includes comprehensive links to a number of comments on how to manage your time while in college or university.

TAKING IT TO THE NET

1 Complete a weekly organizer online. Find a site on the Web that offers shareware or freeware featuring a weekly planner (for example, **www.printablecalendar.ca/** or **www.studygs.net/schedule/weekly.htm**). Create a weekly schedule sheet for yourself based on this design. Be sure to write in all of your classes, job obligations, and any other regular responsibilities that you have. Be sure to set specific times in your daily schedule to study. (If you already use Outlook or another kind of communications software, use its calendar function to do the same thing.)

2 Make a master calendar for the term, using the same software you used for the exercise above. If your calendar does not provide this information automatically, you can go to Yahoo! (**dir.yahoo.com**), click on "Reference," then again on "Calendars." Here you'll find many links to different calendar-related information such as when holidays occur. Be sure to indicate dates when important assignments are due and when exams occur.

The Case of . . .

Time Crunched

Paul Misir couldn't believe it. He was working over-time at his delivery job because one of his co-workers was on vacation. During a break from his shift, he got a text message from a classmate asking if he wanted to study the next day for the exam they had to take the following Monday. Paul had forgotten all about the exam.

Even worse, Paul couldn't study with his classmate the next day because he'd promised his girlfriend he would join her to visit her grandmother, who lived an hour's drive from the city. Although he wasn't looking forward to the two-hour round trip, he knew his girlfriend would be furious if he broke his promise. And on top of all that, he also had to find time in the next few days to work on a term paper due in one of his other classes.

As he was driving home thinking about all this, his car started to sputter and then stalled. He was unable to get it started. That was it. He sat there on the side of the road, feeling as if his life had completely fallen apart and wondering how he'd ever get it back together again.

1. What might you tell Paul that could help solve his predicament?

2. What specific time management techniques might Paul have employed in the past to avoid these problems?

3. Is there anything else Paul could have done to prevent the situation he now faces from occurring in the first place?

4. What strategies might Paul use now to take control over his limited time during the coming days?

5. What advice could you give Paul to try to prevent problems in time management for his next term?

3 Reading and Remembering

Learning Outcomes

By the time you finish this chapter, you will be able to

» LO 3.1   Identify the essential elements of successful reading, and explain how to improve concentration when reading.

» LO 3.2   Demonstrate the use of techniques for memorizing large amounts of information.

» LO 3.3   Analyze how best to retain what you have read.

"Read the next chapter in the textbook by Tuesday." "Read the first two articles in the course pack by next class." "The test will cover the first hundred pages in your book, so be sure you've read them."

One day, three different reading assignments, Jessica Knowles thought as the instructor of her last class of the day delivered this last instruction. It would be hard enough for Jesssica to complete all this reading during an ordinary week. But this week she had to finish painting her bedroom and she had volunteered to help her brother move. On top of that, there was her part-time job as a cashier—and, Jessica suddenly remembered, she'd agreed to work overtime on Friday.

Still, Jessica figured that even with all her work, family, and household obligations, she could still find time to do all her reading—except Jessica believed she was an unusually slow reader. When she pushed herself to read more quickly and absorb more, she actually read and retained less. For Jessica, the problem wasn't just completing the reading—it was remembering it when test time rolled around.

Looking Ahead

For people like Jessica, reading assignments are the biggest challenge in college or university. The amount of required reading is often enormous. Even skilled readers may find themselves wishing they could read more quickly and effectively. On the job, too, many people struggle with all the memos, emails, manuals, and other documents that they need to read.

Fortunately, there are ways to improve your reading skills. In this chapter, we'll go over a number of strategies to make your reading more effective.

We'll also discuss ways to improve memory skills, not just as they relate to reading, but in general. Most of us have experienced the challenge of memorizing a seemingly impossible amount of information, and we tend to focus on our failures far more than on our successes. But the truth is that our memory capabilities are truly astounding. For instance, if you are like the average college or university student, your vocabulary contains some 50 000 words, you know hundreds of mathematical facts, and you can recall detailed images from events you witnessed years ago. In this chapter, you'll learn how to harness the power of your memory.

» LO 3.1 Sharpening Your Reading Skills

One of the reasons many people struggle with reading, especially in college or university, is they feel they *shouldn't* have to struggle with it. Reading, after all, is something almost all of us master as children, right?

In fact, it is not so simple. Reading, as we will see in this chapter, involves more than just recognizing words. The task of reading large amounts of information and remembering the essential points takes time to master.

To begin, consider the way you read now. In other words, what kind of reader are you? Ask yourself first of all about your reading preferences: What do you *like* to read, and why? What makes you pick up a book and start reading—and what makes you put one down?

Before going any further, reflect on your striving style and how it might affect how you read and remember material. Then, examine the suggestions and recommendations provided in the sidebar.

Read for Retention, Not Speed

You may have come across advertisements on the Web promoting reading "systems" that promise to teach you to read so quickly that you'll be reading entire books in an hour and whizzing through assigned readings in a few minutes.

Unfortunately that's not going to happen. Research has shown that claims of speed-reading are simply groundless. But even if it were physically possible to read a book in an hour, ultimately it probably doesn't matter very much. If we read too quickly, comprehension and ultimately retention plunge. Reading is not a race, and the fastest readers are not necessarily the best readers.

The act of reading is designed to increase our knowledge and open up new ways of thinking. It can help us achieve new levels of understanding and get us to think more broadly about the world and its inhabitants. Speed matters far less than what we take away from what we've read. That's not to say we shouldn't try to become more efficient readers who comprehend and recall more effectively. Ultimately, though, the key to good reading is comprehension, not speed.

Reading and Remembering and Striving Styles

Leaders

Try not to get impatient with reading. Set up reading and memorizing challenges to stay engaged. Reading out loud helps focus.

Socializers

Passive learning, such as reading, is de-energizing. Use of visual tools and acronyms are helpful. Helping others helps reinforce learning.

Performers

Read, then review, and talk with others about the subject. Use a visual organizer. Start well in advance and take plenty of breaks.

Adventurers

Try reading while walking or on a treadmill to increase focus. Reading and discussing can help as can having fun with acronyms and word games.

Artists

Take lots of time and space to read and reflect. Use memory cards and repetition to help with rote learning. Connect reading to something personal.

Intellectuals

Checking for inconsistencies when reading is a time-consuming distraction. Use a timer to keep track of time. Make lots of notes.

Visionaries

Read where there are no distractions. Difficulty with rote memory can cause anxiety about remembering. Make plenty of notes and use visual aids.

Stabilizers

Have others help with theory and complex subjects. Take plenty of time to absorb. Check to ensure understanding of exactly what is expected.

P **Prepare**

Approach the written word thoughtfully

O **Organize**

Gather the tools of the trade

W **Work**

Get the most out of your reading

E **Evaluate**

Put it into context of what you already know

R **Rethink**

Get it the second time

P.O.W.E.R. Plan

SQ3R approach

Model for reading and comprehension based on these five steps: Survey, Question, Read, Recite, and Review

In describing how you can use the principles of P.O.W.E.R. Learning to become a better reader with a more complete memory of what you read, we'll focus on the type of reading that is typically called for in academic pursuits—textbook chapters, articles, handouts, and the like. However, the same principles will help you get more benefit and enjoyment out of your recreational reading as well. In addition, the reading skills you learn and employ in the classroom will help you read more efficiently and effectively on the job.

P **Prepare** ## Plan Your Approach

Preparation for reading isn't difficult, and it won't take very long; but it's a crucial first step in applying P.O.W.E.R. Learning (summarized in the P.O.W.E.R. Plan here). In fact, preparation is the first step in the **SQ3R approach to reading,** a model developed during World War II by Professor Francis Robinson, a psychology professor at Ohio State University. His SQ3R model—an acronym for **S**urvey, **Q**uestion, and the three Rs, which in this case stand for **R**ead, **R**ecite, and **R**eview—was developed in response to an urgent need to train soldiers to read and understand thousands of pages of complicated technical manuals in preparation for war. The summary table shown below outlines the main points of the model, which we discuss in more detail throughout the chapter.

SQ3R

S	Survey	Familiarize yourself with the materials that surround the core text
Q	Question	Question the point of view of the material you are reading *and* the credibility of the person writing it
R	Read	Read the material
R	Recite	Recite the material aloud as you read it
R	Review	Go back and review what you've read, along with any notes you've taken

The "S" in SQ3R is for **S**urveying, or familiarizing yourself with the materials that surround the core text. These **advance organizers**—which include prefaces, chapter previews, outlines and overviews, learning outcomes, and other clues to the meaning and organization of new material—are built into most textbooks; for example, every chapter in this book includes a Learning Outcomes list and a Looking Ahead section. You can also create your own advance organizers by skimming material to be read and sketching out the general outline of the material you'll be reading. Another tip is to examine end-of-chapter review material before reading the chapter, as it will point you towards what is most important in the chapter.

Advance organizers pave the way for subsequent learning. They help you tie information that you already know to new material you're about to encounter. This connection between old and new material is crucial in helping build memories of what you read. If you approach each new reading task as something entirely new and unrelated to your previous knowledge, you'll have enormous difficulty recalling it. On the other hand, if you connect it to what you already know, you'll be able to recall it far more easily.

Advance organizers

Broad, general ideas related to material that is to about to be read or heard, which pave the way for subsequent learning

Discover How Advance Organizers Help

Read this passage. What do you think it means?

The procedure is actually quite simple. First you arrange items into different groups. Of course, one pile may be sufficient, depending on how much there is to do. If you have to go somewhere else due to lack of facilities, that is the next step; otherwise, you are pretty well set. It is important not to overdo things. That is, it is better to do too few things at once than too many. In the short run, this may not seem important; but complications can easily arise. A mistake can be expensive as well. At first, the whole procedure will seem complicated. Soon, however, it will become just another facet of life. It is difficult to foresee any end to the necessity for this task in the immediate future, but then one can never tell. After the procedure is completed, one arranges the materials into different groups again. Then they can be put into their appropriate places. Eventually, they will be used once more and the whole cycle will then have to be repeated. However, this is a part of life.[1]

If you're like most people, you don't have a clue about what this all means and you won't be able to remember anything about it in five minutes. Now, suppose you have been given some context in advance, and you know before reading it that the description has to do with doing laundry. Now does it all fall into place? Do you think it will be easier to remember? Read the passage once more, and see how having an advance organizer (in this case, *doing laundry*) helps out.

To Try It online, go to Connect for *P.O.W.E.R. Learning and Your Life.*

In short, the more we're able to make use of advance organizers and our own prior knowledge and experiences, the better we can understand and retain new material. (To prove the value of advance organizers to yourself, complete **Try It! 1**, "Discover How Advance Organizers Help.")

Identify the Purpose of the Reading Assignment

The "Q" in SQ3R involves questioning the purpose of the material you are about to read, and your goal in reading it. Will you be reading a textbook on which you'll be thoroughly tested? Is your reading supposed to provide background information that will serve as a context for future learning but that won't itself be tested? Is the material going to be useful to you personally? Realistically, how much time can you devote to the reading assignment?

Your goal for reading will help you determine which reading strategy to adopt. You aren't expected to read everything with the same degree of intensity. Some material you may feel comfortable skimming; for other material you'll want to put in the maximum effort.

Understand the Author's Point of View

The "Q" in SQ3R also extends to questioning the point of view of the material you are reading and the credibility of the person writing it. What are you reading? Is it a textbook, an essay, an article, a blog? If it is an essay, article, or blog, why was it written? To prove a point? To provide information? To express the author's personal feelings? Knowing the author's purpose (even if his or her specific point and message aren't yet clear) can help you put the material in context. Knowing something about the author can help you determine if the material is based purely on the author's own experience, and, therefore, might suffer from an inherent bias, or whether it is drawn from a broad body of professional research.

Start with the Frontmatter

Frontmatter

The preface, introduction, and table of contents of a book

If you'll be using a text or other book extensively throughout the term, start by surveying the preface and/or introduction and scanning the table of contents—what publishers call the **frontmatter.** Instructors often don't formally assign the frontmatter; but reading it can be a big help because it is there that the author has a chance to step forward and explain, often more personally than elsewhere in an academic book, what he or she considers important. Knowing this will give you a sense of what to expect as you read.

Create Advance Organizers

To provide a context for your reading, you can create your own advance organizers by skimming through the table of contents, which provides the main headings of what you will be reading. Textbooks often have chapter outlines, listing the key topics to be covered, and these also provide a way of previewing the chapter content. As you read over the outline, you can begin to consider how the new material in the book may relate both to what you know and to what you expect to learn—from the reading assignment itself and from the course.

Textbooks also often have end-of-chapter summaries, and many articles include a final section in which the author states his or her conclusions. Take a look at these ending sections as well. Even though you haven't read the material yet and the summary probably won't make complete sense to you, by reading the summary, you'll get an idea of what the author covers and what is important.

Your instructor may also provide an advance organizer for readings. Sometimes instructors will mention things to pay particular attention to or to look for, such as "When you read Thomas Paine's *Common Sense,* notice how he lays out his argument and what his key points are." Sometimes they will tell you why they assigned a particular reading. Such information provides clues that can help you develop a mental list of the reading's key ideas.

However you construct advance organizers, be sure they provide a framework and context for what you'll be reading; this framework and context can spell the difference between fully comprehending what you read and misunderstanding it.

Now it's time to put all these ideas to good use. Create an advance organizer for a textbook chapter by working through **Try It! 2**, "Create an Advance Organizer," on page 67.

Identify What You Need to Remember

No matter how important a reading assignment is to a course, you will not be expected to remember every word of it—nor should you try! The average textbook chapter has something like 20 000 words. Recalling every word of the chapter would be nearly impossible. Furthermore, no matter how much of a perfectionist you may be, memorizing every word would be a waste of your valuable time. Being able to spew out paragraphs of material is quite different from the more important ability to recall and deeply understand material in meaningful ways.

Within those 20 000 words, there may be only 20 different concepts that you need to learn. And perhaps there are only 10 keywords. *Those* are the pieces of information that should be the focus of your efforts to memorize.

How do you know what's so important that you need to recall it? One way is to use the guides built into most textbooks. Key concepts and terms are often highlighted or in boldface type. Chapters often have summaries that recap the most important information. Use such guideposts to understand what's most critical in

Create an Advance Organizer

Use any information you have available to create an advance organizer for a chapter in a text that you are using this term. Skim the section headings in the chapter, read the chapter summary, consult the book's frontmatter, and recall anything your instructor may have said about the chapter.

Complete the following statements to prepare your organizer:

1. The general topics that are covered in the chapter are . . .

2. The most critical topics and concepts in the chapter are . . .

3. The most difficult material in the chapter includes . . .

4. Words, phrases, and ideas that are unfamiliar to me include . . .

5. Ways that the material in this chapter relates to other material that I've previously read in the text include . . .

Use this Try It! as a starting point for advance organizers for future chapters in the book.

To Try It online, go to Connect for *P.O.W.E.R. Learning and Your Life.*

a chapter. Another approach is to use the journalist's trick of asking the Ws—who, what, when, where, and why.

Write down what you determine is important. Putting critical information in writing helps you manage what you need to remember, and the very act of writing it down makes it easier to memorize the information later.

In short, the first step in building a better memory of what you read is to determine just what it is that you wish to recall. By extracting what is important from what is less crucial, you'll be able to limit the amount and extent of the material that you need to recall. You'll be able to focus on what you need to remember.

Organize Gather the Tools of the Trade

It's obvious that the primary item you'll need to complete a reading assignment is the material that you're reading. But there are other essential tools you should gather, potentially including the following:

> Pencils or pens to write notes in the margin.

> Highlighters to indicate key passages in the text.

- A copy of the assignment, so you'll be sure to read the right material.
- A pad of paper and/or index cards for note-taking if the material is particularly complex. If you routinely use a computer to take notes, get it ready.
- A dictionary. You never know what new words you'll encounter while you're reading. If a dictionary is not handy, you'll be tempted to skip over unfamiliar words—a decision that may come back to haunt you. Note that some word-processing software includes a dictionary; there are also many good dictionaries available online (e.g., Merriam-Webster's at **www.m-w.com,** where you will also find an online thesaurus). The point is to use what's available—but use something!

Give Yourself Time

There's one more thing you need in order to prepare successfully for a reading assignment: enough time to complete it. The length of reading assignments is almost never ambiguous. You will typically be given a specific page range, so you will know just how much material you will need to cover.

Now get a watch and time yourself as you read the first three pages of your assignment, being sure to pay attention to the material, not the time! Timing how long it takes to read a representative chunk of material provides you with a rough measure of your reading speed for the material—although it will vary even within a single reading assignment, depending on the complexity of the material.

You'll also need to consider an aspect of your personal learning style: your reading attention span. **Attention span** is the length of time that a person usually is able to sustain attention. People with a long attention span can read for relatively lengthy periods without getting jumpy, while those with a shorter attention span can only maintain attention for a short while. Get a general sense of your own attention span by completing **Try It! 3**, "Discover Your Attention Span," on page 69.

You can use the three pieces of information you now have—the length of the assignment, your per-page reading speed at full attention, and your typical attention span—to estimate roughly how long it will take you to complete the reading assignment. For example, if you are asked to read 12 pages, you have found that you need approximately 4 minutes to read a page, and your reading attention span is, on average, 25 minutes long, you can expect your reading to take at least 60 minutes, assuming you'll take a short break when your attention begins to fade after 25 minutes.

In addition, you may need to interrupt your reading to look up words in the dictionary, get a drink, stretch, or answer the phone. You may also decide to break your reading into several short sessions, in which case your total reading time may be greater since you will have to get reacquainted with the reading assignment each time you approach it.

You can use this strategy for estimating the amount of time you will need for reading tasks outside the classroom, too. If your employer asks you to read a set of customer feedback forms, for example, you can figure out how much time in your day you'll need to block off to complete the work by factoring in the total length of all the forms, your per-page reading speed, and your attention span. Remember, though, that reading on the job is different from reading in a college or university library or at your desk at home. You can expect many more distractions as you try to read—co-workers asking questions, emails coming in, the phone ringing. Take into account these inevitable workplace distractions when making your reading time estimate.

Attention span
The length of time that attention is typically sustained

Try It! **POWER**

Discover Your Attention Span

3

You should be aware of your attention span, the length of time you usually are able to sustain attention to a task, as you prepare for reading assignments. To get an idea of the length of your current attention span for reading, perform this exercise over the next few days.

1. Choose one of the textbooks that you've been assigned to read this semester.
2. Start reading a chapter, without any preparation, noting in the chart below the time that you start reading.
3. As soon as your mind begins to wander and think about other subjects, stop reading and note the time on the chart below.
4. Using the same textbook, but not the same passage, repeat this process four more times over the course of a few days, entering the data on the chart below.
5. To find your reading attention span, calculate the average number of minutes across the five trials.

Trial #1   Starting time: _____   Ending time: _____

Number of minutes between start and end times: _____

Trial #2   Starting time: _____   Ending time: _____

Number of minutes between start and end times: _____

Trial #3   Starting time: _____   Ending time: _____

Number of minutes between start and end times: _____

Trial #4   Starting time: _____   Ending time: _____

Number of minutes between start and end times: _____

Trial #5   Starting time: _____   Ending time: _____

Number of minutes between start and end times: _____

Reading attention span (the average of the number of minutes in the last column, found by adding up the five numbers and dividing by 5) = _____ minutes

---

Ask yourself these questions about your reading attention span:

1. Are you surprised by the length of your reading attention span? In what way?
2. Does any number in the set of trials stand out from the other numbers? For instance, is any number much higher or much lower than the average? If so, can you account for this? For example, what time of day was it?
3. Do the numbers in your trials show any trend? For instance, did your attention span tend to increase, decrease, or stay the same over the course of the trials? Can you explain any trend you may have noted?
4. Do you think your attention span times would be very different if you had chosen a different textbook? Why or why not?
5. What things might you do to improve your attention span?

To Try It online, go to Connect for *P.O.W.E.R. Learning and Your Life.*

Get the Most out of Your Reading

Once you've familiarized yourself with the material as a whole and gathered the necessary tools, it's time to get down to work and start reading. Here are several things that will help you get the most out of the reading process.

Stay Focused

The TV show you watched last night . . . your husband forgetting to meet you at the bus stop . . . the new toothbrush you need to buy for your daughter . . . your grumbling stomach. There are a million and one distractions that can invade your thoughts as you read. Your job is to keep distracting thoughts at bay and focus on the material you are supposed to be reading. It's not easy, but the following are things you can do to help yourself stay focused:

> **Read in small bites.** If you think it is going to take you four hours to read an entire chapter, break up the four hours into more manageable time periods. Promise yourself that you'll read for one hour in the afternoon, another hour in the evening, and the final two hours spaced out during the following day. One hour of reading is far more manageable than a four-hour block.

> **Take a break.** Plan to take several short breaks to reward yourself while you're reading. During your breaks, do something enjoyable—eat a snack, watch a bit of a ball game on television, send a text message to a friend. Just try not to get drawn into your break activity to the point that it takes over your reading time.

> **Deal with mental distractions.** Sometimes problems have a way of popping into our minds and repeatedly distracting us. If a particular problem keeps interrupting your concentration—such as a difficulty you're having on the job—try to think of an action-oriented strategy to deal with it. You might even write your proposed solution down on a piece of paper. Putting it down on paper can get the problem off your mind, making it less intrusive.

> **Manage interruptions.** You can't prevent your children from getting into a fight and needing immediate attention. But there are some things you can do to reduce interruptions and their consequences. For instance, you can schedule reading to coincide with periods when you know you'll be alone. You can also plan to read less critical parts of assignments (such as the summaries or book frontmatter) when distractions are more likely, saving the heavier reading for later. Or, if you are a parent with small children, you can get your children involved in an activity that they can perform independently so you'll be free to concentrate.

Write and Recite While You Read

For those of you who are avid readers or who have a read/write learning style, simply reading the material, which is the first "R" in SQ3R, might be enough to help you remember it. But if you lean more towards a visual/graphic or tactile/kinesthetic learning style, the physical act of writing as you read will actually be an important part of your approach to remembering what you read. If you haven't underlined, jotted notes to yourself, placed check marks on the page, drawn arrows,

If you are reading a long assignment, taking a break can be a reward and reinvigorate you.

Textbook Tips: Starting Off on the Right Page

You've just come back from the bookstore, weighted down with a knapsack filled with textbooks and other materials for the upcoming term. Now is the time to take some preliminary steps to make the most of your investment.

- Make sure you've bought the correct textbooks. Look at each syllabus or course outline from your classes to ensure you've bought the appropriate text. Sometimes there are multiple sections of a course, and each section uses a different text or a particular edition. Be sure the book you've bought matches the description in the syllabus.

- Make the book your own. Write your name, email address, and/or telephone number in the front of the book. If you misplace your book during the term, you want the person who finds it to be able to return it to you easily.

- Orient yourself to each of your textbooks. Take a quick look at each of the books, examining the table of contents, introduction, and/or preface (as we discussed earlier). Get a sense of the content and the general reading level of the book.

- Get yourself online. Many textbooks contain a card or insert with a password that gives you access to online material. Follow the directions and enter the book's website, making sure the password allows you to register. If you have trouble making the site work, call the tech support number that should be included with the password.

constructed diagrams, and otherwise defaced and disfigured your book while you're reading, you're not doing your job as a P.O.W.E.R. reader.

The idea of writing on a book page may go against everything you've been taught in the past. (And, of course, you should never write on a library book or one that you've borrowed.) However, once you've bought your book, you own it and you should make it your own. Don't keep your textbooks spotless so they will fetch a higher price if you sell them later. Instead, think of textbooks as documents recording your active learning and engagement in a field of study. In addition, you should look at your textbooks as the foundation of your personal library, which will grow throughout your lifetime. In short, writing extensively in your book while you're reading is an important tactic for achieving success. (For more on using textbooks, see the **Course Connections** feature above.)

If you have an auditory/verbal learning style, an effective technique is to recite the material aloud as you read it—and recite, coincidentally, is the second "R" in SQ3R. As you learned in Chapter 1, auditory learners prefer to listen to material aloud or hear explanations rather than read them. For this type of learner, it is

A STUDENT To truly
retain what you are read-
ing, you must give your
reading your undivided
attention. Make a list of
your biggest distractions
and consider strategies
for avoiding those distractions when you read.

worth the extra effort to locate an audiobook version of the novel you are reading in English class, or search for a podcast on a particular topic you are discussing in class to reinforce your learning.

The ability to add your own personal notes, underline, and make other annotations to a clean text while you're reading is one of the reasons it usually pays to buy new, rather than used, textbooks. Why would you want a stranger's comments on something you own? Can you really trust that person's judgment over your own regarding what's important enough to underline? You can mark up new books in your own personal style, without the distraction of competing voices.

What should you be writing while you are reading? There are several things you should write down:

> **Rephrase key points.** Make notes to yourself, in your own words, about what the author is trying to get across. Don't just copy what's been said. Think about the material, and rewrite it in words that are your own.
>
> Writing notes to yourself in your own words has several consequences, all good. First, you make the material yours; it becomes something you now understand and part of your own knowledge base. This is an aid to memorization. When you try to recollect your reading, you won't be trying to summon the thoughts of someone else; rather, you'll be trying to remember *your own* thinking.

"What is reading but silent conversation?"

**Walter Savage Landor,
"Aristoteles and Callisthenes,"**
Imaginary Conversations **(1824–53)**

> Second, trying to summarize a key point in your own words will clarify for you whether you truly understand it. It's easy to be fooled into thinking we understand something as we're reading along. But the true test is whether we can explain it to ourselves (or someone else) on our own, without referring to the book or article.
>
> Third, the very act of writing engages an additional type of perception, involving the physical sense of moving a pen or pressing a keyboard. This will help you learn the material in a more active way.
>
> Finally, writing notes and phrases will help you study the material later. The key points will be highlighted, and your notes will also quickly bring you up to speed regarding your initial thoughts and impressions.

> **Highlight or underline key points.** Very often the first or last sentence in a paragraph, or the first or last paragraph in a section, will present a key point. Before you highlight anything, though, read the whole paragraph through. Then you'll be sure that what you highlight is, in fact, the key information. Topic sentences do not always fall at the beginning of a paragraph.
>
> Be selective in your highlighting and underlining. A page covered in yellow highlighter may be artistically appealing, but it won't help you understand the material any better. Highlight only the key information. You might find yourself highlighting only one or two sentences or phrases per page. That's fine. In highlighting and underlining, less is more. One guideline: No more than ten percent of the material should be highlighted or underlined.
>
> Keep in mind as you highlight and underline that the key material you are marking is the material you will likely need to remember for exams or assignments. To aid in your recall of such material, read it over a time or two after you've marked it, and consider reading it aloud as well. This will reinforce the memories you are building of the essential points in the assignment.

> **Use arrows, diagrams, outlines, tables, timelines, charts, and other visuals to help you understand and later recall what you are reading.** If there are three examples given for a particular point, number them. If a paragraph discusses a situation in which an earlier point does not hold, link the original point to the exception by an arrow. If a sequence of steps is presented, number each step.

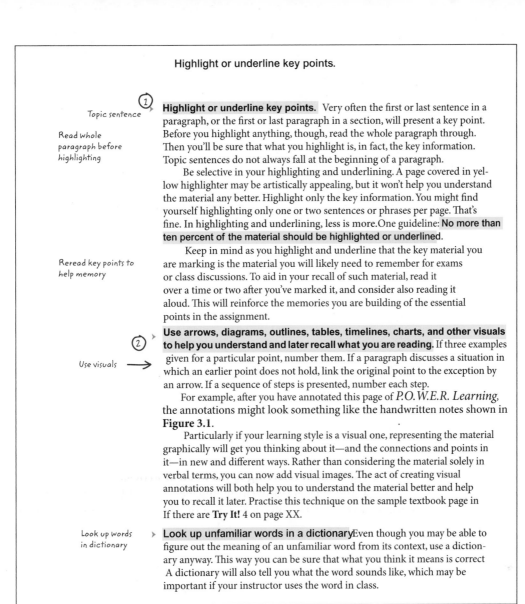

figure 3.1
Sample of Annotated Page

For example, if **Figure 3.1** were a single page of *P.O.W.E.R. Learning,* the annotations might look something like the handwritten notes in the left margin.

Particularly if your learning style is a visual one, representing the material graphically will get you thinking about it—and the connections and points in it—in new and different ways. Rather than considering the material solely in verbal terms, you now add visual images. The act of creating visual annotations will both help you to understand the material better and help you to recall it later. Practise this technique on the sample textbook page in **Try It! 4,** "Mark Up a Book Page," on pages 74 and 75.

›   **Look up unfamiliar words in a dictionary.** Even though you may be able to figure out the meaning of an unfamiliar word from its context, use a dictionary anyway. This way you can be sure that what you think it means is correct. A dictionary will also tell you what the word sounds like, which may be important if your instructor uses the word in class.

4

Mark Up a Book Page

First, working alone, read the excerpt in **Figure 3.2** on the opposite page. Then use the techniques we've discussed for marking up a page to highlight its key points.

Next, working in a group, compare and contrast your annotations with those of some classmates, and answer the following questions:

1. How do others' annotations differ from yours?

2. Why did they use the annotations they did?

3. Which annotation techniques worked best for you? Which did others prefer? Why?

4. How might these annotations help you to remember what is important?

5. If there were different sorts of material presented on the page, such as mathematical formulas, would you use different kinds of annotations?

To Try It online, go to Connect for *P.O.W.E.R. Learning and Your Life.*

4

world, not ... put our foot in our mouths every chance we get." Although a TV ad and commentary from a few politicians do not define the Canadian identity, the flavour of these does reflect distinctions within regional cultures in Canada.

The Self and Culture

So, imagine we replaced the word "Canadian" in the scale we did with some other word from our earlier list (maybe Catholic, or Muslim, or Aboriginal, or any other word that describes a group you belong to). Most of us have multiple identities (e.g., male, Muslim, Canadian and gay; Female, Baptist, Black, and straight), However, can these different identities cause conflict? Do you see conflict in the multiple identities that define who you are? Many immigrants, or children of recent immigrants, report high levels of inter-role conflict. Often, their life satisfaction and well-being is related to their ability to balance the values of their traditional culture with their new language and cultural reality (Lee & Chen, 2000; Liebkind & Jasinskaja-Lhati, 2000; Sam, 2000).

Culture The enduring behaviours, attitudes, and traditions shared by a large group of people and transmitted from one generation to the next.

Culture can be defined as the enduring behaviours, attitudes, and traditions shared by a large group of people and transmitted from one generation to the next For some people, especially those in industrialized Western cultures, individualism prevails as the self-concept. The psychology of Western culture assumes that your life will be enriched by defining your possible selves (that is, the person you could be) and believing in your power of personal control. By the end of the 20th century, individualism had become the dominant voice in Western culture.

Individualism The concept of giving priority to one's own goals over group goals and defining one's identity in terms of personal attributes rather than group identifications.

Cultures native to Asia, Africa, and Central and South America place a greater value on collectivism. They nurture what Shinobu Kitayama and Hazel Markus (1995) call the *interdependent self.* People are more self-critical and have less need for positive self-regard (Heine et al., 1999). Identity is defined more in relation to others. Malaysians, Indians, Japanese, and traditional Kenyans such as the Maasai, for example, are much more likely than Australians, Americans, and the British to complete an "I am..." statement with their group identities (Bochner, 1994; Dhawan et al., 1995; Ma & Schoeneman, 1997; Markus & Kitayama, 1991).

Collectivism Giving priority to the goals of one's groups (often one's extended family or work group) and defining one's identity accordingly.

However, making general statements about a culture's individualistic or collectivist orientations is oversimplified. Even within Canada, there are regional and ethnic differences as well. For example, people in Québec and Ontario tend to be more liberal, whereas people in Western Canada (particularly Alberta) tend to be more individualistic. Conservatives tend to be economic individualists ("don't tax or regulate me") and moral collectivists ("do legislate against immorality"). Liberals tend to be economic collectivists and moral individualists.

With an *inter*dependent self, one has a greater sense of belonging. Uprooted and cut off from family, colleagues, and loyal friends, interdependent people would lose the social connections that define who they are. They have not one self but many selves: self-with-parents, self-at-work, self-with-friends (Cross et al., 1992). As Figure 3-1 suggests, the interdependent self is embedded in social memberships. Conversation is less direct and more polite (Holtgraves, 1997). The goal of social life is not so much to enhance one's individual self as to harmonize with and support one's communities.

figure 3.2
Sample Page to Annotate

Reading Goes Digital

When computers were first introduced in the 1980s, many people sounded the death knell of books and magazines, and the idea of the "paperless office" was born. The reality, however, has been quite different. Fast forward 30 years and the paperless office is nowhere to be seen; and even with the introduction of cheaper e-texts, many students in the first decade of the twenty-first century continued to opt for tangible textbooks.

As we enter the second decade of this century, however, the reading landscape is undergoing a dramatic change. Tools like the Apple iPad, the Sony Reader, Amazon's Kindle, and the Kobo sold through Chapters/Indigo, have made the ability to read anything, anywhere, anytime, a reality for many. In fact, in the first 28 days that the Apple iPad was introduced to the United States market in the spring of 2010, one million were sold, or about one per 300 households. That means more and more of us are going to be doing our reading on electronic devices—and many of these devices incorporate features that will make remembering material even easier. The iPad, for instance, incorporates features that allow you to change font size, highlight and search text, and bookmark specific sections that you can return to later. For auditory learners, there is a built-in screen reader that will read you the page aloud. As more and more applications are built for these devices, you can expect that the task of remembering what you read will only become easier.

When reading material on a traditional computer, there are already a number of tools and techniques available that can make the task easier. The simplest approach is to cut and paste material from the screen into an application like Microsoft Word, and use the "Insert," "Review," and "References" menus to reference the source, research additional material, add comments and insert your own notes, embed images, and so forth. Microsoft also has software called OneNote which is an add-on to its Microsoft Office suite, which provides you with a seamless, organized approach to keeping all of your course materials, including notes, images, and videos, in one place. OneNote has the added advantage of being both shareable with other users (great for group projects!), and searchable by keyword. To download a trial version of OneNote, visit the main Microsoft website.

Web pages are becoming increasingly cluttered with photos, frames, sponsored advertisements, and the like, making it difficult to pinpoint what you actually want to read. A tool that can make reading online easier is Arc90's Readability, a "bookmarklet" that allows you to remove the clutter from any Web page, leaving you with only the text you want to read. To learn more about Readability, view the short video at **www.readability.com**. A similar tool called Readable is also available.

LO 3.2 Memorizing Key Material

Many of the reading strategies discussed earlier will help fix key material in your mind. Rephrasing key points, highlighting or underlining essential material and then rereading it, and creating visuals will all help you recall the information you've read.

Sometimes, though, these strategies are not enough. You may need to memorize a great deal of information, more than you'll be able to recall just through the process of reading, underlining, and so forth. Many people find extensive memorization daunting. But one of the good things about the work of memorization is that you have your choice of literally dozens of techniques. Depending on the kind of material you need to recall and how much you already know about the subject, you can turn to any number of methods.

As we sort through the various options, keep in mind that no one strategy works by itself. (And some strategies don't seem to work; for example, forget about supplements like gingko biloba—there's no clear scientific evidence that they are effective.[2]) Instead, try the following proven strategies and find those that work best for you. Feel free to devise your own strategies or add those that have worked for you in the past.

Rehearsal

Say it aloud: rehearsal. Think of it in terms of the three syllables that make up the word: re—hear—sal. OK, one more time—say the word "rehearsal."

If you're scratching your head over the last paragraph, it's to illustrate the point of **rehearsal**: to transfer material that you encounter into memory. If you don't rehearse information in some way, it will end up like most of the information to which we're exposed—on the garbage heap of lost memory.

Rehearsing is the equivalent of **R**eciting in SQ3R. To test if you've succeeded in transferring the word "rehearsal" into your memory, put down this book and go off for a few minutes. Do something entirely unrelated to reading this book. Have a snack, catch up on the latest sports scores on TSN, or read the front page of the newspaper.

Are you back? If the word "rehearsal" popped into your head when you picked up this book again, you've passed your first memory test. You can be assured that the word "rehearsal" has been transferred into your memory.

Many of us can sing along to popular songs on the radio and know the lyrics by heart. That is because we hear and/or sing the songs over and over again. Rehearsal is the key strategy in remembering information. If you don't rehearse material, it will never make it into memory. Repeating the information, summarizing it, associating it with other memories, and above all thinking about it when you first come across it will ensure that rehearsal will be effective in pushing the material into memory. If you scored high on musical intelligence, try developing a rap or rhyme to help you remember course material.

Mnemonics

This odd word (pronounced in an equally odd fashion, with the "m" silent—"neh MON ix") describes formal techniques used to make material more readily remembered. **Mnemonics** are the tricks of the trade that professional memory experts use, and will probably appeal most to people with an auditory/verbal learning style and a high score on linguistic intelligence.

Among the most common mnemonics are **acronyms.** You're already well acquainted with acronyms—words or phrases formed by the first letters of a series of terms. For instance, although you may not have known it, the word "laser" is actually an acronym for "light amplification by stimulated emissions of radiation," and "radar" is an acronym for "radio detection and ranging." If you took music lessons, you may know that FACE spells out the names of the notes that appear in the spaces on the treble clef of the music staff ("F," "A," "C," and "E," starting at the bottom of the staff).

The benefit of acronyms is that they help us to recall a complete list of items. P.O.W.E.R. stands for—well, by this point in the book, you probably remember.

Rehearsal
The process of practising and learning material to transfer it into memory

Mnemonics
Formal techniques used to make material more readily remembered

Acronym
A word or phrase formed by the first letters of a series of terms

Try It!

5

Do-it-yourself Acronyms and Acrostics

In the first part of this Try It!, work individually to create an acronym and an acrostic.

1. Figure out an acronym to remind you of the names of the five Great Lakes, using the first letters of their names (Erie, Huron, Michigan, Ontario, Superior).

2. The eight multiple intelligences you learned about in Chapter 1 are the following: naturalist, interpersonal, intrapersonal, musical, bodily-kinesthetic, logical-mathematical, spatial, and linguistic. Here is an acrostic to help you remember them: **N**umerous **I**dealistic **I**nventors **M**ake **B**itter **L**e**M**ons **S**weet and **L**uscious. Now, devise your own acrostic to help you remember the learning styles: read/write, visual/graphic, auditory/verbal, and tactile/kinesthetic. Then create another to help you remember the eight striving styles: leader, socializer, performer, adventurer, artist, intellectual, visionary, and stabilizer.

After you've tried to create the acronym and the acrostic, meet in a group and discuss these questions:

1. How successful were you in devising effective acronyms and acrostics?

2. Do some of the group members' creations seem more effective than others? Why?

3. Is the act of creating them an important component of helping to remember what they represent, or would having them created by someone else be as helpful in recalling them?

For your information, a common acronym for the Great Lakes is HOMES (**H**uron, **O**ntario, **M**ichigan, **E**rie, **S**uperior).

To Try It online, go to Connect for *P.O.W.E.R. Learning and Your Life*.

After learning to use the acronym "FACE" to remember the notes on the spaces of the music staff, many beginning musicians learn that the names of the lines on the staff form the acrostic, "Every Good Boy Deserves Fudge." Another type of mnemonic is an **acrostic**—a sentence in which the first letters correspond to something that needs to be recalled. The benefits—as well as the drawbacks—of acrostics are similar to those of acronyms. (You can explore acronyms and acrostics in **Try It! 5,** "Do-it-yourself Acronyms and Acrostics.")

Although mnemonics are helpful, keep in mind that they have a number of significant shortcomings. First, they don't focus on the meaning of the items being remembered. Because information that is learned in terms of its surface characteristics, such as first letters that form a word, is less likely to be retained than information that is learned in terms of its meaning, mnemonic devices are an imperfect route to memorization.

Acrostic

A sentence in which the first letters of the words correspond to material that is to be remembered

There's another problem with mnemonics: Sometimes it takes as much effort to create a mnemonic device as it would to memorize the material in the first place. And because the mnemonic itself has no meaning, it can be forgotten.

Despite their drawbacks, mnemonics can be useful. They are particularly helpful when the material being memorized includes a list of items or a series of steps.

Involve Multiple Senses

No matter what your learning style, the more senses you can involve when you're trying to learn new material, the better you'll be able to remember. Here's why: Every time we encounter new information, all of our senses are potentially at work. For instance, if we witness a car crash, we receive sensory input from the sight of the two cars hitting each other, the sound of the impact, and perhaps the smell of burning rubber. Each piece of sensory information is stored in a separate location in the brain, and yet all the pieces are linked together in extraordinarily intricate ways.

What this means is that when we seek to remember the details of the crash, recalling a memory of one of the sensory experiences—such as what we heard—can trigger recall of the other types of memories. For example, thinking about the *sound* the two cars made when they hit can bring back memories of the way the scene looked.

When you learn something, use your body. Don't sit passively at your desk. Instead, move around. Stand up; sit down. Touch the page. Trace figures with your fingers. Talk to yourself. Think out loud. It may seem strange, but doing this increases the number of ways in which the information is stored.

Visualize

Visualization is a technique by which images are formed to ensure that material is recalled. For instance, memory requires three basic steps: the initial recording of information, the storage of that information, and, ultimately, the retrieval of the stored information. As you read the three steps, you probably see them as logical and straightforward processes. But how do you remember them?

You might visualize a computer, with its keyboard, disks, and monitor (see **Figure 3.3**). The keyboard represents the initial recording of information. The disk represents the storage of information, and the monitor represents the display of information that has been retrieved from memory. If you can put these images in your mind, it will help you to remember the three basic memory steps later.

Visualization
A memory technique by which images are formed to help recall material

figure 3.3
Visualizing Memory

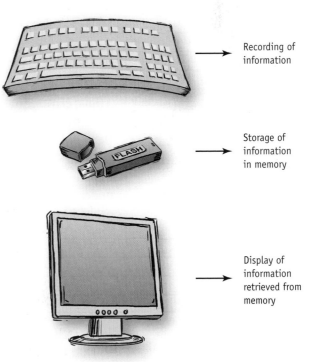

Recording of information

Storage of information in memory

Display of information retrieved from memory

Overlearn

Think back to when you were learning your basic multiplication facts ($1 \times 1 = 1$; $2 \times 2 = 4$; and so forth). Let's suppose you had put each multiplication problem on a flash card, and you decided to go through your entire set of cards, trying to get every problem right.

The first time you went through the set of cards and answered all the problems correctly, would you feel as if you'd memorized them perfectly and believe that you'd never again make an error? You shouldn't. You would need several instances of perfect performance to be sure you had learned the multiplication facts completely.

Lasting learning doesn't come until you have overlearned the material. **Overlearning** consists of studying and rehearsing material past the point of initial mastery. Through overlearning, recall becomes automatic. Rather than searching for a fact, going through mental contortions until perhaps the information surfaces, overlearning permits us to recall the information without even thinking about it.

To put the principle of overlearning to work, don't stop studying at the point when you can say to yourself, "Well, I'll probably pass this test." You may be right, but that's all you'll do—pass. Instead, spend extra time learning the material until it becomes as familiar as an old pair of jeans.

Overlearning
Studying and rehearsing material past the point of initial mastery to the point at which recall becomes automatic

» LO 3.3  **Evaluating What You Have Read**

Evaluation is a crucial step in reading. You need to be able to answer the seemingly simple question, "What does all this mean?"

But there's another aspect to evaluation. You need to evaluate, truthfully and honestly, your own level of understanding. This process of evaluation will help you to retain what you have read. What do you know as a result of your reading? Evaluation, then, consists of the following steps:

From the perspective of . . .

AN EDITORIAL ASSISTANT The ability to discern what is important within what you read is a key job function for editors. How might you apply your reading evaluation skills to an author's first draft?

▸ **Identify the main ideas and themes and their value to you personally.** Try to determine the take-home message of the material you've read. For example, the take-home message of a chapter on accounting ethics might be, "In the long run, honest accounting practices benefit the long-term health of any business."

   Sometimes the main ideas and themes are spelled out, and at other times you will have to deduce them for yourself. Evaluating the main ideas and themes in terms of how they relate to you personally will help you understand and remember them more easily.

▸ **Prioritize the ideas.** Of all the information that is presented, which is the most crucial to the main message and which is the least crucial? Make a list of the main topics covered and try to rank them in order of importance.

▸ **Think critically about the arguments presented in the reading.** Do they seem to make sense? Are the author's assertions reasonable? Are there any flaws in the arguments? Would authors with a different point of view dispute what is being said? How would they build their own arguments?

▸ **Explain the material to someone else.** There is no better way to know if you understand the material than by trying to explain it to someone else. Try explaining the material to a fellow classmate who missed the assignment. In the absence of another person, you can pretend you are explaining the material, talking—out loud!—about what you read. This is one time when talking out loud when no one else is around is not only acceptable, but beneficial.

   Talking out loud does two things. First, it helps you identify weak spots in your understanding and recall; talking to yourself will help you nail down concepts that are still not clear in your own mind. Second, and equally important, because you are transforming the written word into the spoken word, you are thinking about the information in another way, which will help you remember it better.

The Job of Reading

Memos. Annual reports. Instructions. Continuing education assignments. Professional journals.

Each of these items illustrates the importance of developing critical reading skills for on-the-job success. Virtually every job requires reading expertise; and for some professions, reading is a central component. Polishing your reading skills now will pay big dividends when you enter the world of work. The better you are at absorbing and remembering written information, the better you'll be at carrying out your job.

For instance, in many corporations, vital information is transmitted through the written word, via emails, hard-copy memos, technical reports, or Web-based material. The job of repairing broken appliances or automobiles requires the reading of numerous service manuals to master the complex computer diagnostic systems that are now standard equipment. Nurses and others in the health-care field must read journals and reports to keep up with the newest medical technologies.

Furthermore, because not all supervisors are effective writers, you'll sometimes need to read between the lines and draw inferences and conclusions about what you need to do. You should also keep in mind that there are significant cultural differences in the way in which people write and the type of language they use. Being sensitive to the cultural background of colleagues will permit you to interpret and understand what you are reading more accurately.

In short, reading is a skill that's required in virtually every profession. Developing the habit of reading critically while you are in college or university will pave the road for future career success.

> ▶ **Use in-text and online review questions and tests.** Many textbook chapters end with a quiz or a set of review questions about the material or make these available on a companion website. Don't ignore them! Such questions indicate what the writer of the book thought was important for you to learn, and they can also provide an excellent opportunity for evaluating your memory.

> ▶ **Team up with a friend or use a study group.** When it comes to evaluating your understanding of a reading, two heads (or more!) are often better than one, particularly if you scored high on interpersonal intelligence back in Chapter 1. Working with a classmate or study group—especially others who may have a different preferred learning style from your own—can help you test the limits of your understanding and memory of material and assess areas in which you need work.

> ▶ **Be honest with yourself.** Most of us are able to read with our minds on cruise control. But the net result is not much different from not reading the passage at all. If you have drifted off while you've been reading, go back and reread the passage.

 Getting It the Second Time

You're human, so—like the rest of us—when you finish a reading assignment you'd probably like nothing more than to heave a sigh of relief and put the book away.

As an experienced P.O.W.E.R. learner, by now you know that there's a key last step you should take that will assist you in cementing what you've learned into memory: rethinking what you've read. If you do it within 24 hours of first reading the assignment, it can save you hours of work later. This review process also happens to be the third "R" in SQ3R: Going back to something you've read and reviewing it, along with any notes you've taken, is one of the most effective ways of remembering what you have read.

> "Reading furnishes the mind only with materials of knowledge; it is thinking that makes what we read ours."
>
> John Locke, *Of the Conduct of the Understanding*, 1706

Yeah, right, you're probably thinking. *Like I have time for that.* The goal, though, is not a literal rereading. It isn't necessary to reread word for word. You already know what's important and what's not important, so you can skim some of the less important material. But it is wise to review the more difficult and important material carefully, making sure that you fully understand what is being discussed and ensuring that you'll remember the key details.

What's most critical, though, is that you think deeply about the material, considering the take-home message of what you've read. You need to be sure that your understanding is complete and that you're able to answer any questions that you had earlier about the material. Rethinking should be the central activity as you reread the passage and your notes.

The benefits of rethinking the material can't be overstated. Rethinking transfers material from your short-term memory to your long-term memory. It solidifies information so that it will be remembered far better over the long haul.

Time to Reflect: What Did I Learn?

1. Think about times when you read for pleasure compared with times when you read material for a class. How do the ways you read the two types of material differ?

2. Do you prefer reading traditional textbooks or e-books? Why?

3. Based on what you learned about reading and remembering in this chapter, what do you plan to do differently to help you remember what you read in the future? Be specific.

Looking Back

What are the essential elements of successful reading?

> The most important aspect of reading is comprehension, not speed. Finishing a reading assignment quickly is far less important than understanding it fully.

> One problem people have with reading is a limited attention span. However, attention span can be increased with self-awareness and practice.

How can I improve my concentration and read more effectively?

> Reading should be approached with a clear sense of purpose and goals, which will vary from assignment to assignment. Examining the frontmatter of a book and creating advance organizers are useful strategies.

> As your read, identify and focus on the key material you will need to remember later. Don't try to memorize everything you read.

> Maintain focus by breaking down the reading into small chunks, taking breaks as needed, dealing with distractions, and writing while reading.

What are some techniques I can use for memorizing large amounts of information?

> Many memory techniques are available to improve memorization. Rehearsal is a primary one, as is the use of mnemonics such as acronyms and acrostics.

> Other memory techniques are visualization and the use of multiple senses while learning new material.

> Overlearning is a basic principle of memorization.

How can I best retain what I have read?

> Understanding of reading assignments can be cemented in memory by identifying the main ideas, prioritizing them, thinking critically about the arguments, using in-text questions and tests, and explaining the writer's ideas to someone else.

> Quickly rereading assignments and the notes you took as you read can greatly help in solidifying your memory of the material.

[KEY TERMS AND CONCEPTS]

Acronym (p. 77)

Acrostic (p. 78)

Advance organizers (p. 64)

Attention span (p. 68)

Frontmatter (p. 66)

Mnemonics (p. 77)

Overlearning (p. 80)

Rehearsal (p. 77)

SQ3R (p. 64)

Visualization (p. 79)

[RESOURCES]

ON CAMPUS

If you are experiencing unusual difficulties in reading or remembering material, you may have a learning disability, as discussed in Chapter 1. If you suspect this is the case, take action. Many colleges and universities have an office that deals specifically with learning disabilities. You can also talk to someone at your college or university counselling centre; he or she will arrange for you to be tested, and this process can determine whether you have a problem.

IN PRINT

The fourth edition of Joe Cortina and Janet Elder's book, *Opening Doors: Understanding College Reading* (McGraw-Hill, 2008), provides a complete set of guidelines for reading textbooks and other kinds of writing that you will encounter during college or university. Another useful volume is the seventh edition of *Breaking Through: College Reading* (Longman, 2009) by Brenda Smith.

In *Improving Your Memory* (Johns Hopkins, 2005), Janet Fogler and Lynn Stern provide an overview of practical tips on maximizing your memory. Barry Gordon and Lisa Berger provide insight into the functioning of memory and how to improve it in *Intelligent Memory* (Penguin, 2004).

Finally, *The Memory Doctor* by Douglas Mason and Spencer Smith (New Harbinger Publications, 2005) offers simple techniques for improving memory.

ON THE WEB

The following websites provide the opportunity to extend your learning about the material in this chapter.

➤ Check out this excellent 3-minute video on how to help remember what you read. It is an interview with Dr. Cynthia R. Green, psychologist and author of *Total Memory Workout: Eight Easy Steps to Maximum Memory Fitness* (**www.howdini.com/howdini-video-6635124.html**)

➤ *Increasing Textbook Reading Comprehension by Using SQ3R* is the title of this site offered by Virginia Tech University (**www.ucc.vt.edu/lynch/TextbookReading.htm**). Offered here is a clear and detailed outline on how to use the SQ3R reading method, as well as links to other reading comprehension aids such as critical reading, proofreading, and selective reading.

➤ Need a mnemonic? Have one you'd like to share? Then just go to **www.mnemonic-device.com/**, a site devoted entirely to mnemonics. This fun and educational site covers a variety of subjects from astronomy to weather.

➤ *Mind Tools* is a website worth visiting. It offers a number of free online articles on a wide range of topics including reading strategies (**http://www.mindtools.com/rdstratg.html**), techniques for improving memory (**www.mindtools.com/memory.html**) and the SQ3R approach to reading (**http://www.mindtools.com/pages/article/newISS_02.htm**).

TAKING IT TO THE NET

1 Go to a newspaper's website, such as that of *The Globe and Mail* (**www.theglobeandmail.com**) or the *Calgary Herald* (**www.calgaryherald.com/**), and read one of the current editorials, which you can find in the Opinions section. Highlight key points of the editorial. Look up unfamiliar words in the dictionary. Make notes on what you've read. Review your notes. Then, with a classmate, recount the main points made in the editorial.

2 Practise the rehearsal technique for storing information in memory. Go to **http://canadaonline.about.com/od/premiers/Provincial_Premiers_in_Canada.htm** to find the names of five Canadian premiers. Repeat the names several times. Now explore another, unrelated site on the Web. After a few minutes, write down the names of the five premiers from memory. How did you do?

The Case of . . .

The Five-Pound Reading Packet

The instructor dropped the thick packet of course readings on Anjana Garud's desk. It landed with a loud *thunk*.

"We'll be reading this packet over the next four weeks," the instructor announced.

But staring at the packet, all Anjana could think was, *I don't think I could even lift that, let alone read it in just a month!*

Sure, Anjana was interested in the topics of the readings. They all dealt with the history of computer programming, and Anjana was in university to get her degree in that field. She told herself a lot of the information in the readings would probably be very useful, both in university and throughout her programming career.

But all Anjana could focus on as she stared at the packet were nagging questions: How could she possibly read all of it in four weeks? How would she remember all that material for tests or on the job? And perhaps most urgently of all, how would she even get the massive packet home?

1. How would you advise Anjana to prepare for her course reading?

2. How would you suggest Anjana organize her time so she could finish the readings in the allotted four weeks?

3. How might Anjana stay focused on her reading? How might she most effectively use writing as a way to accomplish her task?

4. What techniques might Anjana use to memorize long lists or other key material from her reading?

5. In what ways can Anjana use rethinking techniques to improve her understanding of the readings in the packet?

4 Taking Notes

Learning Outcomes

By the time you finish this chapter, you will be able to

» LO **4.1**   Identify the characteristics of effective notes.

» LO **4.2**   Demonstrate the various methods of note-taking: outlining, the Cornell method, concept mapping, and using a PowerPoint handout.

» LO **4.3**   Demonstrate how to take study notes, which are created for the purpose of reviewing material.

As he took a seat in the front row of his marketing class in his second term of college, Matt Ortiz realized that something fundamental had changed.

For the whole first term, Matt had sat in the back of the room during classes, just as he'd done in high school. He figured that just showing up to class was all that mattered. What difference did it make where he sat? And what difference would it make if he occasionally sent text messages on his cellphone?

But then he had received mostly Cs in his first-term courses.

In a note-taking workshop Matt enrolled in afterward, he learned the importance of active listening and taking good notes in class. He also learned that one way to become more engaged in class is to sit close to the instructor.

Trying out the strategies he was taught in the workshop, Matt found—a bit to his surprise—that they helped. By the end of the term, he'd pulled his grades way up.

Looking Ahead

Matt Ortiz's move from the back to the front of the classroom is both a source and a symbol of his academic success. Matt's ability to take good notes is also likely to pay future dividends, because note-taking skills not only help produce academic success in college but also contribute to career success.

In this chapter, we discuss effective strategies for taking notes during class lectures, during other kinds of oral presentations, and from written sources such as textbooks. There's a lot more to good note-taking than you probably think—and a lot less if you view note-taking as "getting everything down on paper." As we explore the ins and outs of note-taking, we'll pause along the way to discuss the tools of the note-taking trade, how to be an active learner, and how to think your way to good notes.

P Prepare
Consider your goals

O Organize
Get the tools of note-taking together

W Work
Process—don't just copy—information

E Evaluate
Think critically about your notes

R Rethink
Review your notes shortly after class to activate your memory

P.O.W.E.R. Plan

» LO 4.1 Taking Notes in Class

You know the type: the student who desperately tries to write down everything the instructor says. No spoken word goes unwritten. And you think to yourself, "If only I took such thorough notes—I'd do much better in my classes."

Contrary to what many students think, good note-taking does not mean writing down every word that an instructor utters. With note-taking, less is often more. We'll see why as we consider the basic steps in P.O.W.E.R. note-taking.

 **P Prepare**   Consider Your Goals

As with other academic activities, preparation is a critical component of note-taking. The following steps will prepare you for action:

> **Identify the instructor's goals for the course.** On the first day of class, most instructors talk about their objectives, what they hope you'll get out of the class, and what you'll know when it's over. Most instructors restate the information on the class syllabus or course outline, the written document that explains the learning outcomes for the course, the learning objectives for each class, and the reading and assignments for the term. For example, they may say that they want you to "develop an appreciation for the ways that statistics are used in everyday life." The information you get during that first session and through the syllabus is critical. If the instructor's goals aren't stated explicitly, you should consider going up after class and discussing them with the instructor.

> **Identify your own goals for the course.** In addition to those "external" goals, you should have your own goals. What is it you want to learn from the course? What kind of grade do you want, and what are you prepared to do to obtain it? How will the information from the course help you to enhance your knowledge, improve your career prospects, and achieve your dreams?

> **Complete assignments before coming to class.** Always go to class prepared. Complete all of your reading and other assignments beforehand. Instructors assume that their students have done what they've assigned, and their lectures are based upon that assumption. It's virtually impossible to catch on to the gist of a lecture if you haven't completed the assignments. Good note-taking requires being prepared to listen to the material.

> **Be willing to make suggestions to the instructor that can help enhance your note-taking.** For example, if you have a visual/graphic learning style, you may

want to suggest that the instructor put an agenda or outline of the main topics on the board at the beginning of class, to help you follow how the information being presented that day is connected. Students with an auditory/verbal learning style may want to ask for permission to record the lecture, or they may want to find out if a podcast is available.

> **Accept the instructor, whatever his or her teaching style.** Not every instructor teaches in the same way. Accept the fact that, just as students have different learning styles, instructors may approach teaching in different ways. Ultimately, it's your responsibility to adapt to an instructor's teaching style. Where an instructor's teaching style does not fit well with your learning style, you must not use this as an excuse to do poorly or to give up. You cannot afford to let this get in the way of your education or let it interfere with your goals. If you need extra help or clarification, don't be afraid to approach the instructor and ask for it. If need be, investigate whether your college or university offers tutoring, which is often provided at no cost to you.

> "The highest result of education is tolerance."
> Helen Keller

> **Perform a pre-class warm-up.** No, this doesn't mean doing stretches just before each class. As you head to class or settle into your seat, skim your notes from the previous lecture, looking over what the instructor said and where that lecture left off. You should also briefly review the main headings or summary section of the readings you've been assigned.

> The warm-up doesn't have to be long. The goal is simply to refresh yourself, to get yourself into the right frame of mind for the class.

> **Choose a seat that will promote good note-taking.** You should certainly choose a seat that permits you to see and hear clearly, but there's more to your choice than that. Picking the right seat in a classroom can make a big difference.

> Where is the best place to sit? Usually it's front and centre. Instructors make more eye contact with the people near them, and they often believe that the best, most-engaged students sit closest.

Sometimes distracting seats have less to do with location and more to do with the person sitting next to you. Don't be afraid to put some physical distance between yourself and a distracting neighbour.

Furthermore, sitting in the back of the class may make you feel disengaged and out of touch with what is happening at the front of the room. In turn, this lack of engagement may make it easier for your mind to wander.

 **Organize**

Get the Tools of Note-Taking Together

Do you have a favourite pen? A preferred type of notebook?

Most of us have distinct tastes in the type of tools we use for various tasks: a favourite screwdriver, a preferred style of mouse, a brand of running shoes we find most comfortable. You should determine your preferred classroom "tools," too. Taking your favourite kind of notebook and pen to class can give you the confidence and focus you need to take effective notes.

There are several things to consider as you prepare for class:

- **Choose the appropriate writing utensil.** Generally, using a pen is better than using a pencil. Ink is less likely to smudge, and what you produce with ink is usually brighter and clearer—and therefore easier to use when studying. On the other hand, for math and accounting classes, where you may be copying down or even working through formulas in class, a pencil might be better, because it's easier to erase if you make a mistake when copying detailed, complex information.

  Sometimes you may want to use a combination of pen and pencil. And in some cases you might use several different pen colours, or highlighting markers. One colour might signify important information that the instructor mentions will be on the test. Another colour might be reserved for definitions or material that is copied from the board. And a third might be used for general notes on the lecture.

- **Choose a notebook that assists in note-taking.** Loose-leaf notebooks are particularly good for taking notes because they permit you to go back later and change the order of the pages or add additional material in the appropriate spot. But whatever kind of notebook you use, use only one side of the page for writing: keep one side free of notes. There may be times when you're studying when you'll want to spread your notes in front of you, and it's much easier if no material is written on the back of pages.

- **Consider the benefits of taking your textbook to class.** It's generally a good idea to take your textbook to class, unless your instructor advises you otherwise. Sometimes instructors will refer to information contained in it, and they may assign in-class exercises that are in the text. Sometimes it's useful to have the textbook handy to clarify information that is being discussed. You can also use it to look up key terms that may momentarily escape you. But don't, under any circumstances, use class time as an opportunity to read the textbook!

- **Consider the pros and cons of using a laptop computer to take notes in class.** There are several advantages: Legibility problems are avoided, and it's easy to go back and revise or add material after you've taken the notes.

  There are also potential pitfalls. You may end up keyboarding more and thinking less. Or you may succumb to the temptation to check your email or surf the Web, rather than listening to your instructor.

  Because of their drawbacks, some instructors have strong feelings against the use of laptops in class. Consequently, be sure to ask for permission before using your laptop to take notes.

From the perspective of . . .

A STUDENT Using a laptop is advantageous for students who type faster than they write. What are some of the advantages of taking handwritten notes? Of using a laptop to take notes?

W Work

Process—Don't Just Copy—Information

With pen poised, you're ready to begin the work of note-taking. The instructor speaks, and you start to write as quickly as you can, taking down as many of the instructor's words as possible.

Stop! You've made your first mistake. The central act in taking notes is not writing; listening and thinking are far more important. The key to effective note-taking is to write down the right amount of information—not too much and not too little.

Successful note-taking involves not just *hearing* what is said, but *listening actively.* **Hearing** is the involuntary act of sensing sounds. The annoying drip of

Hearing
The involuntary act of sensing sounds

Determine Your Listening Style

Consider the following pairs of statements. Place a check next to the statement in each pair that more closely describes your classroom listening style.

- ☐ 1a. When I'm listening in class, I lean back and get as comfortable as possible.
- ☐ 1b. When I'm listening in class, I sit upright and even lean forward a little.
- ☐ 2a. I let the instructor's words wash over me, generally going with the flow of the lecture.
- ☐ 2b. I try to guess in advance what the instructor is going to say and what direction the lecture is taking.
- ☐ 3a. I regard each lecture as a separate event, not necessarily related to what the instructor has said before or will say the next time.
- ☐ 3b. As I listen, I regularly ask myself how this lecture relates to what was said in previous classes.
- ☐ 4a. When I take notes, I try to reproduce the instructor's words as closely as possible.
- ☐ 4b. When I take notes, I try to interpret and summarize the ideas behind the instructor's words.
- ☐ 5a. I don't usually question the importance of what the instructor is saying or why it's the topic of a lecture or discussion.
- ☐ 5b. I often ask why the content of the lecture is important enough for the instructor to be speaking about it.
- ☐ 6a. I rarely question the accuracy or logic of a presentation, assuming that the instructor knows the topic better than I do.
- ☐ 6b. I often ask myself how the instructor knows something and find myself wondering how it could be proved.
- ☐ 7a. I rarely make eye contact with the instructor.
- ☐ 7b. I often make eye contact with the instructor.

If you tended to prefer the "a" statements in most pairs, you have a more passive listening style. If you preferred the "b" statements, you have a more active listening style. Wherever you selected "a" statements, go back and examine the corresponding "b" response to consider ways that you can become a more active listener.

To Try It online, go to Connect for *P.O.W.E.R. Learning and Your Life*.

a faucet, or the grating sound of a co-worker's voice speaking on the phone in the next cubicle are two examples of how hearing is both involuntary and often meaningless. In contrast, **active listening** is the intentional act of focusing on what is being said, making sense of it, and thinking about it in a way that permits it to be recalled accurately. Listening involves concentration. It also requires shutting out competing thoughts, such as what we need to pick up at the grocery store or why our date last night was so terrific. (To get a sense of your own listening skills, complete **Try It! 1,** "Determine Your Listening Style.")

Keeping the importance of active listening in mind, consider the following recommendations for taking notes in class:

> **Listen for the key ideas.** Not every sentence in a lecture is equally important, and one of the most useful skills you can develop is separating the key ideas from supporting information. Good instructors strive to make just a few main points. The rest of what they say consists of explanation, examples, and other supportive material that expands upon the key ideas.

> Your job, then, is to distinguish the key ideas from their support. To do this, you need to be alert and always searching for your instructor's **meta-message**—that is, the underlying main ideas that a speaker is seeking to convey, or the meaning behind the overt message you hear.

Active listening

The intentional act of focusing on what is being said, making sense of it, and thinking about it in a way that permits it to be recalled accurately

Meta-message

The underlying main ideas that a communicator is seeking to convey; the meaning behind the overt message

How can you discern the meta-message? One way is to listen for key phrases. Instructors know what's important in their lecture; your job is to figure it out, not just from what they say but from how they say it.

For instance, listen for clues about the importance of material. Pay attention to phrases like "don't forget . . . ," "be sure to remember that . . . ," "you need to know . . . ," "the most important thing that must be considered . . . ," "there are four problems with this approach . . . ," and—a big one—"this will be on the test"! These phrases should cause you to sit up and take notice. Another sign of importance is repetition. If an instructor says the same thing in several ways, it's a clear sign that the material being discussed is important.

> ▶ **Be on the lookout for nonverbal signals.** Does an instructor get excited about a particular topic? Does he or she seem unenthusiastic when talking about something? Use nonverbal cues to gauge the importance of a particular part of a message relative to other things being said. Listen also for what is *not* being said. Sometimes silence is not just golden, but informative as well. By noting what topics are not being covered in class, or are presented only minimally, you can gauge the relative importance of ideas in comparison with one another.

This is where preliminary preparation *and* organization come in. The only way to know what's left out of a lecture is to have done the assigned readings in advance. Also, don't be fooled into thinking that if a topic is not covered in class, it's totally unimportant: Most instructors believe students are responsible for all material that is assigned, whether or not it's explicitly covered in class.

> ▶ **Use short, abbreviated phrases—not full sentences—when taking notes.** Forget everything you've ever heard about always writing in full sentences. If you try to write notes in complete sentences, you'll soon become bogged down, paying more attention to your notes than to your instructor. In fact, if you use full sentences, you'll be tempted to try transcribing every word the instructor utters, which, as you now know, is not a good idea at all.

Instead, write in phrases, using only keywords or terms. Save full sentences for definitions or quotations that your instructor clearly wants you to know word for word. For example, consider the following excerpt from a lecture:

There are two kinds of job analyses used by human resource experts: First, there are job- or task-oriented analyses, and second, there are worker- or employee-oriented analyses. Job analyses just describe the tasks that need to be accomplished by a worker; for example, heart surgeons need to be able to perform heart bypass surgery in order to carry out their jobs. In contrast, employee-oriented job descriptions describe knowledge, skills, and abilities the employee must have to get the job done; for example, surgeons need to understand the different types of blood vessels in the heart in order to be successful. Most job analyses include elements of both job-oriented and employee-oriented types.

If you were taking notes, you might produce the following:

2 kinds job analyses:
  1. Job-oriented (=task-oriented): tasks needed to get job done. Ex: heart surgeon operates
  2. Worker-oriented (=employee-oriented): knowledge, skills, abilities, etc. necessary to do job. Ex: surgeon knows blood vessels
Most j.a. a combination

Note how the lecturer used almost 120 words, while the notes used only around 35 words—less than a third of the lecture.

› **Use abbreviations.** One way to speed up the note-taking process is through the use of abbreviations. These are among the most common:

and *& or +*	with *w/*	without *w/o*	
care of *c/o*	leads to; resulting in ⟶	as a result of ⟵	
percent *%*	change *Δ*	number *#*	
that is *i.e.*	for example *e.g.*	and so forth *etc.*	
no good *n.g.*	question *?*	compared with *c/w*	
page *p.*	important! *!!*	less than *<*	
more than *>*	equals, same as *=*	versus *vs.*	

› **Copy key information written on the board or projected from overheads or PowerPoint slides.** If your instructor provides a definition, quotation, or formula, you probably should copy it. In fact, such prominently displayed material has "test item" written all over it. You might want to highlight such material in some way in your notes.

› **Pay particular attention to the points raised by instructors at the end of classes.** Instructors often provide a summary of the discussion, which is worthy of inclusion in your notes.

› **Ask questions.** One of the most important things you can do during a class is to ask questions. Raising questions will help you evaluate, clarify, and ultimately better understand what your instructor is saying. And if you are having trouble understanding something, you can bet there are others just like you who have the same question.

Questions also serve several other purposes. For one thing, raising questions will help you to personalize the material being covered, permitting you to draw it more closely into your own framework and perspective. Furthermore, when you ask a question and it is answered, you become personally engaged in what the instructor is saying. In very large classes, asking questions may be the only way that an instructor can get a sense of you as an individual.

Questioning also increases your involvement in the class as a whole. If you sit back and never raise questions in class, you are much less likely to feel a real part of the class. Becoming an active questioner will rightly make you feel as if you have contributed something to the class. Remember, if you are unclear about some point, it is likely that others share your lack of clarity.

Finally, by asking questions in class, you serve as a role model for other students. Your questions may help break the ice in a class, making it easier for others to raise issues that they have about the material. And ultimately the answers that the instructor provides to others' questions may help you to better understand and/or evaluate your understanding of the material.

›› LO 4.2 Note-taking Methods to Use in Class

Over the years, several note-taking methods have been developed and used successfully by students at all levels of learning. Having a consistent way of taking notes for each of your classes will save you time in the long run. It is, therefore,

figure 4.1
Note-taking in Outline Form

I. Difficulties faced by college students seeking affordable housing

    A. Students subjected to high rents close to campus

        1. Forced to share apartments

        2. Sometimes must live far from campus

    B. Made to sign harsh leases

II. Possible solutions

    A. College offers subsidized housing

        1. Advantage: Housing costs can be lowered

        2. Potential problems

            a. College becomes students' landlord

            b. College uses funds for housing instead of investing in education

    B. Rent control

        1. Advantage: Can provide fixed, reasonably priced rents

        2. Disadvantages

            a. Creates permanent expensive rent-control bureaucracy

            b. Landlords may neglect rent-control property

            c. Little incentive for owners to increase the number of rental units

            d. Strong competition for rent-fixed units

III. Summary

    A. Advantages and disadvantages to both solutions

    B. May need new, creative solutions

worthwhile to explore the various approaches to note-taking to determine which one works best for *you*. The methods we will discuss in this section are the following: outlining, the Cornell method, concept mapping, and using a PowerPoint handout. It is worth trying out each of them before settling on one note-taking method, or perhaps deciding to use a combination.

> **Take notes in outline form.** It's often useful to take notes in the form of an outline. The **outline method of note-taking** summarizes ideas in short phrases and indicates the relationship among concepts through the use of indentations.

When outlining, you can be formal about it, using roman numerals, regular numbers, and capital and small letters (see the example in **Figure 4.1** above). Or, if you prefer, you can also simply use outlining indentations without assigning numbers and letters (as in the short handwritten note on page 92).

Outlining serves a number of functions. It forces you to try to determine the structure of the lecture. Organizing the key points and noting the connections among them helps you remember the material better because you have processed it more. The effort involved in outlining also keeps your mind from drifting away from the lecture.

Use **Try It! 2**, "Outline a Lecture," on page 95, to practise your outlining skills.

outline method of note-taking

A method of taking notes that summarizes ideas in short phrases and indicates the relationship among concepts through the use of indentations.

Try It! **P O W E R**

Outline a Lecture

2

Working with others in a group, take turns slowly reading sections of the following lecture to each other.[2] As the paragraph is being read, outline the main arguments in the space below.

In 1985 Joseph Farman, a British earth scientist working in Antarctica, made an alarming discovery. Scanning the Antarctic sky, he found less ozone than should be there—not a slight depletion but a 30% drop from a reading recorded 5 years earlier in the Antarctic!

At first the scientist thought that this "ozone hole" was an as-yet-unexplained weather phenomenon. Evidence soon mounted, however, pointing to synthetic chemicals as the culprit. Detailed analysis of chemicals in the Antarctic atmosphere revealed a surprisingly high concentration of chlorine, a chemical known to destroy ozone. The source of the chlorine was a class of chemicals called chlorofluorocarbons (CFCs). CFCs have been manufactured in large amounts since they were invented in the 1920s, largely for use as coolants in air conditioners, propellants in aerosols, and foaming agents in making Styrofoam™. CFCs were widely regarded as harmless because they were chemically unreactive under normal conditions. But in the thin atmosphere over Antarctica, CFCs condense on to tiny ice crystals; warmed by the sun in the spring, they attack and destroy ozone without being used up.

The thinning of the ozone layer in the upper atmosphere 25 to 40 kilometres above the surface of the earth is a serious matter. The ozone layer protects life from the harmful ultraviolet (UV) rays from the sun that bombard the earth continuously. Like invisible sunglasses, the ozone layer filters out these dangerous rays. When UV rays damage the DNA in skin cells, it can lead to skin cancer. Every 1% drop in the atmospheric ozone concentration is estimated to lead to a 6% increase in skin cancers. The drop of approximately 3% that has already occurred worldwide, therefore, is estimated to have led to as much as a 20% increase in skin cancers.

Write your outline here.

_____
_____
_____
_____
_____
_____
_____
_____
_____
_____
_____
_____
_____
_____
_____
_____
_____
_____
_____

After you have outlined the passage, compare your outline with that of others who took notes on the same passage.

1. Did you all agree on the main ideas of each passage?
2. How do your notes differ from others? How are they similar?
3. How might you improve your notes to better capture the main points?
4. Would a different topic produce greater or fewer difficulties?

Collectively, produce what you believe is the ideal outline, and compare it with the outlines produced by other groups.

To Try It online, go to Connect for *P.O.W.E.R. Learning and Your Life*.

figure 4.2
Cornell Note-taking Method

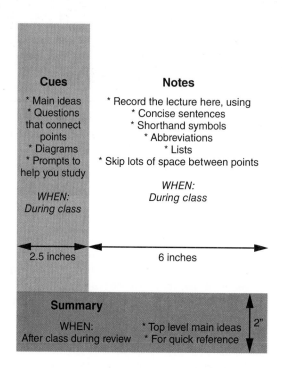

Cues

* Main ideas
* Questions that connect points
* Diagrams
* Prompts to help you study

WHEN: During class

Notes

* Record the lecture here, using
  * Concise sentences
  * Shorthand symbols
  * Abbreviations
  * Lists
* Skip lots of space between points

WHEN: During class

2.5 inches   6 inches

Summary

WHEN: After class during review   * Top level main ideas   * For quick reference   2"

Cornell method of note-taking

A method of structuring one's written notes into three categories: main notes, cues and questions, and a summary.

Concept mapping

A method of structuring written material by graphically grouping and connecting key ideas and themes

From the perspective of . . .

A MEDICAL ASSISTANT

Learning abbreviations is an important aspect of life in a medical office. How can taking notes with abbreviations while in school help you learn important notations for your medical career?

> Use the **Cornell method of note-taking.** If the outline method isn't working for you, you might want to try the Cornell approach to note-taking. This method divides a sheet of paper into three parts, with areas for main notes, cues and questions, and a summary at the bottom, as in **Figure 4.2**, drawn from the Lifehacker website. The site also includes instructions on how to create your own Cornell note-taking templates in Microsoft Word (**http://lifehacker.com/202418/geek-to-live-take-study+worthy-lecture-notes**).

> A third approach to note-taking, one that will appeal particularly to visual learners, is to create **concept maps.** Concept mapping (sometimes called "mind mapping") is a method of structuring written material by graphically grouping and connecting key ideas and themes. In contrast to an outline, a concept map visually illustrates how related ideas fit together. The pictorial summary gives you another handle for storing the information in memory, and it focuses your thinking on the key ideas from the lecture.

In a concept map, each key idea is placed in a different part of the page, and related ideas are placed near it—above, below, or beside it. What emerges does not have the rigid structure of an outline. Instead, a "finished" concept map looks something like a map of the solar system, with the largest and most central idea in the centre (the "sun" position), and related ideas surrounding it at various distances. It has also been compared to a large tree, with numerous branches and sub-branches radiating out from a central trunk. (**Figure 4.3** presents a sample concept map.)

> The final note-taking method we will discuss is the option of creating Power-Point handouts, where you can take advantage of PowerPoint slides provided by your instructor. Some instructors will post online their PowerPoint slides

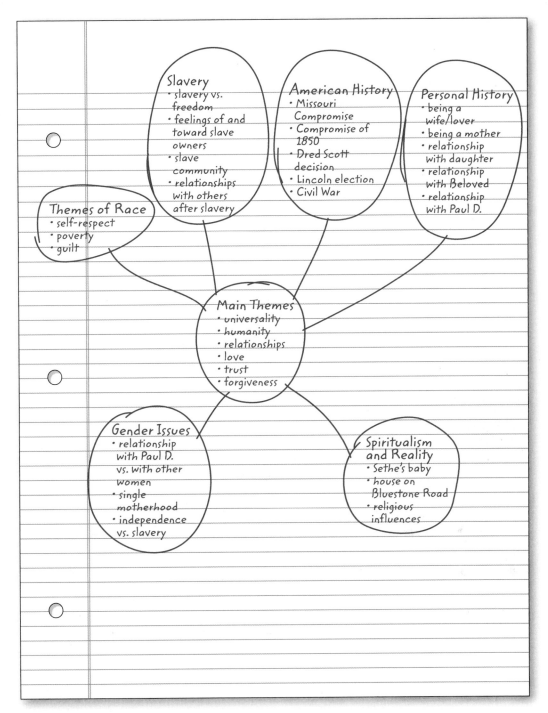

figure 4.3
A Concept Map of Toni Morrison's _Beloved_

before class. (See **Figure 4.4** on page 98 for a sample PowerPoint handout.) To make the most of this opportunity, save the slides to your computer. Then, open them up in PowerPoint and using the print function within PowerPoint, select the option called "handout," and then select "three to a page." This format will produce a sheet containing three slides per page, with a few blank lines next to each slide for your notes.

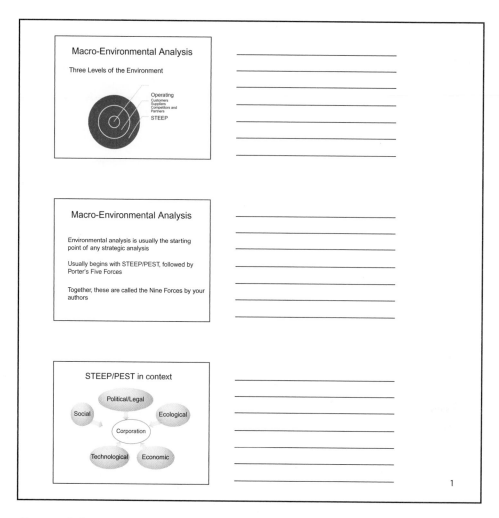

figure 4.4
A PowerPoint Handout, three slides to a page with a place for notes

Create a package of handouts for each chapter, and bring it to class. Then, instead of writing furiously to capture what is on the slide as the teacher speaks, you can listen actively to the value-added explanation and examples provided by your instructor and summarize these next to each slide. The combination of your notes and the PowerPoint slides will be invaluable when reviewing and studying the material later on.

Even if your instructor doesn't post the slides until after class, it's still a good idea to print them out and keep them with the notes you create in class. If your instructor doesn't post slides *at all,* you may want to approach him or her about doing so, explaining the value it provides for all students to be able to create handouts. Students for whom English is a second language find the PowerPoint handout approach to note-taking invaluable, and should approach the instructor on that basis.

Cope with Different Instructional Styles

He talks too fast . . . her accent is difficult to understand . . . he puts people down when they ask a question . . . she rambles . . . he goes off on boring tangents . . . she explains things in a way that doesn't make much sense . . . he won't give me a straight answer.

Not every instructor comes to class with a clear, compelling lecture and then presents it beautifully. All of us have sat through lectures that are deficient in one or more ways. What should you do when you find yourself in such a situation?

> **Remember that "this too shall pass."** First, keep in mind that this is a temporary condition; your experience usually won't last more than one term. Most instructors are conscientious and well prepared; and unless you have enormously bad luck, the unpleasant experience you're having now will not be routine.

> **Ask questions about the material.** Even if you have no idea what is going on in class—or especially if you have no idea—ask questions. You are not the only one struggling with the instructor's shortcomings. You will be doing everyone in the class a favour if you admit you're not following what an instructor is saying and ask for clarification.

> **Ask—privately and politely—for the instructor to alter the way material is presented.** If an instructor has a habit of speaking too quickly, approach him or her privately after class to discuss it. Instructors sometimes get carried away with enthusiasm about their subject and begin speaking faster and faster without being aware of it. Very often a reality check from a student will be welcome. But don't couch your comment in a way that makes the instructor feel inept ("Could you slow down; you're going too fast and losing me"). Instead, keep the comment neutral, without placing blame. For instance, you might simply say, "I'm having trouble keeping up with you; would it be possible for you to speak a little more slowly?"

> **Pool your resources.** Get together with other students in the class and work out a strategy for dealing with the situation. If an instructor speaks too fast and you just can't keep up with the flow of information, meet with your fellow students and compare what you've gleaned from the class. They may have understood or noted material that you missed, and vice versa. (**Figure 4.5** on page 100 shows how two students might take notes on the same material.) Together, you may be able to put the pieces of the puzzle together and get a fuller understanding of the material.

> **Talk with the instructor after class.** If you feel totally lost after a lecture, or even if you've missed only a few points, speak with the instructor after class. Ask for clarification and get him or her to explain again any points that you missed. Such a dialogue will help you to understand the material better.

If you've ever been totally lost following a lecture, you may have discovered that speaking with your instructor immediately after class was helpful. Most instructors are very happy to go over and clarify key points that they've covered during class. They also appreciate your initiative and interest.

Find a Balance between Too Many Notes and Too Few Notes

The key to effective note-taking is to keep a balance between too many and too few notes.

figure 4.5

Sharing lecture notes
with classmates can help
ensure that your notes
are complete.

Student A's Notes
Toni Morrison's Beloved

- Morrison popular and acclaimed author, not easy to be both
- Cloe Anthony?
- effective and intelligent African American writer
- Beloved won National Book Award, Pulitzer 1988, Noble Prize 1993
- gritty reality of spirituality and slavery
- Seth a black woman — what does this tell us?

Student B's Notes
Toni Morrison's Beloved

- M. both popular and respected; many awards
- more than "Afr. Amer. writer" — a great
- Amer. writer
  Beloved:
    blend of personal and historical,
    race and gender themes,
    Black experience and universal
    experience,
    reality and spirituality
- Is it more imp. that Sethe is Black or female? (race/gender?)
- How race & gender move plot?

The best way to achieve this balance is by paying close attention in class. By being alert, engaged, and involved in class, you'll be able to make the most of the techniques we've discussed. The result: notes that capture the most important points raised in class and that will optimize your recall and mastery of the course subject matter.

E Evaluate

Think Critically about Your Notes

Toward the end of class, take a moment to look over your notes. Now's the time—before the class has ended—to evaluate what you've written.

After being sure you can answer yes to the most basic question—can I read what I've written?—ask yourself these questions:

> Do my notes do a good job of representing what was covered in class?

> Do they reflect the emphases of the instructor?

> Are there any key points that are not entirely clear?

> Do I need help clarifying any of the points my instructor made?

Evaluating your notes is a critical part of the note-taking process. You can get a sense of how effective your note-taking has been while you still have a chance to ask your instructor to clarify anything that is not clear.

Perhaps, for example, you've left out a key word in a definition. Maybe you don't understand a concept fully, even though you've written about it in your notes. Possibly you've left out the third step in a list of six steps necessary to accomplish something.

If you look over your notes while you're still in class, you have time to ask your instructor for clarification. Or you can wait until the end of class and raise

Evaluate Your Class Notes

Take a set of notes you made recently during one of your classes and evaluate it using the following criteria.

Statement	Not Even Slightly	Slightly	Moderately	Pretty Well	Very Well
1. I can read my notes (i.e., they are legible).					
2. Someone else can read my notes.					
3. My notes are complete; I missed nothing important.					
4. My notes represent the key points that were covered in class.					
5. My notes reflect the instructor's emphases.					
6. The instructor's key points are clear and easy to understand.					
7. The notes contain only important points, with no extraneous material.					
8. I understand not only the notes but also the class content they reflect.					
9. Using only the notes, I will be able to reconstruct the essential content of the class in 3 months.					

 WORKING IN A GROUP

1. What do your answers tell you about the effectiveness of your note-taking skills?
2. What might you do differently the next time you take notes?
3. Evaluate and compare the notes you took during the previous 20 minutes of the class you are in now. How do your notes compare with those of the other members of your group?

To Try It online, go to Connect for *P.O.W.E.R. Learning and Your Life.*

your question privately. Most instructors will be happy to answer questions from students who have obviously been actively listening. Just make sure that you add what they tell you to your notes so you'll be able to refer to them later. (To practise evaluating your notes, complete **Try It! 3,** "Evaluate Your Class Notes.")

Note-taking: A Collaborative Approach

Different people take notes differently. Some students understand some topics better than others. And let's face it, not everyone is "awake" for every minute of every class. The bottom line is that for every class, students in the same class are unlikely to have the same notes, and most will have notes that are not complete. So why not share? Consider collaborating with other like-minded students and form a note-taking and study group. You can each take notes for a different subject, or for the same class, or for a different part of the same class. Start by trying it out for a week and get together to compare notes, to ensure you are all getting what you expect from each other; if your classmates are not living up to your expectations, set out some guidelines. Note-taking is one student task where sharing can be a good thing!

R Rethink   Activate Your Memory

The lecture has ended, and class is over. You put the top on your pen, close your notebook, stash everything in your bag, and head out for a cup of coffee before your next class.

Wait! Before you close up your notebook, finish the P.O.W.E.R. process. Rethink what you've heard. Spending five or ten minutes reconsidering what you've written right now can save you *hours* of work later. The reason: Rethinking promotes the transfer of information into long-term memory (something we already discussed in Chapter 3). As you integrate the new information you've taken down with what you already know, you plug this information into your memory in a much more meaningful way, which means you can remember it better and more easily.

If you looked over your notes to clarify and evaluate the information in them in class, you've already begun the process. But once class is over, you need to review the material more formally. Here's how to do it:

> "I'd think to myself, 'I don't need to write that down; I'll remember it.' A few days later, it was like, 'What did he say . . .?'"
> Student, Duke University[3]

> **Rethink as soon as possible.** Time is of the essence! The rethinking phase of note-taking doesn't have to take long; five to ten minutes are usually sufficient. The more critical issue is *when* you do it. The longer you wait before reviewing your notes, the less effective the process will be.
>
> There's no doubt that the best approach is to review the material just after the class has ended. As everyone else is leaving, you can just stay seated and go over your notes. This works fine for classes late in the day, when no other class is scheduled in the room. But what if you must vacate the room immediately after class? The next best thing is to find a quiet space somewhere nearby and do your rethinking there.
>
> In any case, don't let the day end without examining your notes. In fact, reconsidering material just before you go to sleep can be particularly effective.

> **Make rethinking an active process.** Some people feel the notes they take in class are akin to historical documents in a museum, with Do Not Touch! signs hanging on them. On the contrary, think of your notes as a construction project and yourself as the project manager.
>
> When you review your notes, do so with an eye to improving them. If any information is not entirely clear, change the wording in your notes, adding to

Practise Your Note-taking Skills

Practise your note taking skills, using any techniques you find helpful, in one of the classes in which you are enrolled this term. Analyze your notes to answer these questions:

1. Which specific techniques did I use in taking notes?

2. Which of the note-taking techniques detailed in this chapter was I unable to use, and why?

3. Could I take the notes I made in class and redo them, using one of the techniques in this chapter, such as creating a concept map?

After you have taken notes, use the techniques discussed in this chapter to evaluate and rethink them. Creating a concept map on a separate sheet of paper may be particularly helpful.

To Try It online, go to Connect for *P.O.W.E.R. Learning and Your Life.*

or amending what's there. If certain words are hard to read, fix them. It won't be any easier to read them the night before a test; chances are you'll have even more trouble.

If, on rethinking the material, you don't understand something, ask your instructor or a friend to clarify it. And when you receive an explanation, add it to your notes so you won't forget it. (You might want to use a different-coloured pen for additions to your notes, so you'll know they came later.)

› **Think critically about the material in your notes.** As you review the information, think about the material from a critical point of view. Go beyond the facts and pieces of information, integrating and evaluating the material.

In addition, as you rethink your notes, don't think of them only in terms of a single lecture or a single class. Take a longer view. Ask yourself how they fit into the broader themes of the class and the goals that you and the instructor have for the term. How will the information be useful to you? Why did the instructor emphasize a particular point?

To practise the techniques we've been discussing, see **Try It! 4**, "Practise Your Note-Taking Skills."

≫ LO 4.3 Creating Study Notes

Weighing as much as five pounds, bulky and awkward, and filled with more information than you think anyone could ever need to know, it's the meat and potatoes of post-secondary work: your course textbook. You might feel intimidated by its size; you might be annoyed at its cost; you might think you'll never be able to read it, let alone understand, learn, and recall the material in it. How will you manage?

Study notes

Notes taken for the purpose of reviewing material

The answer involves taking **study notes,** notes taken for the purpose of reviewing material. They are the kind of notes that you take now to study from later.

Several strategies are useful for taking study notes from written material such as books, magazines, journals, and websites. Which approach works best depends on whether you're able to write directly on the material on which you wish to take notes.

Take Notes on Material You Can Write On

Here are some suggestions for creating study notes for material you own, material you are free to mark up:

>   **Integrate your text notes into your study notes.** Start by annotating the pages, using the techniques that work best for you: highlighting, underlining, circling, and/or making marginal notes. Keep in mind that writing on the text, by itself, is not sufficient to promote learning; it's what you do *next* that counts.

>   Specifically, after you've finished reading and annotating the material, create study notes. The study notes should provide a summary of the key points, in outline form or in the form of concept maps. Either form of summary should supplement the annotations you've made on the printed page.

>   Furthermore, any notes you take should stand on their own; that is, they should include enough information to be useful whether or not you have the book or article on hand.

>   **Use flash cards.** If you feel confident that the annotations you've written in the book are sufficiently comprehensive, you might consider taking notes on flash cards. **Flash cards** are simply index cards that contain key pieces of information that you need to remember.

Flash cards

Index cards that contain key pieces of information to be remembered

>   Flash cards are particularly useful in subjects that present many small bits of information to remember, such as technical vocabulary words or scientific formulas. When you need to learn a new term, for instance, you can write the term on one side of a card and its definition on the other side.

>   One of the greatest virtues of flash cards is their portability. Because they are small, they can fit into your pocket or handbag, and you can look at them at odd times when you have a spare moment.

>   **Create a separate glossary or definitions page.** Having all the definitions in one place can make studying easier.

>   **Keep your notes organized by the chapter they refer to.** Put the date of the lecture on them. Add a reference in your notes to the textbook page they refer to, and vice versa, making it easier for you when it comes time to study and review for a quiz or test.

Take Notes on Material You Cannot Write On

Taking notes on material that can't be written on is a different story. Library books, magazines, journal articles, and materials on library reserve that are shared with others require a different approach.

>   **Approach the written material as you would a class lecture.** The techniques we discussed earlier for taking notes in class can all be adapted for taking notes from written material. In fact, the task is often easier than class note-taking, because the material is in black and white in front of you, and you can refer to it directly.

Taking Notes on the Job: Meetings of the Minds

The principles of good note-taking discussed in this chapter are useful in the classroom, and they can also help you as you make your way in your career. For instance, you may need to take notes on lengthy memos or reports that detail company procedures you will need to master your job.

Further, one of the most important settings in which you'll want to take effective notes is in meetings. Meetings take up a good part of many people's professional workdays and being able to take effective notes can provide a significant career advantage.

Meetings are similar to class discussions. During a meeting, you will want to look for key topics and make note of the ideas that receive the most emphasis or enthusiastic response. Note these areas and keep them in mind as likely priorities.

During meetings, tasks are often assigned. You will want to note clearly what you are supposed to do and when you are supposed to do it; and keeping track of what others are doing will also be helpful, because you may need to get information from them or otherwise coordinate efforts. For instance, if you are assigned the task of managing the development of your company's website, you'll want to clarify in your notes which person has agreed to do what portion of the task.

Taking notes when others are speaking also shows that you are paying attention to what the speaker is saying. It's a kind of compliment that suggests you find what the speaker is saying to be so important that you will want to refer to it later.

Finally, note-taking plays another role: It can make seemingly interminable meetings appear to proceed faster by providing something for you to do that's more active than simply listening. In short, not only can note-taking provide you with a clear record of what occurred in a meeting, but it can also keep you engaged in what is going on.

- ▶ **Laptops can be especially helpful in creating study notes.** If you're a good keyboarder, it's often easier and quicker to take notes using your laptop. On the other hand, don't be lured into typing too much. You need to be just as selective in what you input into your computer as you would be in taking notes during a class lecture.

- ▶ **Use the tricks of the trade we discussed earlier for taking notes from a class lecture.** Look for key ideas, definitions, quotations, and formulas, and include them in your notes. Use the headings that are included in the text, such as chapter and section titles. Bold or italic type is also a clue that an important point is being made. Graphs and charts often provide critical information.

- ▶ **Use the same form of note-taking that you use in class lectures.** If you are a read/write learner and write your notes in outline form, create an outline based on the written material. If you are a visual/graphic learner and prefer to create graphics such as concept maps, create them now. The point is to produce notes that are consistent with those you take during class lectures.

Time to Reflect: What Did I Learn?

1. Overall, how effective are your current note-taking techniques?

2. Describe the way(s) in which you think your note-taking style is a reflection of your learning style.

3. Based on what you learned about note-taking in this chapter, what do you plan to do differently in the future? Be specific.

Looking Back

What is effective note-taking?

➤ The central feature of good note-taking is listening and distilling important information, rather than writing down everything that is said.

How can I take good notes in class?

➤ Prepare for taking notes by identifying the instructor's and your own goals for the course, completing all assignments before arriving in class, and "warming up" for class by reviewing the notes and assignments from the previous class.

➤ Before writing notes, listen to the instructor and carefully process the information that the instructor is attempting to deliver.

➤ One note-taking method is to take down notes as brief phrases rather than full sentences and, if possible, in outline form to reveal the structure of the lecture. Other methods include the Cornell method, concept mapping, and PowerPoint handouts. Material written on the board should usually be copied word for word.

➤ Before leaving class, evaluate your notes, verifying that they are complete and easy to understand, while there is still time to correct them. As soon as possible after class, actively rethink your notes.

What techniques apply to taking notes from written materials?

➤ Taking good study notes from written materials involves many of the principles that apply to taking good notes from oral presentations, although the source material can be consulted repeatedly, making it easier to get the information down accurately.

➤ Concept maps and flash cards can be helpful tools for taking notes from textbooks.

[KEY TERMS AND CONCEPTS]

Active listening (p. 91)

Concept mapping (p. 96)

Cornell method of note-taking (p. 96)

Flash cards (p. 104)

Hearing (p. 90)

Meta-message (p. 91)

Outline method of note-taking (p. 94)

Study notes (p. 104)

[RESOURCES]

ON CAMPUS

If you are having difficulty taking class notes effectively, talk with your course instructor. Bring your notes with you soon after a class has ended, and let the instructor assess what you are doing correctly and what could stand improvement.

If your problems persist, and you have great difficulty translating the spoken word into notes, then there's a small possibility that you suffer from an auditory learning disability. Be tested by your campus learning disabilities office or counselling office to rule this out.

IN PRINT

Judy Kesselman-Turkel and Franklynn Peterson's *Note-Taking Made Easy* (University of Wisconsin Press, 2003) provides a broad overview of how to take good notes in class, as does Bobbi DePorter and Mike Hernacki's *Quantum Notes* (Learning Forum, 2000).

ON THE WEB

The following websites provide the opportunity to extend your learning about the material in this chapter.

> Mount Royal University in Calgary provides some excellent note-taking tips on their website. (**www.mtroyal.ca/AcademicSupport/ResourcesServices/StudentLearning Services/StudyingWritingEffectively/notetaking.htm**)

> California Polytechnic State University offers a good overview of several note-taking systems: Cornell, outline, mapping, charting, and sentence methods. (**http://www. sas.calpoly.edu/asc/ssl/notetakingsystems.html**)

> For online note-taking, you may want to consider a tool like Evernote, which automatically processes, indexes, and allows you to organize and search text-based notes, photos of notes (i.e., notes on a whiteboard), webpages, and screenshots. (**http://www.evernote.com/about/home.php**)

TAKING IT TO THE NET

1 The best way to improve note-taking skills is to practise. One possible strategy is to go to the home page for Canoe.ca, a well-known Canadian website (**http:// en.canoe.ca/home.html**). Click on one of the categories (e.g., News, Sports, Showbiz, Money, Life, etc.), and look for a story that sounds interesting. Locate a story of interest on the Internet and take notes while reading it.

2 Taking notes during lectures is an important part of classroom learning, but keeping up with a speaker for an entire hour can be difficult. You can improve your note-taking skills for lectures by taking notes while listening to recorded speeches on the Internet. For example, go to the TED site (**http://www.ted.com/ talks/steve_jobs_how_to_live_before_you_die.html**) and listen to Apple and Pixar co-founder Steve Jobs's inspiring commencement speech to a Stanford graduating class. Take notes while listening to the speech. Afterward, go back and indicate the key points and terms. You can check your comprehension by comparing the speech to news articles reporting on it. (You can also check the articles for bias!)

The Case of . . .
Not Missing a Thing

Some people write down a few things in class. Others write down most things. Jennifer Beck wrote down *everything*.

The woman was virtually a human dictation machine. She spent her time in class in a whirlwind of note-taking, writing down in a clear, meticulous script seemingly every word her instructor uttered. By the end of a term, her notebooks were so lengthy that they approached the size of telephone books from a small city.

Yet despite her thorough notes, Jennifer was only a mediocre student. She was a hard worker and studied her many notes thoroughly before tests. But she never managed to get grades higher than a C+. It seemed unbelievable to her. She worked incredibly hard in class taking good notes. Why wasn't it paying off?

1. How do you think Jennifer defines "good note-taking"?

2. Why does Jennifer's method of note-taking produce such poor results? What is she missing?

3. If you asked Jennifer to summarize the instructor's main ideas after a class lecture, how successful do you think she would be? Why?

4. Do you think it would be easy or hard to study for a final exam using Jennifer's notes? Why?

5. Do you think Jennifer evaluates her notes during or after class? Do you think she ever rethinks them? What questions would you ask to help her perform these steps?

6. In general, what advice would you give Jennifer on note-taking?

5 Taking Tests

Learning Outcomes

By the time you finish this chapter, you will be able to

>> LO **5.1**   Employ various strategies to prepare for tests.

>> LO **5.2**   Discuss effective strategies for writing tests.

>> LO **5.3**   Analyze the strengths and weaknesses of your performance on a test.

onths of study and classes and reading and commuting to and from his college . . . and now it all came down to a test.

That was the thought that ran through Darvinder's head as he sat down to take the final exam in his computer programming course. Darvinder knew the test would count for 65 percent of his final grade. If he passed, he would have enough credits to get the graphic design diploma he'd been working toward for years. If he failed—well, Darvinder tried not to think about that.

He'd taken tests before, but the stakes had never been so high for a single exam. Although he was fairly confident—he had studied hard—he couldn't altogether relax. He told himself that he had always done well on tests in the past; he wasn't going to fail now. But still, Darvinder couldn't help but feel as if his entire school career, maybe his entire future, was on the line.

Looking Ahead

Although most tests are not as critical as Darvinder's computer programming final, tests do play a significant role in everyone's academic life. Students typically experience more anxiety over tests than over anything else in their college or university careers. If you're returning to post-secondary education after a long break, or perhaps struggled with tests earlier in your academic career, you may find the prospect of taking a test especially intimidating.

But tests don't have to produce so much anxiety. There are strategies and techniques you can learn to reduce your fear of test-taking. In fact, learning how to take tests is, in some ways, as important as learning the content that they cover. Taking tests effectively involves mastering information, but it also requires mastering specific test-taking skills.

One of the most important goals of this chapter is to take the mystery out of the whole process of taking tests. To do that, you'll learn about the different types of tests and about strategies you can start using even before you take a test. You'll gain insight into how different kinds of tests work and how best to approach them. As well, you'll learn about the various types of test questions and strategies for responding most effectively to each type.

This chapter also explores two aspects of test-taking that may affect your performance: test anxiety and cramming. You will learn ways to deal with your anxiety and strategies to keep cramming to a minimum—but you will also learn how to make the most of cramming, if you do have to resort to it.

The chapter ends with suggestions for evaluating your performance toward the end of a test as well as after it's been graded, to learn how to improve your performance the next time around.

What Tests Measure

Tests may be the most unpopular part of college and university life. Students hate them because they produce fear, anxiety, apprehension about being evaluated, and a focus on grades instead of learning for learning's sake. Instructors often don't like them very much either, because they produce fear, anxiety, apprehension about being evaluated, and a focus on grades instead of learning for learning's sake. That's right: Students and instructors dislike tests for the very same reasons.

But tests are also valuable. A well-constructed test identifies what you know and what you still need to learn. Tests help you see how your performance compares with that of others. And knowing that you'll be tested on a body of material is likely to motivate you to learn the material more thoroughly.

However, there's another reason you might dislike tests: You may assume that tests have the power to define your worth as a person. If you do badly on a test, you may be tempted to believe that you've received some fundamental information about yourself from the instructor and the educational institution, information that says you're a failure in some significant way.

This is a dangerous—and wrong-headed—assumption. If you do badly on a test, it doesn't mean you're a bad person. Or stupid. Or that you don't belong in college or university. If you don't do well on a test, you're the same person you were before you took the test—no better, no worse. You just did badly on a test. Period.

In short, tests are not a measure of your value as an individual. They are only a measure of how well (and how much) you studied, and your test-taking skills.

Tests are tools; they are indirect and imperfect measures of what we know. Someone with a great deal of knowledge can do poorly on a test; tension or going at too slow a pace can lead to unwelcome results in some cases. Another person may know considerably less and still do well on the test simply because he or she has learned some test-taking skills along the way.

P Prepare

Prepare to be tested;
work on your course work
every day; study

O Organize

Ready yourself the
day of the test

W Work

Tackle the test
wisely

E Evaluate

Check over your work
before handing in the test

R Rethink

Reflect on what you've learned
when you get the test back

P.O.W.E.R. Plan

How we do on a test depends on a number of considerations: the kind of test it is, the subject matter involved, our understanding of test-taking strategies, and, above all, how well we prepare for it. Let's turn, then, to the first step in test-taking: preparation. (The five steps are summarized in the P.O.W.E.R. Plan on the left.)

LO 5.1    # Preparing to Be Tested

Preparation for tests requires a number of strategies. Many of the most important are listed below.

Course Work as Test Preparation

Many of the things you do during a course will help to prepare you for a test. There is no surer way to get good grades on tests than to take these steps:

> **Read** assigned chapters before every class
> **Attend** class faithfully and pay attention while you are there
> **Review** your notes following each class
> **Create** a set of study notes, as described in Chapter 4
> **Complete** all assignments and review the instructor's feedback when you receive the assignment back

Preparing for tests is a long-term proposition. It's not a matter of "giving your all" the night before the test. Instead, it's a matter of "giving your all" to *every* aspect of the course, throughout the semester.

Know What to Prepare For

Determine as much as you can about the test before you begin to study for it. The more you know about a test beforehand, the more efficient your studying will be.

To find out about an upcoming test, ask these questions of your instructor:

> Is the test called a "test," "exam," "quiz," or something else? As you can see in **Table 5.1,** the names imply different things. For simplicity's sake, we'll use the term "test" throughout this chapter; but you need to know that these distinctions exist, and they should affect the way you prepare.
> What material will the test cover?
> How many questions will be on it?
> How much time is it expected to take? A full class period? Only part of a period?
> What kinds of questions will be on the test?
> How will it be graded?
> Will sample questions be provided?
> Are tests from previous terms available?
> How much does the test contribute to your final course grade?

While an instructor is highly unlikely to tell you what will be on a test, if you can "think like an instructor," you may be able to figure it out yourself. Look for clues in the course outline, in the content of assignments, and in the way the instructor introduces or summarizes certain topics. If the instructor says things like "this is very important" or "you need to pay special attention to the concept I am about to introduce," he or she will probably test on this material. Put an asterisk beside it so it will stand out when you are ready to study for the test.

---

table 5.1 Quizzes, Tests, Exams, Assignments, Term Projects . . . What's in a Name?

Although they may vary from one instructor to another, the following definitions are most commonly used.

Quiz: A *quiz* is a brief assessment, usually covering a relatively small amount of material. Some quizzes cover as little as one class's worth of reading. Although a single quiz usually doesn't count very much, instructors often add quiz scores together, and collectively they can become a significant part of your final course grade.

Test: A *test* is a more extensive, more heavily weighted assessment than a quiz, covering more material. A test may come every few weeks of the term, often after each third or quarter of the term has passed; but this varies with the instructor and the course.

Exam: An *exam* is the most substantial kind of assessment. In many courses, just one exam is given—a final exam at the end of the term. Sometimes there are two exams, one at the midpoint of the term (called, of course, a midterm) and the second at the end. Exams are usually weighted quite heavily because they are meant to assess your knowledge of all the course material covered up to that point.

Assignment: An *assignment* is usually something that is done individually outside of class, has a relatively narrow focus, and is not usually worth more than 10–15% of your final grade. It may involve researching a specific topic or reading a particular article and providing your own perspective on it. Where possible, you should ask the instructor if a "marking rubric" is available for the assignment, so you can see how marks will be allocated and as a result, how to allocate your time and effort.

Term project: A *term project* is completed outside of class, may be done individually or in a group, and spans the full semester or term. It is usually broad in focus, and it can be worth a significant portion of your final grade, depending on the course. Undertaking an analysis of the state of an entire industry and the major competitors within it would be an example of a term project. Again, you should ask your instructor if a marking rubric is available, so you can see how marks will be allocated and where you should put most of your effort.

Test-Preparation Strategies

Match Study Methods to Question Types

Test questions come in different types (see **Table 5.2**), and each requires a somewhat different style of preparation.

> **Essay questions.** Essay tests focus on the big picture—ways in which the various pieces of information being tested fit together. You'll need to know not just a series of facts, but also the connections among these facts; and you will have to be able to discuss these ideas in an organized and logical way. A good study tactic is to play instructor: After carefully reviewing your notes and other course materials, think of likely exam questions. Then, without looking at your notes or your readings, answer each potential essay question, either aloud or by writing out the major points an answer should include. After you've answered the questions, check yourself by looking at your notes and the course readings once again.

> **Short-answer and fill-in questions.** Short-answer and fill-in questions are similar to essays in that they require you to recall key pieces of information rather than finding the information on the page in front of you. However, short-answer and fill-in questions—unlike essay questions—typically don't demand that you integrate or compare different types of information. Consequently, the focus of your study should be on the recall of specific, detailed information.

> **Multiple-choice, true–false, and matching questions.** While the focus of review for essay questions should be on major issues and controversies, studying for multiple-choice, true–false, and matching questions requires more attention to the details.

> Almost anything is fair game for multiple-choice, true–false, and matching questions, so you can't afford to overlook anything when studying. True, these kinds of questions put the material right there on the page for you to react to— e.g., Did Jacques Cartier arrive on New Brunswick's Bay of Chaleur in 1534, or

table 5.2	Types of Test Questions
Essay	Requires a fairly extended, on-the-spot composition about some topic. Examples include questions that call on you to describe a person, process, or event, or those that ask you to compare or contrast two separate sets of material.
Multiple-choice	Contains a question or statement, followed by a number of possible answers (usually 4 or 5 of them). You must choose the best response from the choices offered.
True–false	Presents statements about a topic that are either accurate or inaccurate. You are to indicate whether each statement is accurate (true) or inaccurate (false).
Matching	Presents two lists of related information, arranged in column form. Typically, you are asked to pair up the items that go together (e.g., a scientific term and its definition).
Definition	Requires you to provide the meaning of a word.
Short-answer	Requires brief responses (usually a few sentences at most) in a kind of mini-essay.
Fill-in	Requires you to add one or more missing words to a sentence or series of sentences.

not?—rather than asking you to provide the names and dates yourself (as in the case of the essay or short-answer question). Nevertheless, to do well on these tests you must put your memory into high gear and master a great many facts.

It's a particularly good idea to write down important facts on index cards. Remember the advantages of these cards: They're portable and available all the time, and the act of creating them helps drive the material into your memory. Furthermore, you can shuffle them and test yourself repeatedly until you've mastered the material.

Another helpful strategy is to write the name of a particular concept or theory on one side of a note card, and then to write an example of it on the other side. Studying the cards will ensure that you fully understand the concepts and theories and can generalize them to different situations.

Test Yourself

Once you feel you've mastered the material, test yourself on it. There are several ways to do this. Often textbooks are accompanied by websites that offer automatically scored practice tests and quizzes. (*P.O.W.E.R. Learning* does: Visit Connect for *P.O.W.E.R. Learning and Your Life*.)

You can also create a test for yourself, in writing, making its form as close as possible to what you expect the actual test to be. For instance, if your instructor has told you the classroom test will be primarily made up of short-answer questions, your test should reflect that.

You might also construct a test and administer it to a classmate or a member of your study group. In turn, you could take a test that someone else has constructed. Constructing and taking practice tests are excellent ways of studying the material and cementing it into memory. (To be sure you're fully prepared for your next test, complete **Try It! 1**, "Complete a Test Preparation Checklist," on page 116.)

Form a Study Group

Study groups are small, informal groups of students who work together to learn course material and study for a test. Forming such a group can be an excellent way to prepare for any kind of test. Some study groups are formed for particular tests, whereas others meet consistently throughout the term.

Study groups can be extremely powerful tools because they help accomplish several things:

> They help members organize and structure the material to approach their studying in a systematic and logical way.

> They allow students to share different perspectives on the material.

> They make it more likely that students will not overlook any potentially important information.

> They force members to rethink the course material, explaining it in words that other group members will understand.

From the perspective of . . .

A STUDENT You will take many types of courses during your academic career. Can you think of how test-taking strategies will work in an English course versus a science course?

Study group
Small, informal group of students whose purpose is to help members work together and study for a test

Study groups, made up of a few students who study together for a test, can help organize material, provide new perspectives, and motivate members to do their best. Do you think you would function well in a study group? Why or why not?

Try It!

Complete a Test Preparation Checklist

It takes more than simply learning the material to prepare for a test. You also need a strategy that will help you understand what it is you are studying for. To do that, you need to learn as much as you can about the test. The more you know about the kind of test it is and what it will cover, the better you'll be able to target your studying, and the less anxious you will feel when you first see the test.

To focus your studying, complete the following test preparation checklist before your next test. When it comes to items like the test format or what will be covered, don't be afraid to ask your instructor for input.

TEST PREPARATION CHECKLIST

- ☐ I know whether it's a quiz, test, or exam.
- ☐ I know what kinds of questions will be on the test.
- ☐ I understand what material will be covered.
- ☐ I know how many questions will be on the test.
- ☐ I know how long I will have to complete the test.
- ☐ I know how the test will be graded, and how the grade contributes to my final course grade.
- ☐ I obtained sample questions and/or previous tests, if available.
- ☐ I formed or participated in a study group.
- ☐ I used different and appropriate preparation strategies for different types of questions.
- ☐ I read and studied my class notes.
- ☐ I composed some questions of the kind that will be on the exam.
- ☐ I answered essay questions aloud.
- ☐ I actively memorized facts and details.
- ☐ I made and used index cards.
- ☐ I created and used a test like the real test.

After completing the checklist, ask yourself these questions:

1. How can I use this checklist to study more effectively for tests?
2. How might completing the checklist change the way I study for tests?
3. What new strategies might I follow in order to prepare for tests more effectively in the future?

To Try It online, go to Connect for *P.O.W.E.R. Learning and Your Life*.

There are some potential drawbacks to keep in mind. Study groups don't always work well for students with learning styles that favour working independently. In addition, "problem" members—those who don't pull their weight—may cause difficulties for the group. In general, though, the advantages of study groups far outweigh their disadvantages. To set up your own study group, see **Try It! 2**, "Form a Study Group."

Use On-campus Resources

Many colleges and universities have a learning centre, tutorial centre, or other office that can help you cope with test anxiety and show you how to approach studying for a test. Don't wait until after you do badly on a test to visit your campus learning

Form a Study Group

2

The next time you have to prepare for a test, form a study group with three to five classmates. They may have a variety of study habits and skills, but all must be willing to take the group seriously.

The first time you meet, compare notes about what is likely to be on the test and brainstorm to come up with possible test questions. If the instructor hasn't given you detailed information about the test (i.e., number and types of questions, weighting, etc.), one of you should be delegated to ask for it. Plan to meet once more closer to the test date to discuss answers to the questions you've come up with, share any new insights, and quiz each other on the material.

After you've taken the test and gotten your results, meet again. Find out if members felt the group was effective.

1. Did the members feel more confident about the test?

2. Do you all think you did better than you would have without the group?

3. What worked? What didn't?

4. What could you do differently next time?

To Try It online, go to Connect for *P.O.W.E.R. Learning and Your Life.*

or tutorial centres. A visit prior to your first test is a good use of your time, even if you feel it's not essential. Just knowing what resources are available can boost your confidence.

Deal with Test Anxiety

What does the anticipation of a test do to you? Do you feel shaky? Frantic, like there's not enough time to get it all done? Is there a knot in your stomach? Do you grit your teeth?

Test anxiety is a temporary condition characterized by fears and concerns about test-taking. Almost everyone experiences it to some degree, although for some people it's more of a problem than it is for others. The real danger with test anxiety is that it can become so overwhelming that it can hurt test performance.

You'll never eliminate test anxiety completely, nor do you want to. A little bit of nervousness can energize you, making you more attentive and vigilant. Like other competitive events, testing can motivate you to do your best. You might think of moderate test anxiety as a desire to perform at your peak—a useful quality at test time.

On the other hand, for some, anxiety can spiral into the kind of paralyzing fear that makes their minds go blank. There are several ways to keep this from happening to you:

> **Prepare thoroughly.** The more you prepare, the less test anxiety you'll feel. Good preparation can give you a sense of control and mastery, and it will prevent test anxiety from overwhelming you.

> **Take a realistic view of the test.** Remember that your future success does not hinge on your performance on any single test or exam. Think of the big picture: Put the particular test in context, and remind yourself of all the hurdles you've passed so far.

> **Eat right and get enough sleep.** Good mental preparation can't occur without your body being well prepared.

Test anxiety
A temporary condition characterized by fears and concerns about test-taking

3

Measure Your Test-taking Style

Do you feel anxious at the very thought of a test, or are you cool and calm in the face of testing situations? Get a sense of your test-taking style by checking off every statement below that applies to you.

- [ ] 1. The closer a test date approaches, the more nervous I get.
- [ ] 2. I am sometimes unable to sleep on the night before a test.
- [ ] 3. I have "frozen up" during a test, finding myself unable to think or respond.
- [ ] 4. I can feel my hands shaking as I pick up my pencil to begin a test.
- [ ] 5. The minute I read a tough test question, all the facts I ever knew about the subject abandon me and I can't get them back no matter how hard I try.
- [ ] 6. I have become physically ill before or during a test.
- [ ] 7. Nervousness prevents me from studying immediately before a test.
- [ ] 8. I often dream about an upcoming test.
- [ ] 9. Even if I successfully answer a number of questions, my anxiety stays with me throughout the test.
- [ ] 10. I'm reluctant to turn in my test paper for fear that I can do better if I continue to work on it.

If you checked off more than four statements, you have experienced fairly serious test anxiety. If you checked off more than six statements, your anxiety is probably interfering with your test performance. In particular, statements 3, 5, 6, 7, and 10 may indicate serious test anxiety.

If, based on your responses to this questionnaire and your previous experience, your level of test anxiety is high, what are some of the steps described in this chapter that might be helpful to you?

To Try It online, go to Connect for *P.O.W.E.R. Learning and Your Life*.

> **Learn relaxation techniques.** You can learn to reduce or even eliminate the jittery physical symptoms of test anxiety by using relaxation techniques. The basic process is straightforward: Breathe evenly, gently inhaling and exhaling. Focus your mind on a pleasant, relaxing scene such as a beautiful forest or a peaceful farm, or on a restful sound such as the sound of ocean waves breaking on the beach.

> **Visualize success.** Think of an image of your instructor handing back your test marked with a big fat "A." Or imagine your instructor congratulating you on your fine performance the day after the test. Positive visualizations that highlight your potential success can help replace images of failure that may fuel test anxiety.

To assess your own test-taking style and the degree of anxiety around tests that you experience, see **Try It! 3**, "Measure Your Test-taking Style."

What if these strategies don't work? If your test anxiety is so great that it's getting in the way of your success, make use of your campus resources. Most provide a learning resource centre or a counselling centre that can provide you with personalized help. (For more on dealing with test anxiety, particularly where math is concerned, see the **Course Connections** feature on page 119.)

When Anxiety Leads to Cramming

Cramming
Hurried, last-minute studying

You know, of course, that **cramming**—hurried, last-minute studying—is not the way to go. You know that you're likely to forget the material the moment the test is over because long-term retention is nearly impossible without thoughtful study. But . . .

Special Techniques for Dealing with Math Anxiety

For many students, the greatest test anxiety comes when they're taking a test involving math. Math seems to bring out the worst fears in some people, perhaps because it's seen as a discipline in which answers are either totally right or totally wrong, or perhaps because they've felt they've "hit the wall" and they'll never be able to understand a new concept, no matter how hard they try.

Such feelings about math can be devastating, because they can prevent you from doing well even if you know the material. If you suffer from math anxiety, keep these things in mind:

- Math is like any other subject: The greatest component of success is the effort you put in, not whether you have a "math gene" that makes you naturally good at math. It's not true that you are either born "good at math" or not, or that there's some "secret" about math that some people know and others don't.

- It's also not true that there's only one way to solve a math problem. Sometimes there are a variety of routes to coming up with a solution. And keep in mind that the solution to math problems often calls for creativity, not just sheer logic.

- It's a false stereotype that women are not as good at math as men, but it's a stereotype that many women accept. Research has shown that when men do badly on a math test, they're most likely to think that they haven't put in enough effort; but when women don't do well on a math test, they're three times more likely than men to feel that they don't have enough ability to be successful.[1] That's an erroneous view of the world. Don't become a prisoner of stereotypes.

Use these special strategies to deal with math problems on exams:

BEFORE TESTS:

1. Math is cumulative, building on prior concepts and knowledge. Make sure you review math fundamentals before moving on to more advanced topics.
2. Ask questions in class. Don't be afraid that you'll ask the wrong question in the wrong way. Instructors want you to understand their subject.
3. Make use of review sessions and other study resources.
4. Practise, practise, practise. The more experience you have completing math problems under pressure, the better you'll do. Practise math problems using a timer in order to simulate an actual test.

DURING TESTS:

1. Analyze math problems carefully. What are the known quantities or constants, and what pieces of information are missing? What formula(s) or theorem(s) apply?
2. Consider drawing a diagram, graph, or probability tree.
3. Break down calculations into their component parts.
4. Check your math carefully.
5. Be neat and logical in your presentation, and show every step as you solve problems. Your instructor may give you partial credit if you lay out every step you're going through. In addition, some instructors may require you to show your work.

Cramming can be exhausting, but it is on occasion necessary. With the family and personal responsibilities many students face, sometimes it can't be avoided. There are, however, strategies you can use to help you make the best use of limited time.

. . . it's been one of those weeks where everything went wrong

. . . the instructor sprang a quiz on you at the last minute

. . . you forgot about the test until the night before it was scheduled.

Whatever the reason, there may be times when you can't study properly. What do you do if you have to cram for an exam?

Don't spend a lot of time on what you're unable to do. Beating yourself up about your failings as a student will only hinder your efforts. Instead, admit you're human and imperfect like everyone else. Then spend a few minutes developing a plan about what you can accomplish in the limited time you've got.

The first thing to do is choose what you *really* need to study. You won't be able to learn everything, so you have to make choices. Figure out the main focus of the course—a detailed course outline can help you with this—and concentrate on it.

Once you have a strategy, prepare a one-page summary sheet with hard-to-remember information. Just writing the material down will help you remember it, and you can refer to the summary sheet frequently over the limited time you do have to study.

Next, read through your class notes, concentrating on the material you've underlined and the key concepts and ideas that you've already noted. Forget about reading all the material in the books and articles you're being tested on. Instead, only read the passages that you've underlined and the notes you've taken on the readings. Finally, maximize your study time. Using your notes, index cards, and concept maps, go over the information. Read it. Say it aloud. Think about it and the way it relates to other information. In short, use all the techniques we've talked about for learning and recalling information.

When the exam is over, material that you have crammed into your head is destined to leave your mind as quickly as it entered. If you've crammed for a midterm, don't assume that the information will still be there when you study for the final. In the end, cramming often ends up taking more time for worse results than does studying with appropriate techniques.

Before going any further, reflect on your Striving Style™ and how it might affect your approach to test-taking. Then, examine the suggestions and recommendations provided in the sidebar on page 121.

Reducing Anxiety on the Day of the Test

You've studied a lot, and you're happy with your level of mastery. Or perhaps you have the nagging feeling that there's something you haven't quite gotten to. Or maybe you know you haven't had enough time to study as much as you'd like, and you're expecting a disaster.

Whatever your frame of mind, it will help to organize your plan of attack on the day of the test. What's included on the test is out of your hands, but you can control what you bring to it. Here's how:

> **Bring the right tools to the test.** Have at least two pens with you. It's usually best to write in pen because, in general, writing tends to be easier to read in pen than in pencil. But you also might want to have pencils and a good eraser on hand. Sometimes instructors will use machine-scored tests that require the use of a pencil. Or there may be test questions that involve computations, and solving them may entail frequent reworking of calculations.

- **Bring a watch** to the test, even if there will be a clock on the wall of the classroom. You will want to be able to pace yourself properly during the test. Also, if you usually use a cellphone to determine the time, remember that many instructors will ask you to put it away during the test. If they do so, ask if the instructor can write the time on the board at half-hour intervals.

- **Bring your study notes, if allowed.** Sometimes instructors permit you to use notes and books during the test. If you haven't brought them with you, they're not going to be much help; so make sure you bring them if they're permitted. (Even for closed-book tests, having such material available when you arrive in the classroom allows you a few minutes of review before the test actually starts.) And don't be lulled into thinking an open-book test is going to be easy. Instructors who allow you to use your notes and books during a test may not give you much time to look things up, so you still need to study.

- **Resist the temptation to compare notes with your friends** about how much you've studied. Yes, you might end up feeling good because many of your classmates studied less than you did. But chances are you'll find others who seem to have spent significantly more time studying than you, and this will do little to encourage you.

- **Plan on panicking.** Although it sounds like the worst possible approach, permitting yourself the option of spending a minute feeling panicky will help you to recover from your initial fears.

- **Listen carefully to what an instructor says before the test is handed out.** The instructor may tell you about a question that is optional or worth bonus marks or inform you of a typographical error on the test. Whatever the instructor says just before the test, you can be sure it's information that you don't want to ignore.

≫ LO 5.2

Test-taking Strategies

Take a deep breath—literally.

There's no better way to start work on a test than by taking a deep breath, followed by several others. The deep breaths will help you to overcome any initial panic and anxiety you may be experiencing. It's OK to give yourself over for a moment to panic and anxiety; but, to work at your best, use the relaxation techniques that we spoke about earlier to displace those initial feelings. Tell yourself, "It's OK. I am going to do my best."

Read test instructions carefully. Even if instructors talk about what a test will be like beforehand, at the last minute they may make changes. Consequently, it's critical to read the instructions for the test carefully. In fact, you should skim through the entire exam before you begin. Look at the kinds of questions and pay attention to the way they will be scored. If the weighting of the marks for the various parts of the exam is not clear, ask your instructor to clarify it.

Knowing the weighting of the marks is critical, because it will help you to allocate your time. You don't want to spend 90 percent of your time on an essay that's worth only 10 percent of the marks, and you want to be sure to leave time at the end of the test to check your answers.

An initial read-through will also help you verify that you have every page of the exam and that each one is readable. It may also provide you with

Taking Tests and Striving Styles™

Leaders
Enjoy being tested to demonstrate achievement. Tend to plan and prepare. Prone to over-studying. Organize and lead study groups.

Socializers
Try to do well to please teachers. Study groups lead to more socializing than study. Often unprepared, tend to cram and pull all-nighters.

Performers
Enjoy recognition for achieving top marks but have difficulty disciplining themselves to study. Study sporadically; have difficulty focusing. Will ask for makeup exams.

Adventurers
Dislike studying and exams. Organize study groups which turn into play. Cut corners to get good marks. Would rather show what they know than write about it.

Artists
Diligent around studying because they are afraid of failing. Anxious even when they know their stuff. Perfectionism causes them to underachieve due to pressure they create.

Intellectuals
Enjoy studying subjects they like and will "wing it" on subjects they don't. Can over-focus on one subject and have to cram for others. Don't enjoy study groups.

Visionaries
Do best on theoretical or interpretive tests. Have difficulty memorizing. Have to review excessively to retain facts. Don't trust they know enough.

Stabilizers
Structure and prepare in advance. Excel with factual subjects, have difficulty with theoretical or interpretive. Rarely guess. Feel it is their duty to perform well.

"intratest-knowledge"—sometimes terms defined or mentioned in one part of a test trigger memories that can help answer questions in another part of the test.

If there are any lists, formulas, or other key facts that you're concerned you may forget, jot them down now on the back of a test page or on a piece of scrap paper. You may want to refer to this material later during the test.

Once this background work is out of the way, you'll be ready to proceed to actually answering the questions. These principles will help you to do your best on the test:

> **Answer the easiest questions first.** By initially getting the questions out of the way that are easiest for you, you accomplish several important things. First, you'll be leaving yourself more time to think about the tougher questions. In addition, moving through a series of questions without a struggle will build your confidence. Finally, working through a number of questions will build up a base of marks that may be enough to earn you at least a minimally acceptable grade.

> **Write legibly and only on one side of the paper.** If an instructor can't read what you've written, you're not going to get credit for it, no matter how brilliant your answer. So be sure to keep your handwriting legible.

It's a good idea to write your answers to essay questions on only one side of a page. This will allow you to go back later and add or revise information.

> **Master machine-scored tests.** Tests will sometimes be scored, in part, by computer. In such cases, you'll usually have to indicate your answers by filling in—with a pencil—circles or squares on a computer answer sheet.

Be careful! A stray mark or smudge can cause the computer scanner to misread your answer sheet, producing errors in grading. Be sure to bring a good eraser in addition to a pencil; the biggest source of mistakes in machine grading is incomplete erasing. If you find yourself having to erase more than once, you should probably ask for a fresh answer sheet.

It's best to write your answers not only on the answer sheet, but also on the test itself (if the test is not intended for future reuse). That way you can go back and check your answers easily—a step you should take frequently. It's also a good idea to match up your answers on the test with the numbers on the answer sheet every five or so items. This will help you make sure you haven't skipped a space or gotten off track in some other way. If you catch such problems early, they're easy to fix.

A variant of machine-scored testing is online testing. In such cases, you'll be taking an exam on a computer outside of class. You shouldn't wait until the final deadline to start this type of test, as technical difficulties may not allow you to log in or may not give you enough time to finish. In addition, be sure to have paper and pencil available. Even though you use the computer to record your answers, you'll want to be able to jot down ideas and notes, and to do calculations the traditional way, by hand.

Answer Specific Types of Test Questions Appropriately

Every type of question requires a particular approach. Use these strategies:

> **Essay questions.** Essay questions, with their emphasis on description and analysis, often present challenges because they are relatively unstructured.

Unless you're careful, it's easy to wander off and begin to answer questions that were never asked. To prevent that problem, the first thing to do is read the question carefully. If your essay answer will be lengthy, you might want to write a short outline, or a note using the Cornell note-taking method discussed in Chapter 4 (see page 96).

Pay attention to key words that indicate what, specifically, the instructor is looking for in an answer. Certain action words are commonly used in essays, and you should understand them fully. For instance, knowing the distinction between "compare" and "contrast" can spell the difference between success and failure. **Table 5.3** defines common action words.

table 5.3   Action Words for Essays

These words are commonly used in essay questions. Learning the distinctions among them will help you answer essay questions effectively.

Analyze: Examine and break into component parts.

Clarify: Explain with significant detail.

Compare: Describe and explain similarities.

Compare and contrast: Describe and explain similarities and differences.

Contrast: Describe and explain differences.

Critique: Judge and analyze, explaining what is wrong—and right—about a concept.

Define: Provide the meaning.

Discuss: Explain, review, and consider.

Enumerate: Provide a listing of ideas, concepts, reasons, items, etc.

Evaluate: Provide pros and cons of something; provide an opinion and justify it.

Explain: Give reasons why or how; clarify, justify, and illustrate.

Illustrate: Provide examples; show instances.

Interpret: Explain the meaning of something.

Justify: Explain why a concept can be supported, typically by using examples and other types of support.

Outline: Provide an overarching framework or explanation—usually in narrative form—of a concept, idea, event, or phenomenon.

Prove: Using evidence and arguments, convince the reader of a particular point.

Relate: Show how things fit together; provide analogies.

Review: Describe or summarize, often with an evaluation.

State: Assert or explain.

Summarize: Provide a condensed, precise list or narrative.

Trace: Track or sketch out how events or circumstances have evolved; provide a history or timeline.

Use appropriate language in essays. Be brief and to the point in your essay. Avoid flowery introductory language. Compare the two sentences that follow:

"Management techniques have evolved to a point never before seen in the history of our country, or perhaps even our world."

"Many new management techniques have been developed in recent years."

The second sentence says the same thing much more effectively and economically.

Your response should follow a logical sequence, moving from major points to minor ones, or following a time sequence. Essays are improved when they include examples and point out differences. Above all, your answer should address every aspect of the question posed on the test. Because essays often contain several different, embedded questions, you have to be certain that you have answered every part to receive full credit. (After reviewing Table 5.3, complete **Try It! 4**, "Understand Action Verbs in Essay Questions," on page 125.)

> **Short-answer and fill-in questions.** Short-answer and fill-in questions require you to generate and supply specific information. Unlike essays, which are more free-form and may have several possible answers, short-answer and fill-in questions are usually quite specific, requiring only one answer.

Use both the instructions for the questions and the questions themselves to determine the level of specificity that is needed in an answer. Try not to provide too much or too little information. Usually, brevity is best. Be guided by the mark allocation when deciding how much information to include.

> **Multiple-choice questions.** If you've ever looked at a multiple-choice question and said to yourself, "But every choice seems right," you understand what can be tricky about this type of question. However, there are some simple strategies that can help you deal with multiple-choice questions.

First, read the question carefully. Note any specific instructions. In most cases, only one answer will be correct; but some questions will you ask you to select multiple items.

Then, before you look at the possible answers, try to answer the question in your head. This can help you avoid confusion over inappropriate choices.

Next, carefully read through every possible answer. Even if you come to one that you think is right, read them all—there may be a subsequent answer that is better.

Look for absolutes like "every," "always," "only," "none," and "never." Choices that contain such absolute words are rarely correct. For example, an answer choice that says, "There has never been a woman prime minister in Canada" is incorrect due to the presence of the word "never." On the other hand, less-absolute words, such as "generally," "usually," "often," "rarely," "seldom," and "typically" may indicate a correct response.

Be especially on guard for the word "not," which negates the sentence ("The one key concept that is not embodied in the Canadian Privacy Principles . . ."). It's easy to gloss over "not"; and if you have the misfortune of doing so, it will be nearly impossible to answer the item correctly.

If you're having trouble understanding a question, underline key words or phrases, or try to break the question into different short sections. Sometimes it is helpful to work backwards, *Jeopardy*-style, and look at the possible answers first to see if you can find one that is clearly accurate or clearly inaccurate.

Use an **educated guessing** strategy—which is very different from wild or random guessing. Unless you are penalized for wrong answers (a scoring rule by which wrong answers are deducted from the points you have earned on other questions, rather than merely not counting at all toward your score), it always pays to guess.

Educated guessing
The practice of eliminating obviously false multiple-choice answers and selecting the most likely answer from the remaining choices

Understand Action Verbs in Essay Questions

Part A: Federal Industry Minister Tony Clement claims that new voluntary long-form census "strikes a fair and reasonable balance between ensuring the federal government has the basic information every government requires, and protecting the privacy of Canadian citizens." **(http://www.charityvillage.com/cv/archive/acov/acov10/acov1024.asp)**

Research this topic, then answer the following three questions about the Canadian government's plan to replace the mandatory "long form" of the census with a voluntary form. As you respond to each question, pay special attention to the different action verbs that introduce each question.

1. **Summarize** the government's position on the long census form.

2. **Analyze** the government's position on the long census form.

3. **Discuss** the government's position on the long census form.

Part B:

1. How do your answers differ for the each of the questions?
2. Which of the questions provoked the lengthiest response?
3. Which of the questions could you answer best?

To Try It online, go to Connect for *P.O.W.E.R. Learning and Your Life*.

The first step in educated guessing is to eliminate any obviously false answers. The next step is to examine the remaining choices closely. Does one response choice include an absolute or qualifying adjective that makes it unlikely; for example, "the probability of a leadership review *always* increases when a Canadian prime minister is facing political difficulties"? Does one choice include a subtle factual error? For example, the answer to a multiple-choice question asking why Columbus took his journey to the new world that says "The French monarchy was interested in expanding its colonial holdings" is wrong because it was not the French monarchy, but the Spanish monarchy, that funded Columbus's journey.

▸ **True–false questions.** Although most of the principles we've already discussed apply equally well to true–false questions, a few additional tricks of the trade may help you with this type of question.

Begin a set of true–false questions by answering the ones you're sure you know. But don't rush; it's important to read every part of a true–false question, because key words such as "never," "always," and "sometimes" often determine the appropriate response.

Academic honesty
Completing and turning in only one's own work under one's own name

Plagiarism
Taking credit for someone else's words, thoughts, or ideas

If you don't have a clue about whether a statement is true or false, here's a last-resort principle: Choose "true." In general, more statements on a true–false test are likely to be true than false.

> **Matching questions.** Matching questions typically present you with two columns of related information, which you must link, item by item. For example, a list of terms or concepts may be presented in one column, along with a list of corresponding definitions or explanations in the second column. The best strategy is to reduce the size of both columns by matching the items you're most confident about first; this will leave a short list in each column, and the final matching may become apparent.

About Academic Honesty

It's tempting: A glance at a classmate's test may provide the one piece of information that you just can't remember. But you owe it to yourself not to do it. Copying from a classmate's paper is no different from reaching over and stealing that classmate's cellphone. It is a violation of **academic honesty,** one of the foundations of civility in the classroom, as well as in society. Unless the work you turn in under your own name is your work, you are guilty of academic dishonesty.

A violation of academic honesty can take many forms. It may involve **plagiarism**—taking credit for someone else's words, thoughts, or ideas. Academic dishonesty may also include using a calculator when it's not allowed, discussing the answer to a question, copying an unauthorized computer file, taking an exam for another person, or stealing an exam. It can take the form of ripping a page out of a book in the library, or lying to an instructor about the reason for a late paper. It includes using your textbook or conferring with a friend when taking a closed-book exam in an online, distance-learning course.

You may feel that "everyone does it," so cheating is not so bad. Wrong! Everyone doesn't do it, just as most people don't embezzle from their companies or steal from others. Although you may know of a few cases of exceptionally dishonest classmates, most of your classmates try to be honest—you just don't notice their honesty.

Whatever form it takes, academic dishonesty is just plain wrong. It makes the grading system unfair, it reduces the meaning of your grade, and it lowers the level of civility in the classroom. It certainly hinders academic and personal growth. It can't help but rob the cheater of self-respect. Don't do it!

Finally, academic dishonesty violates the regulations of every college and university (rules that you should familiarize yourself with), and instructors know it is their obligation to uphold standards of academic honesty. Violations of honesty policies will lead to any number of potentially devastating scenarios: failing the exam on which the cheating has taken place, failing the entire course, being brought before a disciplinary board, having a description of the incident permanently placed on your grade transcript, being placed on academic probation, or even being thrown out of school. A single instance of cheating can permanently prevent you from embarking on the career of your choice. Cheating is simply not worth it.

 Check Your Work

The last few minutes of a test may feel like the final moments of a marathon. You need to focus your energy and push yourself even harder. It can be make-or-break time.

Tests for a Lifetime

If you think the last tests you'll ever have to take are the final exams just before you graduate, you're probably wrong.

Increasing numbers of professions require initial licensing exams, and some even require periodic exams to remain in good standing within the profession. For example, in Canada, people who wish to become dental hygienists must pass a licensing exam in the province in which they wish to practise. And even experienced hygienists are expected to remain current with the latest tools and techniques by participating in professional development activities throughout their careers.

In short, good test-taking skills won't just bring you success in college or university. They're something that may benefit you for a lifetime as you pursue your career.

Career **Connections**

Save some time at the end of a test so you can check your work. You should have been keeping track of your time all along, so plan on stopping a few minutes before the end of the test period to review what you've done. It's an important step, and it can make the difference between a terrific grade and a mediocre one. It's a rare person who can work for an uninterrupted period of time on a test and commit absolutely no errors—even if he or she knows the material backwards and forwards. Consequently, checking what you've done is crucial.

Start evaluating your test by looking for obvious mistakes. Make sure that you've answered every question. If there is a separate answer sheet, check to see that all your answers have been recorded on the answer sheet and are in the right spot.

If the test included essay and short-answer questions, proofread your responses. Check for obvious errors—misspellings, missing words, and repetitions. Make sure that you've responded to every part of each question and that each essay, as a whole, makes sense.

Check over your responses to multiple-choice, true–false, and matching questions. If there are some items that you haven't yet answered because you couldn't remember the necessary information, now is the time to take a stab at them. As we discussed earlier, it usually pays to guess, even randomly if you must. On most tests, no answer and a wrong answer are worth the same amount—nothing!

What about items that you initially guessed at? Unless you have a good reason to change your original answer—such as a new insight or a sudden recollection of some key information—your first guess is likely your best guess.

Know When to Stop

After evaluating and checking your answers, there may still be some time left. What to do? If you're satisfied with your responses, it's simply time to tell yourself, "Let it go."

Permit yourself the luxury of knowing that you've done your best, and hand the test in to your instructor. You don't have to review your work over and over just because there is time remaining and some of your classmates are still working on their tests. In fact, such behaviour is often counterproductive, because you might start over-interpreting and reading things into questions that really aren't there.

On the other hand, what if you've run out of time? It's a nightmarish feeling: The clock is ticking relentlessly, and it's clear that you don't have enough time to finish the test. What should you do?

Stop working! Although this advice may sound foolish, in fact the best thing you can do is take a minute to calm yourself. Take some deep breaths to replace the feelings of panic that are likely welling up inside you. Collect your thoughts, and plan a strategy for the last moments of the test.

If there are essays that remain undone, consider how you'd answer them if you had more time. Then write an outline of each answer. If you don't have time even for that, write a few key words. Writing anything is better than handing in a blank page, and you may get at least some credit for your response. The key principle here: Something is better than nothing, and even one mark is worth more than zero marks.

The same principle holds for other types of questions. Even wild guesses are almost always better than not responding at all to an item. So rather than telling yourself you've certainly failed and giving up, do as much as you can in the remaining moments of the exam.

From the perspective of . . .

A LEGAL ASSISTANT
Even though tests are uncommon in professional careers, deadlines are frequent occurrences. How might test-taking strategies help you when you are faced with a tight schedule?

LO 5.3 R Rethink Post-test Analysis

Your instructor is about to hand the graded exams back. All sorts of thoughts run through your head: How did I do? Did I do as well as my classmates? Will I be happy with my results? Will the results show how much I studied? Will I be embarrassed by my grade?

The first thing you should do when you get your test back is to ensure the instructor has added up your mark correctly; instructors are human, and mistakes are sometimes made. It is always worth checking to be sure you have received all the marks you are due. You may also want to ask your instructor about the class average on the test, so you can determine how well you did relative to the rest of the class.

Most of us focus on the evaluative aspects of tests. We look at the grade we've received on a test as an end in itself. It's a natural reaction.

But there's another way to look at test results: They can help guide us toward future success. By looking at what we've learned (and haven't learned) about a given subject, we'll be in a better position to know what to focus on when we take future exams. Furthermore, by examining the kinds of mistakes we make, we can improve our test-taking skills.

When you get your test back, you have the opportunity to reflect on what you've learned and to consider your performance. Begin by actively listening to what your instructor says as he or she hands back the test. You may learn about things that were generally misunderstood by the class. You also may pick up some important clues about what questions will be on future tests.

Then examine your own mistakes. Chances are they'll jump out at you since they will be marked incorrect. Did you misunderstand or misapply some principle? Was there a certain aspect of the material that you missed? Were there particular kinds of information that you didn't realize you needed to know? Or did you lose some points because of your test-taking skills? Did you make careless errors, such as forgetting to fill in a question or misreading the directions? Was your handwriting so sloppy that your instructor had trouble reading it?

Once you have a good idea of what material you didn't fully understand or remember, get the correct answers to the items you missed—from your instructor, your classmates, or your book. If it's a math test, rework problems you've missed. Finally, summarize—in writing—the material you had trouble with. This will help you study for future exams that cover the same material.

Finally, if you're dissatisfied with your performance, talk to your instructor—not to complain, but to seek help. Instructors should be able to point out problems in your test that you can address readily so you can do better in the future. Demonstrate to your instructor that you want to do better and are willing to put in the work to get there. The worst thing to do is crumple up the test and quickly leave the class in embarrassment. Remember, you're not the first person to get a bad grade, and the power to improve your test-taking performance lies within you. (Now, take a deep breath and complete **Try It! 5**, "Take a Test on Taking Tests," on pages 130–31.)

Try It!

Take a Test on Taking Tests

Part A: Take the following test on test-taking skills, which illustrates every question type discussed in this chapter.

Before taking the test, think of the test-taking strategies we've discussed in the chapter and try to employ as many of them as possible.

MULTIPLE-CHOICE SECTION

Choose one of the possible responses following each question.

1. Tests are useful tools for which of the following purposes?
   a. Determining people's likely level of future career success.
   b. Indicating strengths and gaps in people's knowledge.
   c. Defining people's fundamental abilities and potentials.
   d. Evaluating people's individual worth and contributions.

2. One of the main advantages of study groups is that
   a. Every individual must contribute equally to the group.
   b. Group members can help each other during the test.
   c. Each member has to memorize only a fraction of the material.
   d. They allow each member to share different perspectives on the material.

3. Which of the following is a good way to deal with test anxiety?
   a. Visualizing success on the test.
   b. Drinking coffee or other stimulants.
   c. Telling yourself to stop worrying.
   d. Focusing on the importance of the test.

MATCHING SECTION

_____ **1.** Essay question

_____ **2.** Multiple-choice question

_____ **3.** Matching question

_____ **4.** Fill-in question

_____ **5.** Guessing penalty

_____ **6.** Cramming

_____ **7.** Plagiarism

A. A question in which the student supplies brief missing information to complete a statement.

B. Hurried, last-minute studying.

C. A question in which the student must link information in two columns.

D. A question requiring a lengthy response in the student's own words.

E. Deduction of points for incorrect responses.

F. Representing someone else's work as one's own.

G. A question that requires selection from several response options.

FILL-IN SECTION

1. Fear of testing that can interfere with test performance is called _____.
2. The primary source of error on machine-scored tests is incomplete _____.

TRUE–FALSE SECTION

1. The best way to prepare for an essay test is to review detailed factual information about the topic. T _____ F _____

2. True–false questions require students to determine whether given statements are accurate or inaccurate. T _____ F _____

3. You should never permit yourself to feel panicky during a test. T _____ F _____

4. A good evaluation strategy toward the end of a test is to redo as many questions as time permits. T _____ F _____

5. In a multiple-choice question, the words "always" and "never" usually signal the correct response. T _____ F _____

6. If you run out of time at the end of a test, it is best to write brief notes and ideas down in response to essay questions rather than to leave them completely blank. T _____ F _____

SHORT-ANSWER SECTION

1. What are five things you should find out about a test before you take it?

2. What is academic honesty?

ESSAY SECTION

1. Discuss the advantages of using a study group to prepare for an examination.

2. Why is academic honesty important?

(Answers can be found on page 135.)

Part B:
After you have completed the test, consider these questions:

1. Did you learn anything from taking the test that you might not have learned if you hadn't been tested?
2. How effective were the test-taking strategies you employed?
3. Were any types of strategies easier for you to employ than others?
4. Were any types of questions easier for you to answer than others?

 WORKING IN A GROUP

Exchange your essay responses with a classmate, and critique the essays. How do the responses of your partner compare with your own?

To Try It online, go to Connect for *P.O.W.E.R. Learning and Your Life.*

Time to Reflect: What Did I Learn?

1. Generally speaking, how does being tested make you feel?

2. What factors seem to contribute to your success or failure on a particular test or exam? Which of these factors are under your control?

3. What strategies do you plan to use in the future to improve your performance on tests?

Looking Back

What kinds of tests will I encounter in college and university?

▸ There are several types of tests, including brief, informal quizzes; tests, which are more substantial; and exams, which are even more significant and tend to be administered at the midpoint and end of a course.

▸ Although tests are an unpopular fact of college and university life, they can provide useful information about your level of knowledge and understanding about a subject.

What are the best ways to prepare for various kinds of tests?

▸ Good test preparation begins with doing the course assignments, attending class regularly, and paying attention in class. It also helps to find out as much as possible about a test beforehand and to form a study group to review material.

▸ If cramming becomes necessary, focus on summarizing factual information broadly, identifying key concepts and ideas, and rehearsing information orally.

What can I do during the test to maximize my test results?

▸ When you first receive the test, you should skim it to see what kinds of questions are asked, figure out how the different questions and sections will be weighted, and jot down complex factual information you might need for the test.

▸ Answer the easiest questions first, write legibly, use only one side of each sheet of paper, mark answer sheets carefully, and record answers in the test book as well as on the answer sheet.

What are the best strategies for answering specific kinds of test questions?

▸ For essay questions, you should work to understand each question and each of its parts, interpret action words correctly, write concisely, organize the essay logically, and include examples.

▸ The best strategy for short-answer and fill-in questions is to be very sure what is being asked. Keep answers complete but brief.

▸ For multiple-choice items, read the question very carefully and then read all response choices. Educated guessing based on eliminating incorrect response choices is usually a reasonable strategy.

▸ For true–false and matching questions, answer all the items that you are sure of quickly and then go back to the remaining items.

What can I learn from taking the test?

▸ Analyzing the graded test will help you to see weaknesses in your understanding of the material tested. You can study these weak areas further before you take your next test or exam on that material.

▸ You may see places in the test where you have misread questions or misallocated your time. Recognizing these tendencies in yourself can help you to be more "test-wise" in the future.

[KEY TERMS AND CONCEPTS]

Academic honesty (p. 126)

Cramming (p. 118)

Educated guessing (p. 124)

Plagiarism (p. 126)

Study group (p. 115)

Test anxiety (p. 117)

[RESOURCES]

ON CAMPUS

Colleges and universities provide a variety of resources for students having difficulties with test-taking. Some offer general workshops reviewing test-taking strategies. As well, if you are planning to take a specific standardized test, you may be able to sign up for a course offered through your college or university (or through such commercial organizations as Princeton Review or Kaplan).

If you are experiencing difficulties in a specific course, you may be able to find a tutor to help you. Some institutions have tutoring centres or campus learning centres that can provide one-to-one assistance. It's also important to speak to your instructor, who has likely encountered many students with similar problems and may have some useful test-taking strategies.

If you find that you are experiencing significant test anxiety when taking a test or in the days leading up to it, talk to one of the professionals at your campus counselling centre or health centre. They can help you learn relaxation techniques and can provide counselling to help make your anxiety manageable.

IN PRINT

If you have difficulty with test anxiety, you'll want to check out *Insider's Guide to Beating Test Anxiety* (Bedford, 2010).

In *How to Ace Any Test* (Wiley, 2004), Beverley Chin provides a variety of techniques designed to improve your performance on any kind of test.

Eileen Tracy's *The Student's Guide to Exam Success* (Open University Press, 2006) gives an overview of strategies for test-taking success.

ON THE WEB

The following websites provide the opportunity to extend your learning about the material in this chapter.

› "The Multiple Choice Exam," an online handout from the University of Victoria's Learning Skills Program (**www.coun.uvic.ca/learning/exams/multiple-choice.html**) offers some valuable suggestions on how to approach multiple-choice exams. Several types of multiple-choice questions are described and strategies for answering them are explained. There are also helpful hints about what to look for in the wording of both the questions and the answer choices.

› "Simplified Plans of Action for Common Types of Question Words," another online handout from the University of Victoria's Learning Skills Program (**www.coun.uvic.ca/learning/essays/simple-answers.html**), gives examples of question words that are often found in essay assignments or in essay questions on exams. Possible "plans of action" for each of the question types are outlined. These outlines can be useful as a starting point for understanding how to approach essay questions.

› "Tactics for Managing Stress and Anxiety" (**www.coun.uvic.ca/personal/stress-anxiety.html**) offers several suggestions that you might find helpful in managing and reducing your level of stress and anxiety. The techniques may help you deal with test-related anxiety as well as academic anxiety in general. Not all of the techniques work for everyone. Try them and adopt the ones that work best for you.

1 Seeing exams from other classes can help you get an idea of the kinds of questions that are often asked on exams. Use an Internet search engine to locate examples of exams from other colleges and universities. One strategy would be to use the Google search engine at **www.google.ca**, and type "examples of exams" (including the quotation marks) at the search prompt. Look at several exams. How many of the questions on these exams were true–false? How many were multiple-choice? How many were essays?

2 Practise answering essay questions by comparing and contrasting the information different Web pages offer about the same topic. For example, go to Yahoo! (**http://ca.yahoo.com**) and enter the phrase "essay exams" (using quotation marks). Read the strategies for essay exams offered in two different websites. Then write a paragraph describing the information both sites had in common, and another paragraph describing the information that was unique to each site.

[ANSWERS TO ITEMS IN TRY IT! 5]

Multiple-choice: 1b, 2d, 3a

Matching: 1D, 2G, 3C, 4A, 5E, 6B, 7F

Fill-in: test anxiety, erasing

True–False: 1F, 2T, 3F, 4F, 5F, 6T

Short answer:

1. Possible answers include what the test is called, what it will cover, how many questions will be on it, how much time it will take, what kinds of questions will be on it, how it will be graded, whether sample questions will be provided, and whether tests from prior terms are available.

2. Academic honesty is completing and turning in only one's own work under one's own name.

Essay:

1. Strong essays would include a brief definition of a study group, followed by a discussion of the advantages of using study groups (including such things as helping to organize and structure material, providing different perspectives, and rethinking material). A mention of the disadvantages of study groups would also be reasonable.

2. After starting with a brief definition of academic honesty, the bulk of the answer should concentrate on the reasons why academic honesty is important and the consequences of academic dishonesty.

The Case of . . .
That Sinking Feeling

This is going to be easy, Janelle Ross said to herself as she sat down to take her test, a midterm exam covering the basics of restaurant management. She had spent a few hours the previous night and an hour right before class studying key terms and concepts. She felt she knew the material. She felt ready.

Janelle was surprised to see, though, that the exam had two parts: a multiple-choice section and an essay section. Janelle hadn't really thought about what she might say in an essay. But she figured working on the multiple-choice questions might help give her some ideas.

The first two multiple-choice questions Janelle answered easily, but she got stuck on the third one. She went back and forth over two possible answers and finally decided just to leave that question blank. The pattern was the same for the rest of the multiple-choice questions: A few questions Janelle would answer easily, then she'd get stuck on a hard one.

Finally, Janelle finished the multiple-choice questions and came to the essay. Only then did she notice the instructions that indicated the essay was worth 50 marks, and the multiple-choice questions 25 marks. Then Janelle got another shock: She had only ten minutes left to write her essay! Her mind froze—and Janelle had the horrible feeling that she didn't have enough time to complete the test. Even though she had studied, Janelle now felt certain she would fail.

1. What mistakes did Janelle make in her test preparation that probably harmed her performance?

2. What mistakes did Janelle make during the test that hurt her?

3. What was right about Janelle's initial approach to the test?

4. What should Janelle have done differently in calculating the amount of time to devote to each portion of the test? Why?

5. What specific strategies would have helped Janelle with the multiple-choice questions? What strategies could she have used on the essay?

6. If you were in Janelle's shoes, what would you do with only ten minutes left in the test?

6 Leveraging Technology and Doing Research

Learning Outcomes

By the time you finish this chapter, you will be able to

» LO **6.1** Identify technologies that contribute to your efficiency and effectiveness in your academic and everyday life.

» LO **6.2** Determine whether taking a distance learning course is the right choice for you and for your learning style.

» LO **6.3** Discuss the principles of effective online communication and collaboration.

» LO **6.4** Demonstrate information competency by identifying techniques and technologies that help you locate and evaluate information and organize the information that you find.

» LO **6.5** Identify the different types of plagiarism and explain how plagiarism can be avoided through proper citation methods and the use of citation software.

Throughout high school, Melissa Khan had always been a serious student. She did her readings before class, wrote summaries of what she'd learned after each class, and studied hard for tests and exams. Her efforts had resulted in excellent marks, and her goal was to maintain this type of performance now that she was in college. But the one thing Melissa hadn't counted on was how much of her grade would depend on group work. It was one thing to count on herself, but a totally different thing to have to depend on others to get their work done on time and to the same level of quality she expected from herself.

So when Melissa's business analysis instructor announced on the first day of class that the course involved two major group projects worth 40% of the overall course grade, Melissa was far from enthusiastic. And when the instructor went on to say that the teams would be self-managed, and that everyone on the team would get the same mark, Melissa became downright nervous.

But then, the instructor went one step further. He indicated that all documents relating to the project would be worked on in a collaborative space on the Internet (or "in the cloud"), using a tool called Office Live. The instructor did an in-class demonstration of the technology, showing how it would allow members of a group to use the same workspace, track who made changes or additions to a document, and send emails notifying members when changes were made. The technology had its own chat function, as well as tools like calendars and project plans to keep everyone on track. No more wondering if Person A and Person B had done their work and would deliver it on time—it was there for everyone else in the group to see.

Melissa quickly realized that group work would become much more manageable if she used technology like Office Live in all of her classes that involved group work, and went away from the demo feeling much more comfortable with the prospect of working on group projects.

Looking
Ahead

The technology that Melissa's instructor introduced her to didn't even exist five years ago. Like every other aspect of society, education is changing, as "virtual" resources—cloud computing, social media, blogs, Real Simple Syndication (RSS) feeds, social bookmarking, collaborative workspaces, and so forth—become more and more a part of how we learn, and how we live our lives. Today, businesspeople hold meetings and instructors teach courses without even being in the same room with their co-workers or students.

Technology is making a profound difference in how we are taught, the ways we study and carry out our work, and how we communicate with others. It is changing the way you can access the vast quantities of information published each year—tens of thousands of books, journals, and other print materials, and literally billions of Web pages. But successfully wading through all that information to find the "nuggets" requires skills that weren't necessary in the past.

In this chapter, we discuss how technological advances increase your opportunities to achieve success in college and university, and on the job. First, we'll examine some general tools that can help you organize your computer and use it more effectively. Then, we'll talk about some of the technologies that are specific to your role as a student, including course management systems, e-books, and distance learning. Finally, we'll consider how you can use technology to develop information competency—how to locate and assess sources and how to reference them properly—an essential skill in a world where we are drowning in data, but have difficulty finding information that is both relevant and credible.

≫ LO 6.1 You and Technology

It's a great tool that can help you achieve success in your classes. It can save you hours of time on your job, whether you work in a cubicle or a garage. At the same time, it can be extremely frustrating, annoying, and maddening; and it can eat up hours of your time.

"It," of course, is technology. Today, it's as much a necessity to use technology as it was for you to learn to write using pen and paper earlier in your schooling. No one facing the job market in the twenty-first century will want to leave college or university without a strong working knowledge of a variety of technologies and what they can do for you.

Perhaps you are a mature student who is not yet at ease with technology. If so, relax. No one is born with technology expertise. With practice, however, using a broad range of technologies can become second nature.

Use Technology to Get Organized

There are many technologies that can make your life easier, so many that most of us aren't even aware that many of them exist. In this chapter, we introduce you to a number of tools and applications that will probably be new to you. Some you may be interested in adopting; others you may not. Some will work on your computer system; others may not. But all are worthy of exploration. A small investment of time spent downloading some of these tools can add up to a huge increase in your personal efficiency, so it is worth taking a look at a few of them.

We'll begin at the very beginning—your computer's "desktop." When you power up your computer and the main screen comes up, do you find yourself looking at dozens of program shortcuts/icons, from iTunes to MSWord to Second Life, splattered all over the screen every which way like a piece of abstract art? Well, there is a better way. Why not organize those icons in a logical way: utilities like Norton and Adobe in one place, Microsoft programs in another, games and fun in another, and

figure 6.1
**Organizing the icons on
your computer desktop**

so forth? One tool that can help you do this is called Fences. It is a program that allows you to divide up your screen any way you like, and group icons into logical "buckets" or themes. You can read reviews of this free software and download it at **http://download.cnet.com/Fences/3000-2072_4-10909535.html**. You can see the impact of using Fences to organize your desktop icons in **Figure 6.1.**

Now, let's move on to how you organize the files on your computer. Take a look at the files that are on there now. If you are using MS Windows, you can use Windows Explorer to do this. Do you have screens full of individual files, or have you taken the time to organize your files into easily identifiable folders? If you do not have a file management system in place, it's time to invest an hour or so in creating one like the one in **Figure 6.2** on page 140. Examine your individual files and think about the themes that underlie them. Fun and games? Current semester's work? Health and fitness? Recipes? Bring related files together in their own folder, and name the folder appropriately. Use sub-folders to provide even more detail; for your Recipe folder, you could divide it into appetizers, vegetarian meals, meat-based meals, and dessert, for example.

To organize your student life, consider having a folder for each semester, and within that folder, a sub-folder for each course; i.e., Winter 2012–BUSN226. While you are at it, consider creating a desktop shortcut for your current semester's main folder. One click and you are there. When the semester is over, you can put the entire sub-folder into a folder called Archived Semesters. This way, only the most current semester is showing, but you can easily find work that you've done previously. And while we're on the subject of files, consider how much easier your life would be if you used a specific approach (or "convention") to naming your files. For example, what if all your course outlines could be found easily using a

figure 6.2
Organizing your folders

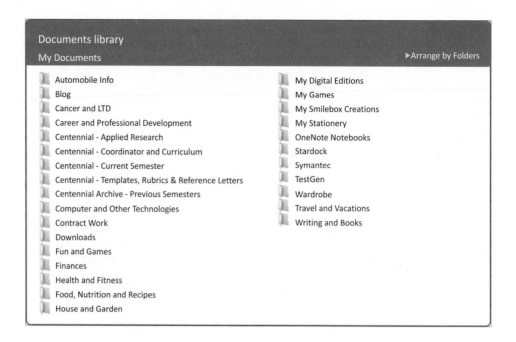

Documents library

My Documents   ▶Arrange by Folders

Automobile Info   My Digital Editions
Blog   My Games
Cancer and LTD   My Smilebox Creations
Career and Professional Development   My Stationery
Centennial - Applied Research   OneNote Notebooks
Centennial - Coordinator and Curriculum   Stardock
Centennial - Current Semester   Symantec
Centennial - Templates, Rubrics & Reference Letters   TestGen
Centennial Archive - Previous Semesters   Wardrobe
Computer and Other Technologies   Travel and Vacations
Contract Work   Writing and Books
Downloads
Fun and Games
Finances
Health and Fitness
Food, Nutrition and Recipes
House and Garden

search function because they are all named in a similar way; i.e., Course outline–BUSN226. Why would you want old course outlines, you might ask? Well, should you ever transfer to another educational institution and want to save yourself both time and money by applying for transfer credits, one of the first things they will ask you for is a course outline for the courses you took at the other institution.

Another area that would probably benefit from organization is your email inbox. For many of us, if our email inbox was a traditional inbox, the mound of paper in it would be several feet high, as we often leave it to build up for months, or even years. A folder system can also be created within most email systems; and if the folders are logically named, finding a specific email should be quick work. If you are not a fan of folders, another alternative is to delete diligently the emails you do not expect to refer back to, and use search functions within your email system to find what you are looking for.

One of the most important technologies available to help you stay on top of your busy life is a calendar like the one in Microsoft Outlook, or an online version like Windows Live Calendar or Google Calendar (see **Figure 6.3**). Use a calendar to put in recurring events like fitness classes, your weekly study group, and even birthdays; and for any event, you can use the "reminder" function. The reminder function can—and should—be used for report due dates, tests, and so forth; but in these cases, they can remind you not only that you are having a test but also that it's time to start studying. Most calendar systems provide you with a "to-do" feature which automatically reminds you of what needs to be done on the day it needs to be done. Why try keeping all of this in your head when it is so easy to use technology to track it for you?

Your browser, which is your entry to the Internet, is yet another tool that can be modified to better suit your needs. Whether you use Internet Explorer, Apple Safari, Google Chrome, or Mozilla's Firefox, one feature worth looking at is the ability to open several pages (or tabs) at once as your home page, rather than just one. For example, when you open your browser, you could have immediate access to your course management system (e.g., Blackboard or WebCT), your college or university's email system, your Facebook home page, the front page of your favourite newspaper, and the local forecast from the Weather Network, each with its own tab, each ready to jump into, as you sip your morning coffee. Indeed, one of the Firefox

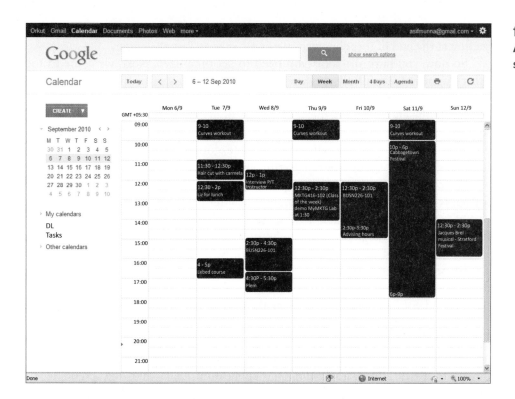

figure 6.3
A calendar and to-do
system are essential.

add-ons that has been developed to allow you to do this is called Morning Coffee! If you don't like having many open tabs, another option is to design your own personalized home page, like iGoogle, that has embedded links. (You will find iGoogle at **www.google.com/ig**.)

The advent of "cloud computing" is making it easier for most of us to stay organized, whether we are sitting home at our computer, or thousands of miles away, vacationing on a sandy beach. In the not-too-distant past, your programs, documents, email, bookmarks, and calendar were probably housed on a specific desktop computer, and were reachable only when you were sitting in front of that computer. These days, all of this information can be housed "in the cloud"—that is, on the Internet—and is available to you anywhere, anytime, as long as you have a device to reach it, like a laptop or smart phone, and access to the Internet.

For those of you who are still tethered to email provided by Internet Service Providers (ISP) like Bell or Rogers, or to a calendar on a system like Outlook, you can still take advantage of cloud computing because you can access your email directly from your ISP's website instead. You can synchronize your Outlook calendar with Web-based applications like Google Calendar; and you can check it online, or even on your iPod.

If you are always on the move and "anywhere, anytime" access is key to you being able to organize your life, then cloud computing is the answer. For documents, you'll want to investigate Google Docs or Live Mesh. Your to-do lists can be stored on sites like Remember the Milk or **www.toodledo.com**. For online access to notes you've created, whether they are based on text, images, audio, or even entire webpages, try Evernote. For access to your bookmarks online, and the ability to share them with others, look to social bookmarking applications like Delicious. Cloud computing also extends to sites where you can share your photos (e.g., Flickr, Picasa), your presentations (e.g., Sliderocket), your music (e.g., Bluetunes), and every single thought going through your head at any moment, as long as you can express it in 140 characters or less (Twitter)! These sites are featured in an excellent little book by Peter Buckley called *The Rough Guide to Cloud Computing*, which reviews the 100 best cloud computing sites. For more details, see the In Print section at the end of this chapter.

So now, you have the tools you need to get organized. Next, we come to the most important step of all: *staying* organized. For many of us, this is the hardest part. To keep on top of your organization, we recommend that you set an hour or so aside at the end of each semester to purge unnecessary files, folders, and emails, to clean up your virtual desktop, and to archive the previous semester's work. To ensure that your software is always up to date, consider signing up for automatic upgrades, which you can program to run while you are sleeping. Frequent upgrades are especially important for your operating system and security software, as the former is prone to attack by hackers, and the latter protects you from them. For the rest of your software, consider setting aside one day every year—preferably *before* the academic year begins—to make all of the necessary upgrades. Often, deeply discounted student rates are available on software in your campus bookstore, so you'll want to check there first. Let's face it—you don't want to find yourself trying to read an important file sent to you by a fellow student in the middle of the night, only to find you can't because you have the previous version of the software!

A final note of caution: There are many, many "free" applications on the Internet, like the ones mentioned above; but as with most things in life, there really isn't a free lunch. The price to be paid for some of these "free applications" can include having to watch advertising before the application loads, allowing a "cookie" or small tracking device to be put on your computer, providing some of your demographic information, or allowing the information you provide, such as your status update, to be harvested and used to deliver targeted advertising to you (this is how Facebook works). Be aware that you are usually giving something up, often your time or your privacy, to get something "free." Before taking advantage of a free application, ensure you *know* what you are giving up in return.

Use Technology to Get the Most out of Your Courses

Technology now plays a big role in everyone's life whether you are proficient with its use or not. Computers run your car's engine, make your digital camera work, allow you to listen to your music on a device that is smaller than a credit card, and make sure the bus you're waiting for runs on time. Technology has revolutionized academic life as well, both inside and outside the classroom. Here are some of the ways technology can be used to support your course work:

> **Course websites.** Many college and university courses have a website associated with them. The website may reside in a course management software system such as Blackboard, WebCT, desire2learn, or eCollege, with which your college has a licensing agreement. In other cases, educational institutions develop their own course management systems.

> Whatever course management system is used, the website will probably contain basic information about the course, such as a copy of the syllabus or course outline, and information on how to contact your instructor. It may also be used provide important emergency updates, such as class cancellations or changes in a paper's due date.

> The course website will often play a central role as a repository for PowerPoint slides, assignments, online quizzes, discussion threads, and even your grades. If your instructor elects to post their slides before class, consider printing them out using the print option in PowerPoint that allows you to create handouts. Select the "three to a page" option, which will provide you with

room for notes, and bring the handouts to class. You will then be able to concentrate on the examples the instructor is using, rather than trying to capture the content of each slide. (For tips on making best use of instructors' presentation slides, see the **Course Connections** box on page 144.)

In some courses, you may electronically deposit papers and essays into a "digital drop box" on the class website. Later, your instructor can read them online, post comments on your submissions, and return them to you on the website. You may carry out group projects on the website, or hold virtual discussions on the site. You may even be required to take your major tests and final exams on the website.

▸ **Textbook Online Learning Centres and Companion Websites.** Many textbooks have a website that is tied to the book. The website typically includes chapter summaries, interactive reviews, flash cards, and practice tests. These resources, which are usually described in the preface to most textbooks, can be extremely valuable study tools. (The companion website for this text is at Connect for *P.O.W.E.R. Learning.*)

▸ **E-Books.** Textbook publishers have responded to the introduction of e-readers like Kobo and Apple's iPad with e-book versions of their texts. In addition to making your backpack significantly lighter, e-books have many other useful features: they are searchable, allowing you to find specific text, highlight that text, and then create a side note and save it as a useful study tool. While the jury is still out on how much you will enjoy reading your textbooks on a screen, there is no question that the lower cost of an e-book, when compared to a traditional paper-based textbook, is very appealing to cash-strapped students.

▸ **Podcasts.** In some classes, instructors produce an audio or a video recording, called a **podcast,** of lectures or other instructional material relevant to the class. You can either access podcasts on the Web or download them to a mobile device (such as an iPod) that permits you to listen to and view them outside of class whenever you want. For podcasts of the best lectures, on any topic, delivered by some of the most dynamic professors in the world, check out iTunesU (**www.apple.com/education/itunes-u**).

Podcast
An audio or video recording that can be accessed on the Internet and viewed on a computer or downloaded to a mobile device

▸ **Blogs and Vlogs.** Some instructors maintain blogs or vlogs of their own. A **blog** is a Web-based public diary in which a writer offers ideas, thoughts, short essays, and commentary; a **vlog** is a video-based version of a blog. If your instructor has a blog or vlog and tells you to take a look at it, get in the habit of checking it routinely. It will contain information relevant to the course, and it also may reveal personal insights that can help you know your instructor better.

Blog/Vlog
A Web-based public diary in which a writer provides written or video commentary, ideas, thoughts, and short essays

Use Technology for Group Work and Networking

As Melissa learned in this chapter's opening vignette, group work is an essential part of post-secondary education; it prepares you for the working world where you will find yourself working daily with others, both inside and outside your company. The increasingly interactive nature of many applications found on the Internet today is evidence of how interconnected our world is becoming. Some of these applications, like Facebook and MySpace, are designed specifically for *social* interaction, but are also being used by employers making hiring decisions, so you need to be wary of what you post, and who you allow to see it, something that *you* control by paying close attention to your privacy settings on these sites.

Websites that are designed to facilitate collaboration among students or employees have many benefits. Aside from the obvious—anyone can access the site, anywhere,

From the perspective of . . .

A STUDENT How can you use technology to improve your effectiveness as a student?

Getting the Most out of Instructors' PowerPoint Presentations

Traditional "chalk-and-talk" lectures are a thing of the past in many classes. Instead, increasing numbers of instructors are using presentation programs such as PowerPoint to project material in their classes.

This technology calls for fresh strategies for taking notes and absorbing the information. Here are some tips:

- **Listening is more important than seeing.** The information that your instructor projects on screen, while important, ultimately is less critical than what he or she is saying. Pay primary attention to the spoken word and secondary attention to the screen.

- **Don't copy everything that is on every slide.** Instructors can present far more information on their slides than they would if they were writing on a blackboard. Often there is so much information that it's impossible to copy it all down. Don't even try. Instead, concentrate on taking down the key points.

- **Remember that key points on slides are . . . key points.** The key points (typically indicated by bullets) often relate to central concepts. Use these points to help organize your studying for tests, and don't be surprised if test questions directly address the bulleted items on slides.

- **Check to see if the presentation slides are available online.** Some instructors make their class presentations available on the Web to their students, either before or after class time. If they do this before class, print the slides out and bring them to class. Then you can make notes on your copy, clarifying important points. If they are not available until after a class is over, you can still make good use of them when it comes time to study the material for tests.

- **Remember that presentation slides are not the same as good notes for a class.** If you miss a class, don't assume that getting a copy of the slides is sufficient. Studying the notes of a classmate who is a good note-taker will be far more beneficial than studying only the slides.

at anytime—these online workspaces can also play an important role in ensuring the accountability of those who participate in them. Introduced in this chapter's opening vignette, Office Live is an example of a Web-based site where a group of people can share and edit Microsoft Office documents. Accountability is addressed because the site allows you to see when others are editing or have edited specific documents. It will even send you an email notifying you of any activity that has taken place on the shared workspace. You can also specify permission levels where, for example, someone can look at a document, but not edit it. Google Docs and Zoho are other options if you are looking for a free collaborative workspace on the Web.

Over the course of your post-secondary education, you will undoubtedly collaborate with many, many people, some of whom you will want to stay in touch with after you graduate. And while Facebook has become the runaway winner in the social media space and might be the first place you would go to maintain these connections, a better choice might be a "professional" alternative known as Linked In. According to its website, Linked In is a networking site that allows you to "Stay informed about your contacts and industry," "Find the people & knowledge you need to achieve your goals," and "Control your professional identity online." Networking is absolutely key to your future, and Linked In is one way to keep your social life and your professional life separate.

The tools available for collaboration and networking will continue to evolve as more and more people take advantage of them. This is, in fact, true of virtually all computer applications; as such, it is probably worthwhile to allocate time during the year to catch up on the many developments that have occurred. You will probably find many applications developed that you didn't even know existed—some of which could make your life a lot easier!

»LO 6.2 Using Technology to Learn at a Distance

Do you find that your schedule changes so much from one day to the next that it's hard to fit in a course that meets at a regularly scheduled time? Interested in an unusual course topic that your own college doesn't offer? Want to take a class during the summer, but your college doesn't have a summer program?

The solution to your problem may be to enrol in a **distance learning** course. Distance learning is a form of education in which students participate via the Web or other kinds of technology. Although most distance learning courses are taught via the Web, some use teleconferencing, fax, and/or express mail.

Distance learning
A form of education in which students participate via the Web or other kinds of technology

The key feature of distance learning courses is the nature of interaction between instructor and students. Rather than meeting in a traditional classroom, where you, the instructor, and the other students are physically present, distance learning classes are most often virtual. Although some schools use "Webcasts" of lectures with virtual discussion rooms or employ lectures on videotape or on CD, most students in distance learning courses will never sit through a lecture or participate in a real-time conversation with students in the class. They may never know what their instructor or classmates look like or hear their voices.

If you take a distance learning course, you may read lecture notes posted on the Web, search and browse websites, write papers, post replies to discussion topics on a message board, and take online quizzes and exams. You will see your instructor's and classmates' responses through comments they post on the Web. You may be expected to read a textbook entirely on your own.

You may already be familiar with the kinds of technologies used in distance learning courses, because many traditional, face-to-face courses already contain elements of distance learning. In **blended (or hybrid) courses,** instruction is a combination of the traditional face-to-face classroom interaction and a significant amount of online learning. Students in blended courses generally spend more time working alone or in collaboration with others online than in traditional classes.

Blended (or hybrid) courses
Instruction is a combination of the traditional face-to-face classroom interaction and a significant amount of online learning

Distance learning is not for everyone. It is important to determine if this type of course suits your preferred style of course-taking. Complete **Try It! 1**, "Assess Your Course-taking Style," on page 146 to see whether you are suited to learn at a distance.

Distance learning classes have both advantages and disadvantages. On the plus side, distance learning courses offer the following:

> **You can take a Web-based distance learning course anywhere that you have access to the Web.** You can take a higher education class no matter where you live. You can be at home, at the office, or on a beach and still participate.

> **Distance learning classes are more flexible than traditional classes.** You can participate in a course any time of the day or night. You set your own schedule. This is particularly helpful for those with time-consuming family obligations such as child care.

> **Distance learning classes are self-paced.** You may be able to spread out your work over the course of a week, or you may do the work in a concentrated manner on one day.

> **You may have more contact with your instructor than you do with a traditional class.** Even though you may not have face-to-face contact, you may have

 Try It!

Assess Your Course-taking Style

Your preferred course-taking style—how you participate in classes, work with your classmates, interact with your teachers, and complete your assignments—may make you more or less suitable for distance learning. Read the following statements and indicate whether you agree or disagree with them to see if you have what it takes to be a distance learner.

	Agree	Disagree
1. I need the stimulation of other students to learn well.		
2. I need to see my teacher's face, expressions, and body language to interpret what is being said.		
3. I participate a lot in class discussions.		
4. I prefer to hear information presented orally rather than reading it in a book or article.		
5. I'm not very good at keeping up with reading assignments.		
6. I'm basically pretty easily distracted.		
7. I'm not very well organized.		
8. Keeping track of time and holding to schedules is NOT a strength of mine.		
9. I need a lot of "hand-holding" while I work on long assignments.		
10. I need a close social network to share my feelings, ideas, and complaints with.		
11. I'm not very good at writing.		
12. Basically, I'm not very patient.		

The more you disagree with these statements, the more your course-taking style is suited to distance learning. Interpret your style according to this informal scale:

Disagreed with 10–12 statements = Excellent candidate for distance learning

Disagreed with 7–9 statements = Good candidate for distance learning

Agreed with 7–9 statements = Probably better taking classes on campus

Agreed with 10–12 statements = Avoid distance learning

To Try It online, go to Connect for *P.O.W.E.R. Learning and Your Life.*

greater access to your instructor than in traditional classes, via email and the Web. You can leave messages for your instructor any time of the night or day; most instructors of distance learning classes respond in a timely way.

› **Shy students may find it easier to "speak up" in a distance learning class.** You can think through your responses to make sure you are communicating just what you wish to say. You don't have to worry about speaking in front of other people. For many people, distance learning is liberating.

› **You can become a better writer.** Because distance learning usually involves more writing than traditional courses, you receive more practice writing— and more feedback about it—than in traditional classes.

On the other hand, distance learning has disadvantages that you should keep in mind:

> **You are a prisoner of technology.** If you lose access to a computer and the Web, you won't be able to participate in the class until the problem is fixed.

> **You won't have direct, face-to-face contact with your instructor or other students.** Distance learning can be isolating, and students sometimes feel alone and lost in cyberspace.

> **You won't get immediate feedback.** In a distance learning class, it may be hours, or sometimes days, before you receive feedback on what you have posted to a message board, depending on how well the pace of other students matches your own.

> **Distance learning classes require significant discipline, personal responsibility, and time management skills.** You won't have a set time to attend class as you do in traditional courses. Instead, you must carve out the time yourself. Although instructors provide a schedule of when things are due, you have to work out the timing to get them done.

Consequently, many students believe that distance learning courses are more difficult than traditional classes. You must be focused and committed to keeping up with the course. You need to be prepared to work hard on your own for a substantial number of hours each week.

Despite these potential challenges to distance learning courses, they are becoming increasingly popular. More and more colleges are offering them. Many companies encourage employees with crowded schedules to take distance learning as a way of providing continuing education.

If you are considering taking a distance learning course, follow these steps, which are summarized in the P.O.W.E.R. Plan in the margin.

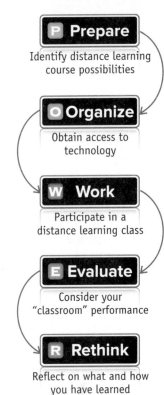

P Prepare
Identify distance learning course possibilities

O Organize
Obtain access to technology

W Work
Participate in a distance learning class

E Evaluate
Consider your "classroom" performance

R Rethink
Reflect on what and how you have learned

P.O.W.E.R. Plan

 **P Prepare**

Identify Distance Learning Course Possibilities

How do you find a distance learning course? In some cases, your own college or university may offer courses on the Web and list them in your course catalogue. In other cases, you'll have to find courses on your own.

The best place to look is on the Web itself. By searching the Web, you can find distance learning courses ranging from agronomy to zoology. Don't be deterred by the physical location of the institution that offers the course. It doesn't matter where the college or university is located, because for most distance learning classes, you'll never have to go to the campus itself.

But before you sign up for a potential course that you would like to count toward your degree, make sure that your own college or university will give you credit for it. Check with your adviser and registrar's office to be certain.

You should also find out what the requirements of a course are before you actually sign up for it. Check the syllabus carefully and see how it meshes with your schedule. If it is a summer course and you are going to be away from your computer for a week, you may not be able to make up the work you miss.

Finally, try to talk with someone who has taken the course before. Was the instructor responsive, providing feedback rapidly? If necessary, could you speak with the instructor by phone? Was the course load reasonable? (**Try It! 2**, "Get Some Distance on the Problem," on page 148 will help you to work through the process.)

Try It!

WORKING IN A GROUP

Get Some Distance on the Problem

Working by yourself initially, see if you can find distance learning courses that might be of interest to you. Start by checking your school's course catalogue to see what is offered there. If you're already comfortable online, you might also try the following:

- Athabasca University offers all of its courses online. Visit **www.athabascau.ca**
- Mount Saint Vincent University in Halifax offers many of its courses online. Visit **www.msvu.ca/en/home/ programsdepartments/distancelearning/default.aspx**

Try to find five courses you would be interested in and list them below. After you have completed your list, share it with others in a group.

1. How diverse were the courses you were able to find?

2. Were particular subject areas better represented than others?

3. Why do you think this might be?

To Try It online, go to Connect for P.O.W.E.R. Learning and Your Life.

O Organize Obtain Access to Technology

Although you don't need to be a computer expert, you will need some chat, email, and basic Web surfing skills to take a distance learning course. If you don't have sufficient technological expertise, beef up your computer skills by taking a computer course or workshop *before* you actually sign up for the distance learning course.

You'll also need access to a computer connected to the Internet. It doesn't have to be your own computer, but you will certainly need regular and convenient access. Make sure that the computer you plan to use has sufficient internal resources to connect quickly to the Internet; a very slow connection is frustrating.

It is a good idea to make all your arrangements for computer access prior to the start of a course. It can take several weeks to set up Internet service on a home computer if you don't have it already.

 ## Participate in a Distance Learning Class

Successfully participating in a distance learning course involves several skills that are distinct from those needed for traditional classes. To get the most out of a distance learning course, you'll need to do the following:

> **Manage your time carefully.** You won't have the luxury of a regular schedule of class lectures, so you'll have to manage your time carefully. No one is going to remind you that you need to sit down at a computer and work. You will need self-discipline to be successful in a distance learning course.

> **Check in frequently.** Instructors may make crucial changes in the course requirements. Make sure to check for any changes in due dates or class expectations.

> **Find a cyber-buddy.** At the start of the semester, try to make personal contact with at least one other student in the class. You can do this by chatting with, emailing, phoning, or actually meeting the student if he or she is geographically nearby. You can share study strategies, form a study group, and share notes. Connecting with another student can help you avoid feelings of isolation that may interfere with your success.

> **Make copies of everything.** Don't assume everything will go well in cyberspace. Make a printed copy of everything you submit, or alternatively have a backup stored on another computer or in the cloud.

> **Have a technology backup plan.** Computers crash, your connection to the Internet may go down, or an emailed assignment may be mysteriously delayed or sent back to you. Don't wait until the last minute to work on and submit assignments, and have a plan in place if your primary computer is unavailable.

 ## Consider Your "Classroom" Performance

As with any class, you'll be receiving feedback from your instructor. But unlike many courses, in which almost all the feedback comes from the instructor, much of the feedback in a distance learning course may come from your fellow students. Consider what you can learn from their comments, while keeping in mind that they are, like you, students themselves.

At the same time you'll be receiving feedback, you will likely be providing feedback to your classmates. Consider the nature of feedback you provide, and be sure that you use the basic principles of classroom civility. (See the sections about "Netiquette" on pages 150–53.)

 ## Reflect on What and How You Learned

Distance learning is not for everyone. If your preferred learning style involves extensive, face-to-face interaction with others, you may find that a distance learning experience is less than satisfying. On the other hand, if you are at ease with computers and enjoy working on your own, you may find distance learning highly effective.

As you reflect on your distance learning experience, go beyond the technology and think about the learning outcomes. Ask yourself whether you learned as much as you would have in a traditional class. You should also consider ways that the experience could have been more effective for you. And think about whether you were so absorbed by the technology that you lost sight of the real goal of the course: learning new material.

Most educational experts believe that distance learning will play an increasingly important role in higher education. Furthermore, because it offers an efficient way of educating people in far-flung locations, it is a natural means of promoting lifelong learning experiences. In short, the first distance learning class you take will likely not be your last.

LO 6.3 Using Netiquette as You Connect and Collaborate with Others

Netiquette

Guidelines for demonstrating civility and respect in an online environment

While we've come a long way from the use of email to connect with others over the Internet, many of us still have a lot to learn about connecting and collaborating with others through the use of technology. Let's start with good manners. The rules of basic etiquette, or **"netiquette"** as it is called on the Internet, may not seem that important to you in your role as a student; but they are essential to your success when communicating with others online, while enrolled in distance learning, and also once you enter the work world.

Show Civility on the Web

Although email and text communication are usually less formal than a letter, it is essential to maintain civility and demonstrate good manners when you communicate electronically. Here are some rules you should follow:

> **Consider having an email address for social purposes and another to communicate with potential employers.** You do *not* want to have an email address at the top of your resumé that says sexygirl@sympatico.ca.

> **Don't write anything in an email or text message that you would regret seeing on the front page of the newspaper.** Yes, email and texts are usually private; but the private message you write can easily be forwarded by the recipient to another person or even scores of other people. Worse yet, it's fairly easy to hit "reply all" when you mean simply to "reply": in this case, you might think that you are responding to an individual, when in fact the email will go to everyone who received the original message.

> **Consider carefully the tone you convey.** It is harder in email and texts to express the personality and subtlety that your voice, your handwriting, or even your stationery can add to other forms of communication. This means that attempts at humour and especially sarcasm can backfire. If you're using humour, consider adding an **emoticon (or smiley)** to clarify the intent of your message.

Emoticons (or smileys)

Symbols used in email messages that provide information on the emotion that the writer is trying to convey.

> **Never write anything in an email or text that you wouldn't say in person.** If you wouldn't say something in a face-to-face conversation, don't say it electronically.

> **Don't use all capital letters.** Using all caps MAKES IT LOOK AS IF YOU'RE SHOUTING.

- **Never send an email or text when you are angry.** No matter how annoyed you are about something someone has written in a message, don't respond in kind. Wait until you've cooled down. Take a deep breath, and wait for your anger to pass.

- **Be professional when writing to instructors and on-the-job supervisors.** In many cases, instructors get dozens, and sometimes hundreds, of emails and texts from their students every week. In many offices, supervisors receive just as many messages. To make sure your message gets maximum attention, use an informative subject line. If you're writing to an instructor, be sure to include the name of the relevant course in the subject line. Address the recipient of the email politely, and always end with a thank you and your full name.

Use Email Effectively

Texting may be the most popular way of keeping in touch with friends and family, but email is still the most widely used tool for communicating in a business setting. Even if you consider yourself a savvy email user, you can still do several things to improve the effectiveness of the messages you send. Keep the following suggestions in mind when writing formal email messages:

- **Use an informative subject line.** Don't say "IMPORTANT" or "meeting" or "question." Those subject lines don't help recipients sort out your message from the dozens of others that may be clogging their inboxes. Instead, something like "Reminder: supervisor applications due 5:00pm 10/11" is considerably more useful. In addition, *always* use a subject line: Some recipients routinely delete messages without a subject line, fearing they contain viruses. If your message is really short, you may want to use *only* the subject line to communicate it!

- **Make sure the recipient knows who you are.** If you are writing someone you know only casually, jog his or her memory with a bit of information about yourself. If you don't know them at all, identify yourself early in the message ("I am a college student who is interested in an internship . . . ").

- **Keep messages short and focused.** Email messages are most effective when they are short and direct. If at all possible, keep your message short enough that it fits on one screen without scrolling down to see the rest. The reason is simple: Recipients sometimes don't read beyond the beginning of a message. If you do need to include a good deal of material, number each point or set them off by bullets so recipients will know they should read down.

- **Try to include only one major topic per email.** It's often better to write separate emails rather than including a hodgepodge of unrelated points in an email. This is especially true if you want a response to each of the different points.

- **Put requests near the beginning of the email.** If you want the recipient to do something in response to your message, respectfully put the request at the very beginning of your message. Be explicit, while being polite.

- **Keep attachments to a minimum.** If possible, include all relevant information in the body of your email. Large attachments clog people's email accounts and may be slow to download. In addition, recipients who don't know you personally may fear your attachment contains a virus and will not open it.

- **Avoid abbreviations and emoticons in formal emails.** When writing informal emails to friends, abbreviations such as AFAIK ("as far as I know"), BTW ("by the way"), CYA ("see ya"), OIC ("oh, I see"), and WTG ("way to go") are fine. So are emoticons, which signal the emotion that you are trying to

Try It!

Using Email Netiquette

Read the email below, written by a student to his instructor, and respond to the questions that follow.

| ○ ○ ○ | Class | ⬭ |

| Send | Chat | Attach | Address | Fonts | Colors | Save As Draft |

To: Professor@ketchum.edu

Cc:

Subject: Class

Yo, Professor!!!

    I'm in your class, and I couldn't come yesterday because I had something I had to do. Did I miss anything important? Can u send me any assignments u gave out AS SOON AS POSSIBLE so I can work on it?

    I'm attaching the worksheet that was do. Hope it doesn't fill up your mailbox too much :-) !!

        BTW, when is ur next test?
          BJ

---

1. What rules of "netiquette" does the email violate?

2. If you were the instructor to whom the email message was sent, how do you think you would react to receiving it? What questions would you have about the message?

3. Based on the email, what opinion might you have of the student who wrote it?

4. Rewrite the email so that it is consistent with good netiquette.

To Try It online, go to Connect for *P.O.W.E.R. Learning and Your Life*.

---

convey. However, they should be avoided in formal emails. Recipients may not be familiar with them, and they may make your email seem overly casual.

> **Above all, be respectful and courteous.** It *always* pays to be polite.

To consider email netiquette more closely, do **Try It! 3**, "Using Email Netiquette."

In-Person Netiquette

There are standards for appropriate use of technology. An instructor does not want you to answer a cellphone call while he or she is speaking; neither does your boss.

Follow these guidelines to ensure you don't offend anyone with your use of technology:

> **Turn off your cellphone in formal settings.** If you're in a meeting or a class, keep your cellphone off (or set in "vibrate" mode). Cellphones ringing at random times are distracting and annoying.

> **Don't send text messages or make calls while someone else is speaking to you.** You should be paying attention to what co-workers, classmates, or instructors are saying, rather than what's going on in the rest of the world. This goes for times when you are with friends as well. Texting one friend while you are with another friend is disrespectful and demeaning to the person you are with, unless, of course, you are all making plans together.

> **If you use your laptop to take notes in class, stay on task.** No matter how tempting it is to check your email messages, IM with a friend, or surf the Web, avoid the temptation. When in class, use your laptop to take notes, and nothing else.

> **Never use your cellphone to text answers to problems in class.** Cheating is cheating, whether done using high-tech or low-tech methods. Don't do it.

» LO 6.4 Developing Information Competency

Learning *how* to learn in the twenty-first century is about understanding where and how to locate the information and expertise you need, how to evaluate the credibility of an information source, and how to credit sources that you use. In other words, learners today need to develop **information competency**. To view a short but fascinating video that summarizes how all of these skills come together under the umbrella term "connectivism", visit YouTube and find a video written by Wendy Drexler called "The Networked Student."

Students are often mystified by the notion that anyone would want to make the effort of going to a library database to find information, when the Web is at their fingertips. Why bother? **Table 6.1** on page 154 will help you understand why the library is the hands-down winner in this battle.

Information competency
The ability to determine what information is necessary, and then to locate, evaluate, credit, and effectively use that information

Locate Information in the Library

No matter how imposing or humble their physical appearance, whether they contain only a few hundred volumes or hundreds of thousands, libraries are a good place to focus your efforts as you seek out and gather information. Although every library is different, all share two key elements: the material they hold—whether paper-based or electronic—and tools available to help you locate the material you need.

table 6.1   The Web vs. Library Databases—A Comparison*

	The Web (Google, Wikipedia, About.com, etc.)	Library Databases (Business Source Complete, Lexis-Nexis, etc.)
Authority	Varies at best. Difficult to verify. Cannot limit to professional, scholarly literature. Information on the Web is seldom regulated, which means authority is often in doubt	Easy to determine. Most databases have scholarly/peer-reviewed filter or contain only scholarly literature. Authority and trustworthiness are virtually guaranteed.
Number of Hits	Thousands, sometimes millions of hits, much of the same information repackaged or duplicated. Duplicates are not filtered out.	Dozens to hundreds of hits (sometimes thousands but not hundreds of thousands)—a more manageable number, and duplicates can be filtered out.
Relevance	Lack of subject focus resulting in numerous irrelevant hits—or "junk"—to wade through. Much Web information is opinionated and biased. Unless you are using a subject-specific search engine, expect "everything including the kitchen sink" in the results. Quantity ≠ Quality	Focus by subject (business, art, Canadian history) and/or format (journals, books, book reviews), often meaning more relevant information and less time wasted dealing with junk. Information comes from legitimate, quality-controlled sources.
Search Features	Varies by search engine, but often limited. Can limit by document type (.doc, .pdf) or language, but limiting by publication date, format (article, book, etc.), scholarly/peer-reviewed, and more is unavailable.	Numerous advanced search features determined by database subject focus, e.g., limiting by publication type, date, language, document format, scholarly/peer-reviewed status. The list of features is as long as the number of databases available.
Access to Published Information	Web information often lives and dies on the Web and can come from anyone with Internet access. Information seldom coming from legitimate published sources: magazines, academic journals, books, etc. When it is, the user usually has to pay to access it.	Databases dealing only with published information; that is, information that originally appeared in print: magazine and journal articles, books, etc. More stable than the Web. Through the library's paid access, all of this information is available to you, the user, for free.

*Source: Yale University

What Can Be Found in a Library's Basic Collection?

Libraries obviously contain books—some of which are now available in the form of e-books—but they typically have a lot more than that, including some or all of the following:

> **Paper-based periodicals.** Periodicals include magazines published for general audiences, specialized journals for professionals in a field, and newspapers. While recent issues may be found in paper form, older issues are usually available through **online databases.**

Online database

An electronic, organized body of information on a related topic, or dealing with related media

> **Online databases.** A significant proportion of your college or university's library holdings are actually not in the library itself; instead, they can be found online. Most university or college libraries subscribe to a wide variety of online databases that are accessible to enrolled students anywhere, anytime, without the students ever having to set foot in the library.

An online database usually includes a searchable listing of periodical articles by title, author, subject, and key word. These databases contain advanced search options that allow you to perform these functions:

• search in particular kinds of publications; e.g., academic journals versus newspapers or trade magazines

- specify date ranges; e.g., only articles published after 2010
- choose to obtain a short summary (called an *abstract)* of the contents of available articles, or to see only articles that appear with "full text"; i.e. the entire contents of the article, including images.
- select articles by subject (Lexis-Nexis, for example, contains many articles relating to the legal profession). Some libraries will create separate folders or guides that contain databases used most often by particular faculties or programs.
- trust the credibility of what you locate. The source of the information is easy to identify and the references themselves can often be exported directly to a program such as RefWorks which stores references and automatically creates a bibliography.

➤ **Encyclopedias.** Some encyclopedias, such as the *Encyclopaedia Britannica* or *World Book Encyclopedia,* attempt to cover the entire range of knowledge; they will take up many volumes. Others are more specialized, covering only a particular field, such as the *Encyclopedia of Human Behavior* or the *Encyclopedia of Religion.* Encyclopedias provide a good general view of a topic, but they lack depth. Use them at the earliest stage of your hunt for information for an overview of key issues, and move from there to more specific and current sources.

➤ **Government documents.** Census records, laws, and tax codes are some of the millions of government documents that are stored in libraries.

➤ **Musical scores.** The music to *Rent, Alto Rhapsody* by Brahms, and The Beatles' greatest hits are among the musical scores you can find in libraries.

➤ **Reserve collections.** Reserve collections hold heavily used items that instructors assign for a class. Sometimes reserve material can be checked out for only an hour or two to be used in a designated room; in other cases, the material can be used overnight or for a few days.

The place to begin searching for information in a library is the library catalogue. The catalogue lists all materials that are held in the library and provides their locations. Most library catalogues are computerized, though a few still use cards filed in drawers or microform (microfiche or microfilm). You are usually able to access computerized catalogues from home or your room in residence as well as from computers housed in the library itself.

Library catalogues traditionally allow searches by title, author name, and subject; electronic catalogues also typically allow searching by key word. Individual catalogue entries generally include additional information about the material, such as the publisher, date of publication, and number of pages. If you are having difficulty finding the material you are looking for, or need help figuring out how to use an online database, ask your librarian for help. Today's librarians are generally very

Searching for materials in the library stacks can be frustrating if the materials you need are not on the shelves. Don't forget to ask your librarian whether what you are looking for can be found in an online database instead.

adept with computers and can show you how to search efficiently and effectively for the information you need. Some even host regular chat sessions to help students with their research.

Locate Information on the Web

The Web is vast—sometimes frustratingly so. In fact, no one knows how much material exists on the Web. Not only is more information added to the Web every day, but the information also resides on thousands of individual computers. Anyone with minimal Web savvy and access to a server (a computer with a permanent Internet connection) can set up a personal website.

The fact that anyone can put information on the Web is both the biggest asset and the greatest disadvantage of using the Web as an information source. Because minimal computer skill is the only expertise a person needs to set up a web page, there may be as much misinformation on the Web as there is information. Consequently, keep the usual consumer rule in mind: Buyer beware. Unless the website has been established and is maintained by a reliable organization, the information it contains may not be accurate.

Unlike the library, there is no central catalogue of the contents of the Web; instead, there are a number of different search engines. Furthermore, depending on the search engine you use and the type of search you do, you'll identify different information.

Search engines themselves are located on the Web, so you have to know their addresses. After you reach the home page of a search engine, you enter your search terms. The search engine then provides a list of websites that may contain information relevant to your search.

Some search engines, such as Yahoo!, specialize in organizing information by subject, making it easy to search for information on, say, different dog breeds, the Islamic religion, or car repair. Using Yahoo! for its subject directories is like searching for information using the subject entries in a library catalogue (see **Figure 6.4**).

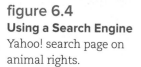

figure 6.4
Using a Search Engine
Yahoo! search page on animal rights.

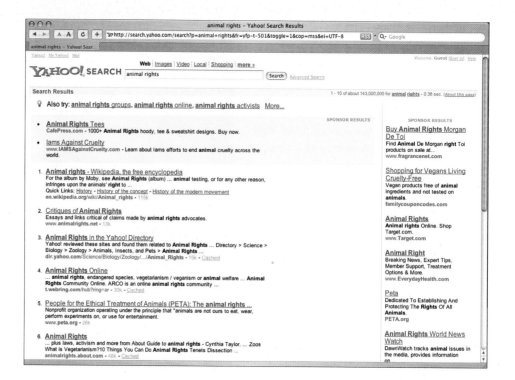

Work the Web: Information, Please!

4

Part A: Try to find the answer to the first question below on Yahoo! (**http://ca.yahoo.com**), Google (**www.google.ca**), and Dogpile (**www.dogpile.com**). Then use whichever search engine you prefer to find answers to the remaining questions.

1. What was Bill 101, and where and when was it passed?

2. Who is Jason Reitman?

3. Actor Kiefer Sutherland's grandfather was famous in his own right. What was his name, and what is he known for?

4. Is the birth rate in Canada higher or lower than that in Brazil?

5. What is an ECU?

Part B:

1. How easy was it for you to find the answers to the questions?
2. Which search engine(s) did you prefer, and why?

To Try It online, go to Connect for *P.O.W.E.R. Learning and Your Life.*

Other search engines, such as Google or AltaVista, index many more pages than Yahoo! but don't group them by subject. Due to the breadth of their coverage, they might be more useful when you are looking for obscure pieces of information or for numerous sources for different perspectives on a topic. Using Google or AltaVista is like performing a key word search in a library catalogue.

Finally, a third type of search engine is exemplified by Ask.com and AlltheWeb.com. Known as meta-search tools, these sites send your search commands to other search engines, compiling the results into a single, unified list.

There's no single search engine that works best. Most people develop their own preferences based on their experience. The best advice: Try out several of them and see which works best for you. To get started, work through **Try It! 4**, "Work the Web: Information, Please!"

Evaluate the Credibility of a Website

While you can be pretty much assured of the credibility of what you find in a library's online database, the same cannot be said for what you find on the Web. You must carefully assess the content of every website you choose to reference in

From the perspective of . . .

A LAW ENFORCEMENT PROFESSIONAL Technology is changing the approach to many long-established career fields. What technology changes could potentially impact your chosen profession?

your academic work. Yale University, working from a tool developed by the University of Maryland and the University of Dallas, developed five criteria for evaluating websites. (These criteria are applicable to any medium.) To determine whether a site's contents can be trusted, it is best that you carefully evaluate the site. Ask yourself the following questions to determine whether a site (or other media source) contains sound information:

1. **Audience:** To whom is the site directed—children, adults, students; a certain ethnicity, gender, or political affiliation? Is it understandable by the layman, or is it highly technical requiring specialized knowledge?

2. **Authority:** Is the author of the site listed? Can you determine his/her expertise? Is contact information given—phone number, address, email? With what organization is he/she associated?

3. **Bias:** Does the language, tone, or treatment of its subject give the site a particular slant or bias? Is the site objective? Is it designed to sway opinion? (Note that the organizational affiliation can often indicate bias.)

4. **Currency:** Is the site up to date? Do the links work? Are dates given for when the site was created and last updated? Is the topic current?

5. **Scope:** Is the site an in-depth study of the topic going several pages deep, or is it a superficial, single-page look at the subject? Are statistics and sources that are referenced properly cited? Does the site offer unique information not found anywhere else; e.g., not found in print sources?

Find the Information You Need Efficiently and Effectively

Whether you are searching an online library database or the Web, the process is very similar and is based on your ability to use key words appropriately to find what you are looking for. Use too few key words, and your search will turn up too many documents, many of which will not be directly relevant to your topic. On the other hand, use too many key words or use quotation marks around them, and you may find nothing at all.

"First, they do an online search."

Once you have narrowed your search appropriately, using the list of sites generated by the search is simple. With the mouse, click on the site address of the relevant document, and the site will appear on your computer screen. You can then take notes on the material, in the same way you'd take notes on material in a book.

Consider the search illustrated in **Figure 6.5** on page 159. It is the result of entering "How do I use the Web?" into the home page of Google. The search identified over 2.8 *billion* websites related to the topic. Many of the million sites Google returned, however, may well be of little use. It's easy in such a search to end up in a virtual dead end, in which the information you have found is only minimally related to the topic you're researching. If you do find yourself at a site that's of no use to you, simply hit the "back" button on your browser until you return to where you started.

How can you limit your search in the first place, so that you find sites that are more directly relevant to your research topic? The following tips can help you to get the most from a search[1]:

- **Phrase your search as a question** before you type anything into your computer.
- **Identify the important words in that question.** Then think of words that are related to the important words. Write all of these words down.
- **Type these keywords into a search engine** like Google.

You can do several things to limit the number of results returned, thus making your search more efficient and effective. Most search engines (including those on online databases) have advanced search features (see **Figure 6.6** on page 160) which allow you to use some or all of the following:

- **Quotation marks**, to denote a phrase—words that should appear together, in a specific order (e.g., "animal rights").
- **Plus signs**, used before terms that must appear in all results returned (+ "animal rights" + experimentation).
- **Minus signs**, before terms you do not want to appear in results (+ "animal rights" + experimentation − fur).
- **An asterisk**, to denote that the word can have more than one ending (auto * can be automobile or automotive) or to be a placeholder for an unknown term, e.g. Harper voted * on the bill).
- **Boolean operators**—words like AND, OR, AND NOT, and NEAR (e.g., "animal rights" AND experimentation NOT fur).

> "Don't let that little glowing screen become an adversary. If you plan correctly, the computer can become your most useful tool at college— next to your brain."
>
> Greg Gottesman, author

figure 6.5
Starting a Search
This search on Google on How do I use the Web? identified more than 2.8 billion sites.

figure 6.6
Using Advanced Search in Google

Advanced search functionality is also available on many search engines. Google allows you to specify language, date, region, and so forth.

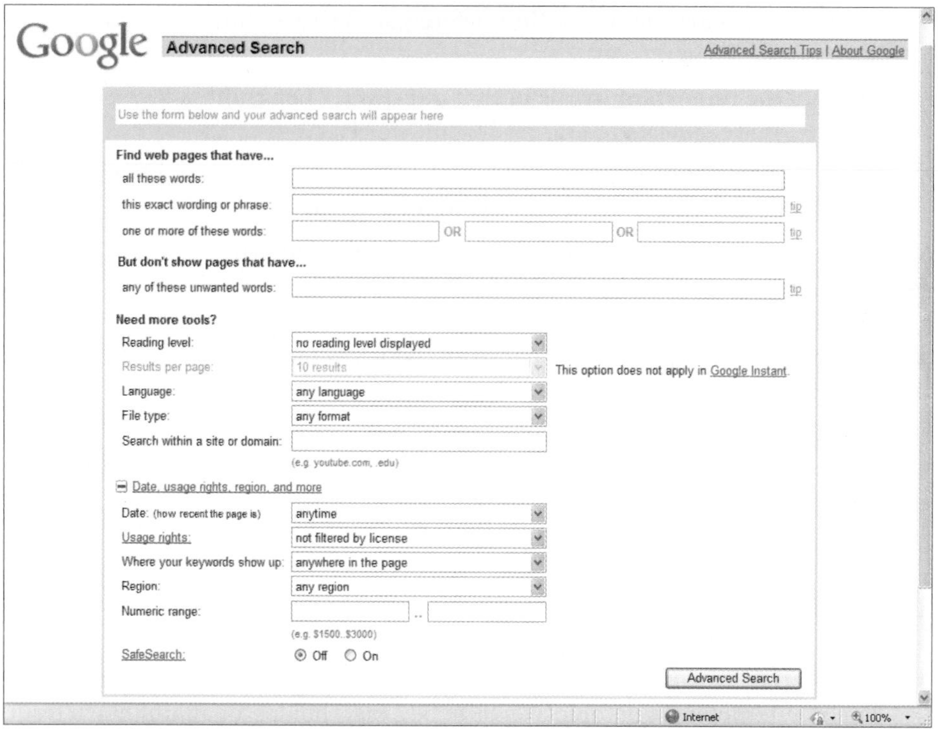

Another approach to consider, particularly when you are working on a specific report or assignment, is to have the information come to you, rather than you going to the Web to retrieve the information. Sound intriguing? Well, it's really not hard to do. For instance, let's say that you are doing a group report on the auto industry, and you've been assigned to work on Toyota. Through Google Alerts, you can specify that any article on the Web or in a blog that mentions Toyota be emailed to you on a regular basis—as it happens, daily, or weekly, for example. The email will contain a short description of each article and a link to it that can be accessed immediately. It's a simple way to stay on top of the latest information about a particular topic.

RSS feeds are one more way to stay on top of what interests you. RSS stands for Real Simple Syndication, and is best described as a way of subscribing to information sources over the Internet. News feeds, blog posts, and other sources are delivered directly to you as they are updated. In the case of Google, this functionality is provided through Google Reader, which can be added to your iGoogle home page. You can subscribe to all or specific parts of a newspaper (e.g., *The Globe and Mail*'s Money section), or to a blog that you like; and you can see the very latest feeds whenever you visit your iGoogle home page (see **Figure 6.7**), or, if you prefer, when you go directly to Google Reader and sign in to your Google account.

And last, but certainly not least, Twitter offers you an opportunity to follow some of the leading thinkers on a subject, and perhaps even get their (140-character) answer to one of your burning questions. At **www.listorious.com**, you can find and interview experts who are willing to exchange tweets with you, from K'naan Warsame, who wrote "Wavin' Flag," to Mitch Joel, President of Twist Image and interactive marketing expert.

Evaluate the Information You Find

In most instances, you'll find more information than you need. Once you have determined that the website you are looking at is reliable, you will then have to evaluate the information you have found there. Some of the important questions

figure 6.7
Organizing Information Feeds
You can add Google Reader to your personalized iGoogle home page to stay on top of your RSS subscriptions.

you must address before you can feel confident about what you've found include the following:

▶ **How authoritative is the information?** It is absolutely essential to consider the source of the material. Approach every piece of information with a critical eye, trying to determine what the author's biases might be. The best approach is to use multiple sources of information. If one source diverges radically from the others, you may reasonably question the reliability of that source.

Another approach is to consider the publisher of the material or sponsoring institution. For instance, sites established by well-known publishers and organizations are more likely to contain accurate information than those created by unknown (and often anonymous) authors. Remember, the Web is completely unregulated: *Anyone* can put *anything* on the Web. The best example of this is Wikipedia, a widely used online encyclopedia created by people just like you. *Anyone* can contribute to Wikipedia—from a prison inmate to your grandmother. You do *not* have to be an established authority on a subject to contribute. For this very reason, Wikipedia should NEVER be used as a source for academic work.

> *"On the Internet, nobody knows you're a dog."*

▶ **How current is the information?** No matter what the subject, information is changing at a rapid rate. Consider whether what you've found is the most recent and up-to-date material. Compare older sources to newer ones to identify changes in the ways in which the topic is considered.

▶ **How well are claims documented?** Are there references and citations to support the information? Are specific studies identified?

Using the Web at Work

The skills you learn for finding and sorting information on the Web will have many uses in your working life. Nearly every modern office is equipped with Internet-ready computers. Your employer will probably expect you to be able to find specific pieces of information—addresses, dates, phone numbers, and so forth—using the Web, regardless of your specific profession. Further, in many industries, Web skills are crucial. Real estate agents, for example, need to be able to use the Web to assess markets and post offerings; accountants need to be able to research costs; salespeople need to be able to get background on present and potential clients.

Even if you don't work in an office setting, you will find great use for the Web. Whatever professional problem you are facing—from an engine you can't fix to a patient who won't cooperate—there are others who have faced it before, and probably more than one of these people has shared his or her experiences online. Your evaluation skills will be crucial in applying what you find on the Web to your job, but it's likely that there is helpful, reliable information to be found online.

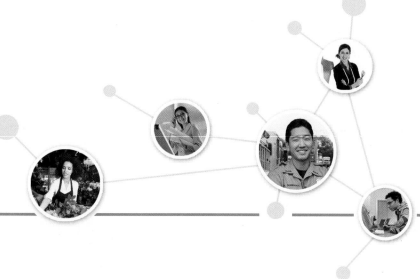

» LO 6.5 Plagiarism: What It Is and How to Avoid It

Not so long ago, aspiring scholars would find that one of their most difficult tasks came not *during* the research process but, rather, at the *end* of the process, when they found themselves having to pull together the many sources used in their work to ensure they avoided plagiarism. Depending on the nature of their research, they might use the Modern Language Association (MLA) or American Psychological Association (APA) standard of citing sources, making careful note of the type of source being cited, what needed to be italicized or underlined, and the order in which to place each part of the reference. They had to capture all their in-text citations, and then they would find themselves collecting all of their sources in a bibliography at the end of their research document. To call this a major effort is an understatement; and if a researcher was collaborating with other authors who had their own list of references, this last step was a nightmare. For many students, the temptation to "lift" the information, without bothering to cite the source, became increasingly hard to resist: it was simply too much effort to do it right.

But times have changed.

The recent introduction of user-friendly citation or reference management software has made it much, much easier to be an ethical researcher. Products like Zotero, Noodlebib, Endnote, and RefWorks help you collect, manage, cite, and share your research sources and to avoid plagiarism by making it easy to practise proper citation methods. Much of this citation software is either free online or available free of charge through your school's library.

So what exactly is plagiarism? As discussed in Chapter 5, in simplest terms, plagiarism is taking credit for someone else's words, thoughts, or ideas. The website **www.plagiarism.org** provides a detailed explanation:

> Anyone who has written or graded a paper knows that plagiarism is not always a black and white issue. The boundary between plagiarism and research is often unclear. Learning to recognize the various forms of plagiarism, especially the more ambiguous ones, is an important step towards effective prevention. Many people think of plagiarism as copying another's work, or borrowing someone else's original ideas. But terms like "copying" and "borrowing" can disguise the seriousness of the offense.

Types of Plagiarism

Sources Not Cited

1. **"The Ghost Writer"**

   The writer turns in another's work, word-for-word, as his or her own.

2. **"The Photocopy"**

   The writer copies significant portions of text straight from a single source, without alteration.

3. **"The Potluck Paper"**

   The writer tries to disguise plagiarism by copying from several different sources, tweaking the sentences to make them fit together while retaining most of the original phrasing.

4. **"The Poor Disguise"**

   Although the writer has retained the essential content of the source, he or she has altered the paper's appearance slightly by changing key words and phrases.

5. **"The Labor of Laziness"**

   The writer takes the time to paraphrase most of the paper from other sources and make it all fit together, instead of spending the same effort on original work.

6. **"The Self-Stealer"**

   The writer "borrows" generously from his or her previous work, violating policies concerning the expectation of originality adopted by most academic institutions.

Sources Cited (But Still Plagiarized)

1. **"The Forgotten Footnote"**

   The writer mentions an author's name for a source, but neglects to include specific information on the location of the material referenced. This often masks other forms of plagiarism by obscuring source locations.

2. **"The Misinformer"**

   The writer provides inaccurate information regarding the sources, making it impossible to find them.

3. **"The Too-Perfect Paraphrase"**

The writer properly cites a source, but neglects to put in quotation marks text that has been copied word-for-word, or close to it. Although attributing the basic ideas to the source, the writer is falsely claiming original presentation and interpretation of the information.

4. **"The Resourceful Citer"**

The writer properly cites all sources, paraphrasing and using quotations appropriately. The catch? The paper contains almost no original work! It is sometimes difficult to spot this form of plagiarism because it looks like any other well-researched document.

5. **"The Perfect Crime"**

Well, we all know it doesn't exist. In this case, the writer properly quotes and cites sources in some places, but goes on to paraphrase other arguments from those sources without citation. This way, the writer tries to pass off the paraphrased material as his or her own analysis of the cited material.

(Used with permission from **plagiarism.org** website)

Virtually every college and university today has a policy with respect to plagiarism. Increasingly, institutions are turning to plagiarism detection programs like the one found at **www.turnitin.com** to identify students who contravene their policy. The penalties for plagiarism can range from getting a 0 on an assignment or on the course to being expelled.

Resist the temptation to simply cut and paste the material into a new document, once you've found the information you're looking for. It's too easy to succumb to plagiarism if you simply copy material. Instead, take notes on the material using the critical thinking and note-taking skills you've been developing throughout this course. If you must quote a source directly, use proper citation methods: Put quotation marks around the quotation, insert an in-text citation, and ensure that you have the full reference in your bibliography or Works Cited list. It is not worth taking the chance—especially when there are now so many tools available that can make citing easy.

A Final Word

The Information Age presents us with great promise and opportunity. Through the use of media such as email and the Internet, we have at our fingertips the ability to communicate with others around the world. We can break the bounds of our physical location and reach across geographical barriers to learn about others. The computer keyboard can be said to contain keys to the entire earth and its peoples.

Time to Reflect: What Did I Learn?

1. In an average day, how much time do you spend using technology; e.g. cellphone, computer?

2. Thinking about both the positive and the negative, in what way does technology affect your relationships with others?

3. What technological device could you live without? What device could you *not* live without? Why?

Looking Back

How is technology used in education?

> Course websites (including instructor's presentation slides), textbook websites, e-books, podcasts, blogs, and vlogs are among the major educational uses of technology.

How can I use technology to become a better student?

> You can organize your desktop, your files, your time, and your tasks using technology.

> You can use technology as a support to your in-class learning or to take courses at a distance.

> You can use technology to connect and collaborate with your fellow students.

> You can use technology to network with your peers and to maintain contact with your industry and potential employers.

What is distance learning?

> Distance learning is a form of education that does not require the physical presence of a student in a classroom. It is usually conducted over the Web.

> Distance learning requires some adjustments for students, but it is becoming an increasingly popular choice, as people try to balance their lives and as their competency with technology increases.

What is netiquette, and why does it matter?

> Netiquette is the guidelines for interacting politely on email and other electronic devices.

> Your manners on electronic devices, like your manners in person, contribute to people's overall impression of you. If you behave inappropriately in cyberspace, you will present an image of yourself that could undermine your effectiveness in groups, interfere with your friendships, and even effect job and career prospects.

How can I develop information competency?

> There are two main sources of information today: libraries and the Web.

> Information in libraries is available in print form and in electronic form.

> Library resources can be found by using the library catalogue, which may be digital or print-based.

> Your library likely subscribes to several online databases, which are an excellent source of information.

> The Web is another major source of information, although it needs to be used with some caution.

What do I need to keep in mind as I use the Web to gather information?

> Using the Web effectively to find information can be tricky. It has many dead ends, false trails, and distractions; and the accuracy of the information presented as fact can be difficult to assess.

> You must carefully evaluate information on the Web by considering how reliable the source is, how current the information is, and how well the source's claims are documented.

How can I avoid plagiarism?

> The only way to avoid plagiarism is to cite your sources, both in the context of your report (called in-text citations) and in a bibliography at the end.

[KEY TERMS AND CONCEPTS]

Blended (or hybrid) courses (p. 145)　　Emoticons (p. 150)　　Online database (p. 154)

Blog and Vlog (p. 143)　　Information competency (p. 153)　　Plagiarism (p. 163)

Distance learning (p. 145)　　Netiquette (p. 150)　　Podcast (p. 143)

[RESOURCES]

ON CAMPUS

If you are having difficulty connecting to or surfing the Web, the first place to turn is your college's computer centre. Most campuses have consultants who can help you with the technical aspects of computer use.

If you need access to computers, most colleges have computer labs. Typically, these labs provide computers with Web access, as well as printers. It's important to check their hours, as they usually are not open 24/7. In addition, you may have to wait in line for a computer, so it is a good idea to bring some other work to the lab so you have something to do while waiting. You may also need to provide printer paper if you want to print something out.

The librarians at your college library are the people to whom you should turn first if you need help in locating information. In recent years, librarians—most of whom hold advanced degrees—have undergone a significant change in what they do. Most are equally at home using traditional print material and searching electronic information storehouses.

IN PRINT

A good introductory guide to computers is Michael Miller's *Absolute Beginner's Guide to Computer Basics,* 5th edition (Que, 2009).

For a guide to going beyond Google when searching the internet, take a look at Randolph Hock's *The Extreme Searcher's Internet Handbook: A Guide for the Serious Searcher,* 3rd edition (Information Today, Inc., 2010)

Peterson's Guide to Online Learning (Peterson's, 2010) offers clear instruction on becoming an effective online learner.

For more cloud computing sites, check out Peter Buckley's *The Rough Guide to Cloud Computing: 100 websites that will change your life,* 1st edition (Penguin Books, 2010).

ON THE WEB

The following websites provide the opportunity to extend your learning about the material in this chapter.

▸　Imperial College (London)'s Department of Computing offers FOLDOC (Free Online Dictionary of Computing) at **http://foldoc.org**. If you're having a hard time trying to figure out some computer jargon, this site—a dictionary of computer terminology— might help. Topics are listed alphabetically and a search engine helps locate specific information.

▸　The WWW Virtual Library (**http://vlib.org/**) is one of the oldest catalogues of the Web, providing useful links to thousands of subjects.

▸　Questia (**www.questia.com**) is the world's largest online library of books, with over 72 000 full-text books, two million articles, and an entire reference set complete with a dictionary, encyclopedia, and thesaurus.

▸　For a shot of "YouTube for the *brain"* spend a few minutes on **www.ted.com**. The site, which has as its tag line "ideas worth spreading," contains videos of some of the most compelling people in the world speaking on every topic imaginable. A good place to start is with *Wired* magazine's Chris Anderson on the concept of technology's "long tail," or, on a lighter note, Canadian Malcolm Gladwell's talk on why there are so many versions of spaghetti sauce available.

▸ If you are having difficulty with a concept discussed in class and need more explanation, or you simply want to dig deeper into a subject that interests you, you'll want to visit **www.academicearth.org**, which contains video lectures on topics ranging from viral marketing to brain–computer interfaces.

TAKING IT TO THE NET

1 Using the search engine of your choice, find the address for the website of the libraries of the University of California at Berkeley. Once there, find "Finding Information on the Internet: A Tutorial." Try the tutorial, which will help you understand many of the basic skills needed to use the Internet effectively. (Would taking the tutorial *first* have helped you to find it?)

2 To see for yourself how the Web can be a great resource for locating information on important issues, try to find the answer to this question: "What are the effects of media violence on children?" Go to a search engine (try **www.google.ca**) and type in the phrase, "media violence and children." (Be sure to include the quotation marks.) Look over the first page of documents that the search engine turns up. Are they, in fact, about the effects of media violence on children? Do they answer the question you are asking? What is the answer to the question?

The Case of . . .

The Empty Page

It had already been a long day for Joelle.

She'd worked two hours of overtime at her job supervising a call centre. She'd driven home and immediately sat down at her computer to start work on a paper for her marketing class the next day. It was already 11:00 P.M. by the time she finished her research on the Web. Then she began writing, opening a new file in her word processing program.

Joelle worked hard, drinking coffee to help her concentrate on the paper—and to keep her eyes open. When she was about three-quarters of the way done, her computer screen suddenly froze. Joelle pushed every button she could think of, but finally had to switch her computer off and then switch it back on. She opened the file for her paper . . . and saw an empty page.

To her horror, Joelle realized that her paper had been lost. She looked at the clock—it was almost 3:00 A.M. Did she really need to start her paper all over again?

1. How well did Joelle use her time to work on her paper? What advice would you give her about the preparation stage of working on a paper?

2. Clearly, Joelle should have saved her work frequently while she was working. What else should she have done while working on her paper to help her recover from such a catastrophe?

3. Do you think Joelle's instructor would be sensitive to her problem? Do you think he or she would be willing to give her an extension? What could Joelle do to make her case that she had nearly finished the paper?

4. What should Joelle do next to begin reconstructing her paper and recovering as much of her work as possible?

7 Writing and Presenting

Learning Outcomes

By the time you finish this chapter, you will be able to

» **LO7.1**   Describe the type of writing done at the post-secondary level.

» **LO7.2**   Explain the process involved in preparing and writing a report or case analysis.

» **LO7.3**   Discuss the process involved in creating and delivering effective presentations.

Maria was terrified. It was only the third week of classes and it was gradually sinking in that she was not going to be able to avoid making presentations in class; in fact, it was looking like presentations were going to account for an important part of her mark in several courses. She had always been a good student, turning in well-thought-out written reports; but when it came to having to explain her findings to others in her class—well, let's just say it was not her strong suit. But now, with her college marks depending on it, she knew she had no choice. Maria was going to have to find some help.

Maria confided her fears to a classmate, who, as it turned out, was a member of Toastmasters, an organization which has helped hundreds of thousands of people get over their fear of speaking in public. After some gentle prodding, Maria agreed to accompany her friend to the next Toastmasters meeting, where she observed that the participants learn by doing, giving impromptu speeches on specific topics and delivering prepared speeches to an audience that is able to provide useful feedback in a supportive environment.

In just over a year, Maria worked her way through Toastmasters' Competent Communication manual, a series of self-paced speaking assignments that teach the foundations of public speaking. Feeling far more confident about her ability to speak in public, Maria now looked forward to the opportunity to practise her newfound skills through the remainder of her college career and beyond.

Looking Ahead

As Maria discovered, communication is the foundation of education. Being able to speak and write clearly and communicate your ideas with conviction orally and in writing are skills that will go a long way towards getting you through college or university, irrespective of your major. But the need for good communication skills doesn't end when you graduate. Whether it's writing a resumé, interviewing for a job, pitching an idea to your co-workers, or coming up with a unique way to propose to your girlfriend, learning how to get your ideas across to others is an investment that offers a lifetime payout.

In the first half of this chapter, you'll learn the "how to" of good writing: how to generate ideas and come up with a main thesis, how to structure your report in a logical fashion, how to make a compelling argument for your point of view, how to cite supporting evidence, and how to produce a conclusion that ties the whole report together. In the second half of the chapter, the focus will be on transforming your thoughts and ideas into vivid and memorable presentations. You'll get tips for creating effective presentations, suggestions on how to reduce the anxiety associated with public speaking, and ways to make your presentations come alive with visuals.

» LO 7.1 Writing at the Post-secondary Level

With the arrival of texting and email, where abbreviations like LOL, BTW, and TTFN are ubiquitous, and with the increasing reliance on simple PowerPoint slides to communicate increasingly complex ideas, writing in the traditional sense is starting to look downright quaint. You'll soon find out, however, that it has *not* gone out of style in post-secondary educational institutions, where it remains the main method of communicating thoughts and ideas.

Thesis
A closely related set of ideas that suggest an angle or way of approaching a topic

Arguments
Facts, research findings, or other evidence used to support a thesis

Some General Guidelines

There are many different types of writing that you may be called upon to use in college or university, and these will depend on your area of study. English majors may be asked to analyze a poem, art majors might be asked to describe a famous painting, chemistry students may be asked to write a lab report, and business students may be asked to complete a case analysis to recommend a specific course of action.

While there are different types of writing, there are still some general guidelines to keep in mind when you are asked to write at the college or university level. First, you need to write with a specific **thesis** or "angle" in mind. Writing an essay on "Aboriginals in Canada" is far too broad a topic for the post-secondary level; instead, try writing a critique of "the policy of 'aggressive assimilation' of Aboriginal children in residential schools in Canada in the 19th century." In the next section, we introduce mind mapping, an excellent way to uncover an appropriate thesis or angle for your essays. Second, you will need to produce **arguments**; i.e., facts or evidence that support your thesis. This means you need to keep track of your research sources, as academic writing requires that you cite sources and produce a

The longer you wait to start writing an essay or report, the harder it will be to produce a good result.

Prepare

Figure out what to write about; do the necessary research

O **Organize**

Identify major themes, find an angle, and outline the flow

W **Work**

Write the initial draft

E **Evaluate**

Rest, reread, revise; rewrite, if necessary

R **Rethink**

Reflect on instructor feedback

P.O.W.E.R. Plan

Mind mapping

A visual technique which involves writing a central idea in the middle of a sheet of paper, then drawing "branches"; i.e., subtopics or themes which stem from the central idea. These subtopics can then be used to form a new thesis

figure 7.1

Here is an example of a mind map—created on the subject of mind maps!

comprehensive bibliography of these sources. And finally, outlining a logical progression of your ideas and the evidence supporting them, and doing so *before* you actually begin to write, is essential to high-quality writing.

» LO 7.2 The Process of Writing

Writing is *not* a one-step process. In fact, the writing process follows the five steps in the P.O.W.E.R. Learning framework. Procrastinators, take note: This means that sitting down and attempting to write a complete essay in one sitting is unlikely to produce a good outcome. To write a good report, you need to take the time to proceed through each of the steps in sequence. Before you begin, consider drawing up a "workback" schedule, a technique you learned back in Chapter 2: work your way back from the report due date, give specific deadlines for each step in the writing process, and record these deadlines on your work calendar. This approach will ensure that you don't find yourself trying to "wing it" the day before the report is due.

P **Prepare**   Explore Your Topic

How do you prepare to start writing? The first thing you need to do is to figure out what to write about. Instructors at the post-secondary level will often assign a broad topic, and it will be up to you to determine what angle or perspective you want to bring to that topic. To get started, you'll want to use some of the research techniques you learned about in Chapter 6 to find articles about the topic that interests you most. Then, do some reading to get a sense of what others have already written on the issue. This part of the process can take almost as much time as the writing itself, so be sure to include it in your workback schedule! Next, you'll want to engage in a free-form exercise such as brainstorming or **mind mapping** to identify existing approaches and come up with new angles and unique approaches to the topic.

Mind mapping allows you to explore your associations with a main idea or theme and to uncover subtopics or supporting ideas that you can use in your report (see **Figure 7.1**). Mind mapping is a technique that can also be used to identify

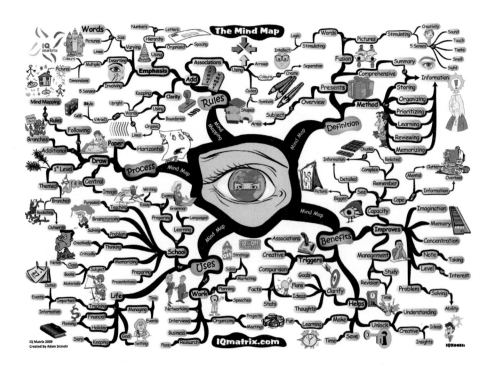

Create a Mind Map

One way to generate ideas and angles for a report is to create a mind map.

Try making your own mind map for a topic assigned by one of your instructors. Follow the example in Figure 7.1 on page 172.

To Try It online, go to Connect for *P.O.W.E.R. Learning and Your Life.*

tasks in a project, components of a new website, and so forth. While a mind map is usually created by linking a central idea on a piece of paper to other ideas, you can also create a mind map by using "sticky notes" on a table or wall. The sticky note approach works well if you are generating ideas in a group. This approach can save you organizational time as it allows you to go back and put your ideas into a logical order simply, thereby creating a framework for your report writing or presentation planning. (See **Try It! 1**, "Create a Mind Map.")

○ Organize Create an Outline

The second step in the writing process is getting organized to write. At this point, you've completed your mind mapping exercise and should have identified a number of different approaches or themes from which to select. Now is the time to narrow down your focus and select a major thesis or angle for your essay or report. Your selection can be based on what interests you most, which angle is most contentious, or even which thesis has the most supporting evidence available. It's entirely up to you, although you may wish to check with your instructor to ensure you are on the right track before proceeding.

Once you are clear on your topic, it's time to outline it. You may be thinking that this is a step you can afford to skip, but it is actually one of the most important steps in the writing process. An **outline** is a framework that sets out a logical progression of your ideas; i.e., what will come first, what will come next, and so forth. A good outline is a planning tool that can guide you painlessly through the rest of the writing process. Once you have outlined your topic into a set of subtopics, you may want to check back again with your instructor to see if you are on still the right track. The instructor may also be able to guide you towards specific texts or resources that could help you with your research. Once your outline is finalized, you'll want to categorize your research materials in the order in which you'll draw on them in your paper, perhaps putting them in separate folders to make them easy to refer to as you write.

Outline
A framework that sets out a logical progression or flow of ideas, prepared before the writing process begins

W Work Write the Initial Draft

The first draft of any report is usually the hardest draft to write. Being human, we have a tendency to want to "get it right the first time"; but, unfortunately, writing simply doesn't work that way. Using your outline as your guide, the next step in the writing process is about doing the work: getting the words into your computer.

Try It!

2

Overcoming Writer's Block

For some of you, just getting that first draft completed may seem impossible. You may find yourself experiencing "writer's block," the inability to clear your mind and start writing. In *The Artist's Way,* author Julia Cameron talks about the need for writers to write "Morning Pages" immediately upon awakening. According to her website, "morning pages are three pages of longhand, stream of consciousness writing, done first thing in the morning." Cameron's rationale is that this exercise allows you to get all of your inconsequential thoughts out of the way, so you can focus on what you really need to write.

If you are having difficulty getting started on a report, you may wish to give Morning Pages a try. Take out a notebook and pen and leave them by the side of your bed. Every morning for a week, immediately upon waking, try writing whatever comes to your mind until you've filled up three pages. Then, see if later in the day you find it easier to focus on writing the report that is due.

For more tips, aspiring writers will want to visit Julia Cameron's website at **JuliaCameronLive.com**.

To Try It online, go to Connect for *P.O.W.E.R. Learning and Your Life.*

You can create a writing framework or outline by using sticky notes and moving them around until you get a logical flow.

This is not the time to be concerned about the precise wording, whether a sentence is out of place, or if a diagram would be better than a paragraph to illustrate your point. And this is definitely not the time to censor your thoughts or do grammar or spelling checks. There will be plenty of time for that later. It is simply the time to put your initial thoughts into words, in a logical order.

Because you need to leave yourself time to reflect on what you have written before you make revisions, you'll want to write your first draft as soon as you can. Once you've completed the first draft—and it may require several sessions to do so—you should set it aside for at least a day to gain the perspective you'll need to see what requires revision.

Even with the systematic preparation we have outlined here, you may still occasionally experience writer's block. If that ever happens to you, **Try It! 2**, "Overcoming Writer's Block," may help you to overcome this challenge.

▣ Evaluate

Rest, Reread, Revise—then Rest, Reread, and Revise Again

Your final report will probably not look anything like your first draft, and that first draft will undoubtedly end up in your recycle bin—not because you can't write, but because that's how writing works. It is a process of ongoing evaluation, reflection, and revision. That's also why you need to give yourself time to work through the process. After you've written the first draft in its entirety, leave it for a day or two, then come back to it and reread what you've written. Then ask yourself these questions:

- ▶ Have I covered all of the main points?
- ▶ Are my points well supported by my research findings?
- ▶ Does each topic flow easily into the next?
- ▶ Is there any new evidence I've become aware of that I need to include?

Now, go back and fill in the gaps. Once you've done so, leave it for another day; then come back and reread it once again. (See **Figure 7.2** for a "before and after" writing sample.) Once you are satisfied with the content, create headings for each section, then run a spell check and grammar check. When running these checks, don't simply accept all recommended changes, though, or you may be in for some nasty surprises. After you have printed out your report, give it to a friend, colleague, or family member for their feedback. Once you've thoughtfully incorporated this feedback, give it a last once-over before handing it in.

Do not try to draft, review, and revise in the same session. The sections that need to be rewritten will be more obvious to you once you've had a chance to sleep on it.

 **R Rethink**

Reflect on Instructor Feedback

Once you've received your graded report, take the time to read the instructor's comments to learn how to improve your next report.

As with anything you submit for evaluation, you'll be receiving a grade and some feedback from your instructor. While it may be tempting to focus only on the grade, it is also important to take the time to go through your report and read your instructor's comments carefully. If you aren't sure what some of the comments mean, ask to meet with your instructor after class to go over them. Take the comments to heart and reflect on them the next time you are asked to write something. It is only through continuously incorporating instructor feedback that you can hope to improve your writing over time.

Avoid Plagiarism

We talked briefly about avoiding plagiarism in Chapter 6, where you were encouraged to use citation management software to ensure that all of your sources are properly referenced. However, where you may not have access to this software, you still have the option of citing the old-fashioned way. Depending on your area of study and/or instructor's preference, you may be asked to cite using the APA (American Psychological Association) guideline, the MLA (Modern Language Association) guideline, or the Chicago Style Guide. The latter two were updated in 2010. For an excellent resource on all three styles, with sample in-text citations and Works Cited/References, you'll want to visit 'Research and Citation Sources' on the website known as Online Writer's Lab (or OWL) at Purdue University, which can be found at **http://owl.english.purdue.edu/owl/**.

figure 7.2
"Before and After" Writing Sample

Editing should result in a more *precise*, but not necessarily more *concise*, version of the original. This example was prepared by Barbara McNichol Editorial © Barbara McNichol Editorial. All rights reserved.

BEFORE EDITING . . .

"How to Improve Your Proofreading Skills"

The written word is often the first impression a business makes on prospective clients or customers. You can lose credibility by having just one typo in the volumes of words produced by your company.

Everything written in an office should be read for errors, and this includes email. There is a guide to proofreading and it includes checking for errors methodically. You should never proof your own copy because you are too familiar with it. If this is not feasible, leave the copy alone for a while, a day preferably, before trying to find errors. A good way to trick your mind when reading for spelling errors is to read the copy backwards.

The first time you read through your copy, you should check for deviations in text, i.e., doubly typed words (the the), typographical errors and incorrect word breaks. One of the most common erroneous word-breaks is the word "therapist," if this word is hyphenated at just the right spot it could become the "the-rapist."

Secondly read for fact or format inconsistency, word usage, sentence structure, subject/verb agreement, repetition of thought or phrases and incorrect math. Next check for language mechanics, such as capitalization, punctuation, spelling and grammar. The fourth read through includes checking overall format—type size, margins, alignment, spacing, positioning (headlines, subheads, copy, footnotes, indentations), pagination, and general appearance.

Always leave time for proofing. You will never be sorry for the costly mistakes you avoid.

AFTER EDITING . . .

"How to Avoid Costly Mistakes with Better Proofreading"

The first impression a business often makes on prospective clients or customers comes from the written word. Your company can lose credibility by having just one typo in the volumes of words it sends out.

To minimize mistakes, therefore, proofread everything that's written in your office—and this includes email. Use a guide to help you methodically check for errors. Avoid proofing your own copy because you have likely become too familiar with it. If it isn't feasible to delegate this task, leave the copy alone for a while—a day preferably—before searching for errors. Read it backwards, too. It's a good way to trick your mind into seeing common mistakes.

I recommend rereading your copy four times. The first time, check for deviations in text; e.g., words typed twice in a row (the the), typographical errors, and incorrect word breaks. A common erroneous word break is "therapist." If this word is hyphenated in the wrong place, it becomes the "the-rapist." Not a good impression!

The second time, read for fact or format inconsistency, poor word usage, weak sentence structure, subject/verb disagreements, repetition of thoughts or phrases, and incorrect math.

On the third read, check for language mechanics such as capitalization, punctuation, spelling, and grammar.

The fourth read includes checking overall format—type size, margins, alignment, spacing, positioning (headlines, subheads, copy, footnotes, indentations), pagination, and general appearance. Doing a good job of this makes your designer's life much easier!

If you always set aside time to proofread your piece, you'll avoid costly mistakes and leave your prospects with a positive first impression.

How to Approach Business Report Writing and Case Analysis

You probably learned a lot about essay writing before you arrived at college or university. However, writing a business report or case analysis requires an approach that your teachers may not have taught in high school.

In the case of a business report, your instructor may provide you with a preferred format; but if he or she does not, then a general outline looks something like this:

> ▸ **Title page.** A page listing the title of the assignment, your name and student number, your professor's name, the course code, and the date the assignment is due.

- **Executive summary.** A one- or two-page summary of the highlights and recommendations contained in your report.

- **Table of contents.** A list of topics and subtopics, with page numbers. Consider using Word's Table of Contents function to make the job of putting this together easy.

- **Introduction.** A few paragraphs that outline the scope of the report and introduce the main topics that will be addressed in the remainder of the report.

- **Body of the report.** The major topics and subtopics the report addresses.

- **Conclusions and/or recommendations.** What should be done, given the situation you've outlined, and why.

- **Works cited or bibliography.** A list, in alphabetical order by author, of all sources used. Ask your instructor which format he or she prefers; e.g., MLA, APA, or Chicago.

- **Appendices.** The place to put graphs, diagrams, and supporting articles.

If you are analyzing a business or marketing case, the preferred approach once again may vary from instructor to instructor; but a general outline of what needs to be done will look something like this:

- **Identify the main issue** raised in the case. This can be a problem or an opportunity. Ensure that you distinguish symptoms of a problem—e.g., decreasing sales—from the problem itself—e.g., our competitor's recently introduced product is receiving rave reviews, and our version is outdated.

- **Analyze the *external* environment.** Sometimes called the "uncontrollables," the external environment is the social, economic, ecological, technological, and political/regulatory trends that are affecting the industry in which the company is operating. This step can also include an examination of the competition and the structure of the industry. From this analysis comes the identification of opportunities and threats.

- **Analyze the *internal* environment.** Usually referred to as the "controllables," the internal environment refers to what is happening inside the organization; e.g., marketing, finance, human resources, etc. From this analysis comes the identification of the company's strengths and weaknesses.

- **Create the integrated SWOT analysis.** SWOT is an acronym for strength/weakness/opportunity/threat. Your SWOT analysis integrates your findings about the opportunities and threats in the environment with the company's specific strengths and weaknesses; e.g., there may be an opportunity to introduce a new product, and one of the company's strengths is research and development.

- **Generate alternative courses of action.** Here, you are putting forth potential solutions to the problem or opportunity identified. These alternatives should be viable given the abilities and constraints of the company and its current situation.

- **Evaluate the courses of action** against criteria that you have drawn up; e.g., the alternative that is selected must have minimal impact on the environment.

- **Recommend a course of action.** Provide your rationale, based on the decision criteria identified.

- **Develop an implementation plan.** This should include a detailed outline of the tasks to be undertaken by each area of the company, major milestones, risks, and costs involved.

From the perspective of . . .

A STUDENT How can you use technology to improve your effectiveness as a writer?

- **Create the necessary exhibits.** A formal project plan, a budget, and a proforma income statement are a few of the exhibits often used to support a case analysis.
- **Put together a Works Cited page or Bibliography.** Prepare a list, in alphabetical order by author, of all research sources used. Ask your instructor if he or she prefers MLA, APA, or Chicago format.

» LO 7.3 Creating and Delivering Effective Presentations

In our wired and wireless society, communication has never been easier. The informality and immediacy of text messages, tweets, and Facebook updates mean that most of us are doing more communicating in more ways than ever before. But *more* communication does not necessarily translate into *better* communication. A fundamental skill that all students need to master is how to present complex ideas compellingly in front of an audience. This entails learning not only how to deliver a proper formal presentation, but also how to quell anxiety about speaking in public, how to prepare for the presentation, and how to develop visuals that can make that presentation come alive for your audience.

Overcome Presentation Anxiety

Afraid to speak in public? You're in good company. Public speaking is the number one fear of most North Americans. Comedian Jerry Seinfeld said it best: "According to most studies, people's number one fear is public speaking. Number two is death. Death is number two. Does that sound right? This means to the average person, if you go to a funeral, you're better off in the casket than doing the eulogy."

It is absolutely normal to feel **presentation anxiety**; and while it will probably decrease each and every time you present, it will likely never go away completely—and that is a good thing. Even the most practised presenters usually feel a bit anxious before a presentation, mainly because they cannot control the audience's reaction. To assess your level of anxiety about speaking in public compared to the average, fill out the survey in **Try It! 3**, "Measuring Your Anxiety about Speaking in Public." Note that the average score on this survey is 114.6, which is categorized as "moderate anxiety," further proof that anxiety about speaking in public is the rule rather than the exception!

When making a presentation, remember that *you* are the expert.

Presentation anxiety
Fear related to speaking in public

Measuring Your Anxiety about Speaking in Public

Directions: Below are 34 statements that people sometimes make about themselves. Please indicate whether or not you believe each statement applies to you, using these rankings:

Strongly Disagree = 1; **Disagree = 2;** **Neutral = 3;** **Agree = 4;** **Strongly Agree = 5.**

_____ 1. While preparing for giving a speech, I feel tense and nervous.

_____ 2. I feel tense when I see the words "speech" and "public speech" on a course outline when studying.

_____ 3. My thoughts become confused and jumbled when I am giving a speech.

_____ 4. Right after giving a speech, I feel that I have had a pleasant experience.

_____ 5. I get anxious when I think about a speech coming up.

_____ 6. I have no fear of giving a speech.

_____ 7. Although I am nervous just before starting a speech, I soon settle down after starting and feel calm and comfortable.

_____ 8. I look forward to giving a speech.

_____ 9. When the instructor announces a speaking assignment in class, I can feel myself getting tense.

_____ 10. My hands tremble when I am giving a speech.

_____ 11. I feel relaxed while giving a speech.

_____ 12. I enjoy preparing for a speech.

_____ 13. I am in constant fear of forgetting what I prepared to say.

_____ 14. I get anxious if someone asks me something about my topic that I don't know.

_____ 15. I face the prospect of giving a speech with confidence.

_____ 16. I feel that I am in complete possession of myself while giving a speech.

_____ 17. My mind is clear when giving a speech.

_____ 18. I do not dread giving a speech.

_____ 19. I perspire just before starting a speech.

_____ 20. My heart beats very fast just as I start a speech.

_____ 21. I experience considerable anxiety while sitting in the room just before my speech starts.

_____ 22. Certain parts of my body feel very tense and rigid while giving a speech.

_____ 23. Realizing that only a little time remains in a speech makes me very tense and anxious.

_____ 24. While giving a speech, I know I can control my feelings of tension and stress.

_____ 25. I breathe faster just before starting a speech.

_____ 26. I feel comfortable and relaxed in the hour or so just before giving a speech.

_____ 27. I do poorly on speeches because I am anxious.

_____ 28. I feel anxious when the teacher announces the date of a speaking assignment.

_____ 29. When I make a mistake while giving a speech, I find it hard to concentrate on the parts that follow.

_____ 30. During an important speech, I experience a feeling of helplessness building up inside me.

_____ 31. I have trouble falling asleep the night before a speech.

_____ 32. My heart beats very fast while I present a speech.

_____ 33. I feel anxious while waiting to give my speech.

_____ 34. While giving a speech, I get so nervous I forget facts I really know.

Scoring: To determine your score on the Personal Report of Public Speaking Anxiety (PRPSA), complete the following steps:

Step 1. Add the scores for items 1, 2, 3, 5, 9, 10, 13, 14, 19, 20, 21, 22, 23, 25, 27, 28, 29, 30, 31, 32, 33, and 34

Step 2. Add the scores for items 4, 6, 7, 8, 11, 12, 15, 16, 17, 18, 24, and 26

Step 3. Complete the following formula:

PRPSA = 72 − Total from Step 2 + Total from Step 1

(Your score should be between 34 and 170. If your score is below 34 or above 170, you have made a mistake in computing the score.)

Low Anxiety = < 98 **Moderate Anxiety = 98–131** **High Anxiety = > 131**

To Try It online, go to Connect for *P.O.W.E.R. Learning and Your Life.*

Source: McCroskey, J.C. (1970). Measures of communication-bound anxiety. *Speech Monographs*, 37, 269–277. Available at **www.jamescmccroskey.com/measures/prpsa.htm.**

Plan the Presentation

While most students focus on the actual delivery of the presentation, there are a number of things to think about well before that day comes. First, know who will be in your audience. It is the composition of your audience that will help you determine which topics to cover and in how much depth. It is the composition of your audience that will guide your choice of visuals. It is the composition of your audience that will suggest how you should dress for the occasion. No matter what you are presenting, you *first* need to understand who will be in your audience.

In many ways, preparing for a presentation is like preparing to write a report or essay. You need to do your research, you need to organize your thoughts and findings into a working outline for logical presentation, and then you have to figure out what exactly to say. The main differences are that you will be presenting your material in front of a live audience; and instead of a page or word requirement, you will mostly likely be given a finite time in which to present.

There are, however, some planning considerations that are unique to the oral presentation. You obviously need to consider ahead of time what needs to be covered in the presentation. To do this properly, you need to know enough about your audience to know what they already know; e.g., there is no point using valuable presentation time to regurgitate company history to the president of that company. Find out how much time you are allotted, and think carefully about what you can communicate well in that amount of time. What are your main messages? What evidence must you present to support those messages? What do you want your audience to remember after they leave? What action do you hope they will take as a result of seeing your presentation? These are critical questions to ask yourself as you narrow down the topic of your presentation to a few key themes.

Once you've identified your key themes, you need to be ruthless in structuring your presentation around only those key themes. Conventional wisdom suggests that you should always approach a presentation by "telling them what you are going to tell them, telling them, then telling them what you told them." This is no different from saying that every presentation needs an introduction, a body, and a conclusion. It does, however, emphasize the importance of repeating your main messages more than once.

Dry Run

A rehearsal for a presentation in its entirety, from beginning to end, with all visuals and audio effects

Finally, always make time for a "**dry run**"; if at all possible, make a video of it. A dry run is a rehearsal of the entire presentation, to check the flow of the material and the time it takes to get through it. Videotaping it allows you to see it from the audience's perspective. Do you have an obvious vocal tic; e.g., always saying "OK . . ." in between slides, or "eh?" after each question? Are your transitions from one slide to another choppy? Do you have your hands in your pockets throughout the presentation? Watching yourself on video is always a rude awakening, but it is also one of the best ways to zoom in on what needs improving.

Note that a dry run is even more critical if you are presenting as part of a team. Not only do you need to work out the transitions from one person to the next to ensure that the presentation flows properly, but you also need to make sure you have enough time for all parts of the presentation. A dry run is the best way to assess this.

Creating Effective Presentation Slides and Visuals

Have you heard of "Death by PowerPoint"? Perhaps you have experienced it! This is an expression used for presentations where the presenter thinks that PowerPoint slides should do all

Buddy believed that successful presentations began with the entrance.

of the work, and the presenter need only stand there and read aloud the contents of slide after slide after slide. This is *not* an effective way to present your material. PowerPoint is like perfume—it can enhance the senses, but only if it is applied in small doses. Here are some recommendations for you as you consider visuals for your presentation:

> **Number of slides.** As a general guideline, you should allot one or two minutes of talking time per slide. That means a 15-minute presentation should have no more than 15 slides, and that *includes* a title slide, an agenda, and a slide asking if your audience has questions! Venture capitalist Guy Kawasaki, who listens to pitches from aspiring entrepreneurs day after day, recommends abiding by the 10–20–30 rule: a maximum of 10 slides, a maximum 20-minute presentation, and a minimum font size of 30. That's excellent advice for classroom presentations as well.

> **Choice of template.** When selecting a template for your slides, you need to consider if they will be projected in a well-lit room or in a dark room. In a well-lit room, your background should be light-coloured, and the print colour should be dark, preferably black. If you are presenting in a room where the lights are low, the opposite is true: dark background, light letters. To help you remember this, think, for example, of watching the credits roll in a dark movie theatre. The background in this case is always dark, and the credits are usually white.

> **Font size and style.** Whatever template you select, you need to ensure that the smallest font size on your slide can be seen at the very back of the room by the oldest person in the audience. Going back to Guy Kawasaki's suggestion, use nothing less than a 30-point font size. As for font style, presentation guru Garr Reynolds recommends using a sans serif font for presentation slides, because it is easier to see at high resolutions. To see the difference between serif and sans serif fonts, check out the example below.

Times roman is a **serif** font	Arial is a **sans serif** font.

> **Don't get too fancy.** As a general rule, simpler is better when it comes to presentation slides. That means your background should not involve anything that competes with the words on the slide; illustrations or graphics should only appear along the border of the slide. It also means judicious use of custom animation effects like transition fadeouts or flyouts, or audio effects like applause. To adapt the phrase coined by legendary Canadian scholar and visionary Marshall McLuhan, don't let the medium overtake the message.

> **Limit yourself** to three bullets per slide, and no more than seven or eight words per bullet. To ensure that your audience is concentrating on the point you are currently talking about, show only one bullet at a time.

> **Use pictures instead of words** where possible. There is a good reason for the expression "a picture is worth a thousand words." You can use the free clipart images that come with Microsoft Word or you can obtain royalty-free images on the Internet on sites like **freedigitalphotos.net**. If you are presenting data, use pie charts, bar charts, and graphs that summarize your findings rather than showing the raw data.

"There are many true statements about complex topics that are too long to fit on a PowerPoint slide."
Edward Tufte, author

> **Add variety.** Switch it up a bit. Feel free to go from a slide with bullet points over to a website and back, or from a bullet point to a visual and back. Your audience will appreciate the break from words, words, and more words.

Kevin finds that one hand-out between 20 people makes for difficult reading.

> **Plan for questions.** Decide ahead of time whether you want the audience to hold its questions until the end. If so, ensure you have a "Questions?" slide to wrap up your talk—and make sure you've left enough time to field questions.

> **Prepare a handout** of your presentation slides by printing them out three to a page. Be sure to put your detailed contact information somewhere in the handout, and print more than enough copies for the number of people you are expecting in the audience.

Dressing the Part

Whether you are speaking in front of your instructor and fellow students, or at a convention of the best minds in the world, your clothing should be inwardly comfortable and outwardly presentable. This is *not* the time to wear your shortest miniskirt and highest heels, or your torn hoodie and grubby running shoes. Your clothing choices should convey a crispness and professionalism that conveys the message "I am the expert," while at the same time allowing you to move freely across a stage or into an audience. Think about what you'll wear several days before you make your presentation. This will give you time to ensure that the clothing you've selected is clean and in good repair, and that your shoes are shined and ready to go. The extra care you take with dress and grooming on presentation day will be noticed—and first impressions being what they are, it could even have an impact on your grade.

You're On!

The day of your presentation has arrived. You've done all the recommended preparation, your slides and visuals have been created, your USB stick is in your pocket, and you are raring to go. Whoa, Nelly . . . as Canadian singing superstar Nelly Furtado might exclaim. Not so fast. There are still a few things to do *before* the presentation actually begins.

Owning Your Environment

Always be sure to arrive early for your presentation, and check out the room in which it will take place. Examine the room carefully. Is there a podium or lectern? Where is the projector? Do you need to move anything around? Own your environment by ensuring that it is optimized for the type of presentation you plan to deliver. Now, check and double-check that the technology is working. There is nothing more distressing than having to troubleshoot a projector or a laptop while your audience waits for the presentation to start. Bring up the programs and content you plan to use, then minimize them or bring up your title slide. If you are planning to use videos from YouTube or the Internet, make sure they have time to buffer before the presentation starts. In a nutshell, make sure everything is ready ahead of time.

Beginning Confidently

Your opening statement is an important one. It needs to engage your audience and pique their interest for what is to come in the remainder of the presentation. The traditional recommendation of opening with an elaborate entrance or some sort of

From the perspective of . . .

A BUSINESS PROFESSIONAL

Making presentations is a frequent task in the lives of most business professionals.

joke is *not* the way to go unless you are a standup comedian. Canned humour generally sounds contrived and rarely achieves the objective of leaving the audience wanting more. Instead, consider starting with a visual, an anecdote, or a pointed question that introduces one of your main themes. You want your audience to sit up and take notice of what you have to say. A good opening statement can pave the way.

Next, always have an agenda slide. It introduces your audience to the structure and flow of the presentation, so your audience knows where you are headed and how you plan to get there. The agenda slide, because it is relatively straightforward, and something you should be able to present without having to think too much about it, gives you a moment to get physically comfortable in front of the audience. It will give you an opportunity to size up the audience.

Never, ever stand in front of a projector.

Switching it Up

To keep your audience interested, you need to make a conscious effort to vary your tone of voice and move around the room. Do not stand perfectly still, glued to a podium. Your slides, while benefitting from a consistent background look and feel, should also be varied: Switch up traditional bullet point slides with video, audio, charts, and website links. The use of a variety of techniques to make your points will appeal to the varied learning styles of your audience and keep them engaged.

Involving Your Audience

You'll need to determine ahead of time whether you want members of your audience to ask questions as you go along, or whether you prefer that they wait until the question period at the end of your presentation. Let them know your preference early in the presentation; but always, always make time for questions. People may not remember half of what you said in your presentation but they *will* remember how you answered their question—and you just never know who might be in your audience asking the question. Finally, if you *don't* know the answer, the simple reply is "I'm sorry, I don't know the answer to that, but I will find out for you." Then get their contact information, and make sure you follow up as promised.

Always encourage your audience to ask questions.

Finishing Memorably

How you end your presentation is just as important as how you begin. There are many different ways to end a presentation. A common one is to reiterate your main themes one last time, and invite your audience to ponder on some take-away questions. Another is to use a cartoon, quotation, or other visual that sums up what you've presented. Another is to thank those who invited you to present, and offer to stay after the presentation should anyone have

The 10 Dos and Don'ts of Making Effective Presentations

1. DO remember that YOU are the expert—the person who knows the most about the presentation—so speak with confidence.
2. DO use a font size that can be seen from the back of the room.
3. DO involve your audience by inviting their comments and questions.
4. DO provide a means for your audience to provide anonymous feedback.
5. DO prepare handouts for everyone in the audience, but DON'T hand them out until after the presentation.
6. DON'T bore your audience by speaking in a monotone voice and standing perfectly still. Vary your tone and volume, and feel free to gesture and move around as you speak.
7. DON'T try too hard by attempting elaborate or contrived presentation openers.
8. DON'T show a slide that has more than three bullet points on it.
9. DON'T stand in front of the projector when you are showing slides.
10. DON'T rely exclusively on PowerPoint bullet slides. Use photos, quotations, illustrations, graphs, and other visuals to make your presentation come alive.

further questions. You'll need to decide what makes sense for you, given the topic and purpose of your presentation.

Using Handouts Effectively

If you want your audience focused on what you are saying during the presentation, never give them a handout of your slides in advance. Indicate at the beginning of your presentation that a handout is available and will be distributed at the end of the presentation. Always make a few extras; and in your contact information, be sure to include your email address so audience members can request additional electronic copies if they are interested.

"Well, Ladies and Gentlemen, I'm sure my little talk has made you all think."

After the Presentation

While you might assume your message got through to the members of your audience, you will never know for sure unless you invite them to provide feedback. If you are given the opportunity to obtain feedback from your audience, be ready with a quick survey that can be handed out along with the copy of your slides. Check out **Try It! 4**, "Getting Feedback on Your Presentation," for a sample survey. Once you've received feedback—and it should be provided *anonymously*—take it to heart and use it to make improvements in future presentations.

Getting Feedback on Your Presentation

The very best way to improve your presentation skills is to practise, practise, practise. It is a good idea to get feedback from your audience after each presentation. Most folks don't like to make critical comments out loud, and they would probably be more honest if their comments were anonymous. To get their honest feedback, consider making copies of the short survey shown below, and have your audience members hand it in anonymously after you've made your presentation.

Feedback on my Presentation

1. What is the *one* thing that stood out for you in this presentation; i.e., the one idea or fact that you will take away from it?
2. What is the *one* thing that could have been done differently to make *this* presentation more effective for *you*?
3. What is the *one* thing that could have been done differently to make this presentation more effective for *everyone in the audience*?

To Try It online, go to Connect for *P.O.W.E.R. Learning and Your Life*.

Presenting Yourself in a Job Interview

It is one thing to create and deliver a presentation that you've had the luxury of practising over and over; it is quite another to find yourself having to present your own skills and abilities in the context of a job interview. Since you don't have any control over the questions that will be asked, interviews are never predictable. You might face an interviewer who starts with an open-ended question like "Tell me about yourself"; or you might find yourself in a highly structured group interview, where several individuals ask you questions in turn. The interviewer may decide to approach the interview using behaviour-based questions like "Tell me about a time when . . ." This lack of predictability—and the high stakes—are what make job interviews so fraught with anxiety.

But in spite of their unpredictability, there are concrete steps you can take to prepare more thoroughly for job interviews. Aside from doing research on the company and having a well-constructed resumé and cover letter that are tailored to the job in question, you should also consider preparing your own "tip sheet"—a few pages where you've summarized your main skills and abilities and listed at least one concrete example that illustrates each. It is also worthwhile to get a friend or parent to ask you typical interview questions and provide feedback on your responses. For sample questions and more tips on preparing for job interviews, download the free Interview Booklet developed by York University, which can be found at **www.yorku.ca/laps/sowk/pdf/Interview_Booklet.pdf**.

Career Connections

A Final Word

Communication is the lifeblood of the twenty-first century. You cannot have an impact on the world around you if you keep your thoughts and ideas to yourself. You may choose to start a blog, upload a video to YouTube, and communicate with friends and family by text message, Twitter, or email; or you may write a traditional report or make a formal presentation. Use the methods that best suit your learning style and Striving Style™, and examine the suggestions and recommendations provided in the sidebar.

Don't be afraid to get your message out there. The world is waiting to hear from you.

Leaders

You think you have enough time to write your report or expand your arguments when you don't. Have a time budget. Presenting can make you feel out of control; but you are a natural, so learn to relax and enjoy.

Performers

Try not to get stuck creating the perfect report or exhausting yourself by over-delivering. Don't get so caught up in your enjoyment of presenting that you ramble or lose focus. Use cue cards or PowerPoint.

Socializers

Stay with facts when developing reports. Test the logic of your analysis with a trusted friend or teacher. Don't worry so much about being judged by others when you present.

Adventurers

Use a digital recorder to capture what you want to write instead of labouring over writing a report. You can entertain your audience during presentations but fail to make your points. Use PowerPoint or cue cards to stay focused.

Artists

Ask for help with the structure and analysis so you don't stall before you even begin. You can make yourself overly anxious about presenting when you can't separate what you are presenting from who you are.

Intellectuals

Don't focus so much on pursuing one argument that you fail to add breadth to a case or report. You can excel as a presenter when you are not afraid of engaging your audience.

Visionaries

Try not to go into information overload when preparing your report and business case. Keep your excitement about the content of your presentation in your voice when you present.

Stabilizers

Don't adhere so much to the literal instructions that you fail to provide a broader scope to your case analysis. When presenting, let your personality come through rather than just factually recounting information.

Time to Reflect: What Did I Learn?

1. Review the material in Chapter 1 on the four learning styles: read/write, visual/graphic, auditory/verbal, and tactile/kinesthetic (pages 18–19). Thinking about your own learning style, what approaches are likely to be most effective for you when you are generating ideas for a report or presentation?

2. When you are beginning work on a group report or presentation, and thinking again about your *own* learning style, what tasks should you volunteer to do?

3. When you are preparing a presentation for a diverse audience, what steps can you take to ensure that the content of your presentation will appeal to *their* learning styles?

Looking Back

Why is communication so important?

- Virtually all course work at the post-secondary level relies on good communication skills.
- Without effective communication skills, you will not be able to maximize your impact on the world around you.

What do I need to do before I actually start writing a report?

- Research your topic thoroughly. Then use mind mapping or brainstorming techniques to explore themes and possible subtopics for your report.
- Determine what your main thesis will be.
- Organize your arguments and research findings.
- Create a "workback" schedule to ensure you leave yourself enough time to rest, reread, and revise. (You can apply these concepts to the preparation of a presentation as well.)

How can I ensure that I get my message across in a report?

- Focus on a specific thesis and ensure you have a cohesive set of supporting arguments.
- Make sure your report is organized in a logical fashion and that each section of the report flows readily into the next.

How can I avoid plagiarism?

- Cite all of your sources, both in the context of the report (in in-text citations) and in a bibliography or Works Cited page at the end.

How can I become a better presenter?

- Know your audience.
- Prepare your materials well ahead of time.
- Rehearse, preferably in front of a video camera.
- Invite audience feedback and take it to heart.
- Consider joining an organization like Toastmasters.

[KEY TERMS AND CONCEPTS]

Arguments (p. 171)

Dry run (p. 180)

Mind mapping (p. 172)

Outline (p. 173)

Presentation anxiety (p. 178)

Thesis (p. 171)

[RESOURCES]

ON CAMPUS

Contact your student association to find out if there is a Toastmasters (or similar) group operating on campus, and attend a meeting. You might also want to consider taking on volunteer positions that require you to write and/or present, such as the campus newspaper or various committees or clubs.

Colleges and universities will often sponsor a "Speaker Series." Take the time to attend and learn from these speakers.

Free tutoring is often available on campus. You can use this service to have a "second pair of eyes" proofread your reports prior to submitting them or to have someone watch a dry run of your presentations before you do them in front of the class.

IN PRINT

Nancy Duarte's book, *Slide-ology: The Art and Science of Creating Great Presentations,* is a wonderful resource to call upon when you are preparing a presentation (O'Reilly Media, 2008).

If you are interested in how to present data in a compelling way, you'll want to examine *The Wall Street Journal Guide to Information Graphics: The Dos and Don'ts of Presenting Data, Facts, and Figures* by author Dona M. Wong (W.W. Norton & Co., 2009).

Barcharts Publishing Inc. offers a 3-panel laminated guide on MLA and APA citation styles that can be purchased for under $10 at **www.chapters.indigo.ca.**

ON THE WEB

The following websites provide the opportunity to extend your learning about the material in this chapter.

➤ Garr Reynolds, author of the book *Presentation Zen* and its companion blog, has an excellent three-part series of tips on presentations that is divided into organizing and preparation, delivery, and slide tips. If you do nothing else before planning your presentation, check out this series at **www.garrreynolds.com.**

➤ Mike Parkinson's website, **http://billiondollargraphics.com**, contains free templates and graphics that can be used in a report or presentation.

➤ At **www.presentationmagazine.com**, you'll find plenty of tips on making good presentations.

➤ For a funny take on "Life After Death By PowerPoint 2010", check out manager-turned-stand-up-comedian Don McMillan's routine at **http://vodpod.com/watch/2505919-life-after-death-by-powerpoint-2010**.

TAKING IT TO THE NET

1   After you have written a paper or report for one of your courses, copy and paste it into **www.paperrater.com**. This free site, which has been developed and is maintained by linguistics professionals and graduate students, will provide you with a detailed analysis of your report, including grammar suggestions, plagiarism detection, and writing suggestions. To top it all off, it will give you a "grade" for your paper, based on the analysis. While your instructor obviously gets the last word on your grade, this is still a good way to avail yourself of an excellent proofreader—at no cost to you!

The Case of . . .
The "Creative" Presenter

Zenobia was excited. She was going to get an opportunity to make a presentation to her psychology class on a topic that she'd recently researched for a report: creativity.

She immediately set to work, planning a grand entrance: She would enter the class dressed in a clown suit (last year's Halloween costume) with her dachshund, Soprano, at her side. She would open her presentation by asking the audience for their definition of creativity and bring candies to throw out to those who answered. To show just how creative she could be, she decided to develop a set of "wild and crazy" slides. She spent days lovingly designing the slides, each one with a different background and colour scheme. She experimented with several different-coloured fonts on each slide, although she decided on lavender for all the titles—it was, after all, her favourite colour. She ended up spending so much time designing the slides that she didn't have much time left over to think about what to put on them; but she came up with a creative solution, cutting and pasting paragraphs from her recently submitted report onto each slide. Her plan was to end the presentation with a bang by having her dog—who wasn't called Soprano for nothing—sing for the audience. What a splash she'd make . . . people would be talking about her presentation the rest of the semester!

Well, Zenobia did make her presentation, and people were certainly talking about it; but mainly, they were commenting on the negative feedback Zenobia received from the instructor, who decided to use the occasion to teach Zenobia and the rest of the students what *not* to do.

1. How well did Zenobia use her time to plan her presentation? What advice would you give her about the preparation stage of planning a presentation?

2. Clearly, Zenobia was enthusiastic about the topic of creativity, and she tried hard to make it "come alive" for her audience. Where did she go wrong?

3. What was Zenobia's priority when preparing this presentation? What *should* have been her priority?

4. Do you agree with Zenobia's instructor's decision to provide feedback publicly? Why or why not?

8 Making Decisions and Solving Problems

Learning Outcomes

By the time you finish this chapter, you will be able to

>> LO **8.1**   Outline a framework for decision-making.

>> LO **8.2**   Discuss how critical thinking can be applied to the problem-solving process.

>> LO **8.3**   Apply critical thinking to everyday problems.

Bayani Soriano had a tough decision coming up. In three weeks, he would earn his Construction Engineering Technician diploma. It had taken a great deal of effort and the sacrifice of a lot of free time, but he was almost there. It was what to do next, though, that was giving Bayani problems.

All through college, he had worked for a local contractor, picking up construction jobs when the contractor needed an extra pair of hands. Now that Bayani was graduating as a construction engineering technician, the contractor had offered to make him a permanent member of his construction crew. In short, he was being offered more work at a better salary.

Bayani knew it was a great offer—but it was not his only option. A friend he had met in college wanted to start his own house inspection business, and he wanted Bayani to be his partner. Working together, Bayani's friend said, they could build the business quickly; and they would earn more and have more flexibility than if they worked for someone else.

As graduation approached, Bayani knew he had to make up his mind. But he kept going around in circles. Was security more important than flexibility? How much was running his own business worth to him?

Bayani knew he had to make up his mind. But how?

Like Bayani, all of us face important life decisions at one time or another. How can we make the right decisions? The best way is to employ some basic techniques that can help improve the quality of our decision-making.

This chapter gives you a sense of what decision-making is and is not, and it discusses a structured process that can help make your decisions the right ones. But what happens when you make the wrong decision? That's where problem-solving skills come into play. Most students confront a variety of problems as they proceed through college or university and throughout their career. In this chapter, we'll look at a number of proven techniques that will help you find solutions to the problems you might face. We'll also examine some common problems that can affect our thinking and discuss several biases that can make us jump to the wrong conclusions.

» LO 8.1 Making Better Decisions: A Framework

Neither making decisions nor solving problems is easy. Sometimes the best decision or solution to a problem is one that we don't see at first; we all have mental blind spots. The best problem-solvers and decision-makers have learned how to use critical thinking to see around these blind spots. To use Robert Ennis's classic definition, "critical thinking is reasonable, reflective thinking that is focused on deciding what to believe or do."[1] In other words, it is the ability to reflect on your views and opinions about the world around you and on what gave rise to these views; i.e., *why* you think the way you do.

Decision-making is the process of deciding among various alternatives. Whether you are trying to decide between a Ford and a Honda, between an apartment that is close to your job and one that is close to family, or simply between a hamburger and a pizza, every choice requires a decision. Some decisions are easily made and have few consequences; but others, such as whether to take one job or another, can involve the deepest examination of our beliefs and values.

Whatever you're deciding, you need to think critically in order to make a reasoned decision. You need to actively apply your past knowledge, synthesize and evaluate alternatives, and reason and reflect on a course of action. The greater your depth of thinking about the components of the decision, the more likely it is that you'll come up with the best choice.

To make a good decision, map out a strategy for making the choice that is best for you. Every decision can benefit from your thinking systematically through the options involved, based on the P.O.W.E.R. Plan illustrated here.

Decision-making
The process of deciding among various alternatives

P Prepare
Examine your goals

O Organize
Consider and assess your alternatives

W Work
Make your decision and carry it out

E Evaluate
Consider the outcome

R Rethink
Reconsider your goals and options

P.O.W.E.R. Plan

P Prepare   Examine Your Goals

Every decision starts with the end you have in mind: the goals you wish to accomplish by making the decision.

For example, suppose you are trying to decide on something as simple as where to sit in a classroom. Your long-term goal is to make the Dean's List. You know that sitting near the front of the room means you'll probably pay attention more, the teacher will get to know who you are, and it will be easier to ask or answer questions. On the other hand, sitting at the back means you can sit with your friends; and if the class gets boring, you can text without the teacher noticing. Also, if you are at the back, it's unlikely that the teacher will call on you to answer questions. Your seat selection must be seen in light of your long-term goal: doing well enough to make the Dean's List. Where you sit in each classroom will very likely have an impact on your grade in each course; the closer you sit to the front, the more likely you will be able to reach your goal.

In short, every decision should start with a consideration of what our short- and long-term goals are. Identifying the goals that underlie decisions ensures that we make decisions in the context of our entire lives and not just to provide short-term answers to immediate problems.

 ## Consider and Assess Your Alternatives

Identifying Alternatives

Making a decision requires weighing various alternatives. Determining what those alternatives are, and their possible consequences, is often the most difficult part of decision-making. It's important not only to think thoroughly about the obvious alternatives, but also to consider alternatives that are less obvious. For many decisions, there are choices beyond the "this or that" alternatives that can dominate our thinking. How can you be sure that you've considered all the possible alternatives? Do your research. What have others done in a similar situation? Investigate, either through reading about the life journeys of others in your situation, or by interviewing them personally.

There are also more creative approaches to identifying alternatives that you may wish to consider. If you have a visual/graphic learning style, you might want to use the mind mapping technique introduced in Chapter 7. If your learning style leans more towards read/write, using a technique called freewriting may be the best way to go.

In **freewriting**, you write continuously for a fixed period of time, perhaps five or ten minutes. During this period, the idea is to write as many different ideas as possible, without stopping. It makes no difference whether the alternatives are good or bad or even whether they make sense. All that matters is that you let yourself brainstorm about the topic for a while and get the ideas down on paper.

Freewriting
A technique involving continuous writing, without self-criticism, for a fixed period of time

With freewriting, evaluating the worth of the ideas you've generated comes later. After you have produced as many possibilities as you can, then you go back and sift out the reasonable ones from those that are unlikely or just plain wacky. It's OK if you have to delete quite a few alternatives from your list; the process is likely to have liberated some reasonable alternatives that you might not otherwise have come up with. (Try this technique in **Try It! 1**, "Use Freewriting," on page 194.)

Assessing Alternatives

Once you have generated as extensive a list of alternatives as possible, assess them. You need to follow three key steps when assessing each alternative:

"Nothing is more difficult, and therefore more precious, than to be able to decide."
Napoleon I, *Maxims*, 1804–15

1. **Determine the possible outcomes for each alternative.** Some outcomes are positive, some negative. Consider as many as you can think of. For example, if you are considering ways of solving transportation problems, one alternative might be to purchase a car. That alternative produces several potential outcomes. For example, you know that it will be easier to get wherever you want to go, and you might even have a

Try It!

Use Freewriting

Part A: Use freewriting to think of as many answers as you can to each of the following questions. The ground rules are that you should spend three minutes on each question, generating as many ideas as possible—regardless of whether they are feasible. To give yourself maximum freedom, write each answer on a separate sheet of paper.

1. How can you make room in your schedule to take one more course next term than you're taking this term?

2. Thinking about past relationships, what will you look for in future partners?

3. How can you make some extra money while going to school full-time?

4. What activities can you participate in while in school that will make your resumé more attractive to potential employers?

Part B: After generating ideas, go back and evaluate them.

1. How many were actually feasible?
2. Do you think freewriting led to the production of more or fewer ideas than you would have come up with if you hadn't used the technique?
3. Did the quality of ideas change?

 WORKING IN A GROUP

After you have answered the questions above, form a group and compare your answers with those of others in your group. As a group, try to identify the best answers to each question.

To Try It online, go to Connect for *P.O.W.E.R. Learning and Your Life.*

better social life—clearly positive outcomes. But it is also true that buying and owning a car will be expensive, and that it may be difficult to find convenient parking—both significant negative outcomes.

2. **Determine the probability that those outcomes will take place.** Some outcomes are far more likely than others. To take this into account, make a rough estimate of the likelihood that an outcome will come to pass, ranging from 100 percent (you are certain that it will occur) to 0 percent (you are certain that it will never occur). Obviously, the probabilities are just guesses, but going through the exercise of estimating them will make the outcomes more real and will permit you to compare the various alternatives against one another more easily.

3. **Compare the alternatives, taking into account the potential outcomes of each.** Systematically compare each of the alternatives. A simple pro/con list like the one shown in **Figure 8.1,** which examines the decision to get a tattoo, can help you make this comparison. Then ask yourself the key question: Which alternative, on balance, provides the most positive (and most likely) outcomes?

The Pros & Cons of Getting a Tattoo

figure 8.1
Creating a list of pros and cons can help you make a better decision.

Pros

1. It expresses my individuality

2. It would represent something special to me

3. My friends all have one

4. It's the style these days to have a tattoo

5. I think tattoos can be really pretty

6. My style icon, Lady Gaga, has several

Cons

1. My parents would be angry

2. It's expensive to remove

3. I don't like needles or pain

4. There's a risk of infection

5. Will it still look good when I'm 60?

6. It might not look good if I'm in a wedding dress or business attire

Obviously, not every decision requires such an elaborate process. In fact, most won't. But when it comes to major decisions, those that could have a large impact upon you and your life, it's worthwhile to follow a systematic process.

Take a look at **Career Connections** on page 197 for another process that you can follow to help you make a career decision.

 ## Make Your Decision and Carry It Out

Working through the previous steps will lead you to the point of decision: choosing one of the alternatives you've identified. Having carried out the steps will make the actual decision easier, but not necessarily easy.

Choosing among Alternatives

The reason that important decisions are difficult is that the alternatives you have to choose from carry both benefits and costs. Choosing one alternative means that you have to accept the costs of that choice and give up the benefits of the other alternatives. A decision can also mean a "fork in the road": One decision can lead to a number of other decisions; and as you become more and more committed, you find it almost impossible to go backwards. A graphic representation of that process is captured by what is called a "decision tree." Examine the decision tree in **Figure 8.2,** which shows a person who has already taken a fork in the road by deciding to get a tattoo. Now they must decide what the subject of that tattoo should be. They are torn between a text-based tattoo (either a song lyric or a line from a poem) or an illustration of a fish (goldfish or dolphin) or a flower (tulip or rose). As they move through the decision process, they compare one alternative against the other, narrowing their preference down each time and finally coming to the

figure 8.2
Developing a decision tree can help you select among a set of alternatives.

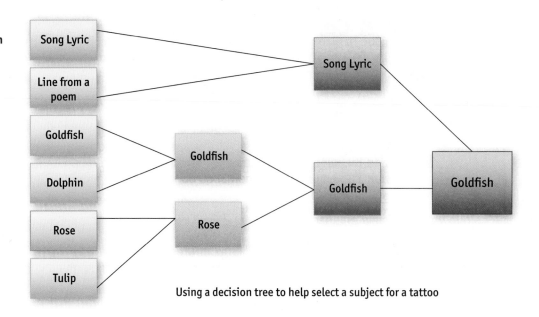

Using a decision tree to help select a subject for a tattoo

conclusion that they will get a tattoo of a goldfish. While this decision tree is rather simple, consider what a similar tree might look like as you try to choose between five or six majors at college or university.

What if, after going through the steps of the process laid out here, you still can't make up your mind? Try these strategies:

> **Give the decision some time.** Sometimes waiting helps. Time can give you a chance to think of additional alternatives. Sometimes the situation will change, or you'll have a change in viewpoint.

> **Make a mental movie, acting out the various alternatives.** Many of us have difficulty seeing ourselves in the future and envisioning how various options would play out. One way to get around this difficulty is to cast yourself into a series of "mental movies" that have different endings depending on the decision you make. Working through the different scripts in your head makes potential outcomes far more real and less abstract than they would be if you simply left them as items on a list of various options.

> **Toss a coin.** This isn't as crazy as it sounds. If each alternative seems equally positive or negative to you, pull out a coin—make option A "heads" and B "tails." Then flip it.

> The real power of the coin-toss strategy is that it might help you discover your true feelings. It may happen while the coin is in the air, or it may be that when you see the result of the coin toss, you won't like the outcome and will say to yourself, "No way." In such a case, you've just found out how you really feel.

> **Ask for advice.** Although Western society teaches the virtues of rugged individualism, asking others for their advice is often an excellent strategy. Friends, instructors, parents, or a counsellor can provide helpful recommendations—sometimes because they've had to make similar decisions themselves. You don't have to take their advice, but it can help to listen to what they have to say.

> **Go with your gut feeling.** Call it what you like—gut feeling, intuition, hunch, superstition—but sometimes we need to go with our hearts and not our minds. If you've thought rationally about a decision and have been unable to

From the perspective of . . .

A STUDENT Balancing education and other aspects of life can be fraught with many alternatives and choices. How do you prioritize options when making a decision?

Weighing Options

After choosing what type of education and career to pursue, one of the most important decisions you'll ever make is choosing how to apply this education in an employment setting that will stimulate you and that you will enjoy. Your long-term goals, as well as your personality, your striving style, and your learning style, should all factor into this decision. Here's one method that can help you decide what might be best suited to you:

- Generate a selection of choices to consider. Include not only the obvious options that your current education prepares you for, but also alternative ideas such as pursuing a position in a different environment (e.g., dental hygienist in a public health setting), earning a degree, starting your own business, and so forth. Even if you doubt you'll select one of these other options, considering them will help you assess what you truly want to do.

- Determine life-satisfaction considerations that are important to you. Generate a list of criteria to use in weighing the possibilities. For instance, you might want to consider the following:

   Benefits (vacation, health insurance, etc.)
   Salary
   Spouse's opinion
   Friends' opinions
   Interest in the activity
   Prestige
   Job security
   Flexible hours
   Benefit to society
   Practicality/attainability
   Everyday working conditions
   Clients you will be working with
   Opportunities to learn
   Opportunities to travel

- Determine how well a particular option fulfills each of the life-satisfaction factors you consider important. By systematically considering how a potential path fulfills each of the criteria you use, you'll be able to compare different options. One easy way to do this is to create a chart like the one in **Table 8.1,** which shows an example of how job options for a massage therapist might fulfill the various criteria, using a scale of 1-10, where 1 means worst and 10 means best.

- Compare different choices. Using the chart, evaluate your possibilities. Keep in mind that this is just a rough guide and that it's only as accurate as (a) the effort you put into completing it and (b) your understanding of a given choice. Use the results in conjunction with other things you find out about the jobs—and yourself.

table 8.1	Making Career Decisions		
Life-satisfaction considerations on a scale of 1-10	Massage therapist at a local spa	Sports massage therapist at a university	Massage therapist on a cruise ship
Benefits	4	8	5
Income	8	7	5
Spouse's opinion	8	6	1
Friends' opinions	4	7	7
Interest in the activity	5	6	8
Prestige	5	9	7
Job security	4	7	5
Flexible hours	8	5	6
Benefit to society	6	8	6
Practicality/attainability	9	4	2
Everyday working conditions	7	8	6
Clients you will be working with	5	7	8
Opportunity to learn	3	8	5
Opportunity to travel	1	5	10
Other			
Total	**77**	**95**	**81**

determine the best course of action but have a gut feeling that one choice is better than another, follow your feelings.

Following a gut feeling does not mean that you don't need to consider the pros and cons of a decision rationally and carefully. In fact, generally our "intuition" is best when informed by the thoughtfulness of a more rational process.

Carrying Out the Decision

Ultimately, decisions must move from thought to action—they have to be carried out. Consequently, the final stage in making a decision is to act upon it. You need to turn your decision into behaviour.

 **Evaluate** Consider the Outcome

Did you make the right decision?

Even if you've spent time and mental effort in thinking through a decision, you still need to consider the results. Even well-considered decisions can end up being

If all else fails, toss a coin to decide what alternative to follow. Tossing a coin at least brings you to a decision. Then, if you find you're unhappy with the result, you'll have gained important information about how you really feel regarding a particular choice.

wrong, either because you neglected to consider an alternative or because something has changed: either you or the situation.

Remember, it's never too late to change your mind. In fact, even major life decisions are often reversible. That's why it's so important to evaluate your choices. If you chose the wrong alternative, reverse course and reconsider your options.

It's not a bad thing to change your mind. In fact, admitting that a decision was a mistake is often the wisest and most courageous course of action. You don't want to be so rigidly committed to a decision that you're unable to evaluate the consequences objectively. Give yourself permission to be wrong.

> "In any moment of decision, the best thing you can do is the right thing, the next best thing is the wrong thing, and the worst thing you can do is nothing."
> **President Theodore Roosevelt**

 ## Reconsider Your Goals and Options

We can get to most places by multiple routes. There's the fastest and most direct route, which will get us to our destination in the smallest amount of time. Then there's the longer, more scenic route, where the trip itself provides pleasure. You can "take the long way home," as the song goes. Is one route better than the other? Often not. Both take us to our destination. However, the experience of reaching our goal will have been very different.

Decisions about how to achieve a goal are similar to travelling down different routes. There's often no single decision that is best, just as there's often no single road to a particular place. Consequently, it's important now and then to reconsider the major decisions that we've made about our lives.

Ask yourself these questions:

> Are my decisions still producing the desired consequences?
> Are my decisions still appropriate, given my circumstances and changes in my life?
> Are my decisions consistent with what I want to get out of life?

Periodically taking stock like this is the best way to make sure that your decisions are taking you where you want to go. Taking stock also helps you to be more effective in making future decisions.

»LO 8.2 Problem-Solving: Applying Critical Thinking to Find Solutions

Two trains are approaching one another, each moving at 60 miles an hour. If the trains continue moving at the same speed, how long will it be before . . .

If this is what comes to mind when you think of problem-solving, think again. **Problem-solving** encompasses more than the abstract, often unrealistic situations portrayed in math texts. It involves everyday, commonplace situations: How do we divide the restaurant bill so that each person pays a fair share? How do I keep my 1-year-old from tumbling down the stairs when there seems to be no way to fasten a gate at the top? How can I stop a faucet from dripping? How do I manage to study for a test and do the laundry the same evening?

While decision-making is most focused on choosing among various alternatives, the central issue in problem-solving is generating alternatives. Since many problems require that decisions be made regarding alternatives, decision-making and problem-solving are related.

What's the Problem?

The first step in solving any problem is to be as clear as you can about what the problem is. This may sound easy, but often it isn't. In fact, it may take some time to figure out just what is at stake. Some problems, such as mathematical equations or the solution to a jigsaw puzzle, are quite precise. Determining how to stop terrorism or finding peace in the Middle East, on the other hand, are big, ill-defined problems. Simply determining what information is required to solve such problems can be a major undertaking.

To determine what the problem is and set yourself on a course for finding a solution, ask yourself these questions:

> What is the initial set of facts?

> What is it that I need to solve? Which parts of the problem am I actually able to solve?

> Which parts of the problem appear to be most critical to finding a solution?

> Is there some information that can be ignored?

> "Problems are only opportunities in work clothes."
>
> Henry J. Kaiser (1882–1967), entrepreneur, *Maxim*

The more systematically you approach a problem, the better. For instance, you can apply the five P.O.W.E.R. steps to problems, similar to the way you can apply them to making decisions. When you consider a problem systematically and think through your options, your choices will become clearer to you.

As you clarify what the problem is, you may find that you have encountered similar problems before. Your experience may suggest the means to the solution of the current problem. For example, consider the problem of the trains rushing toward each other. If you have worked on this kind of problem before, you might know a fairly simple equation you can write to determine how long it will take before they meet. If someone asks you about the problem she has in keeping her toddler from tumbling down the stairs, you might offer your experience in keeping your own children from visiting an off-limits area of your house.

On the other hand, to solve many of the problems we face in our daily lives, we have to do more than reach into our memories of prior situations. Instead, we need to devise novel approaches. How do you do this? There are several strategies you might use.

Strategies for Solving Life's Messier Problems

> **Break the problem down into smaller, more manageable pieces, a process called "chunking."** Divide a problem into a series of sub-goals. As you reach

each sub-goal, you get closer to your overall goal of solving the problem. For example, if your goal is to find a job in Montreal, a sub-goal should be to learn French. By reaching this sub-goal, you move closer to reaching your ultimate goal—a job in a city that interests you.

> **Work backward.** Sometimes you know the answer to the problem, but not how to get there. Then it's best to work backward. A workback strategy starts at the desired solution or goal and works backward, moving away from the goal. For example, if you have a project due in eight weeks, and you aren't sure how to start it, you might imagine the end result—the finished project—and then work backward to consider how to prepare it.

> **Use a graph, chart, or drawing to redefine the problem.** Transforming words into pictures often can help you to devise solutions that otherwise would elude us. For ideas on how drawing pictures can help you solve problems, you'll want to take a look at the international best-seller *The Back of the Napkin: Solving Problems and Selling Ideas with Pictures*, as well as author Dan Roam's website **www.thebackofthenapkin.com.**

> **Consider the opposite.** You can sometimes solve problems by considering the opposite of the problem you're seeking to solve. For example, to define "good mental health," you might try to define "bad mental health."

> **Use analogies.** Some problems can be solved through the use of an **analogy,** which is a comparison between concepts or objects that are alike in some respects, but dissimilar in most others. For instance, if you liken a disastrous family vacation to a voyage on the *Titanic,* you're using an analogy.

> Analogies may help us gain additional insight into the problem at hand, and they may provide an alternative framework for interpreting the information that is provided. For instance, the manufacturers of Pringles potato chips found that they could cut packaging costs if they slightly moistened the chips before packaging them—an idea that came when researchers noticed that dry tree leaves, which normally crumble easily, could be packed together tightly when they were wet.

Analogy
A comparison between concepts or objects that are alike in some respects but dissimilar in most others

> **Take another's perspective.** By viewing a problem from another person's point of view, it is often possible to obtain a new perspective on the problem that will make it easier to solve.

> **Forget about it.** Sometimes it's best simply to walk away from a problem for a while. Just a few hours or days away from a problem may give us enough of a break to jar some hidden solutions from the recesses of our minds. The idea of "sleeping on it" also sometimes works; we may wake up refreshed and filled with new ideas.

> **Approach it in the spirit of "trial and error."** Whether you are solving a problem or making a decision, recognize that what you choose to do is often reversible. You can "dip your toe in," by volunteering part-time in a field that interests you. If it doesn't turn out the way you expected, you can always change gears later. If you research the requirements in advance, you can even try out a "major" in English, and later switch to Psychology, without losing credits towards your degree.

> **Recognize that NOT making a decision IS making a decision.** Keeping things as they are is as much a decision as choosing to change them, and the status quo can sometimes be a viable alternative. But don't let inaction be the result of procrastination, of letting time slip away without making a decision. Let it be a *true* choice.

Try It!

2

Exercise Your Problem-solving Skills

Part A: Working in a group, try to solve these problems.[2] To help you devise solutions, a hint regarding the best strategy to use is included after each problem.

1. A college student has a flat tire on a dark, deserted stretch of country road. He pulls onto the shoulder to change it. After removing the four lug nuts and placing them into the hubcap, he removes the flat tire and takes his spare out of the trunk. As he is moving the spare tire into position, his hand slips and he upsets the hubcap with the lug nuts, which tumble off into the night where he can't find them. What should he do? (*Hint:* Instead of asking how he might find the lug nuts, reframe the problem and ask where else he might find lug nuts.)

2. A construction worker is paving a walk, and needs to add water quickly to the just-poured concrete. She reaches for her pail to get water from a spigot in the front of the house, but suddenly realizes the pail has a large hole in it and cannot be used. As the concrete dries prematurely, she fumbles through her toolbox for tools and materials with which to repair the pail. She finds many tools, but nothing that would serve to patch the pail. The house is locked, and no one is home. What should she do? (*Hint:* When is a pail not a pail?)

3. What day follows the day before yesterday if two days from now will be Sunday? (*Hint:* Break it up, or draw a diagram.)

4. Sadia has four chains, each three links long. She wants to join the four chains into a single, closed chain. Having a link opened costs 2 cents and having a link closed costs 3 cents. How can she have the chains joined for 15 cents? (*Hint:* Can only end links be opened?)

5. What is two-thirds of one-half? (*Hint:* Reverse course.)

6. Toby has three separate large boxes. Inside each large box are two separate medium-sized boxes, and inside each of the medium boxes are four small boxes. How many boxes does Toby have altogether? (*Hint:* Draw it.)

Part B: After working together to solve these problems, consider these questions:

1. Which problems were the easiest to solve, and which were more difficult? Why?

2. Were the hints helpful?

3. Do you think there was more than one solution to any of the problems?

4. Did your initial assumptions about the problem help or hinder your efforts to solve it?

Note: Answers to the problems are found on page 212.

To Try It online, go to Connect for *P.O.W.E.R. Learning and Your Life.*

Test these problem-solving strategies in **Try It! 2**, "Exercise Your Problem-solving Skills," above.

Assess Your Potential Solutions

If a problem clearly has only one answer—a math problem, for example—this step in problem-solving is relatively easy. You should be able to work the problem and figure out whether you've been successful. In contrast, messier problems have several possible solutions, some of which may be more involved and costlier than others. In these cases, it's necessary to compare alternative solutions and choose the best one. For example, suppose you want to surprise your best friend on her birthday. She is studying at a school about 100 kilometres from you, and you need to find a way to get there. You could rent a car, take a bus, or find some other way.

Money is an issue. You will want to figure out how much each alternative costs before choosing one as your solution to the problem. Since every penny you spend getting there is a penny less that you will have to celebrate, you will want to weigh the options carefully.

Finally, spend a bit of time seeing whether there is a way to refine the solution. Is the solution you've devised adequate? Does it address all aspects of the problem? Are there alternative approaches that might be superior? Answering these questions, and refining your solution to address them, can give you confidence that the solution you've come up with is the best. For example, if you're trying to get to your friend's school, you might decide to use the ride board at your school to try to find a ride with someone going there that day. Maybe your friend's family is going to be driving in and could pick you up or could even lend you a car for the trip.

Remember that not every problem has a clear-cut solution. Sometimes we need to be satisfied with a degree of uncertainty and ambiguity. For some of us, such a lack of clarity is difficult, making us uneasy; it may push us to choose a solution—any solution—that seems to solve the problem. Others of us feel more comfortable with ambiguity; but this may lead us to let problems ride without taking steps to resolve the situation.

Either way, it's important to consider what your own problem-solving style is when you seek to identify solutions. And keep in mind that often there is no perfect solution to a problem—only some solutions that are better than others.

Reflect on the Process of Problem-Solving

It's natural to step back and bask in the satisfaction of solving a tough problem. That's fine—but take a moment to consider your success. Each time you solve a problem, you end up a couple steps ahead, but only if you've thought about the process you went through to solve it.

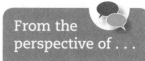

From the perspective of . . .

A PHARMACY TECHNICIAN The ability to ask questions is a trait that will continue to matter in your career. What are some of the potential consequences of not asking questions in a field that presents possible health risks?

Go back and consider what it took to solve the problem. Can the means you used to come up with your solution be applied to more complex kinds of problems? If you arrived at a solution by drawing a chart, would this work on similar problems in the future? Taking a moment to rethink your solution can provide you with an opportunity to become an expert problem solver and, more generally, to improve your critical thinking skills. Don't let the opportunity slip away.

» LO 8.3 Applying Critical Thinking to Everyday Problems

Being able to think clearly and without bias is the basis for critical thinking. As you have probably noticed already, the quality of the thinking you do regarding problems and decisions plays a crucial role in determining how successful you are.

Unfortunately, it is sometimes the alternative you *didn't* think of that can end up being the most satisfactory decision or solution. So how can we learn to think critically and avoid blind spots that hinder us in our decision-making and problem-solving? We can start by considering these common obstacles to critical thinking:

> **Don't assume that giving something a name explains it.** The mere fact that we can give an idea or problem a name doesn't mean we can explain it. Yet we often confuse the two.

For instance, consider the following sequences of questions and answers:

Q. Why do I have so much trouble falling asleep?

A. Because you have insomnia.

Q. Why is he so unsociable?

A. Because he's an introvert.

Q. Why did the defendant shoot those people?

A. Because he's insane.

Q. How do you know he's insane?

A. Because only someone who was insane would shoot people in that way.[3]

It's clear that none of these answers is satisfactory. All use circular reasoning, in which the alleged explanation for the behaviour is simply the use of a label.

> **Don't accept vague generalities dressed up as definitive statements.** Read the following personality analysis and think about how well it applies to you:

You have a need for other people to like and admire you and a tendency to be critical of yourself. You also have a great deal of unused potential that you have not turned to your advantage; but although you have some personality weaknesses, you are generally able to compensate for them. Nonetheless, relating to members of the opposite sex has presented problems to you; and while you appear to be disciplined and self-controlled to others, you tend to be anxious and insecure inside.

If you believe that these statements provide an amazingly accurate description of your unique qualities, you're not alone: Most college and university students believe that the description is tailored specifically to them.[4] But how is that possible? It isn't. The reality is that the statements are so vague that they are virtually meaningless. The acceptance of vague but seemingly useful and significant statements about oneself and others has been called the *Barnum effect*, after showman and circus master P. T. Barnum, who coined the phrase "there's a sucker born every minute."

▸ **Don't confuse opinion with fact.** Opinions are not facts. Although we may be aware of this simple formula, almost all of us can be fooled into thinking that someone's opinion is the same as a fact.

A fact is information that is proven to be true. In contrast, an opinion represents judgments, reasoning, beliefs, inferences, or conclusions. If we accept some bit of information as a fact, we can use it to build our opinions. But if we are presented with an opinion, we need to determine the facts on which the opinion is built to judge its reliability.

The difference between fact and opinion can sometimes be subtle. For instance, compare these two statements:

1. Every student needs to take a writing course during the first term of college or university.

2. Many students need to take a writing course during the first term of college or university.

The first statement is most likely an opinion, because it is so absolute and unqualified. Words such as "every," "all," and "always" are often evidence of opinion. On the other hand, the second statement is more likely a fact, since it contains the qualifier "many." In general, statements that are qualified in some way are more likely to be facts.

Complete **Try It! 3**, "Distinguish Fact from Opinion," on page 206, to see the difficulties sometimes involved in distinguishing between fact and opinion.

▸ **Avoid jumping to conclusions.** Read this riddle and try to answer it:

> *A father and his son were driving along the Trans Canada Highway when the father lost control of the car, swerved off the road, and crashed into a utility pole. The father died instantly, and his son was critically injured. An ambulance rushed the boy to a nearby hospital. A prominent surgeon was summoned to provide immediate treatment. When the surgeon arrived and entered the operating room to examine the boy, a loud gasp was heard.*
>
> *"I can't operate on this boy," the surgeon said. "He is my son."*

How can this be?

If you find this puzzling, you've based your reasoning on an assumption: that the surgeon is a male. But suppose you had assumed that the surgeon was a female. Suddenly, the riddle becomes a lot easier. It's far easier to guess that the surgeon is the son's mother if we don't leap to embrace a faulty assumption.

Why is it so easy to jump to conclusions? One reason is that we sometimes aren't aware of the assumptions that underlie our thinking. Another is our reliance on "common sense."

▸ **Be skeptical of "common sense."** Much of what we call common sense makes contradictory claims. For example, if you believe in the notion "Absence makes the heart grow fonder," you may assume that your girlfriend, now working at a job in another city, will arrive home at Christmas even more in love with you than before. But what about "Out of sight, out of mind," which

Try It!

Distinguish Fact from Opinion

Read the following statements and try to determine which are facts (put "F" on the line that follows the item) and which are opinions (put "O" on the line that follows the item).

1. College and university students should get at least seven hours of sleep every night. _____

2. The average college or university student sleeps less than seven hours a night. _____

3. Nike offers better styling and comfort than any other brand of shoe. _____

4. Two out of five sports figures surveyed preferred Nike over Converse shoes. _____

5. Government figures show spending in Canada is much higher for health than for education. _____

6. Sidney Crosby is the most outstanding, most exciting, and certainly most successful hockey player who ever stepped onto the ice. _____

Items 1, 3, and 6 are opinions; the rest are facts. What are the main differences between opinion and fact?

To Try It online, go to Connect for *P.O.W.E.R. Learning and Your Life*.

Using Critical Thinking in Your Classes

Nowhere is critical thinking more important to use—and demonstrate to your instructors—than when you're in your classes. Here are some strategies to foster your skills as a critical thinker when you are in class:

- **Ask questions.** Most instructors welcome questions. Even if an instructor doesn't have time to provide a full response, the very act of formulating a question will help you think more critically about the course material.

- **Accept that some questions have no right or wrong answers.** Understanding that some questions have no simple answer is a sign of mental sophistication. Sometimes the best an instructor can do is present competing theories. Although you may want to know which theory is right, accept that sometimes no one knows the answer to that question—that's why they're theories, not facts!

- **Keep an open mind.** Your instructor and classmates have their own perspectives and opinions. Even if you disagree with them, try to figure out why they hold their views. It will help you to see the multiple sides of different issues.

- **Don't deny your emotional reactions—manage them.** There may be times when an instructor or classmate says something that is bothersome or even makes you angry. That's OK. But be sure to manage your emotions so that they don't overwhelm your rational self. And use your emotional reactions to gain understanding of what's important to you.

- **Don't be afraid of looking unintelligent.** No one wants to look foolish, especially in front of a roomful of classmates. But don't let self-defeating feelings prevent you from expressing your concerns. Take intellectual risks!

suggests a less positive outcome? Common sense often presents us with contradictory advice, making it a less than useful guide to decision-making and problem-solving.

> **Don't assume that just because two events occur together one causes the other.** Just because two events appear to be associated with one another, we cannot conclude that one event has caused the other to occur. Suppose you read that a study showed that 89 percent of juvenile delinquents use marijuana. Does this mean that smoking marijuana *causes* juvenile delinquency?

No, it doesn't. It is pretty safe to say that 100 percent of juvenile delinquents grew up drinking milk. Would you feel comfortable saying that milk causes delinquency? With the association between marijuana use and delinquent behaviour, it is very likely that there's some third factor—such as the influence of peers—that causes people both to (a) try drugs and (b) engage in delinquent behaviour. The bottom line: We do not know that marijuana use is the cause of the delinquency just because delinquents often smoke marijuana.

In short, we need to be careful in assuming causality. Even if two events or other kinds of variables occur together, it it is not necessarily true that one causes the other. To see this for yourself, take a look at the statements in **Try It! 4**, "What's the Real Explanation?" on page 208.

4

What's the Real Explanation?

Even though two events are related to each other, it doesn't mean that one causes the other. Instead, there is often some other factor that is the actual cause of the relationship.

To see this for yourself, consider each of the following (actual!) findings. What might be a plausible explanation for each one?

1. Ice cream sales and the timing of shark attacks are highly related. Why?

2. The number of cavities children have and the size of their vocabulary are closely related. Why?

3. Skirt hemlines tend to rise as stock prices rise. Why?

4. Women with breast implants have a higher rate of suicide than those without breast implants. Why?

5. People who own washing machines are more likely to die in car accidents than those who don't. Why?

Once you've completed this **Try It!,** look at the possible explanations on page 212. Keep in mind that these are simply theories; we don't know for sure if they're correct.

To Try It online, go to Connect for *P.O.W.E.R. Learning and Your Life.*

Apply Decision-making and Problem-solving Techniques to Everyday Life

In this chapter, you've learned about many tools and techniques that can help you with the problems you encounter and the decisions you have to make while pursuing your post-secondary education. You may be under the impression that it's only worth using these techniques to solve the *big* problems and make the *big* decisions—should you have children, should you change careers, or when should you retire, for example—but they apply equally to the little decisions. And it doesn't stop there. Whether it's a pro/con list, a decision tree, a chart to help you weigh alternatives, or freewriting, you will find that you will return to the techniques introduced in this chapter again and again, in all facets of your life, and through its many stages. For suggestions on the decision-making and problem-solving techniques that best suit your striving style, see the recommendations provided in the sidebar.

Decision-making, Problem-solving, and Striving Styles™

Leaders
Approach problems logically, systematically, and objectively. Weigh options and alternatives. Can be reactive to problems when stressed.

Socializers
Use value judgments to decide (good/bad, right/wrong). Consider impact of decisions on people. Can ignore facts and details.

Performers
Approach problems as a challenge. Great at weighing pros and cons and arguing both sides. Can change their minds many times in process and fail to conclude.

Adventurers
Prefer using instincts to decide. Don't like to delve into weighing options. Need to move to action to attempt to solve the problem.

Artists
Use subjective criteria for decision-making. Value judgments (good/bad, right/wrong) influence approach. Problems that evoke emotion are challenging.

Intellectuals
Gather information to assess alternatives. Can spend too much time weighing options. Can come up with unique solutions and alternatives.

Visionaries
Arrive at a decision intuitively, and then support it with facts and details. Generate lots of options. Try to make facts fit their decision even when they don't.

Stabilizers
Use a prescribed framework for making decisions. Like to decide quickly without too much consideration. Can get overwhelmed by too many alternatives.

Time to Reflect: What Did I Learn?

1. Generally speaking, how would you characterize your decision-making skills?

2. In what way(s) does your approach to decision-making reflect your Striving Style?

3. Based on what you learned about decision-making in this chapter, what do you plan to do differently when making decisions in the future? Be specific.

Looking Back

How can I improve the quality of my decisions?

▸ A structured process of decision-making can clarify the issues involved, expand your options, and improve the quality of your choices.

▸ Good decision-making begins with understanding your short- and long-term goals.

▸ Decision-making is improved if you have a large number of alternatives.

▸ For difficult decisions, strategies include taking time to make the decision, acting out alternatives, tossing a coin to test your feelings, seeking advice, and acting on gut feelings.

What strategies can I use for problem-solving?

▸ Problem-solving entails the generation of alternatives to consider.

▸ You need to first understand and define the problem and to determine the important elements in coming to a solution to a problem.

▸ Approaches to generating solutions include breaking problems into pieces, working backward, using pictures, considering the opposite, using analogies, taking another's perspective, and "forgetting" the problem.

▸ Problem-solving ultimately requires the evaluation and refinement of the solutions that have been generated.

What are some problems that affect critical thinking?

▸ Labelling, using vague generalities, accepting opinion as fact, jumping to conclusions, mistaking common sense for logic, and assuming causation all pose threats to critical thinking.

[KEY TERMS AND CONCEPTS]

Analogy (p. 201)

Critical thinking (p. 192)

Decision-making (p. 192)

Freewriting (p. 193)

Problem-solving (p. 200)

[RESOURCES]

ON CAMPUS

Some colleges and universities offer courses in critical thinking, and they are a good bet to help increase decision-making and problem-solving skills. In addition, courses in logic and philosophy will help improve critical thinking skills.

If you are having a personal problem that is difficult to solve, don't hesitate to turn to staff at the counselling centre at your college or university or to your local mental health centre. Trained counsellors and therapists can help you sort through the different options in an objective manner. They may help you to identify possibilities for solutions that you didn't even know existed. Even if the person with whom you speak initially is not the right one, he or she can direct you to someone who can help.

If you need career counselling, staff at your campus counselling centre or career centre are the people to approach for assistance. They have access to a wide range of resources that can help you narrow down your career choices.

IN PRINT

If you have trouble making good decisions, then check out *Learning to Think Things Through: A Guide to Critical Thinking Across the Curriculum,* by Gerald M. Nosich (Prentice Hall, 2008). It is an excellent, concise guide to improving your decision-making skills.

In addition, *Asking the Right Questions: A Guide to Critical Thinking,* 9th ed. (Prentice Hall, 2009) teaches readers how to effectively consider alternative points of view while making personal choices.

ON THE WEB

The following websites provide the opportunity to extend your learning about the material in this chapter.

➤ "Guidelines to Problem-Solving and Decision-Making" (**www.managementhelp.org/ prsn_prd/prob_slv.htm**) by Carter McNamara, PhD, provides seven steps to effective problem-solving and decision-making. This site is rich in links to comprehensive approaches to decision-making, critical and creative thinking, time management, and organizing yourself.

➤ Metropolitan Community College's Critical Thinking Project site (**http://mcckc. edu/main.asp?L=CoreNotesIntro**), coordinated by Michael Connelly of Longview Community College, presents principles of critical thinking with exercises and examples. The site contains a short history of logic and answers the question, "What is the point of studying critical thinking?"

[ANSWERS TO TRY IT! 2 PROBLEMS]

1. Remove one lug nut from each of the other three tires on the car and use these three to attach the spare tire. This will hold until four more lug nuts can be purchased.
2. Dump the tools out of the toolbox and use it as a pail.
3. Thursday.
4. Open all three links on one chain (cost = 6 cents) and use them to fasten the other three chains together (cost = 9 cents; total cost = 15 cents).
5. It is the same as one-half of two-thirds, or one-third.
6. 33 boxes (3 large, 6 medium, 24 small).

[ANSWERS TO TRY IT! 4 PROBLEMS]

1. The actual cause is probably the temperature, which causes both sales of ice cream and ocean swimming to increase.
2. Both the number of cavities children have and the size of their vocabularies are related to their age.
3. Skirt hemlines go up, as does the stock market, when people are feeling less conservative and more optimistic.
4. Having breast implants and committing suicide both may be a result of unhappiness or a poor self-image.
5. People who own washing machines are more likely to own cars, and therefore they stand a higher risk of dying in a car crash.

TAKING IT TO THE NET

1   Making good decisions can depend on distinguishing legitimate appeals (good reasons) from fallacious appeals (bad reasons). Go to San Jose State University's "Mission: Critical," an interactive tutorial in critical thinking (**www.sjsu.edu/depts/itl/graphics/adhom/appeal.html**). After reading the description of the different kinds of fallacious appeals, do the related exercises.

2   Locate three problem-solving strategies on the Internet. Possible strategy: Go to Yahoo! (**http://ca.yahoo.com**) or AltaVista (**www.altavista.com**), and enter the key phrase "problem-solving." Search the results until you find at least three different problem-solving strategies. Are these strategies similar to the ones described in the book? If not, how are they different?

The Case of . . .
The Missing Roommate

Megha had a problem.

In June, she and her cousin had rented a three-bedroom apartment near the university and had signed a lease for the two semesters from September to April. They had advertised for a third person on the university's website, and had interviewed several applicants, finally settling on a young nursing student called Neha to be their third roommate. That wasn't the problem, though. The problem was that it was now the day after Labour Day and classes were starting, and Neha had still not shown up.

Concerned, Megha called her—and the nursing student brusquely told her she'd found a better place and wouldn't be sharing the apartment with Megha and her cousin after all. Then she hung up. Suddenly Megha was left with an empty room, and without Neha's share of the rent money.

1. Of the problem-solving strategies outlined in this chapter, which would you use to approach this problem?

2. What alternatives does Megha have for dealing with the situation?

3. How should Megha go about evaluating the outcomes for each alternative?

4. Based on your analysis of the problem, what advice would you give Megha for dealing with the situation?

5. Is there anything Megha could have done to avoid this problem in the first place?

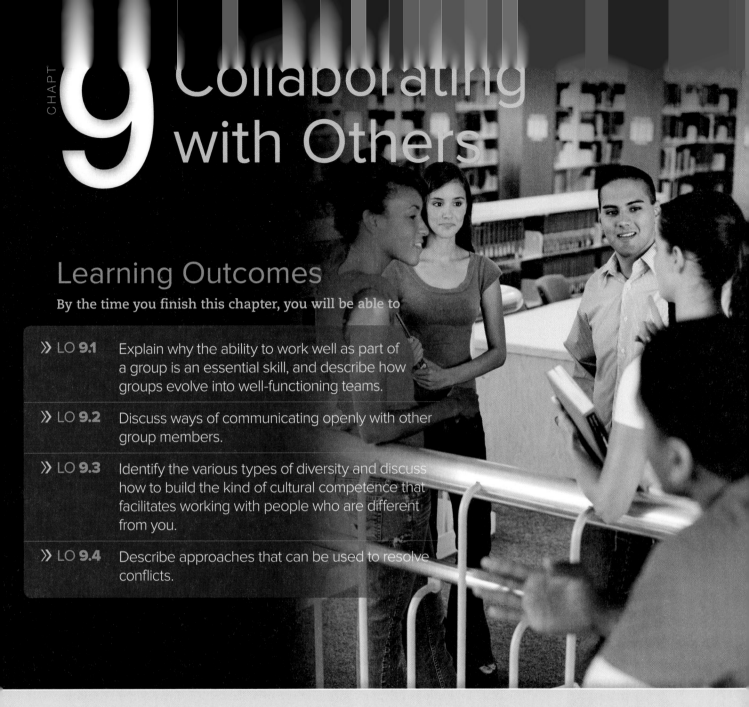

9 Collaborating with Others

Learning Outcomes

By the time you finish this chapter, you will be able to

>> LO **9.1**   Explain why the ability to work well as part of a group is an essential skill, and describe how groups evolve into well-functioning teams.

>> LO **9.2**   Discuss ways of communicating openly with other group members.

>> LO **9.3**   Identify the various types of diversity and discuss how to build the kind of cultural competence that facilitates working with people who are different from you.

>> LO **9.4**   Describe approaches that can be used to resolve conflicts.

His parents immigrated to Canada from Tanzania. He was born in Toronto and moved to Calgary as an infant. He attended public schools in northeast Calgary and went on to graduate with a Bachelor of Commerce degree in 1994 from the University of Calgary, where he also served as President of the Student Union. By 1998, he had obtained a Master's degree in public policy from Harvard University and had jump-started his career at highly respected global consulting firm McKinsey & Company. By the age of 30, he became a Board member and eventually Chair of the Board of the EPCOR Centre for the Performing Arts in Calgary, the largest performing arts centre in western Canada. A few years later, he started his own business and became the first tenured professor of non-profit management in Canada. He was one of 190 people chosen from a pool of nearly 5000 candidates for the World Economic Forum's list of Young Global Leaders (YGLs) for 2011. Bill Graveland of the Canadian Press described him as "young, funny, educated, a visible minority and a Muslim." Supporters on his website, **www.purplerevolution.ca**, referred to him as "a real people person," "a team player," and "willing to listen to people's ideas." His grassroots election campaign was built from the ground up, using the power of collaboration and the leverage of social media.

He is Naheed Nenshi, who at age 38 became mayor of Calgary, the first Muslim mayor of a major Canadian city.

Looking Ahead

Whether you are Catholic or Muslim or Hindu, have a Stabilizer or a Visionary Striving Style, were born in India or China or Lethbridge, are able-bodied or physically challenged—whatever your background, post-secondary education presents a world of new opportunities for you to encounter people with very different backgrounds and perspectives from your own. If you take the opportunity to work with and form relationships with a variety of individuals, you will increase your understanding of the human experience and greatly enrich your life. This will also benefit you enormously in your career, because, whatever your field, you will inevitably find yourself in situations where success will depend on your ability to collaborate effectively with people different from yourself.

In this chapter, we address the issue of teamwork as an essential life skill. We examine how groups are formed and how they evolve into smoothly functioning teams. We put forth practical strategies for communicating with others and working well in a group environment. We look at how diversity can enhance your academic and life experience and the importance of being receptive to others based on their own merits. Finally, the chapter addresses the conflicts that can arise between people and what you can do to resolve them.

» LO 9.1 Working Productively in Groups

Naheed Nenshi's story is not remarkable because he is Muslim. Nor is it remarkable because he is a visible minority. It isn't even particularly remarkable because he was only 38 years old when he became mayor. What is remarkable about Nenshi's story is that his faith was never an election issue. It was Nenshi's passion for his city, his drive to get things done, and his power to leverage his contacts and social networks like Facebook and Linked In that got him elected—and it will be his ability to work collaboratively with city council that will determine how successful he is as Calgary's mayor. In our increasingly connected and interconnected world, learning to work collaboratively is now, more than ever before, an essential life skill.

No matter where you end up—whether in a lab working on a cure for cancer or in a classroom, teaching six-year-olds—you cannot get there without working with other people and learning from other people. "Plays well with others" is a comment commonly found on elementary school report cards, so it may come as a surprise to you that years later, in college and university and even on the job, your ability to work well with others continues to have a significant impact on your success. Take a look at your course outline or syllabus. It is increasingly common to find that a significant portion of your course grade is related to group work. In some schools, group work has become so important that figuring out whom to work with, how to communicate within a group, and how to move towards a common goal can make the difference between getting a B grade and achieving an A. Building a well-functioning team proceeds in several steps, outlined in the P.O.W.E.R. Plan.

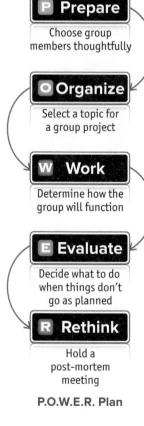

P Prepare

Choose group members thoughtfully

O Organize

Select a topic for a group project

W Work

Determine how the group will function

E Evaluate

Decide what to do when things don't go as planned

R Rethink

Hold a post-mortem meeting

P.O.W.E.R. Plan

P Prepare Choose Group Members Thoughtfully

In some courses, you may not have the luxury of picking your own group members; but if you do, think very carefully about who you want to work with and why. Left to their own devices, students will often make the mistake of working with their friends or will seek out the students with the highest GPAs. While it *is* important that the people you choose to work with have a similar end goal in mind—e.g., you all want a minimum B grade—and that you have compatible schedules to allow for meetings, you do not need to all be extremely intelligent. A recent study published in *Science* magazine found that the most important variables for optimal group performance were these: the average social sensitivity of the group's members, the degree to which each person in the group was allowed to speak in turn, and the proportion of females in the group.[1] The emphasis on social sensitivity and speaking in turn is consistent with the notion advanced by author Daniel Goleman, that "**emotional intelligence**," or EQ, is a better predictor of success in life than the traditional measure known as IQ, or intelligence quotient.

In any group, there will be a leader and there will be followers. Some group members will be smarter than others. There will be people who enjoy doing research, and others who prefer to write up the results. There will be people who understand the content deeply, and others who excel at presenting it in a simple manner that their classmates will understand. What *is* important when selecting group members is to ensure that you have a mix of the skills required to complete the project you've been assigned, that you respect one another and are willing to listen to each other, and finally, that you are sensitive to each other's needs.

 ## Select a Topic for a Group Project Creatively

If your group is given an opportunity to select the topic of the group report, you may want to consider holding a **brainstorming** session to allow everyone in the group an opportunity to contribute ideas. A brainstorming session is a structured process whereby group members generate as many ideas as they can within a specific time frame; no censoring of ideas is permitted, no matter how inane the idea might seem at first. The process allows everyone to contribute and is designed to make everyone feel that "any idea is a good idea." Once the session is over, ideas can be categorized and weeded out, as required, to come up with the best of the best. See **Try It! 1**, "Organize a Brainstorming Session," on page 218, for specific guidelines on how to hold a brainstorming session.

 ## Determine How the Group Will Function

Some years ago, psychologist Bruce Tuckman proposed that a highly functioning team, whether set up for a temporary purpose or as a permanent group, would pass through five stages: He called those **stages in a group's evolution** forming, storming, norming, performing, and adjourning. Recognizing this evolution and adjusting to what happens in each stage can help you and your group members understand how groups evolve and how to become a high-performing group.

Emotional intelligence (EQ)

According to Daniel Goleman, having high emotional intelligence, or EQ, means possessing "abilities such as being able to motivate oneself and persist in the face of frustrations; to control impulse and delay gratification; to regulate one's moods and keep distress from swamping the ability to think; to empathize and to hope"[2]

Brainstorming

A process whereby ideas are generated by a group following a specific set of rules that do not permit censoring or critiquing of ideas as they are generated

Stages in a group's evolution

According to psychologist Bruce Tuckman, all well-functioning groups go through five stages: forming, storming, norming, performing, and adjourning

Analyzing the results of a brainstorming session

Try It!

Organize a Brainstorming Session

Task: Your marketing instructor would like your group to come up with ideas for a new application for the iPhone.

1. Explain the rules of brainstorming:
   a) Don't censor your own ideas before stating them. Allow every thought to come out as you are thinking it. Feel free to suggest your wildest, craziest ideas.
   b) Every idea is a good idea. Don't critique anyone else's ideas.
   c) Build on the ideas of others. You are going for quantity, *not* quality.
2. Assign someone to capture every idea. He or she can write the ideas on a flip chart, or record them on individual sticky notes and stick them to a wall. Keep generating ideas until no one can think of any more. When everyone runs out of steam, the brainstorming part of your session is over.
3. Either with the same group, or with a different group, develop a set of criteria against which you can assess the ideas that have been generated; e.g., can implement immediately, cheap to do, interesting to all/most members of group, etc.
4. Go back through each idea, assessing it against your set of criteria, eliminating some and creating a list in order of priority with the others.

To Try It online, go to Connect for *P.O.W.E.R. Learning and Your Life*.

The "Forming" Stage

In the forming stage of a group's evolution, which may last only as long as the very first group meeting, group members usually feel one another out, trying to determine how the group will work and what role each person will play. Some members may want to jump right in and get to work, but an upfront investment in planning will pay off later on. At the forming stage, some of the things that should be established are these:

> Members' grade expectations, and the time commitment they are willing to make to achieve it (if this has not already been determined during the group selection stage).

> When, where, and how often the group will meet. Exchanging timetables and detailed contact information is critical at this stage, as is identifying a time and meeting spot that is convenient to all group members.

> How the workload will be divided up. You may want to get the instructor's guidance on this to ensure that some group members are not shouldering a heavier load than others.

> Who will be responsible for what. This includes responsibilities for the actual functioning of the group, including who will lead meetings and take minutes. As for the actual project, try to allocate the work in a way that leverages group members' individual strengths. If someone is good with Excel, for example, they should be assigned the section on spreadsheets and graphs.

Team charter

A set of written guidelines that outline the rules, roles, and responsibilities of team members, and set out how a team plans to operate towards achieving its goals.

The group may wish to consider drawing up a **team charter** that puts rules, roles, and responsibilities for the group and its project into writing. A sample charter is shown in Figure 9.1 on the next page. For detailed guidelines on how to draw up a team charter, see the "On the Web" resource section at the end of this chapter.

> *Sample Team Charter*
>
> 1. *Group members will attend all group meetings.*
> 2. *Group meetings will be held every Friday from 12:30–2:30 in B416.*
> 3. *We will start and end group meetings on time & all meetings will have an agenda.*
> 4. *Each member of the group is responsible for getting his/her work done by the agreed-upon time.*
> 5. *Group members will use the team's Office Live site as the repository for all of their work.*

figure 9.1
A team charter

 **Evaluate**

React Positively When Things Don't Go as Planned

The "Storming" Stage

It is normal and natural in the evolution of a team for disagreements and conflict to arise. These might involve who should be the leader, or how the work should be done, or even what the work should entail. Many groups disintegrate at this point, with some members giving up entirely and deciding not to do the work they'd promised. During this stage, it is useful to evaluate where team members stand with respect to their ongoing commitment to the team and its objectives. Keeping lines of communication open, ensuring everyone has an opportunity to contribute, and dealing with situations as soon they arise are important to moving to the next stage.

How might your striving style affect how you collaborate with others? You'll want to examine the sidebar for suggestions. Specific suggestions for communicating with other team members and resolving conflicts are also provided in this chapter.

The "Norming" Stage

At this stage of a group's evolution, the group is beginning to gel: Members have settled into their roles and accepted their responsibilities, and there is palpable commitment to achieving the group's objectives. There may be an occasional lapse back into the storming stage; but for the most part, the foundation work of getting the team to move in one direction has been accomplished.

The "Performing" Stage

Once groups have reached the performing stage, most of the friction has gone out of the equation: The focus has shifted to working together to get the task done. Unfortunately in the case of groups who tend to procrastinate, this stage is reached far too close to the project deadline, and quality suffers as a result.

 **Rethink**

Hold a Post-mortem Meeting

The "Adjourning" Stage

Unless there is another project in the offing, the adjourning stage is usually reached once the group disbands, after having received a grade on the project they have

Collaborating with others and Striving Styles™

Leaders
Organize and lead groups. Create rules, roles, and structure and hold others accountable. Will take over when others don't contribute.

Socializers
Do best cooperating and working on teams. Try to get others to work together, managing conflict and helping with work of others.

Performers
Enjoy working on teams, but want to be recognized for own contribution. Project must reflect their abilities even if it means doing the work of others.

Adventurers
Need to work with others to stay motivated. Will make the team process fun, but won't always meet commitments.

Artists
Take a low key role on teams and contribute what is expected. Prefer to work independently. Expectation of others creates anxiety.

Intellectuals
Prefer to work independently or in the role of researcher on the team. Can procrastinate and fail to deliver. Play devil's advocate.

Visionaries
Independent thinkers who prefer to work alone. On a team, will encourage people to think outside the box. Need for ideas and insight contributed to be used.

Stabilizers
Need clear roles and rules on the team. Will deliver precisely what is expected Frustrated by others who don't follow rules.

CHAPTER NINE Collaborating with Others **219**

submitted. One of the most important things a group can do at this stage is to hold a "post-mortem" meeting, where they discuss what worked and what didn't, and how to do things differently the next time. Unfortunately, student groups rarely bother with this stage, and it is often left up to the individual—that's you!—to reflect on what he or she has learned from the process.

LO 9.2 Communicating Well with Others

Communicating well in a group setting is a blend of talking and listening. Not only does it help to do both well, but it is also important to know when it's time to listen and when it's time to speak up. Listening is an often underrated skill. When working closely with others, we may be so busy trying to communicate our opinions and perspective that we overlook the need of the others to be heard. As you work collaboratively with others towards a common goal, doing all the talking simply isn't enough. Knowing when to talk and when to stop talking and listen, and knowing how to express yourself, especially in moments of difficulty, can be very important to getting your message across.

Be a Good Listener

Supportive silence is very powerful. When it comes to working with others on a group project, how you listen is sometimes more important than what you say. The silence involved in listening is a powerful force, one that can bind us more closely to others.

We've already discussed the art and science of listening as it applies to academic success in Chapter 4. The same principles that promote learning about lecture topics also promote learning about the people we work with in an academic setting and in our future career. You can't call yourself a team player without knowing what others are like and what they are thinking. Good listening is one of the ways to enhance your understanding of others.

When we feel we are heard, we get the message that our listeners care about our opinions, not just their own. Similarly, when we listen, we show that we have respect for those who are speaking, that we are interested in their ideas and beliefs, and that we are willing to take the time to pay attention to them.

There are several ways you can improve your ability to listen:

> **Stop talking!** Are you the kind of person who revels in giving your opinions on every subject? Do you wait eagerly for others to finish what they are saying so that you can jump in with your perspective? Do you accidentally cut other people off or finish their sentences while they are still speaking?

>   No one likes to be interrupted, even in casual conversation. People who are more introverted, or for whom English is a second language, may need more time to organize and present their thoughts. Ensure that all group members are given an opportunity to voice an opinion. And when they do, don't interrupt—you may be amazed by what you learn.

> **Demonstrate that you are listening.** Linguists call them **conversational markers**—those nonverbal indications that we're listening. They consist of head nods, uh-huhs, OKs, and other signs that we're keeping up with the conversation. Eye contact is important too. Listening this way shows that we're paying attention and are interested in what the other person is saying.

What you *don't* say also matters. Good teamwork is often built on good listening skills.

Conversational markers

Non-verbal indications that we are listening to what someone else is saying.

When you are listening, *truly* listening, you should not be multi-tasking. If you're having a serious conversation, turn off your cellphone. If your phone rings, don't look at caller ID. Even glancing at your phone for a moment shows you're not paying full attention.

> **Use reflective feedback.** Carl Rogers, a respected therapist, developed a very useful way to lend support to someone and draw him or her out. In **reflective feedback**, a listener rephrases what a speaker has said, trying to echo the speaker's meaning. For example, a listener might say, "If I understand what you're saying, . . ." or "You seem to feel that . . ." or "In other words, you believe that . . ."

Reflective feedback
A technique of active listening in which a listener rephrases what a speaker has said, trying to echo the speaker's meaning

In each case, the summary statement doesn't just "play back" the speaker's statements literally. Instead, it is a rephrasing that captures the essence of the message in different words.

Reflective feedback has two big benefits. First, it provides speakers with a clear indication that you are listening and taking what they're saying seriously. Second, and equally important, it helps ensure that you have an accurate understanding of what the speaker is saying.

> **Ask questions.** Asking questions shows that you are paying attention to a speaker's comments. Questions permit you to clarify what the speaker has said, and he or she can move the conversation forward. Further, people feel valued when others ask them about themselves.

> **Deal with distractions.** We've all had those moments: Something is bothering you and you can't get it out of your mind, or you've simply got to finish something and don't really have time to chat. If at the same time someone wants to engage you in conversation, your distraction will undoubtedly show, making the other person feel you are not interested in her or him.

The way to deal with this situation is to admit that you're distracted. Simply say, "I'd love to talk, but I've got to finish reading a chapter." That should be enough to explain the situation to a classmate who just wants to chat.

You should work to avoid distractions during a preplanned group meeting. Don't hold your meeting in a busy student centre, or where the smell of coffee or food, or the presence of people outside your group, can distract you.

» LO 9.3 Living in a Diverse World

No matter where we live, our contacts with others who are different from us are increasing. The Web is bringing people from across the globe into our homes, as close to us as the computer sitting on the desk in front of us. Businesses now operate globally, so co-workers are likely to come from many different countries and cultures. Being comfortable with people whose backgrounds and beliefs may differ from our own is a necessity, not only socially, but also for career success.

As you can see in the Diversity Wheel in **Figure 9.2** on page 222, diversity encompasses characteristics such as ethnicity, gender, sexual orientation, and age; it also includes mental and physical characteristics, and even work style. Layer on top of all of that factors such as language, religion, and income level, and the complexity of others—and ourselves—becomes apparent.

Ethnicity and Culture

Are you Québécois? Italian? South Asian? Chinese? Aboriginal?

The language we use to describe our ethnic membership, and those of other people, is in constant flux. And what we call people matters. The subtleties of

figure 9.2
Diversity wheel

Diversity is composed of many different characteristics as exemplified by the Diversity Wheel.[3]

Ethnicity

Shared national origins or cultural patterns

Culture

The learned behaviours, beliefs, and attitudes that are characteristic of an individual society or population, and the products that people create

language affect how people think about members of particular groups, and how they think about themselves.

Ethnicity refers to shared national origins or cultural patterns. In Toronto, North America's most multicultural city, half of the city's residents were born outside of Canada. According to the city's website, 200 distinct ethnic origins and 140 languages and dialects are spoken there, and just over 30 per cent of Toronto residents speak a language other than English or French at home.

Culture comprises the learned behaviours, beliefs, and attitudes that are characteristic of an individual society or population. But it's more than that: Culture also encompasses the products that people create, such as architecture, music, art, and literature. Culture is created and shaped by people, but at the same time it contributes to people's behaviour.

Ethnicity and culture shape each of us to an enormous degree. They profoundly influence our view of others, as well as who we are. They affect how others treat us, and how we treat them in turn. They determine whether we look people in the eye when we meet them, how early we arrive when we're invited to dinner at a friend's house, and even, sometimes, how well we do in school or on the job. If many ethnic backgrounds are represented in your class and you'd like to learn more about them, ask your instructor if he or she would consider devoting a class to a potluck, where students bring in a dish that in some way reflects their ethnicity. Then, during the potluck, have each person deliver a short presentation; e.g., "five things I love about being Korean."

One example of cultural differences is related to the decade of your adolescence. The 60s brought us the hippie culture, a subculture within a larger group that became known as the Baby Boomers. The 70s ushered in the "Me Generation." Then came the Generation Xers, the Millennials, the Echo Boomers, and so forth. There was a time in the not-too-distant past when college and university students were drawn from a relatively homogeneous population. These days, universities and colleges are a mosaic of students coming straight out of high school, people returning after a few years off, and those in middle age who've been laid off and are now returning to post-secondary institutions to prepare for a new career. In spite of their different experiences and the fact that they may have grown up in very different times, these students may find themselves collaborating with one another, studying together, and working on group projects. They bring different skill sets to the table, and often they also bring different expectations that can affect group dynamics, as can be seen in **Table 9.1**.

Because some of us grow up in neighbourhoods that are not ethnically diverse, we may have little or even no experience interacting with people who are different

table 9.1 Different Generations View Work Differently

	WORKPLACE CHARACTERISTICS			
	Veterans (1922–1945)	**Baby Boomers (1946–1964)**	**Generation X (1965–1980)**	**Generation Y (1981–2000)**
Work Ethic and Values	Hard work Respect authority Sacrifice Duty before fun Adhere to rules	Workaholics Work efficiently Crusading causes Personal fulfillment Desire quality Question authority	Eliminate the task Self-reliance Want structure and direction Skeptical	What's next Multi-tasking Tenacity Entrepreneurial Tolerant Goal-oriented
Work Is . . .	An obligation	An exciting adventure	A difficult challenge A contract	A means to an end Fulfillment
Leadership Style	Directive Command-and-control	Consensual Collegial	Everyone is the same Challenge others Ask why	*TBD
Interactive Style	Individual	Team player Loves to have meetings	Entrepreneur	Participative
Communications	Formal Memo	In person	Direct Immediate	Email Voice mail
Feedback and Rewards	No news is good news Satisfaction in a job well done	Don't appreciate it Money Title recognition	Sorry to interrupt, but how am I doing? Freedom is the best reward	Whenever I want it, at the push of a button Meaningful work
Messages that Motivate	Your experience is respected	You are valued You are needed	Do it your way Forget the rules	You will work with other bright, creative people
Work and Family Life	Ne'er the twain shall meet	No balance Work to live	Balance	Balance

*As this group has not spent much time in the workforce, this characteristic has yet to be determined.
Source: **www.fdu.edu/newspubs/magazine/05ws/generations.htm**

Try It!

2
Determine the Diversity of Your Community

Try to assess the degree of diversity that exists in your community. "Community" can be a loosely defined term; but for this **Try It!**, think of it as the group of people you encounter and interact with on a regular basis. When thinking of diversity, remember to include the many different ways in which people can be different from one another, including ethnicity, culture, sexual orientation, physical challenges, and so on.

1. Overall, how diverse would you say your community is?

2. Are there organizations in your community that promote diversity? Are there organizations that work to raise the visibility and understanding of particular groups within your community?

3. What is the nature of your university or college's student diversity in terms of statistics regarding membership in different ethnic or cultural groups? (You may be able to find these statistics on your university or college's website.)

4. Is your student community more or less diverse than your community at large? Why do you think this might be?

To Try It online, go to Connect for *P.O.W.E.R. Learning and Your Life*.

Workplace colleagues are increasingly diverse.

Cultural competence
Knowledge and understanding about other ethnic groups, cultures, and minority groups

from us. Depending on where your college or university is located, some campuses don't have much diversity either; and consequently, even in college or university, your exposure to people who have different backgrounds may be limited. But as you move to the larger urban centres, you will quickly realize that Canada is a country of astonishing diversity; and it's not a matter of "if" you will be exposed to people who have profoundly different backgrounds from your own, but "when." Whether in the workplace or the neighbourhood in which you reside, living in a diverse environment will be part of your life. You can examine the diversity around you by completing **Try It! 2**, "Determine the Diversity of Your Community," above.

Accept Diversity as a Valued Part of Your Life

We're not born knowing how to drive a car or cook. We have to learn how to do these things. The same is true of developing a basic understanding of other ethnic groups and cultures. Called **cultural competence,** this knowledge of customs, perspectives, background, and history of others can teach us a great deal, about others and about ourselves. Cultural competence also provides a basis for civic engagement, permitting us to act with civility toward others and to make the most of our contributions to society.

In the title of her book on social diversity, psychologist Beverly Tatum asks, *"Why Are All the Black Kids Sitting Together in the Cafeteria?"*[4] She might just as well have asked a similar question about the white kids, the Asian Canadian kids, and so forth. It often appears as if the world comes already divided into separate ethnic and cultural groups.

It's more than appearances: We form relationships more easily with others who are similar to us than with those who are different. It's more comfortable to interact with others who look the same as we do, who come from similar backgrounds, and who share our ethnicity and culture; we can take for granted certain shared cultural assumptions and views of the world.

But that doesn't mean that "easy" and "comfortable" translate into "good" or "right." We can learn a great deal more, and grow and be challenged, if we seek out people who are different from us. If you look beyond surface differences and find out what motivates other people, you can become aware of new ways of thinking about family, relationships, earning a living, and the value of education. It can be liberating to realize that others may hold very different perspectives from your own and that there are many ways to lead your life.

Letting diversity into your own life also has very practical implications: As we discuss in **Career Connections** on page 226, learning to accept and work with people who are different from you is a crucial skill that will help you in whatever job you hold.

Explore Your Own Prejudices and Stereotypes

South Asian. Gay. Female. Disabled. Overweight.

Quick: What comes into your mind when you think about each of these labels? If you're like most people, you don't draw a blank. Instead, a collection of images and feelings comes into your mind, based on what you know, have been told, or assume about the group. The fact that we don't draw a blank when thinking about each of these terms means that we already have a set of attitudes and beliefs about them and the groups they represent. Acknowledging and then examining these pre-existing assumptions is a first step toward developing cultural competence: We need to explore our own prejudices and stereotypes.

Prejudice refers to evaluations or judgments of members of a group that are based primarily on their membership in the group, rather than on their individual characteristics. For example, the auto mechanic who doesn't expect a woman to understand auto repair or a job supervisor who finds it unthinkable that a father might want to take a leave for child care are engaging in gender prejudice. *Gender prejudice* is evaluating individuals on the basis of their being male or female and not on their own specific characteristics or abilities. Similarly, prejudice can be directed toward individuals because of their ethnic origin, sexual orientation, age, physical disability, or even physical attractiveness.

Prejudice leads to discrimination. **Discrimination** is behaviour directed toward individuals on the basis of their membership in a particular group. Discrimination can result in exclusion from jobs and educational opportunities. It also may result in members of particular groups receiving lower salaries and benefits.

Prejudice and discrimination are maintained by **stereotypes,** beliefs and expectations about members of a group. For example, do you think that women don't drive as well as men? Do you agree that "white men can't jump"? Do you believe that people raised in the less developed countries are less intelligent than those raised in a western society? Do you think that people on welfare are lazy? If you answered yes to any of these questions, you hold stereotypes about the group being referred to. It is the degree of generalization involved that makes stereotypes inaccurate. Some white men can't jump. But the fact is, many can—and do—and the stereotypes ignore this diversity.

To develop cultural competence, it's important to identify our prejudices and stereotypes and to fight them. Sometimes they are quite subtle and difficult to detect. For instance, a wealth of data taken from observing elementary school classrooms shows that teachers are often more responsive to boys than to girls. The teachers don't know they're doing it; it's a subtle, but very real, bias.

From the perspective of . . .

A STUDENT Having a varied classroom can help you see the world in a broader way. Have you ever had a classmate relate an experience that had a major impact on your thought process?

Prejudice
Evaluations or judgments of members of a group that are based primarily on membership in the group and not on the particular characteristics of individuals

Discrimination
Behaviour directed toward individuals on the basis of their membership in a particular group

Stereotypes
Beliefs and expectations about members of a group that are held simply because of their membership in the group

Diversity in the Workplace

Diversity, and issues relating to it, are a part of today's workplace. Employers must deal daily with issues ranging from whether time off for religious holidays should count as vacation time to whether the partner of a gay or lesbian worker should be covered by the worker's medical insurance.

The gulf in the workplace between people with different cultural backgrounds may be wide. For instance, an immigrant from Japan might consider it the height of immodesty to outline his or her accomplishments in a job interview. The explanation? In Japan, the general cultural expectation is that people should stress their incompetence; to do otherwise would be considered highly immodest and inappropriate.

The increasing diversity of the workplace means that increasing your cultural competence will serve you well. It will help you perform on work teams that are composed of people of different ethnic backgrounds; it will help you supervise people whose native language and customs may be different from yours; and it will help you to work for a boss from another country and cultural background.

Equally important, gaining cultural competence will help you respond to the legal issues that surround diversity. It is illegal for employers to discriminate on the basis of ethnic background, age, gender, and physical disability. Cultural competence will help you not only to deal with the letter of the law, but also to understand why embracing diversity is so important to getting along with others in the workplace.

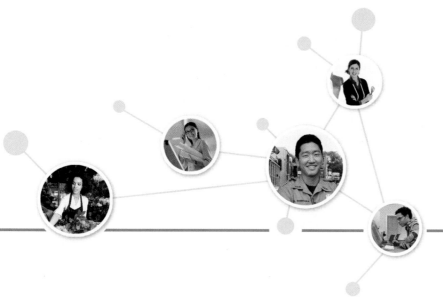

Why does this happen? In part it's because we're exposed to stereotypes from a very young age. Parents and relatives teach them to us, sometimes unwittingly, sometimes deliberately. The media illustrate them constantly and often in very subtle ways. For instance, men in the movies are often portrayed as action heroes, career women like Miranda in *Sex and the City* are seen as strident, and gay men are frequently depicted as effeminate.

> "Honouring one's own identity need not mean rejecting others"
>
> **The Aga Khan**

But it's not only stereotypes that lead us to view members of other groups differently from those of our own. For many people, their own membership in a cultural or ethnic group is a source of pride and self-worth. There's nothing wrong with this. However, these feelings can lead to a less desirable outcome: the belief that their own group is superior to others. As a result, people inflate the positive aspects of their own group and belittle groups to which they do not belong. The bottom line is continuing prejudice.

To fight prejudice and to overcome stereotypes, work to develop cultural competence. Identify and conquer your own prejudices.

Develop Cultural Competence

Although it's neither easy nor simple to increase your understanding of and sensitivity to other cultures, it can be done. Several strategies are effective:

> **Study other cultures and customs.** Take an anthropology course, study religion, or learn history. If you understand the purposes behind different cultural customs, attitudes, and beliefs, you will be able to understand the richness and meaning of other people's cultural heritage.

> **Become more aware of your own culture.** We tend to believe that the way our culture does things is the way everyone does things. But this is not the case. Look at some of your own celebrations to raise your awareness of practices that you take for granted but which people from other cultural backgrounds might find strange.

Travel provides us with an opportunity to become immersed in very different cultures and to see the world—and ourselves—through different eyes.

> **Travel.** There is no better way to learn about people from other cultures than to see those cultures firsthand. Investigate student exchange programs at your college or university. Volunteer for study or work terms in other provinces or overseas. If you have some time off in the summer or between semesters, consider buying a cross-Canada student pass for the bus or the train. If you are short on time or money, focus on exploring the different neighbourhoods in the city or town that you are living in. No matter where you go, just finding yourself in a new context can aid your efforts to learn about other cultures.

> **Participate in community service.** By becoming involved in community service, such as tutoring middle-school students, volunteering to work with the homeless, or working on an environmental cleanup, you get the opportunity to interact with people who may be very different from those you're accustomed to.

> **Don't ignore people's backgrounds.** None of us is blind to ethnicity. Or to culture. It's impossible to be completely unaffected by people's ethnic and cultural backgrounds. So why pretend to be? Cultural heritage is an important part of everyone's identity, and to pretend that someone's background doesn't exist and has no impact on them is unrealistic at best, and insulting at worst. It's important, though, to distinguish between accepting the fact that other people's backgrounds affect them and pigeonholing people, expecting them to behave in particular ways.

> **Don't make assumptions about who people are.** Don't assume that someone is heterosexual just because most people are heterosexual. Don't assume that someone with an Italian-sounding last name is Italian. Don't assume that a Filipino has two Filipino parents.

> **Accept differences.** Different does not mean better. Different does not mean worse. Different just means different—not looking, acting, or believing exactly the same as you. We shouldn't attach any kind of value to being different; it's neither better nor worse than being similar.

In fact, even people who seem obviously different on the surface probably share many similarities with you. Like you, they have commitments to family or loved ones; they have fears and anxieties like yours; and they have aspirations and dreams, just as you do.

The important point about differences is that we need to accept and embrace them. Think about how different you may be even from people who are similar to you in culture and upbringing. Perhaps you really can't stand baseball, yet one of your childhood friends has followed the game since he was five and loves it. Chances are you both accept that you have different tastes and see this difference as part of who you are.

Check Your Progress in Attaining Cultural Competence

Because you will often meet and work with people from other cultural groups, developing cultural competence is an ongoing process. To evaluate where you stand, ask yourself the following questions:

> Do I make judgments about others based on external features, such as skin colour, ethnic background, cultural customs, gender, weight, or physical appearance?

> Who are my friends? Do they represent diversity, or are they generally similar to me?

> Do I openly express positive values relating to diversity? Do I sit back passively when others express stereotypes and prejudices, or do I actively question their remarks?

> Am I educating myself about the history and varying experiences of different ethnic and cultural groups?

> Do I give special treatment to members of particular groups, or am I even-handed in my relationships?

> Do I recognize that, despite surface differences, all people have the same basic needs and desires?

> Do I feel so much pride in my own ethnic and cultural heritage that it leads me to look less favourably upon members of other groups?

> Do I seek to understand events and situations through the perspectives of others and not just my own?

Understand How Your Own Ethnic and Cultural Background Affects Others

If you are a member of a group that traditionally has been the target of prejudice and discrimination, you probably don't need to be told that your ethnicity and cultural background affect the way that others treat you. But even if you are a member of a traditionally dominant group in society, the way in which others respond to you is, in part, a result of others' assumptions about the group of which you are a part.

In short, both how we view others and how we ourselves are viewed are affected by the groups to which we—and others—belong. But keep this in mind: No matter how different other students, co-workers, or community members are from you in terms of their ethnicity and cultural background, they undoubtedly share many of the same concerns you do. Like all of us, they question themselves, wonder whether

Diversity in the Classroom

The increasing diversity of classrooms presents both opportunity and challenge. The opportunity comes from the possibility of learning on a first-hand basis about others and their experiences. The challenge comes when people who may be very different from us call into question some of our most fundamental beliefs and convictions.

Here are some ways that you can be better equipped to deal with the classroom challenges involved in diversity:

- **Present your opinions in a respectful manner.** Don't get annoyed or angry when others disagree with your point of view. Be tolerant of others' perspectives and their thinking.

- **Don't assume you can understand what it's like to be a member of another ethnicity, cultural group, or gender.** Talk about your own experiences, and don't assume you know what others have experienced.

- **Don't treat people as representatives of the groups to which they belong.** Don't ask someone how members of his or her ethnic or cultural group think, feel, or behave with respect to a particular issue. No single individual can speak for an entire group. Group members are likely to display little uniformity on most issues and in most behaviours. Consequently, this type of question is ultimately impossible to answer.

- **Seek out students who are different from you.** If you are assigned a group project, volunteer to work with students who are different from you. You may learn more working with them than with those who are like you.

- **Don't be afraid to offer your opinion out of concerns for "political correctness."** If you offer an opinion in a respectful, thoughtful, and tolerant manner, you should feel free to voice your opinion. Even if your views are minority opinions, they deserve to be considered.

they will be successful, and fret about making ends meet. Bridging the surface difference between you and others can result in the development of close, lasting social ties. (See Course Connections, above, for more insights related to diversity in your college or university.)

LO 9.4 Managing and Resolving Conflicts

Group work is an unavoidable part of the academic experience and, for many students, it is often the most frustrating. Group members don't show up for meetings, or they don't do what they said they'd do, or they drop out of the class you share midway through the semester and don't tell anyone. Disagreements may arise through cultural misunderstanding. When conflicts of any type occur—as they will from time to time—communication can fall apart. These situations test your ability to communicate effectively. Using the active listening strategies discussed earlier will be helpful. Here are some other approaches that will help you resolve conflict in your group. (These approaches will also serve you well at work and in personal relationships.)

Use "I" Statements to Defuse Anger

Suppose a group member says something with which you disagree: "All you guys are the same—you always expect to get everything your way!" You might respond by directing anger at the other person, directly or indirectly accusing the person of some imperfection. "You're always looking for something to complain about!" Such responses (and, as you will notice, the initial statement) typically include the word "you." For instance, consider these possible responses to indicate disagreement: "*You* really don't understand", "*You're* being stubborn", and "How can *you* say that?"

These types of statements cast blame, make accusations, express criticism, and make assumptions about what's inside the other person's head. And they inevitably lead to defensive replies that will probably do little to move the conversation forward: "I am *not!*", "I do so understand", "I'm *not* being stubborn", and "I can say that because that's the way I feel."

A far more effective approach is to use "I" statements. **"I" statements** cast responses in terms of yourself and your individual interpretation. Instead of saying, for example, "You really don't understand," a more appropriate response would be, "I think we're misunderstanding each other." "You're being stubborn" could be rephrased as "I feel like you're not really listening." And "Why don't you call when you're going to be late?" becomes "I worry that something has happened to you when you don't call if you are going to be late." In each case, "I" statements permit you to state your reaction in terms of your perception or understanding, rather than as a critical judgment about the other person. (Practise using "I" statements in **Try It! 3**, "Switch 'You' to 'I'.")

"I" statements

Responses spoken in terms of oneself and one's individual interpretation, rather than casting blame on the other person

From the perspective of . . .

A HUMAN RESOURCES SPECIALIST Relationships are a key part of a productive professional environment. What might you need to know about fostering positive relationships in your professional life?

Create a Win–Win Proposition

Even with careful attention to putting our own feelings forward instead of making accusations, whenever people share their thoughts, concerns, fears, and opinions with each other, the chances are that sooner or later some sort of conflict will arise.

Conflict is not necessarily bad; in fact, it is often necessary to achieve progress.

Often, people are upset simply by the fact that they are having a conflict. It is as though they believe conflicts don't occur in a "good" group. But the opposite is true. Conflict can be helpful in some very important ways: It can force us to say what is really on our minds, it can encourage us to clear up misconceptions and miscommunications before they begin to undermine the team, it can lead to creative solutions, and it can even give us practice at resolving conflicts with others outside the group.

Outside the context of academic group work, conflict is not necessarily a bad thing, either. In the working world, conflict is often inevitable. Yet as with school, conflicts on the job can be beneficial. Inefficiencies can be removed, misconceptions cleared up, and new processes devised when co-workers engage in honest, passionate discussion.

Like anything else, though, there are good ways to resolve conflict, and there are bad ways. Good ways move people forward, defining the problem and promoting creative problem-solving. Bad ways make the situation worse, driving people apart rather than bringing them together. The following are some fundamental principles of conflict resolution that you can use when conflict occurs in academic, professional, and personal relationships:

> **Stop, look, and listen.** In the heat of an argument, all sorts of things that otherwise would go unsaid get said. If you find yourself making rash or hurtful statements, stop, look at yourself, and listen to what you and the other person are saying.
>
> Stopping works like a circuit breaker that prevents a short circuit from causing a deadly fire. You've probably heard about counting to 10 to cool off when you're angry. Do it. Take a break and count to 10 . . . or 20 . . . or more. Whether you count to 10 or 100, stopping gives you time to think and not react rashly. You don't want to say things you will regret later.

Switch "You" to "I"

Working in a group or in pairs, turn the following "you" statements into less aggressive "I" statements. For example, a possible "I" statement alternative to "You just don't get it, do you?" would be "I don't feel I'm making my feelings clear."

1. You just don't get it, do you?

2. You never listen to what I say.

3. You don't see where I'm coming from.

4. You don't really believe that, do you?

5. You never try to see my point of view.

6. Please stop interrupting me and listen to what I'm saying for a change.

7. Stop changing the subject!

8. You're not making sense.

9. You keep distorting what I say until I don't even know what point I'm trying to make.

10. You use too many "you" statements. Use more "I" statements when you're talking to others.

To Try It online, go to Connect for *P.O.W.E.R. Learning and Your Life*.

- **Defuse the argument.** Anger is not an emotion that encourages rational discourse. When you're angry or annoyed with someone, you're not in the best position to evaluate logically the merits of various arguments others may offer. It may feel exhilarating to get our fury off our chests in the heat of an argument, but you can bet it isn't taking anyone any closer to resolving the problem.

  Don't assume that you are 100 percent right and the other person is 100 percent wrong. Make your goal solving the problem rather than winning an argument.

- **Admit personal responsibility.** Perhaps you've heard others suggest that you shouldn't get personal in an argument. In one sense that's true: Accusing people you're arguing with of having character flaws does nothing to resolve real issues.

  At the same time, you should be willing to admit personal *responsibility* for at least part of the conflict. The conflict would not exist without you, so you need to accept that the argument has two sides and that you are not automatically blameless. This creates some solid ground from which you and the other person can begin to work on the problem.

- **Listen to the real message.** When people argue, what they say is often not the real message. There's typically an underlying communication—a subtext—that is the actual source of the conflict.

  It's important, then, to dig beneath what you're hearing. If someone accuses you of being selfish, the real meaning hidden in the accusation may be that you don't give anyone else a chance to make decisions. Remember, arguments are usually about behaviour, not underlying character and personality. What people *do* is not synonymous with who they *are*.

  If you rephrase the person's statement in your own mind, it moves from an insult ("You're a bad person") to a request for a change of behaviour ("Let me participate in decision-making"). You're much more likely to respond reasonably when you don't feel that the essence of your being is under attack.

- **Show that you're listening.** It's not enough only to listen to the underlying message that someone is conveying. You also need to acknowledge the *explicit* message. For example, say something like "OK, I can tell you are concerned about sharing the burden on our group project, and I think we should talk about it." This acknowledges that you see the issue and admit that it is worthy of discussion. This is a far more successful strategy than firing back a countercharge each time someone makes a complaint.

- **If you are angry, acknowledge it.** Don't pretend that everything is fine if it isn't. Ultimately, teams that have members that bottle up their anger may suffer more than those in which the group members express their true feelings. If you're angry, say so and explain why.

- **Ask for clarification.** As you're listening to another person's arguments, check out your understanding of what is being said. Don't assume that you know what's intended. Saying something like "Are you saying . . ." or "Do you mean that . . ." is a way of verifying that what you think someone means is really what is meant.

- **Make your requests explicit.** If you're upset that a team member isn't providing you with the quality of work you'd expected, remarking that he or she is stupid shows more than that you are angry: It also shows that your intent is to hurt rather than to solve the problem.

It's far better to be explicit in your concerns. Say something like "It would make our group report better if you put more effort into your submission." Couching your concern in this way changes the focus of the message from your group member's personality to a specific behaviour that can be changed.

> **In an argument, there doesn't have to be a loser.** Many of us act as if life were a **zero-sum game,** a situation in which when one person wins, the other person automatically loses. A zero-sum game is what happens when you make a bet: If one person wins the bet, the other person loses.

Life is not like that. If one person wins an argument, it doesn't mean that others automatically have to lose it. And if someone loses an argument, it doesn't mean that others have automatically won. In fact, all too often conflict escalates so much that the argument turns into a lose-lose situation, where everyone ends up a loser.

However, life can be a win-win situation. The best resolution of conflict occurs when both parties walk away with something they want. They may not have achieved *every* goal but at least they have enough to feel satisfied.

Zero-sum game
A situation in which when one person wins, the other person automatically loses

Time to Reflect: What Did I Learn?

1. Generally speaking, do you prefer doing individual work or group work? Why?

2. Thinking about the eight striving styles outlined in Chapter 1, which do you think is most amenable to doing group work? Which is least amenable? Why?

3. If you had to put together a group of four people to work on a research/analysis project, which Striving Styles would you most want represented? Why? Would your answer be different if you were working on a creative project? In what way?

Looking Back

Why is learning to work well as part of a team an essential life skill?

> There are very few jobs out there where you can operate as a "lone wolf." Most organizations today are complex and the projects they undertake often require combining the talents of many people from different backgrounds and/or with different perspectives. Whether it's a group project in college or university or a job-related challenge, learning to work well with other people is an investment that will pay positive dividends and help lead to success in many areas of your life.

How can I communicate openly with other group members?

> Be a good listener and let others have their say.

> Provide conversational markers that demonstrate that you are listening.

> Use reflective feedback, ask questions of the person who is speaking, and deal with distractions so you can concentrate on what your group members have to say.

How can I become more at ease with differences and diversity?

> Being aware of diversity can allow you to accept the challenge and opportunity of living and working with others who are very different.

> Cultural competence begins with accepting diversity by seeking out others who are different, as well as by exploring your own prejudices and stereotypes.

> Consider joining clubs or student associations that bring you into contact with people from different backgrounds.

> Read about and/or join organizations that fight against injustice and discrimination.

> You can learn about other cultures by travelling to other countries and geographic areas. It also helps to accept differences simply as differences.

How can I deal with conflict?

> Listening is an important skill for team building, demonstrating that the listener really cares about the views of other group members.

> Conflict is an inevitable part of the evolution of a team and sometimes it is useful because it permits us to clear up misconceptions and miscommunication before they escalate.

[KEY TERMS AND CONCEPTS]

Brainstorming (p. 217)

Conversational markers (p. 220)

Cultural competence (p. 224)

Culture (p. 222)

Discrimination (p. 225)

Emotional intelligence (or EQ) (p. 217)

Ethnicity (p. 222)

"I" statements (p. 230)

Prejudice (p. 225)

Reflective feedback (p. 221)

Stages of a group's evolution (p. 217)

Stereotypes (p. 225)

Team charter (p. 218)

Zero-sum game (p. 233)

[RESOURCES]

ON CAMPUS

Anyone who feels he or she is facing discrimination based on gender, ethnic background, sexual orientation, or national origin should contact a university or college official *immediately*. Often there is a specific office that handles such complaints. If you don't know which campus official to contact, speak to your academic adviser or someone in the dean's office, and you'll be directed to the appropriate person. The important thing is to act and not to suffer in silence. Discrimination is not only immoral; it is against the law.

IN PRINT

To get a sense of the statistics that underlie Canada's growing diversity, take a look in your local library for the Canada Yearbook published every year by Statistics Canada (the pdf version is available free of charge at the **www.statcan.gc.ca**).

Beverly Tatum's *"Why Are All the Black Kids Sitting Together in the Cafeteria?" And Other Conversations about Race*, rev. ed. (HarperCollins, 2003), explores race, racism, and the everyday impact of prejudice.

In *Affirming Diversity* (Allyn & Bacon, 2007), Sonia Nieto examines how ethnic and cultural factors affect student success.

ON THE WEB

The following websites provide the opportunity to extend your learning about the material in this chapter.

> Visit the Mind Tools website at **www.mindtools.com** for more information on working in groups, team charters, and conflict resolution.

> To measure your own level of emotional intelligence, or EQ, visit Discovery Health's website at **http://health.discovery.com/games/games-tab-05.html**, and scroll down to "What Is Your Emotional IQ?

> The Conflict Resolution Network (**www.crnhq.org**) website offers free training materials and self-study guides on the subject of conflict resolution.

[TAKING IT TO THE NET]

1 Explore cultural differences using the Internet. Go to Yahoo! (**dir.yahoo.com**), choose "Society and Culture," and then "Cultures and Groups." Click on "Cultures" and type a topic that you find interesting into the search field. Make sure to limit your search to just this category. How many pages did you find? Read and compare the information from different cultural groups.

2 Use the Internet to help find a volunteer organization that sounds interesting to you. Using either Google (**www.google.ca**) or Bing (**www.bing.com**), enter "volunteer organizations" and the name of your city or town into the search field. Examine the volunteer organizations listed and write down the ones that you find interesting. Consider contacting one or more to explore possibilities of participating in the organization that will mesh with your other responsibilities.

The Case of . . .
Keeping Your Mouth Shut

Jorge Azar immigrated with his parents to Canada from the Dominican Republic when he was 11 years old. Although Jorge has become fluent in English, he still speaks with an accent. Jorge has never felt self-conscious about it before. He's lived most of his life in Toronto, surrounded by dozens of different accents.

Now, though, Jorge has relocated with his wife to a small city located several hours outside of Toronto. He's enrolled in university to earn his degree in software engineering. Sitting in a classroom in which he is the only Hispanic, Jorge suddenly feels too nervous to open his mouth. He is sure that no matter what he says, his classmates will disregard it because of his accent. Despite graduating from high school at the top of his class, Jorge has been struck dumb at the idea of answering the questions his instructors are asking.

One day, Jorge can't avoid the problem anymore. In one of his programming classes, his instructor has called on him by name to explain a technical term. Jorge knows what the term means and how to explain it . . . but he is afraid that as soon as he speaks, he'll be laughed at. As the moments tick by and the class waits for Jorge's response, Jorge starts to wonder why he's enrolled in university in the first place.

1. Can you identify with Jorge's situation? Are there aspects of yourself that you feel self-conscious about?

2. What assumptions does Jorge fear his classmates will make?

3. What assumptions about his classmates is Jorge making?

4. What advice would you give Jorge to help him feel more comfortable, not just speaking in class but in university in general?

5. Have you ever judged someone based not on what they say, but on how they say it? What did you learn from this incident, and how could you avoid it in the future?

10 Managing Stress and Money

Learning Outcomes

By the time you finish this chapter, you will be able to

>> LO **10.1** Define stress and analyze its effects in your life.

>> LO **10.2** Identify practical ways of managing stress.

>> LO **10.3** Differentiate between needs and wants, prepare a budget, and explain how to stick to it.

>> LO **10.4** Discriminate between good and bad debt, discuss how student loans and credit cards work, and explain how to use credit wisely.

It had been a long day for Alexandre Durand—and now, lying in bed, he couldn't fall asleep.

The many stresses and worries of his day kept repeating in his mind. The babysitter he relied on to watch his children in the afternoon when he went to accounting classes had told him she wanted a raise. Alexandre, a single father, wasn't sure he could afford to pay more and still pay his other bills: utilities, rent, car insurance, tuition, books, and everything else. His paycheque from his job as a bank teller was already stretched thin. And given that he worked full-time and was going to college, he didn't think he could find time to take on a new job or even additional shifts.

Alexandre reassured himself that he could figure out a way to save a little more money. He told himself that at the moment what he really needed was sleep. He had to get up at 5:00 A.M. to exercise, then get his children to school, then go to work, then go to class. But all he could do was toss and turn, worrying about all the many challenges he had to face in the morning.

Looking
Ahead

Do you ever feel like Alexandre? Do you ever stay awake wondering how you'll meet the demands of college or university, work, bills, and family? Then you're no stranger to stress, and you are definitely not alone. All of us experience stress from time to time, and studying at a post-secondary institution can often exacerbate it. It isn't easy to be a student on top of being a parent, a spouse, an employee, and so forth.

Coping with stress is one of the challenges that virtually all college and university students face at one time or another. Almost a third of first-year college students report feeling frequently overwhelmed with all they need to do.[1] The many demands on your time can make you feel that you'll never finish what needs to get done. This pressure produces wear and tear on your body and on your mind, and it's easy to fall prey to ill health as a result.

However, stress and poor health are not inevitable outcomes. In fact, by following simple guidelines and deciding to make health a conscious priority, you can maintain good physical and mental health. It's not easy to balance the many responsibilities of study, work, and family, but it is possible; and in this chapter, we discuss how this delicate balance can be achieved.

Perhaps the greatest source of stress for college and university students, if not for people in general, is money. Even under the best of circumstances, our finances present us with many challenges. But money stress is not inevitable, either. In the second part of this chapter, we address the basics of managing your money. We begin by discussing how to distinguish your needs from your wants, then we examine how to track your spending and prepare a realistic budget for the coming year—the basis for sound money management. The chapter then goes on to look at the difference between good and bad debt, and how to discriminate between smart and stupid borrowing. We take a close look at how credit cards work and why credit card companies target college and university students, and we examine how to manage your student loans. Finally, we address the role of credit reporting agencies and discuss why you need to build up a good credit rating and how to use credit effectively to do just that.

» LO 10.1 Living with Stress

Stressed out? Tests, papers, job demands, family problems, volunteer commitments . . . It's no surprise that these can produce stress. But it may be a surprise to know that stress can also result from positive life events such as graduating from high school, starting your dream job, falling in love, getting married, and even winning the lottery.

Stress
The physical and emotional
response to events that
threaten or challenge us

Virtually anything—good or bad—is capable of producing stress if it presents us with a challenge. **Stress** is the physical and emotional response we have to events that threaten or challenge us. It is rooted in the primitive "fight or flight" response wired into all animals. You see it in cats, for instance, when confronted by a dog or other threat: Their backs go up, their fur stands on end, their eyes widen, and, ultimately, they either attack or take off. The challenge stimulating this revved-up response is called a *stressor*. For humans, common stressors can range from a first date or losing our wallet to driving in a winter storm.

Because our everyday lives are filled with events that can be interpreted as threatening or challenging, stress is commonplace in most people's lives. There are three main types of stressors:

Cataclysmic events
Sudden, powerful events that
occur quickly and affect many
people simultaneously

1. **Cataclysmic events** are events that occur suddenly and affect many people simultaneously. Avalanches, tornadoes, and plane crashes are examples of cataclysmic events.

2. **Personal stressors** are major life events that produce a negative physical and psychological reaction. Failing a course, losing a job, and ending a relationship are all examples of personal stressors. Positive events—such as getting married or starting a new job—can also act as personal stressors. Although the short-term impact of a personal stressor can be difficult, the long-term consequences may decline as people learn to adapt to the situation.

Daily hassles
The minor irritants of life which,
individually, produce little
stress, but which can add up
and produce more stress than a
single, larger-scale event

3. **Daily hassles** are the minor irritants of life that, singly, produce relatively little stress. Waiting in a traffic jam, receiving a tuition bill riddled with mistakes, and being interrupted by noises of major construction while trying to study are examples of such minor irritants. However, daily hassles add up, and cumulatively they can produce even more stress than a single larger-scale event. (**Figure 10.1** indicates the most common daily hassles in people's lives.[2])

What Is Happening When We Are Stressed?

Stress does more than make us feel anxious, upset, and fearful. Beneath those responses, we are experiencing many different physical reactions, each placing a high demand on our body's resources. Our hearts beat faster, our breathing

figure 10.1
Daily Hassles

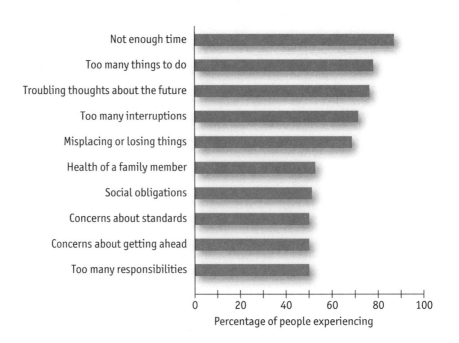

Percentage of people experiencing

becomes more rapid and shallow, and we produce more sweat. Our internal organs churn out a variety of hormones. In the long run, these physical responses wear down our immune system, our body's defence against disease. We become more susceptible to a variety of diseases, ranging from the common cold and headaches to strokes and heart disease. In fact, surveys have found that the greater the number of stressful events a person experiences over the course of a year, the more likely it is that he or she will have a major illness.

According to the Canadian Mental Health Association (CMHA), good mental health is related to your ability to enjoy life, your resilience in the face of life's challenges, your level of work–life balance, your degree of self-actualization, and how flexible you are. To assess your current level of mental fitness, complete **Try It! 1**, "Assess Your Level of Mental Health," on pages 242–243. (See also **www.cmha.ca/bins/meter_page.asp?cid=2-267-1304&lang=1.**)

LO 10.2 Managing Stress

Stress is an inevitable part of life. In fact, a life with no stress at all would be so boring, so uneventful, that you'd quickly miss the stress that had been removed.

That doesn't mean, though, that we should sit back and accept stress when it does arise. **Coping** is the effort to control, reduce, or tolerate the threats that lead to stress. Students with high Emotional Intelligence tend to cope better with stress than students who are more emotionally reactive. The characteristics of these two types of students are contrasted in **Table 10.1**

There are many tactics you can employ to cope with the stress in your life, regardless of its cause or intensity.

Being in good physical condition is an excellent way to alleviate future stress. Stress takes its toll on your body, so it makes sense that the stronger and fitter you are, the less negative impact stress will have on you. For example, a regular exercise program—even something as simple as walking briskly for 30 minutes three times a week—reduces heart rate, respiration rate, and blood pressure at times when

Coping
The effort to control, reduce, or tolerate the circumstances that lead to stress

table 10.1 Emotional Intelligence and Stress Management*	
Characteristics of Emotionally Reactive Students	**Characteristics of Emotionally Intelligent Students**
Overwhelmed too often	Resilient
Reactive to stress	Proactive, planned responses to stress
Driven by emotion	Do things with reflection and intention
Self-doubting	Self-confident
Resistant to change	Flexible, open to change
Aggressive or non-assertive communicators	Assertive communicators
Performance decreases under stress	Performance improves under stress
Pessimistic, sarcastic	Optimistic, positive, hopeful focus
Continually make the same mistakes	Learn from experience

*Adapted from Nelson, Darwin. B, and Low, Gary R. (2011). *Emotional intelligence: Achieving academic and career excellence* (2nd ed.). Prentice Hall.

Try It!

Assess Your Level of Mental Health*

Ability to enjoy life	Agree	Disagree
1. I tend to live in the moment and appreciate the "now."		
2. I often dwell on past experiences and daydream about different outcomes.		
3. I recognize that some things can't be changed.		
4. My feelings of happiness are often overshadowed by worry about the future.		
5. My home is a comfortable, pleasant place.		
6. I worry a lot about my friends and family.		
Resilience	Agree	Disagree
1. When life gets tough, I retreat from friends and family.		
2. When I'm under serious stress, I can't lead a normal life.		
3. I believe that I can learn from difficult times.		
4. After an emotional upheaval, it makes me feel guilty to feel happy.		
5. I exercise regularly and eat right, even when life gets busy or stressful.		
6. I have a great support network.		
Balance	Agree	Disagree
1. There aren't enough hours in the day to accomplish everything I want to do.		
2. I always make time for my hobbies.		
3. My friends often complain that they never see me.		
4. If life is a juggling act, then I think I'm a pretty good juggler.		
5. I practise a relaxation technique regularly.		
6. Focusing on work will get me where I want to be.		
Self-actualization	Agree	Disagree
1. Compliments make me uncomfortable.		
2. I have good self-esteem.		
3. When people say I have positive qualities, I have trouble believing what they are saying.		
4. I know what my strengths are and I work to develop them.		
5. I feel I am reaching my potential.		
6. Taking chances is risky, but it's worth the risk.		
Flexibility	Agree	Disagree
1. I don't always know what to expect from people.		
2. My problems are usually caused by other people.		
3. Life is smoother when I keep my emotions level at all times.		
4. I accept things the way they are, even if I don't like them.		
5. I'm often frustrated when other people don't share my point of view.		
6. I cope well with change.		

*DISCLAIMER

This information provides general information only and may or may not reflect the position of the Canadian Mental Health Association (CMHA). It is not a scientific test. Information provided is not a substitute for professional advice. If you feel that you may need advice, please consult a qualified health care professional.

Scoring:

Give yourself one point for each correct answer. Then, tally the number of correct answers in each category.

Ability to enjoy life:	1. Agree.	2. Disagree.	3. Agree.	4. Disagree.	5. Agree.	6. Disagree
Resilience:	1. Disagree.	2. Disagree.	3. Agree.	4. Disagree.	5. Agree.	6. Agree.
Balance:	1. Disagree.	2. Agree.	3. Disagree.	4. Agree.	5. Agree.	6. Disagree.
Self-actualization:	1. Disagree.	2. Agree.	3. Disagree.	4. Agree.	5. Agree.	6. Agree.
Flexibility:	1. Agree.	2. Disagree.	3. Disagree.	4. Agree.	5. Disagree.	6. Agree.

Ability to enjoy life

- If you scored fewer **than 3 points,** your enjoyment of life is being diminished by anxiety and worry. Some of your concerns are based on real problems, but many are "what ifs" and "maybes".
- If you scored **3-6 points,** your ability to enjoy life is good to excellent. The higher your score, the stronger your capability to live in the moment and accept that there are some things you cannot predict or change.

Resilience

- If you scored **fewer than 3 points,** your resilience may be too low. You isolate yourself during tough times, and the lack of support and other perspectives means you tend to stay focused on the negative.
- If you scored **3-6 points,** your resilience is good to excellent. The higher your score, the more strongly you feel that even though life can be full of tough times, it's important to keep your perspective.

Balance

- If you scored **fewer than 3 points,** your life is out of balance. Whether it's work, family, or personal interests, one or more aspects of your life are being neglected.
- If you scored **3-6 points,** your life has a fair to good degree of balance. The higher your score, the stronger your realization that there are many facets to your life that are important to you and deserving of your interest and attention.

Self-actualization

- If you scored **fewer than 3 points,** you are lacking in self-esteem. You tend not to trust other people's good opinions of your abilities and talents, nor do you feel that you could truly make more of your life.
- If you scored **3-6 points,** you have a good to high degree of self-actualization. The higher your score, the more you are able to value your own unique strengths and potential, and work to develop them to enhance your life.

Flexibility

- If you scored **fewer than 3 points,** you are not as flexible as you could be in your opinions or expectations. This rigidity can create a strong sense of frustration.
- If you scored **3-6 points,** you have a fair to good level of flexibility. The higher your score, the stronger your belief that change is a fact of life, and that seeing things from other points of view helps you adapt to change and make the most of your life and the people in it.

If you add together all of your scores across all of the five categories and the total is 10 or less, it suggests that you are overwhelmed and not coping particularly well. You should make an appointment as soon as possible with your campus counsellor to discuss coping strategies. If you score fewer than 3 points in a specific category, you still may want to make an appointment with a counsellor to focus specifically on identifying strategies that address this category.

To Try It online, go to Connect for *P.O.W.E.R. Learning and Your Life.*

the body is at rest, making us better able to withstand the negative consequences of stress.

If you drink a lot of coffee, tea, carbonated soft drinks, or energy drinks, simply reducing your consumption of these caffeine-packed liquids may be enough to bring about a reduction in stress. Caffeine can make you feel jittery and anxious even without outside stressors; add a stressor, and the reaction can be very intense and unpleasant.

Eating right is also key. A daily "diet" consisting of a bagel or donut for breakfast, a burger and fries at lunchtime, and a couple of pizza slices for supper may sound like food heaven to a student who is always on the go; but the sugar, saturated fat, and high sodium found in fast food will leave you feeling sluggish and can increase your cholesterol and blood pressure over the long term. Consider taking a daily vitamin supplement if you are not finding the time to eat properly.

Over-indulgence in fast food can also lead to another problem: obesity. Being overweight can bring on stress for several reasons. For one thing, the extra pounds drag down the functioning of the body. This can lead to fatigue and a reduced ability to bounce back when we encounter challenges to our well-being. In addition, feeling heavy in a society that values slimness can be stressful in and of itself.

Of course, stress is not just a question of diet and exercise. To cope with stress, you need to understand what is causing it. In some cases, it's obvious—a series of bad test grades in a course, a family problem that keeps getting worse, or a job supervisor who seems to delight in making things difficult, for example. In other cases, however, the causes of stress may be more subtle: Perhaps your relationship with your girlfriend or boyfriend is rocky, and you have a nagging feeling that it isn't going to work out.

Whatever the source of stress, the first thing you need to do is pinpoint it. To organize your assault on stress, then, take a piece of paper and list the major circumstances that are causing you stress. Just listing them will help put you in control, and you'll be better able to figure out strategies for coping.

Sources of Stress

1. Psychology professor talks so fast that notetaking is nearly impossible
2. Difficulty paying rent this month.
3. Not enough time to study for Tuesday's accounting test

Develop Effective Coping Strategies

A wide variety of tactics can help you deal with stress once you've identified its sources. In addition to the lifestyle changes outlined above, among the most effective approaches to coping are these:

> **Take charge of the situation.** Stress is most apt to arise when we are faced with situations over which we have little or no control. If you take charge of the situation, you'll reduce the experience of stress. For example, if several work assignments are given to you all on the same day, you might try recruiting a co-worker to help lighten your load.

> **Don't waste energy trying to change the unchangeable.** There are some situations that you simply can't control. You can't change the fact that you have come down with a case of the flu, and you can't change your performance on a test you took last week. Don't hit your head against a brick wall and try to modify things that can't be changed. Use your energy to improve the future, not try to rewrite the past.

> **Look for the silver lining.** Stress arises when we perceive a situation as threatening. If we can change how we perceive that situation, we can change our reactions to it. For instance, if your computer instructor requires you to learn a difficult spreadsheet program in a very short time, the saving grace is that you may be able to use the skill to your advantage in getting a high-paying job down the road. (You can practise finding the silver lining in **Try It! 2**, "Look for the Silver Lining," on page 246.)

> **Talk to friends and family, or to a campus counsellor. Social support,** assistance and comfort supplied by others, can help us through stressful periods. Turning to our friends and family and simply talking about the stress we're under can help us tolerate it more effectively. Most colleges and universities also provide free counselling services to their students. Trained counsellors have the benefit of "fresh eyes" and can both offer practical strategies and direct you to resources for dealing with your specific circumstances.

Social support
Assistance and comfort supplied by others in times of stress

> **Relax.** Because stress produces constant wear and tear on the body, it seems possible that practices that lead to the relaxation of the body might lead to a reduction in stress—and that's just what happens. Using any one of several techniques for producing physical relaxation can help you to cope with stress. Among the best relaxation techniques is meditation. Though often associated with its roots in the ancient Eastern religion of Zen Buddhism, meditation, a technique for refocusing attention and producing bodily relaxation, is practised in some form by members of virtually every major religion. Meditation reduces blood pressure, slows respiration, and in general reduces bodily tension. Mindfulness-based stress reduction, or MBSR, is an eight-week meditation-based program focused specifically on stress reduction that was developed by Dr. Jon Kabat-Zinn at the University of Massachusetts Medical Center. To learn more about the benefits of MBSR and about meditation in general, check online, at the library, or at a meditation centre in your area.

> **Wimping out doesn't work—so live up to your commitments.** Suppose you've promised a friend that you'll help him move, you've agreed to participate in a marketing case competition that involves six hours of intensive training each week, and you are also helping your boyfriend build a website for his new business. Plus, you have two midterms next week and a major group assignment to work on. You are facing all the demands connected to these commitments and feeling stressed.

You may be tempted to cope with the feeling by breaking some or all of your commitments, thinking, "I just need to sit at home and relax in front of the television!" This is not coping. It is escaping, and it doesn't reduce stress. Ducking out of commitments, whether to yourself or to others, will make you feel guilty and anxious and will be another source of stress—one without the satisfaction of having accomplished what you set out to do.

Find ways to keep your promises; and in future, think carefully before you over-commit yourself. Learning how and when to say no will prevent you from becoming overwhelmed in the future.

Try It!

2

Look for the Silver Lining

Consider the following list of potentially stressful situations. Try to find something positive—a silver lining—in each of them. The first two are completed to get you started.

Situation	Silver Lining
1. Your car just broke down and repairing it is more than you can afford right now.	1. *This is the perfect time to begin exercising by walking and using my bicycle.*
2. Your boss just yelled at you and threatened to fire you.	2. *Either this is a good time to open an honest discussion with my boss about my job situation, OR this is a good time to get a more interesting job.*
3. You have two papers due on Monday and there's a great concert you wanted to go to on Saturday night.	3.
4. You just failed an important test.	4.
5. You're flat broke. You promised your friend you'd visit him, and you can't afford the tickets right now.	5.
6. Your last date went poorly, and you think your girlfriend/boyfriend was hinting that it was time to break up.	6.
7. You just found out you missed the due date for your cellphone payment.	7.
8. You just got cut from a sports team or club activity you loved.	8.
9. Your best friend is starting to turn weird and seems not to enjoy being with you as much as before.	9.
10. You just realized you don't really want to pursue the career you're training for in college or university.	10.

 WORKING IN A GROUP

After you have considered these situations on your own, discuss each of them in a group.

1. What similarities and differences in others' responses did you find?
2. Evaluate the different responses, and consider whether—and why—some ways of reframing the situations were better than others.

To Try It online, go to Connect for *P.O.W.E.R. Learning and Your Life.*

Place Stress in Perspective

It's easy to think of stress as an enemy. In fact, most approaches to coping are geared to overcoming its negative consequences. But consider the following two principles, which in the end may help you more than any others in dealing with stress:

> **Don't sweat the small stuff . . . and it's all small stuff.** Stress expert Richard Carlson[3] emphasizes the importance of putting the circumstances we encounter into the proper perspective. He argues that we frequently let ourselves get upset about situations that are actually minor.
>
>   So what if someone cuts us off in traffic, or does less than his or her share on a group project, or unfairly criticizes us? It's hardly the end of the world. If an unpleasant event has no long-term consequences, it's often best to let it go. One of the best ways to reduce stress, consequently, is to maintain an appropriate perspective on the events of your life.

> **Make peace with stress.** Think of what it would be like to have no stress in your life. Would you really be happier, better adjusted, and more successful? The answer is "probably not." A life that presented no challenges would probably be, in a word, boring. So think about stress as an exciting, although admittedly sometimes difficult, friend. Welcome it, because its presence indicates that your life is stimulating, challenging, and exciting—and who would want it any other way?

From the perspective of . . .

A STUDENT The educational process can be stressful. When you consider your future career path, what are the areas of stress you may need to address?

Keep Well

Eat right. Exercise. Get plenty of sleep.

Sounds pretty simple, doesn't it? We learn the fundamentals of fitness and health in the first years of elementary school.

Yet for millions of us, wellness is an elusive goal. We eat on the fly, stopping for a bite at the drive-in window of a fast-food restaurant. Most of us don't exercise enough either, because we feel we don't have enough time or because it's not much fun for us. And as for sleep, our long commutes and increasingly busy schedules are leading to sleep deprivation on a nationwide scale.

For many post-secondary students, the bad habits are only made worse by the need to manage so many different sets of responsibilities. It is hard to concentrate on keeping well when you also need to complete your schoolwork, keep your boss happy, care for your children, and manage your household. Personal health can easily get lost in the shuffle of all these competing demands. At the end of the day, too many students feel as if they've run themselves ragged just trying to do the minimum to meet their many obligations.

Yet your health is too important to ignore. There are strategies you can use to balance your commitments, and you can begin to eat more properly, exercise effectively, and sleep better.

> "The first wealth is health."
> Ralph Waldo Emerson, author and poet

Juggle Your Responsibilities

> **Identify your priorities.** Taking your child to the dentist and studying for a final exam are examples of tasks that absolutely have to be accomplished. Updating your blog and cleaning out your garage are things that can be left to another day. This distinction seems obvious, yet too often we allow lower-priority tasks to crowd out the high-priority ones. Identify what is most important for you to achieve, and use your time and energy to accomplish

these high-priority goals. (Think back to the decisions you made when completing the priority setting exercise in Chapter 2 [see page 42].)

> **Use proven time management techniques.** There are only 24 hours in a day. Often, though, it can seem there is 25 hours' worth of work to do—or more. To get a handle on your schedule, use the time management strategies outlined in Chapter 2. Creating daily to-do lists, calendars, and so forth will be a huge help in effectively meeting your many responsibilities.

> **Communicate with others about your obligations.** Remember that the people in your life—bosses, family members, instructors, fellow students—can't know you are managing a wide set of responsibilities unless you tell them. And while you can't expect special treatment just because you have a child at home or a second job to go to, you'll be surprised at how understanding others will be of such circumstances. At the beginning of the semester, see what can be done about making your class schedule work for you. If you have to bring a child to daycare each morning, or you need three mornings off during the week to work, find out if your schedule can be changed to accommodate your obligations. By communicating with those around you, you can work with them to find solutions before your life starts to feel overwhelming.

> **Multi-task.** Don't draw strict limits regarding what you do and when. If you have a free 20 minutes at your job or while waiting for the doctor, use it to catch up on reading for classes. When your children are napping or when a commercial comes on the TV, see if there is work you can accomplish at home. You don't want to fill every spare minute with work, but you do want to take advantage of the gaps in your hectic day.

> **Don't put your own needs last.** It's easy to cut corners in your schedule by giving yourself the least attention—sleeping less, skipping leisure activities, eating on the go. But this sort of lifestyle is not sustainable. You need to treat yourself well if you are going to be an effective student, parent, and employee.

Eat Right

> **Eat a variety of "whole" foods, including fruits, vegetables, and grain products.** Strive to eat a range of different foods. If you make variety your goal, you will end up eating the right foods. Avoid processed foods. Make an effort to choose "whole" foods, or foods in a state as close as possible to their natural state: brown rice is better than white rice, and both are better than a preservative-filled, packaged "rice casserole" mix.

> **Avoid foods that are high in sugar and salt content.** Read labels on product packages carefully and beware of hidden sugars and salts. Many ingredients that end in -ose (such as dextrose, sucrose, maltose, and fructose) are actually sugars; salt can lurk within any number of compounds beginning with the word sodium.

> **Strive for a diet low in fat.** The fat that is to be especially avoided is saturated fat—the fat that is the most difficult for your body to rid itself of. For starters, try weaning yourself off that Tim Horton's double-double by gradually reducing the amount of cream in your coffee and eventually replacing it with milk. Do the same with the sugar. Over time, like anything else, you'll get used to it—and on an extra-large double-double, you'll be saving yourself an astounding 280 calories, 14 grams of fat, and 9 grams of saturated fat per cup!

> **Less is more.** You don't need to walk away stuffed from every meal. Avoid all-you-can-eat restaurants; people try to "get their money's worth" by eating as

much as possible, and most continue to eat long after they are full and should stop eating. Moderation is the key. To be sure you don't eat more than your body is telling you to eat, pay attention to internal hunger cues.

> **Eat three regular meals a day and snacks in between.** Eating should be a priority—a definite part of your daily schedule. Avoid skipping meals. Breakfast is particularly important; get up early enough to eat a full meal. Consider preparing large batches of filling foods like chili or stew on the weekend and freeze portions to reheat later. Always have healthy snacks nearby; keep them in your locker, in your car, or on the way out the door for easy access as you leave for school. Apples, high-fibre/low-sugar granola bars, and unbuttered popcorn are all good choices for snacking.

> **Be sensitive to the hidden contents of various foods.** Soft drinks and chocolate can contain substantial quantities of caffeine, which can disrupt your sleep and, along with coffee, become addictive. Many cereals—even those labelled "low fat"—contain a considerable amount of sugar or salt. Pay attention to labels. And watch out for fast foods: Research finds that eating fast foods just a few times a week leads to significant weight gains over the long run.[4]

> **If you want to lose weight, follow a sensible diet.** There's really only one proven way to lose weight: control your food portions, eat a well-balanced diet, and increase the amount of exercise you get. Fad, quick-fix diets are not effective and will eventually lead to regaining any weight you might have lost.

Make Exercise a Part of Your Life

Exercise produces a variety of benefits: Your body will run more efficiently, you'll have more energy, your heart and circulatory system will run more smoothly, and you'll be able to bounce back from stress and illness more quickly.

> **Choose a type of exercise that you like.** Exercising will be a chore you end up avoiding if you don't enjoy what you're doing.

> **Incorporate exercise into your daily activities.** Take the stairs instead of the elevator. Leave your car at home and walk to the campus or to work. When you're on campus, take the longer way to reach your destination.

> **Make exercise a group activity.** Exercising with others brings you social support and turns exercise into a social activity. You'll be more likely to stick to a program if you have a regular "exercise date" with a friend.

> **Vary your routine.** You don't need to do the same kind of exercise day after day. Choose different sorts of activities that will involve different parts of your body and keep you from getting bored. For example, for cardiovascular fitness, you might alternate between running, swimming, biking, and using a cardio training machine.

One note of caution: Before you begin an exercise program, it is a good idea to have a physical checkup, even if you feel you're in the peak of health. This is especially true if you're starting an exercise program after years of inactivity. You also might consult a personal trainer at the gym to set up a program that gradually builds you up to more vigorous exercise.

Get a Good Night's Sleep

Do you feel as if you don't get enough sleep? You probably don't. Most college and university students are sleep-deprived, a condition that causes them to feel fatigued, short-tempered, and tense. Sleep deprivation makes staying alert in class nearly impossible (see the **Course Connections** feature on page 252).

Ultimately, insufficient sleep leads to declines in academic, work, and physical performance. You can't do your best at anything if you're exhausted, or even tired.

Often the solution to the problem is simply to allow yourself more time to sleep. Most people need around eight hours of sleep each night, although there are wide individual differences. In addition to sleeping more, there are also some relatively simple changes you can make in your behaviour that will help you to sleep better. They include the following:

> **Exercise more.** Regular exercise will help you sleep more soundly at night, and it will help you cope with stress that might otherwise keep you awake.

> **Have a regular bedtime.** By going to bed at pretty much the same time each night, even on weekends, you give your body a regular rhythm and make sleep a habit.

> **Use your bed for sleeping and not as an all-purpose area.** Don't use your bed as a place to study, read, eat, or watch TV. Let your bed be a trigger for sleep.

> **Avoid caffeine after lunch and dinner.** The stimulant effects of caffeine (found in coffee, tea, energy drinks, and some soft drinks) may last as long as 8 to 12 hours after you have consumed the drink.

When we have more responsibilities than time, sleep is often the first thing to suffer. Getting an appropriate amount of sleep can actually help you get more done in the time you do have.

> **Drink a glass of milk at bedtime.** Your mom was right: Drinking a glass of milk before you go to bed will help you get to sleep. The reason: Milk contains a natural chemical that makes you drowsy.

> **Steer clear of sleeping pills.** Although sleeping pills may be temporarily effective, in the long run they impair your ability to sleep because they disrupt your natural sleep cycles.

> **Don't try to force sleep on yourself.** Although this advice sounds odd, it turns out that one of the reasons that we have trouble sleeping is that we try too hard. Consequently, when you go to bed, just relax, and don't even attempt to go to sleep. If you're awake after 10 minutes or so, get up and do something else. Only go back to bed when you feel tired. Do this as often as necessary. If you follow this regimen for several weeks—and if you don't take naps or rest during the day—eventually getting into your bed will trigger sleep.

≫ LO 10.3 Managing Your Money

When it comes to addressing the stress in our lives, it's probably hard to overstate the impact of money. Few things command the attention—and worry—that money does. That's why it's essential to learn to manage your money effectively while you are attending college or university, and to keep doing so throughout your life. Not only are many of your choices and opportunities influenced by money, but so too is your mental well-being. Take a look at **Try It! 3**, "Test Your Knowledge of Personal Finance," before reading on.

Do you know where your money goes? Do you spend more than you think you should? Do you never have quite enough money to buy the things you want? Does the arrival of your credit card bill send you into a tailspin?

Try It!

Test Your Knowledge of Personal Finance

3

Understanding the basics of personal finance is the key to living within your means and building a solid financial future. Use this **Try It!** to get started.

1. What is the average Canadian family's largest annual expenditure?
   a. Food
   b. Shelter
   c. Taxes
   d. Utility bills

2. What is the average amount of student loan(s) outstanding after graduation for a community college student in Canada? For a student graduating with a Bachelor's degree from a Canadian university?
   a. college $5300; university $7300
   b. college $9400; university $15 300
   c. college $11 800; university $22 700
   d. college $12 700; university $32 000

3. You have a $3000 balance on your credit card, which charges 19% on outstanding balances. If you make only the minimum payment each month (usually 2.5% of the outstanding balance), how many months will it take you to pay off the entire balance?
   a. 283 months (more than 23 years)
   b. 125 months (more than 10 years)
   c. 62 months (more than 5 years)
   d. 38 months (more than 3 years)

4. If you graduate from college with a two-year diploma, how much more money will you earn in total over a 37-year working life than someone who has only a high-school diploma?
   a. $38 925
   b. $58 825
   c. $96 825
   d. $173 825

5. A Canadian couple decides to marry and plan to invite 100 people to their wedding. How much does the average couple budget for this size of wedding? How much do they actually spend?
   a. budget $8000, spend $7000
   b. budget $9000, spend $14 000
   c. budget $14 000, spend $27 000
   d. budget $19 000, spend $19 000

 WORKING IN A GROUP

Compare your answers to the following questions with those of your classmates.

1. What surprised you the most?
2. What misconceptions about personal finance did most of you share?

Quiz answers (and data sources) are:

1.c (Fraser Institute, 2008)
2.d (Coalition for Student Loan Fairness, 2006)
3.a (personal-debt-management.suite101.com)
4.d (ACAATO)
5.c (Today's Bride)

To Try It online, go to Connect for *P.O.W.E.R. Learning and Your Life.*

Staying Alert in Class

If you're having trouble staying alert or, even worse, staying awake in class, the best solution is to get more sleep. Short of that, you can try the following strategies to help stay awake:

- Throw yourself into the class. Sit near the front, pay close attention, take notes, ask questions, and generally be fully engaged in the class. You should do this anyway, but making a special effort when you're exhausted can get you through a period of fatigue.
- Sit up straight. Pinch yourself. Stretch the muscles in different parts of your body. Fidget. Any activity will help you thwart fatigue and feel more alert.
- Eat or drink something cold in class. If your instructor permits it, the mere activity of eating a snack or drinking can help you stay awake.
- Avoid heavy meals before class. Your body's natural reaction to a full stomach is to call for a nap, the opposite of what you want to achieve.
- Stay cool. Take off your coat or jacket and sit by an open window. If it's warm, ask your instructor if there's a way to make the classroom cooler.
- Take off one shoe. This creates a temperature difference, which can be helpful in keeping you awake.

Understanding the role money plays in your life is the first step toward wise money management. If you have money problems—and there's virtually no one who doesn't have some concerns about finances at some point in life—there are a number of different things you can do. We discuss solutions in the remainder of this chapter. Let's start by taking a look at what is often at the root of money problems: mistaking a want for a need.

Distinguish Needs from Wants

Disposable income
The amount left over after payment of taxes and contributions to social insurance plans (such as the Canada Pension Plan and Employment Insurance) and other fees

If you are living on your own for the first time, one of the first things you'll probably notice is that your amount of **disposable income**—money you used to be able to spend on clothing or electronics or partying—is now needed for other things: feeding yourself, keeping a roof over your head, buying books, and paying for tuition. Those of you who've always worked part-time in high school and considered shopping a harmless pastime are in for a shock: what you used to think was a "need"—the latest iPod, for instance—is actually a "want", something that you can do without. You may *need* winter boots, but you *don't* need a $200 pair of UGGs. You may *need* transportation to and from school, but there are many ways to address this need and a shiny new Mazda3 isn't one of them for most students. And on a day-to-day basis, you may *need* a coffee, but you *don't* need a Starbucks Venti NonFat Caramel Macchiato.

How do you make distinguishing needs from wants a part of your daily life? It starts with asking yourself a simple question. With every expenditure you make, no matter how small, ask yourself this: Is this a need or a want? If you experience even the slightest hesitation, it's probably a want.

How do you stop yourself from spending excessively on wants? One way is to postpone the purchase. It is amazing how many things we think we want are just fleeting desires that go away when we are no longer in the mall. A week later, you probably won't even remember what it was that you wanted. Another way is to replace the want with a cheaper substitute: A serviceable pair of winter boots does *not* have to cost $200. And a final strategy to avoid overspending, which will probably cause the fashionistas among you to recoil in horror is simply this: Avoid shopping unless you have a real need. Strolling through your local mall or searching Zappos.com is a surefire way to uncover items you that didn't know existed, items that now seem essential to your life. Don't do it. While you are in college or university, stay away from shopping as a way to pass the time. Try studying instead!

As a student attending an institution of higher learning, you are probably not in a position to entertain having several lofty financial goals. But you are at a point in your life where you should definitely have one overriding financial goal: graduating from college or university with as little debt as possible. Let's now discuss how strategies like budgeting and the wise use of credit can help you get there.

What Is a Budget?

A **budget** is a formal plan that accounts and plans for the money that comes into your life (income) and the money that goes out (expenditures). Taking your needs into account, a budget helps you determine how much money you should be spending each month, and on what. Budgets can also help you prepare for the unexpected, such as the loss of a job that would reduce your income, or for sudden, unanticipated expenses, such as a major car repair, by giving you a sense of the financial impact on the rest of your expenses.

Although all budgets are based on an uncomplicated premise—expenditures should not exceed income—budgeting is not simple. There are several times during the year that involve especially large expenditures, including the start of each semester, when you must pay your tuition and purchase books. Furthermore, your income can be erratic; it can rise and fall depending on overtime, on whether another member of your family starts or stops working, and so forth. But a budget will help you deal with the ups and downs in your finances, smoothing the bumps and extending your view toward the horizon. Learning budgeting skills can also help you at work, as discussed in this chapter's **Career Connections** on page 257.

Most of all, a budget provides security. It will let you take control of your money, permitting you to spend it as you need to without guilt, because you have planned for the expenditure. It also makes it easier to put money aside because you know that your current financial sacrifice will be rewarded later, when you can make the purchase that you've been planning for.

Budgeting is very personal: What is appropriate for one person doesn't work for another. For a few people, keeping track of their spending comes naturally; they enjoy accounting for every dollar that passes through their hands. For most people, though, developing a budget—and sticking to it—does not come easily.

Budget
A formal plan that accounts for income and expenditures

> "There was a time when a fool and his money were soon parted, but now it happens to everybody."
> **Adlai Stevenson, politician**

P.O.W.E.R. Plan

P Prepare
Track the money coming in and going out

O Organize
Prepare a budget

W Work
Balance your budget, and stick to it!

E Evaluate
Review your budget regularly

R Rethink
Revisit your budget when circumstances change

P Prepare ── Track the Money Coming In and Going Out

Do you open your wallet for the $10 that was there yesterday and find only a dollar? Spending money without realizing it is a common affliction. There's only one way to get a handle on where your money is going: Keep track of it.

To get an overview of your income for the coming year, take a look at your paycheques from work, and focus in on the bottom line, your take-home pay.

As you can see from the Dilbert cartoon on the next page, what your employer tells you is your salary is not the last word. In Canada, deductions for everything from Canada Pension Plan to Employment Insurance to income taxes will reduce the amount that ends up in your bank account. There is no point whining about

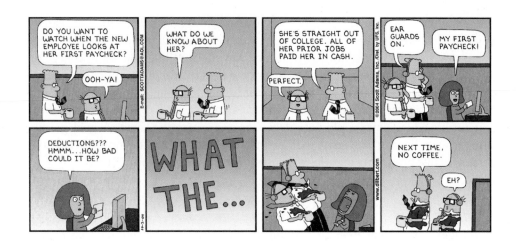

it—just be aware that, when looking at incoming sources of cash, you have to look at it after deductions and after tax. And if you plan to reduce your hours while attending college or university, ask your employer to help you estimate how this will impact your take-home pay.

Aside from job-related income, you'll also want to get a sense of other sources of funds you can count on for the coming year. This might include money from family members, bursaries or scholarships, and financial aid from the government in the form of grants and student loans. According to site **www.sayfutostudent debt.com**, 31% of all Canadian households carry debt relating to student loans and the average outstanding debt two years after graduation is $20 000. In addition, 27% of students carry an additional $9200 of debt from other sources. As you can see, if you borrow to fund your education, you are certainly not alone.

To get an overview of your expenditures for the coming year, the first thing you should do is go through any records you've kept to identify where you've spent money over the last year. If, like most Canadians, you prefer to bank and pay bills online, the easiest way to do this is to bring up your account summary and look at it on a month-by-month basis. Otherwise, you'll have to rely on cancelled cheques, rent and utility receipts, and tuition and book receipts from past years to help you estimate what you spend.

To track all of the little items that you tend to pay for with cash, the best thing to do is for one week, keep track of everything you spend. *Everything*. When you spend $1.25 for a chocolate bar from a vending machine, write it down. When you buy lunch for $6.99 at a fast-food restaurant, write it down. When you buy a double-double at Tim Horton's, write it down. Record your expenditures in a small "dollar store" notebook that you carry with you all the time. It may be tedious, but you're doing it for only a week. And it will be eye-opening: People are usually surprised at how much they spend on little items without thinking about it.

 Prepare a Budget

Once you have the information you need to put your budget together, it's time to categorize it and list it in an organized fashion, putting the sources of income together, and separating them from the uses of income.

How Much Money Do I Have Coming In?

You probably have a pretty good idea of how much money you have each month. But it's as important to list each source of income as it is to account for everything you spend.

table 10.2 Estimated Income, Next 12 Months

Category	The next 3 months	4–6 months from now	7–9 months from now	10–12 months from now
Take-home pay				
Family Support (e.g., RESPs)				
Financial Aid				
Bursaries				
Grants				
Scholarships				
Student Loans				
Gifts of $ (birthday, etc.)				
Other				
TOTAL				

Add up what you make from any jobs you hold. Also list any support you receive from family members, including occasional gifts you might get from relatives. Finally, include any government aid or financial aid, such as bursaries, student loans, or scholarships you receive from your college or university. Use **Table 10.2** to record this information. When you do, be sure to list the amounts you receive in terms of disposable income.

How Much Money Do I Have Going Out?

Make a list of everything you think you'll need to spend over the next year. Some items are easy to think of, such as rent and tuition payments, because they occur regularly and the amount you pay is fixed. Others are harder to budget for because they can vary substantially. For example, the price of gasoline changes frequently. If you have a long commute, the changing price of gasoline can cause substantial variation in what you pay each month. Use **Table 10.3** on page 256 to estimate your expenditures for the coming year. For a template of this form online, go to Connect for *P.O.W.E.R. Learning and Your Life*.

Always Include Some Savings in Your Budget

When you are listing your upcoming expenditures, be sure to include an amount that you will routinely put aside in a savings account, a way of "Paying Yourself First." The best way to do this is to automate the process, so it is "out of sight, out of mind." Ask your financial institution to set up an automatic withdrawal, where a specific amount is taken out on a regular basis from your main account and moved to an interest-bearing savings account. For obvious reasons, this is best scheduled to coincide with the day you normally get paid. Some online banking services, like the one offered by ING Direct, allow you to set up specific savings goals and create your own "automatic savings program." For instance, if you are planning to buy a car in a few years, start socking away a regular amount in your "Car Account," so you'll have a down payment when the time comes. If you are planning to travel to Mexico during study week next year, estimate the amount you'll need, divide it by

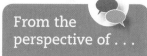

From the perspective of . . .

A RECENT GRADUATE
Have you considered how your new career may impact your personal budget? What preparations might you need to make to ensure that a higher monthly income results in a better standard of living?

table 10.3 Estimated Expenditures, Next 12 Months

Category	The next 3 months	4–6 months from now	7–9 months from now	10–12 months from now
Personal Necessities				
Groceries & eating out				
Shelter				
Utilities (e.g., heat, hydro)				
Cellphone & Internet				
Clothing				
Personal care (haircuts, toiletries, medication, etc.)				
Transportation (car payments, gas, car repairs, bus tickets, etc.)				
Loan and credit card payments				
Child-care expenses				
Savings fund				
Other				
Educational Necessities				
Tuition and fees				
Books				
School supplies				
Computer expenses				
Other				
Social Needs				
Relationships				
Clubs and teams				
Charitable contributions & gifts				
Other				
Entertainment				
Movies and concerts				
Trips				
Recreation and sports				
Other				
TOTAL				

Budgeting on the Job

If you've ever held a job, the salary you received was determined, in part, by your employer's budget.

Although the financial plan of an employer may not always be accessible to every employee, budgets are part of the world of work. Regardless of who the employer is—be it a small dry cleaning business or the federal government—there is a budget outlining anticipated income and expenditures. Managers are expected to keep to the budget, and if their expenditures exceed what is budgeted, they are held accountable.

For this reason, the ability to create and live within a budget is an important skill to acquire. Not only will it help keep your own finances under control, but it will also prepare you to be financially responsible and savvy on the job—qualities that are highly valued by employers.

the number of pay periods between now and study week, and start putting that amount into an account every time you get paid. Most money stress comes from poor choices or poor planning. Saving regularly is a very potent way to ward off financial stress. Knowing you have savings to fall back on should something unexpected come up is like having an umbrella on a rainy day!

 ## Balance Your Budget

If you've prepared and organized your income and expenditures, actually constructing your budget is as easy as adding 2 + 2. Well, not exactly; the numbers will be larger. But all you need to do is transfer your total income and total expenses for each time period to a table like the one shown in **Table 10.4**. Then, subtract the expenses from the income. In a perfect world, the result will be 0, or there will be some money left over.

table 10.4 Budget, Next 12 Months				
Category	The next 3 months	4–6 months from now	7–9 months from now	10–12 months from now
Money coming in (income)				
Money going out (expenditures)				
Leftover or Shortfall (+ or −)				

But most of the time, the world is not perfect: Most of us find that expenditures are larger than our income, and we are left with a shortfall. If you find you are expecting to spend more than you make, there are only two things to do: Find places in your budget either to decrease your spending or to increase your income. This is where the real work of balancing your budget begins. It's often easiest to decrease expenditures, because your expenses tend to be more under your control. For instance, you can do many things to save money, including the following:

› **Control impulse buying.** If you shop for your groceries, read your weekly grocery flyer ahead of time (most are online), plan your menus around sale items, always take a list with you (and stick to it), and don't shop when you're hungry.

› **Make and take your own lunch.** Brown-bag lunches can save you a substantial amount of money over purchasing your lunches, even if you go to a fast-food restaurant or snack bar.

› **Plan major purchases to coincide with sales.** When making major purchases, like a new laptop, plan to buy when these items are usually on sale. Take advantage of price-matching policies by doing your research first.

› **Shop at consignment stores and thrift stores.** Stores like the Salvation Army Thrift Store and Value Village sell household goods like dishes and furniture, as well as clothing, at deep discounts.

› **Buy used rather than new.** Check out your school's "buy and sell" web page, your local Kijiji site, or Ebay for items like used textbooks, bicycles, and electronics.

› **Share and trade.** Pool your resources with friends. Carpool, share computers, and trade clothes.

› **Live more simply.** Is it really necessary to subscribe to the premium cable TV package? Do you absolutely *have* to have an iPad? Is it really necessary to eat out once a week? Do you buy clothes because you need them or because you want them? It goes back to needs and wants. Because you are foregoing a full-time income to go to school, and you are probably borrowing to attend school, this is a time in your life when it is critical that you keep your expenses low. Living simply really is your best strategy.

There are as many ways to save money as there are people looking to save it. But keep in mind that saving money should not necessarily be an end in itself. Don't spend hours thinking of ways to save a dime, and don't get upset about situations where you are forced to spend money. The goal is to bring your budget into balance, not to become a tightwad who keeps track of every penny and feels that spending money is a personal failure. To help you get started, get a sense of your current style of saving money in **Try It! 4**, "Determine Your Saving Style."

Finally, it's important to remember that budgets may be brought into balance not only by decreasing expenditures, but also by increasing income. The most direct way to increase income is to get a job if you don't already have one, or to work more hours at the job you have.

 Review Your Budget Regularly

Budgets are not meant to be set in stone. You should review where you stand financially preferably at the end of each month, but at the very least, at the end of each semester. Only by monitoring how closely actual expenditures and income match your budget projections will you be able to maintain control of your finances.

Try It! POWER

4

Determine Your Saving Style

Read each of the following statements and rate how well it describes you, using this scale:

    1 = That's me

    2 = Sometimes

    3 = That's not me

	1	2	3
1. I count the change I'm given by cashiers in stores and restaurants.			
2. I always pick up all the change I receive from a transaction in a store, even if it's only a few cents.			
3. I don't buy something right away if I'm pretty sure it will go on sale soon.			
4. I feel a real sense of accomplishment if I buy something on sale.			
5. I always remember how much I paid for something.			
6. If something goes on sale soon after I've bought it, I feel cheated.			
7. I have money in at least one interest-bearing bank account.			
8. I rarely lend people money.			
9. If I lend money to someone repeatedly without getting it back, I stop lending it to that person.			
10. I share resources (e.g., books, magazines) with other people to save money.			
11. I'm good at putting money away for big items that I really want.			
12. I believe most generic or off-brand items are just as good as name brands.			

Add up your ratings. Interpret your total score according to this informal guide:

    12–15: Very aggressive saving style

    16–20: Careful saving style

    21–27: Fairly loose saving style

    28–32: Loose saving style

    33–36: Nonexistent saving style

    1. What are the advantages and disadvantages of your saving style?

    2. How do you think your saving style would affect your ability to keep to a budget?

    3. If you are dissatisfied with your saving style, how might you be able to change it?

To Try It online, go to Connect for *P.O.W.E.R. Learning and Your Life*.

You don't need to keep track of every penny you spend to evaluate your success in budgeting. As you gain more experience with your budget, you'll begin to get a better sense of your finances. You'll know when it may be possible to consider splurging on a gift for a friend, and when you need to operate in penny-pinching mode.

 ## Revisit Your Budget When Circumstances Change

Reviewing your budget on a regular basis is one thing, but most budgets should be revisited whenever your personal circumstances change in a significant way. Perhaps you've decided to move in with a friend and you plan to share expenses. Maybe the funds from your Registered Education Savings Plan (RESP) have run out and you still have a year of university to finish. Maybe you have to move and your rental costs are about to take a major jump. Or maybe the store where you work is closing and you are losing your job. Whatever the change in circumstances, you need to take immediate steps to rethink and revise your budget accordingly.

» LO 10.4 Using Credit Wisely

The first thing to learn about borrowing and credit is that there is good debt and there is bad debt. When you borrow money to invest in your education, it is considered good debt. Why? Because graduating from college or university is an investment in your future, one that can add well over $100 000 to your lifetime earnings, as you learned in **Try It! 3.** Bad debt is the kind that stems from borrowing to buy something you don't really need and can't really afford, like taking a trip to Florida during spring break and putting it on your credit card, knowing full well you don't have the money to pay for it now, and won't have the money to pay for it when the bill comes due. You are left with $1500 on your credit card and you can barely make the minimum payment. That's called bad debt.

While the return on your investment in education is generally very good, the upfront outlay of money is high; and for most students, borrowing is the only answer. But just as there is good debt and bad debt, there is also smart borrowing and stupid borrowing.

Smart borrowing is getting a loan that will provide you with the funds you need at the lowest possible interest rate and with the most flexible payment terms, then paying it off as quickly as you can.

Stupid borrowing is putting a major purchase on a department store credit card that charges 28% interest, then making only the minimum payment every month. Or buying something on the basis of "no money down, no interest, no payments for a year," paying a $99 fee for the privilege of doing so (read the fine print!), then not having the money available a year down the road, so you end up paying a year's worth of accrued interest and then some—at a horrifying interest rate—plus the $99 fee. All on top of the initial purchase price.

Credit does have a purpose, and there are ways to use it without getting in over your head. We'll discuss some of them in this next section.

How Credit Cards Work

You see them in the campus cafeteria: a couple of students, sitting at a table, with a poster behind them advertising a free T-shirt, a free Frisbee, free tickets to a basketball game. All free—just for signing up for ABC credit card. By now, you've learned that there is no such thing as a free lunch. So what is the catch? It's simple. Credit card companies make their money from cardholders who have difficulty making their payments every month, and students just happen to be one of the groups that fit that description perfectly. Now, you may consider yourself different from the average student, and maybe you are. Maybe you *will* be the exception to the rule, using your card only for emergencies, spending only what you can pay back when the bill arrives, paying every bill in full on the due date. But the hugely profitable credit card companies are betting against you—and their profits suggest they know their market rather well.

So how do credit cards work, and how can you make them work for you? Used properly, credit cards are tools that can help you manage your money. Here's how they work. When you use a credit card to make a purchase, you are essentially being given an interest-free loan for a period of up to 21 days (known as a "grace period"), after which you will have to pay the credit card company the amount of the original purchase in full, or begin paying interest on the amount they lent you.

According to the Canadian Bankers Association, 70 percent of households pay their credit card balance in full each month. Those households have had the use of someone else's money for 21 days, while their own money was hopefully collecting interest in a bank account somewhere. That's smart borrowing.

But 30% of households don't pay off their balance in full—and there are, unfortunately, lots and lots of students in that group. With interest rates for major credit cards usually hovering around 19.5%, and department store credit cards charging an obscenely high 28%, it doesn't take long for the interest charges to start to pile up. Now, that's we call stupid borrowing. Even stupider than that is using that same credit card to take out a "cash advance," where you get no grace period and the interest starts getting charged immediately, often at a higher interest rate than for a purchase, and with a transaction fee tacked on for good measure. A credit card cash advance should *never* be used unless there is truly a dire emergency. And while we're on the subject, ditto for a payday loan.

So why even bother getting a credit card in the first place? There are a few good reasons:

1) Credit cards are one of the most accepted forms of payment worldwide.

2) Sometimes there is no other payment alternative; e.g., try booking a hotel room or renting a car without one.

3) You need to start building up your credit rating.

What is a credit rating? A **credit rating** is a judgment about your credit worthiness given to you by an external agency called a credit reporting agency. Equifax and TransUnion are the two credit reporting agencies currently operating in Canada. These companies monitor and record every aspect of your credit history: when and where you've applied for credit, how much credit you can currently access, whether you've been paying your bills on time, and whether any of your payments are in arrears and by how much. The data they collect are reproduced in a credit *report* and summarized in a credit *score* that establishes your overall credit worthiness. While no one can access a report of your credit history without your express permission, you'll find that something as simple as renting an apartment will be difficult to do without giving a potential landlord that permission. If you have already built up a credit history and would like to see your credit *report,* you can obtain it free of charge by mail. However, if you need immediate online access to your credit report or you want access to your credit score, you will be charged. Visit **www.equifax.ca** or **www.transunion.ca** for details.

Credit rating
A judgment by a credit reporting agency about your credit worthiness

How Student Loans Work

Because the student loan programs in Canada vary from province to province, you will need to visit the website for your province to get specific details. That said, there are several things you need to know about student loans. First and foremost, for many students, while they provide you with a very good return on your investment, they are a significant financial liability. According to a report released in 2010 by Statistics Canada, undergraduate students paid an average of $5138 in tuition fees and another $702 in compulsory fees for things like athletics and student associations in 2010. And tuition is just the beginning. Based on figures from Statistics Canada and Université de Sherbrooke[5], the projected total cost of education for a student living at home and entering a four-year university program in 2013 is $34 321. This climbs to $59 599, if you choose to live away from home. That is a *lot* of potential debt. It is, therefore, not surprising that in a 2010 survey conducted for BMO by Leger Marketing, 64% of Canadians believe the cost of education is more than they can afford.[6]

When do you have to start making payments on your student loan? In the case of Canada Student Loans, they are interest-free while you are pursuing your education, but **they begin accumulating interest as soon as you complete your program.** While there is a six-month "grace period" before you have to start making payments, don't be fooled: If you wait six months, you will have an additional six months of interest tacked on to your overall payment, so start making payments as soon as you can. And graduation from your program is not the only condition for repayment of your loan to begin. The requirement to repay your loan also kicks in if you switch to part-time studies or stop going to school altogether. You need to stay in regular contact with your loan provider to ensure that they know you are still a student; otherwise, you may find yourself being asked to repay a loan when you simply chose to take six months off to make some money. If you are unable to make the payments, you will want to look into the Repayment Assistance Plan, which can provide you with some relief until your circumstances change.

What payments can you expect to have to make? Taking the projected average of $34 321 for a student in a 4-year program living at home, and assuming you decide to take advantage of the six-month grace period (when interest on the loan continues to accumulate and adds $1373 to your overall liability), you would find yourself paying $448/month for 120 months—that's ten years! If you elected to live away from home and paid the projected average of $59 599 over 4 years, you'd find yourself making payments (following the six-month grace period) of $778/month for ten years. The grace period alone would tack on $2384 to the overall payment due. By the time you'd finished paying off this loan, you would have paid a total of $88,688—and $26,705 of that is interest! To obtain your own estimate, go to **www.canlearn.ca** and look for the Loan Repayment Calculator.

How can you pay a student loan off sooner? Live simply, and borrow only as much as you absolutely need. Start paying it back as soon as you finish school, make lump sum payments whenever you can, and increase the amount you pay whenever you get a raise or your circumstances allow you to increase your payment.

If You Get In Over Your Head

All of us face financial difficulties at one time or another. Sometimes it happens suddenly and without warning. Other times people sink gradually into financial problems, each month accumulating more debt until they reach a point at which they can't pay their bills.

table 10.5 Steps to Help You Deal with Financial Difficulties

Assess the Problem	Make a list of what you owe and to whom. Figure out a reasonable amount you can put toward each debt. Work out a specific plan.
Contact Each of Your Creditors	Start with your bank, credit card companies, and landlord. Explain the situation. Show them your plan to pay off debt.
See a Credit Counsellor	If you cannot work out a repayment plan on your own, visit a credit counselling service. Your bank or creditor can help you identify a credit counsellor.
Stick to the Plan	Once you have a plan, make a commitment to stick to it.

However it happens, finding yourself with too little money to pay your bills requires action. You need to confront the situation and take steps to solve the problem. The worst thing to do is nothing. Hiding from those to whom you owe money makes the situation worse. Your creditors—the institutions and people to whom you owe money—will assume that you don't care, and they'll be spurred on to take harsher action.

There are several steps to take if you do find yourself in financial difficulty (see also **Table 10.5**):

> **Assess the problem.** Make a list of what you owe and to whom. Look at the bottom line and figure out a reasonable amount you can put toward each debt. Work out a specific plan that can lead you out of the situation.

> **Contact each of your creditors.** Start with your bank, credit card companies, and landlord, and if necessary continue through other creditors. It's best to visit personally, but a phone call will do.

> When you speak with them, explain the situation. If the problem is due to illness or unemployment, let them know. If it's due to overspending, let them know that. Tell them what you plan to do to pay off your debt, and show them your plan. The fact that you have a plan demonstrates not only what you intend to do, but also that you are serious about your situation and capable of financial planning.

> If you've had a clean financial record in the past, your creditors may be willing to agree to your plan. Ultimately, it is cheaper for them to accept smaller payments over a longer time than to hire a collection agency.

> **See a credit counsellor.** If you can't work out a repayment plan on your own, visit a credit counselling service. These are non-profit organizations that help people who find themselves in financial trouble. They can advise you on whether you need to consider a "consumer proposal." They can explain to you what bankruptcy involves, and show you how to dig yourself out of debt. To locate one near you, visit **www.creditcounsellingcanada.ca/**.

> **Stick to the plan.** Once you have a plan to get yourself out of debt, follow it. Unless you diligently make the payments you commit to, you'll find your debt spiraling out of control once again. It's essential, then, to regard your plan as a firm commitment and stick to it.

Time to Reflect: What Did I Learn?

1. Generally speaking, how would you characterize your money management skills?

2. Research has shown that although winning the lottery or other large sums of money brings an initial surge in happiness, a year later the winners' level of happiness returns to what it was before.[7] Why do you think this is true in general, and do you think it would it be true for you?

3. Based on what you learned about money management in this chapter, what changes do you plan to make in the way you handle your money in the future? Be specific.

Looking Back

What is stress, and how can I control it?

> Stress is a common experience. Three main types of stressors are cataclysmic events, personal stressors, and daily hassles. Excessive stress is not only unpleasant and upsetting, but it also has negative effects on the body and mind.

> Coping with stress involves becoming prepared for future stress through proper diet and exercise, identifying the causes of stress in your life, taking control of stress, seeking social support, practising relaxation techniques, training yourself to redefine and reinterpret stressful situations, and keeping your promises.

What is involved in keeping fit and healthy, and why is it important for me to do so?

> For all people, keeping fit and healthy is both essential and challenging. Balance your responsibilities by identifying your priorities and using time management techniques.

> Eating properly means eating a variety of foods on a regular schedule and restricting your intake of fat, cholesterol, and salt.

> Exercise is valuable because it improves health and well-being. Choosing exercises that you like, making everyday activities a part of exercise, and exercising with others can help form the habit of exercise.

> The third key element of good health is sleeping properly. Good exercise and eating habits can contribute to sound sleep, as can the development of regular sleeping habits and the use of sleep-assisting practices.

What are reasons for keeping to a budget, and how can I prepare and stick to one?

> Concerns about money can be significantly reduced through the creation of a budget by which spending and income can be planned, accounted for, and aligned with your goals.

> Budgets provide security by helping you control your finances and avoid surprises.

> The process of budgeting involves identifying sources of income, keeping track of current expenses, estimating future expenses, and making the necessary adjustments to keep income and spending in balance.

What is the difference between good and bad debt, and how do I ensure I use credit wisely?

> Good debt involves borrowing for the purpose of investing in your future earnings; it promises a future financial return. Bad debt involves borrowing for immediate consumption, with no possibility of future gain.

> Credit cards, when used wisely, are a very convenient payment instrument. To use them wisely, get a no-fee card, use it sparingly, and always pay the amount outstanding in full, and on the due date.

> If financial difficulties relating to credit do arise, contact your creditors and arrange a plan for paying off the debt. If you need help in designing a repayment plan, non-profit credit counsellors can help.

[KEY TERMS AND CONCEPTS]

Budget (p. 253)	Credit rating (p. 261)	Personal stressors (p. 240)
Cataclysmic events (p. 240)	Daily hassles (p. 240)	Social support (p. 245)
Coping (p. 241)	Disposable income (p. 252)	Stress (p. 240)

[RESOURCES]

ON CAMPUS

Many post-secondary institutions have mental health counsellors who can help you deal with emotional problems. If you are depressed, have trouble sleeping, or have other problems coping with the challenges of life, speaking with a counsellor can be extremely helpful. Check with your school's counselling centre or health centre to identify someone appropriate with whom to speak.

The office of the registrar, bursar, or treasurer handles money affairs at your college or university. Not only does it collect money owed for tuition, but it also may perform other services such as cashing cheques.

If you are receiving financial aid, there is usually a particular office devoted to the complexities of scholarships, loan processing, and other forms of aid. The personnel in the office can be very helpful in maximizing your financial aid package as well as in solving financial problems related to your schooling. If you have a problem with your finances, see them sooner rather than later.

IN PRINT

10 Simple Solutions to Stress: How to Tame Tension and Start Enjoying Your Life (New Harbinger Publications, 2007) provides 10 techniques for coping with stress and its effects on your health and your life.

Emotional Intelligence: Achieving Academic and Career Excellence, 2nd edition (Prentice Hall, 2011) is an interactive book that takes the theory of emotional intelligence and applies it to your academic life and career.

YOU: The Owner's Manual, Updated and Expanded Edition: An Insider's Guide to the Body that Will Make You Healthier and Younger (Collins Living, 2008) is an engaging and comprehensive book that provides practical information on how the body works, and also offers hundreds of pointers on how to live healthier, resist disease, and maintain a high quality of life.

A sequel to David Chilton's Canadian classic, *The Wealthy Barber* (Stoddard, 1989) will be published in 2011. In the meantime, the original book offers a clear and simple path to getting all your finances under control.

Murray Baker's national bestseller, *The Debt-Free Graduate* ((Money$marts Publishing, 2009) is a must-read for any student enrolled in a post-secondary institution. You can also visit the website at **www.debtfreegrad.com.**

ON THE WEB

The following websites provide the opportunity to extend your learning about the material in this chapter.

> You can learn more about maintaining variety in your diet by visiting the Health Canada's website (**www.hc-sc.gc.ca**), where you can download Canada's Food Guide, which is available not only in English and French, but also in Arabic, Chinese, Farsi, Korean, Russian, Punjabi, Spanish, Tagalog, Tamil, and Urdu. On the website, you can also construct a personalized food guide that involves choosing from a

large list of ingredients, including many commonly used in cooking by various ethnic groups; e.g., bok choy, paneer, couscous, bannock, lentils, and tortillas.

▸ Visit **www.mindfullivingprograms.com/whatMBSR.php** to learn more about Mindfulness Based Stress Reduction (MBSR) programs.

▸ The Government of Canada's **www.canlearn.ca** website is an excellent online resource, offering videos, quizzes, and plenty of information on funding your post-secondary education. The site also provides you with interactive tools such as a budget planner, a student financial assistance estimator, and a loan repayment estimator

▸ For budget trackers, credit and savings calculators, and other financial tools, check out these sites: **www.globecampus.ca/money-finder/financial-calculators, www. moneyville.ca,** and **www.nomoredebts.org.**

TAKING IT TO THE NET

1 Find two stress reduction techniques. One possible strategy: Go to Google (**www.google.ca**) and enter the phrase "stress reduction techniques" into the search field. Examine the sites identified until you find two stress reduction techniques that you like. Try each of the techniques. Do you feel less stressed and more relaxed? Which of the techniques works better for you? Why?

2 Discover three new ways to save money. Using the search engine of your choice, enter the phrase "saving money." Examine the sites for tips and tricks to help you hold on to what you earn.

The Case of . . .
The Breaking Point

Staring at the balance in his chequing account on the computer screen, Antonio Gagliardi thought to himself, *It is all over.*

"It" was his college career. For three semesters, Antonio had worked two jobs to pay his way through school. He'd been careful with his money, only rarely indulging in major new purchases such as a new computer and a refurbished car stereo.

Now, though, financial events beyond his control had taken their toll. His brother had broken his leg on a construction site and couldn't return to work for months. While details of compensation were being worked out, Antonio had helped support his brother and his young niece.

Staring at his chequing account, Antonio realized that supporting his brother had added up to a lot more than he thought. Now his tuition was due—and Antonio simply did not have the money. Antonio had never felt the sinking sensation he now experienced: After everything he'd done, he believed his college career was finished.

1. Is Antonio's college career really over? What should his next steps be if he wants to stay in college?

2. What can Antonio do in the long term to make sure he doesn't face a similar crisis down the road?

3. Is there anything Antonio could have done to have avoided this situation in the first place?

4. Do you think Antonio was right to support his brother while he was injured? Would you have done the same thing in a similar circumstance in your own life?

5. Have you ever had a moment when you thought your financial plans had been ruined? In the end, was the situation as bad as it first appeared?

Glossary

Academic honesty: Completing and turning in only one's own work under one's own name (Chapter 5)

Acrostic: A sentence in which the first letters of the words correspond to material that is to be remembered (Chapter 3)

Acronym: A word or phrase formed by the first letters of a series of words (Chapter 3)

Active listening: The intentional act of focusing on what is being said, making sense of it, and thinking about it in a way that permits it to be recalled accurately (Chapter 4)

Advance organizers: Broad, general ideas related to material that is about to be read or heard, which pave the way for subsequent learning (Chapter 3)

Analogy: A comparison between concepts or objects that are alike in some respects but dissimilar in most others (Chapter 8)

Arguments: Facts, research findings, or other evidence used to support a thesis (Chapter 7)

Attention span: The length of time that attention is typically sustained (Chapter 3)

Auditory/verbal learning style: A style that favours listening as the best approach to learning (Chapter 1)

Blended courses: Courses in which instruction is a combination of the traditional face-to-face classroom interaction and a significant amount of online learning; also called **hybrid courses** (Chapter 6)

Blog: A Web-based public diary in which a writer provides written commentary, ideas, thoughts, and short essays (Chapter 6)

Brainstorming: A process whereby ideas are generated by a group following a specific set of rules that do not permit censoring or critiquing of ideas as they are generated (Chapter 9)

Budget: A formal plan that accounts for income and expenditures (Chapter 10)

Career Portfolio: A dynamic record that documents your skills, capabilities, achievements, and goals, and provides a place to keep notes, ideas, and research findings related to careers (Chapter 11)

Cataclysmic events: Sudden, powerful events that occur quickly and affect many people simultaneously (Chapter 10)

Concept mapping: A method of structuring written material by graphically grouping and connecting key ideas and themes (Chapter 4)

Conversational markers: Non-verbal indications that we are listening to what someone else is saying (Chapter 9)

Coping: The effort to control, reduce, or learn to tolerate the circumstances that lead to stress (Chapter 10)

Cornell method of note taking: A method of structuring one's written notes into three categories: main notes, cures and questions, and a summary (Chapter 4)

Cramming: Hurried, last-minute studying (Chapter 5)

Credit rating: The judgment of a credit reporting agency about your credit worthiness (Chapter 10)

Critical thinking: A process involving reanalysis, questioning, and challenge of underlying assumptions (Chapter 1); the ability to reflect on our views about the world around us and why we think the way we do (Chapter 8)

Cultural competence: Knowledge and understanding about other ethnic groups, cultures, and minority groups (Chapter 9)

Culture: The learned behaviours, beliefs, and attitudes that are characteristic of an individual society or population, and the products that people create (Chapter 9)

Daily hassles: The minor irritants of life that, individually, produce little stress, but which can add up and produce more stress than a single, larger-scale event (Chapter 10)

Daily to-do list: A schedule showing the tasks, activities, and appointments due to occur during the day (Chapter 2)

Decision making: The process of deciding among various alternatives (Chapter 8)

Discrimination: Behaviour directed toward individuals on the basis of their membership in a particular group (Chapter 9)

Distance learning: A form of education in which students participate via the Web or other kinds of technology (Chapter 6)

Dry run: A rehearsal for a presentation in its entirety, from beginning to end, with all visuals (Chapter 7)

Educated guessing: The practice of eliminating obviously false multiple-choice answers and selecting the most likely answer from the remaining choices (Chapter 5)

Emoticons: Symbols (☺ ☹) used in email messages that provide information on the emotion that the writer is trying to convey; also called **smileys** (Chapter 6)

Emotional intelligence (EQ): According to Daniel Goleman, "abilities such as being able to motivate oneself and to persist in the face of frustrations; to control impulse and delay gratification; to regulate one's moods and to keep distress from swamping the ability to think; to empathize and to hope." (Chapter 9)

Ethnicity: Shared national origins or cultural patterns (Chapter 9)

Evaluation: An assessment of the match between a product or activity and the goals it was intended to meet (Chapter 1)

Flash cards: Index cards that contain key pieces of information to be remembered (Chapter 4)

Freewriting: A technique involving continuous, nonstop writing, without self-criticism, for a fixed period of time (Chapter 8)

Frontmatter: The preface, introduction, and table of contents of a book (Chapter 3)

Hearing: The involuntary act of sensing sounds (Chapter 4)

Hybrid courses : Instruction is a combination of the traditional face-to-face classroom interaction and a significant amount of online learning; also called blended courses (Chapter 6)

"I" statements: Responses spoken in terms of oneself and one's individual interpretation, rather than casting blame on the other person (Chapter 9)

Information competency: The ability to determine what information is necessary, and then to locate, evaluate, credit, and effectively use that information (Chapter 6)

Learning disabilities : Difficulties in processing information when listening, speaking, reading, or writing; in most cases, characterized by a discrepancy between learning potential and actual academic achievement (Chapter 1)

Learning style : One's preferred manner of acquiring, using, and thinking about knowledge (Chapter 1)

Long-term goals : Aims relating to major accomplishments that take some time to achieve (Chapter 1)

Master calendar: A schedule showing the weeks of a longer time period, such as a term or semester, with all assignments and important activities noted on it (Chapter 2)

Meta-message: The underlying main ideas that a speaker is seeking to convey; the meaning behind the overt message (Chapter 4)

Mind mapping: A visual technique which involves writing a central idea in the middle of a sheet of paper, then drawing "branches"; i.e., subtopics or themes which stem from the central idea. These subtopics can then be used to form a new thesis (Chapter 7)

Mnemonics: Formal techniques used to make material more readily remembered (Chapter 3)

Motivation: The inner power and psychological energy that directs and fuels our behaviour (Chapter 1)

Netiquette: Guidelines for demonstrating civility and respect in an online environment (Chapter 6)

Online database: An electronic, organized body of information on a related topic, or dealing with related media (Chapter 6)

Outline: A framework that sets out a logical progression or flow of ideas, prepared before the writing process begins (Chapter 7)

Overlearning: studying and rehearsing material past the point of initial mastery to the point at which recall becomes automatic (Chapter 3)

Personal stressors: Major life events that produce stress (Chapter 10)

Plagiarism: Taking credit for someone else's words, thoughts, or ideas (Chapter 5)

Podcast: An audio or video recording that can be accessed on the Internet and viewed on a computer or downloaded to a mobile device (Chapter 6)

P.O.W.E.R. Learning: A system designed to help people achieve their goals, based on five steps: *Prepare, Organize, Work, Evaluate,* and *Rethink* (Chapter 1)

Prejudice: Evaluations or judgments of members of a group that are based primarily on membership in the group and not on the particular characteristics of individuals (Chapter 9)

Presentation anxiety: Fear related to speaking in public (Chapter 7)

Priorities: The tasks and activities one needs and wants to do, rank-ordered from most important to least important (Chapter 2)

Problem solving: The process of generating alternatives to work on (Chapter 8)

Procrastination: The habit of putting off tasks that need to be accomplished (Chapter 2)

Read/write learning style: A style that involves a preference for written material, favouring reading over hearing and touching (Chapter 1)

Reflective feedback: A technique of active listening in which a listener rephrases what a speaker has said, trying to echo the speaker's meaning (Chapter 9)

Rehearsal: The process of practising and learning material to transfer it into memory (Chapter 3)

Short-term goals: Relatively limited steps you would take on the road to accomplishing your long-term goals (Chapter 1)

SMART approach to goal setting: A framework for goal setting that emphasizes that goals should be specific, measurable, achievable, realistic, and time-bound (Chapter 3)

Smileys: Symbols (☺ ☹) used in email messages that provide information on the emotion that the writer is trying to convey; also called **emoticons** (Chapter 6)

Social support: Assistance and comfort supplied by others in times of stress (Chapter 10)

SQ3R approach: Model for reading and comprehension based on these five steps: Survey, Question, Read, Recite, and Review (Chapter 3)

Stages in a group's evolution: According to psychologist Bruce Tuckman, all well-functioning groups go through five stages: forming, storming, norming, performing, and adjourning (Chapter 9)

Stereotypes: Beliefs and expectations about members of a group that are held simply because of their membership in the group (Chapter 9)

Stress: The physical and emotional response to events that threaten or challenge us (Chapter 10)

Study groups: Small, informal groups of students whose purpose is to help members work together and study for a test (Chapter 5)

Study notes : Notes taken for the purpose of reviewing material (Chapter 4)

Tactile/kinesthetic learning style: A style that involves learning by touching, manipulating objects, and doing things (Chapter 1)

Team charter: A set of written guidelines that outline the rules, roles, and responsibilities of team members, and set out how a team plans to operate towards achieving its goals (Chapter 9)

Test anxiety: A temporary condition characterized by fears and concerns about test taking (Chapter 5)

Thesis: A closely related set of ideas that suggest an angle or way of approaching a topic (Chapter 7)

Time log: A record of how one spends one's time (Chapter 2)

Visual/graphic learning style: A style that favours material presented visually in a diagram or picture (Chapter 1)

Visualization: A memory technique by which images are formed to help recall material (Chapter 3)

Vlog: A video version of a blog; Web-based public video diary (Chapter 6)

Weekly timetable: A schedule showing all regular, prescheduled activities due to occur in the week, together with one-time events and commitments (Chapter 2)

Workback: Planning when to start a project by working your way back from its due date (Chapter 2)

Working backward strategy: In problem solving, the strategy of starting at the desired solution or goal and working toward the starting point of the problem (Chapter 8)

Zero-sum game: A situation in which when one person wins, the other person automatically loses (Chapter 9)

Endnotes

Chapter 1

1. Day, J.C., & Newburger, E.C. (2002). The big payoff: Educational attainment and synthetic estimates of work–life earnings. *Current population reports, special studies*, p23-210. Washington, DC: Commerce Department, Economics and Statistics Administration, Census Bureau. Retrieved August 10, 2011 from http://www.census.gov/prod/2002pubs/p23-210.pdf
2. Gottesman, G. (1994). *College survival.* New York: Macmillan. 70.
3. *The American freshman: National norms for 2006.* American Council on Education and University of California at Los Angeles Higher Education Research Institute.

Chapter 2

1. Adapted from Ferner, J.D. (1980). **Successful time management.** New York: Wiley. 33.
2. Retrieved from http://www.marketingcharts.com/interactive/37-of-canadians-have-visited-a-social-network-29-have-a-profile-1898/ipsos-reid-canada-online-social-network-time-spent-usingjpg/

Chapter 3

1. Bransford, J.D., & Johnson, M.K. (1972). Contextual prerequisites for understanding: Some investigations of comprehension and recall. *Journal of Verbal Learning and Verbal Behavior*, 11, 722.
2. Gold, P.E. Cahill, L., & Wenk, G.L. (2003, April). The low-down on ginkgo biloba. *Scientific American*, 86–91.

Chapter 4

1. Tyler, S. (1997). *Been there, should've done that.* Haslett, MI: Front Porch Press. 117.
2. Adapted from Johnson, G. (2000). *The living world* (2nd ed.). New York: McGraw-Hill.
3. Tyler, S. (1997). *Been there, should've done that.* Haslett, MI: Front Porch Press. 114.

Chapter 5

1. Tobias, S. (1995). *Overcoming math anxiety.* New York: W. W. Norton & Company.
2. Tyler, S. (1997). *Been there, should've done that.* Haslett, MI: Front Porch Press. 128.

Chapter 6

1. Liebovich, L. (2000, August 10). Choosing quick hits over the card catalog. *The New York Times,* 1, 6. Based on material from Eliot Soloway, University of Michigan, School of Education.

Chapter 8

1. Nosich, G. (2005). *Learning to think things through: A guide to critical thinking across the curriculum* (2nd ed.) Pearson Prentice Hall. 2.
2. Adapted from Halpern, D.F. (1996). *Thought and knowledge: An introduction to critical thinking* (3rd ed.). Mahwah, NJ: Erlbaum; and Bransford, J.K, & Stein, B.S. (1993). *The ideal problem solver* (2nd ed.). New York: W.H. Freeman.

3. Forer, B. (1949). The fallacy of personal validation: A classroom demonstration of gullibility. *Journal of Abnormal and Social Psychology*, 44, 118–123.
4. Byrne, D., & Kelley, L. (1981). *An introduction to personality* (3rd ed.). Englewood Cliffs, NJ: Prentice Hall. 304.

Chapter 9

1. Woolley, A.W, Chabris, C.R., Pentland, A., Hashmi, N., & Malone, T.W. (2010, October 29). Evidence for a collective intelligence factor in the performance of human groups. Science 330 (6004), 686–88.
2. Goleman, D. Quoted at Big Dog & Little Dog's Performance Juxtaposition website. Retrieved August 10, 2011, www.nwlink.com/~donclark/performance/ei.html
3. Nolan, M.F. (1997, April 26). Tiger's racial multiplicity. *The Boston Globe*, A11.
4. Tatum, B.D. (1997). *"Why are all the black kids sitting together in the cafeteria?" And other conversations about race.* New York: Basic Books.

Chapter 10

1. Sax, L.J., Astin, A.W., Korn, W.S., & Mahoney, K. (1999). *The American freshman: National norms for fall 1999.* Los Angeles: Higher Education Research Institute, UCLA.
2. Chamberlain, K., & Zika, S. (1990). The minor events approach to stress: Support for use of daily hassles. *British Journal of Psychology*, 81, 469–481.
3. Carlson, R. (1997). *Don't sweat the small stuff . . . and it's all small stuff.* New York: Hyperion.
4. Pereira, M., Kartashov, A.I., Ebbeling, C.B., Van Horn, L., Slattery, M.L., Jacobs, Jr., D.R., & Ludwig, D.S. (2005, January 1). Fast-food habits, weight gain, and insulin resistance (The CARDIA Study): 15-year prospective analysis. *The Lancet, 365*, 36–42.
5. Desjardins Funds. The cost of postsecondary education. Retrieved August 1, 2011, from www.fondsdesjardins.com/en/produits/reee-cout.jsp. The figures used represent costs in the province of Quebec for a student starting post-secondary education in 2013. Students should note that tuition in Quebec is lower than in the rest of Canada.
6. BMO Financial Group (2010). Retrieved August 11, 2011, from http://www2.bmo.com/news/article/0,1083,contentCode-10390_divId-4_langId-1_navCode-112,00.html.
7. Diener, E., & Biswas-Diener, R. (2002). Will money increase subjective well-being? *Social Indicators Research, 57*, 119–169.

Chapter 11

1. Geist, S., referenced in Schacter, H. (2011, January 3). 10 must-ask job interview questions. *The Globe and Mail.* Retrieved August 10, 2011 from http://www.theglobeandmail.com/report-on-business/managing/morning-manager/ten-must-ask-job-interview-questions/article1855882/

Credits

Photo Credits

Page 1: Mel Yates/Stone+/Getty Images

Page 7: Commercial Eye/Iconica/Getty Images; Nick White/Digital Vision/Getty Images

Page 13: Jupiterimages/Workbook Stock/Getty Images

Page 18: Photos 12/Alamy

Page 28: Library of Congress, Prints and Photographs Division

Page 34: curved-light/Alamy

Page 45: Brand X Pictures/PunchStock

Page 48: Used with the permission of the Zits Partnership, King Features Syndicate and the Cartoonist Group. All rights reserved.

Page 55: George Doyle & Ciaran Griffin/Stockbyte/Getty Images

Page 62: Ken Banks/CORBIS

Page 70: Ian Shaw/Alamy

Page 71: Peanuts by Charles Schultz © United Feature Syndicate, Inc. Reprinted by permission.

Page 87: NEED FROM INDU

Page 89: Simon Jarratt/CORBIS

Page 99: Photodisc/Alamy

Page 110: Simon Jarratt/CORBIS

Page 115: Dennis MacDonald/Alamy

Page 120: Andersen Ross/Stockbyte/Getty Images

Page 126: Red Chopsticks/Getty Images

Page 137: Royalty-Free/CORBIS

Page 139: Used with permission from Microsoft.

Page 140: Used with permission from Microsoft.

Page 155: BananaStock/Jupiterimages

Page 158: © The New Yorker Collection 1993 Peter Steiner from cartoonbank.com. All Rights Reserved.

Page 161: © The New Yorker Collection 1993 Peter Steiner from cartoonbank.com. All Rights Reserved.

Page 170: © Petar Chernaev/iStockPhoto

Page 171: © Images.com/Corbis

Page 172: Reprinted with permission by IQ Matrix

Page 174: © Andrew Watt

Page 175: © geotrac/iStockPhoto

Page 178: © Monalyn Gracia/Corbis

Page 180: © Andrew Toos/www.CartoonStock.com

Page 182: © Kate Taylor/www.CartoonStock.com

Page 183: © Royalty-Free/Masterfile; © Cultura/Masterfile

Page 184: © RGJ -Richard Jolley/www.CartoonStock.com

Page 191: Satchan/CORBIS

Page 198: Eyebyte/Alamy

Page 199: © 2009 Charles Barsotti from cartoonbank.com. All Rights Reserved.

Page 203: FoxTrot © 2009 Bill Armend. Reprinted by permission of Universal Press Syndicate. All Rights Reserved.

Page 215: BananaStock/Jupiterimages

Page 217: Hiep Vu/Masterfile

Page 220: John Giustina/Iconica/Getty Images

Page 224: Ryan McVay/Getty Images

Page 227: Roy Hsu/UpperCut Images/Getty Images

Page 238: The McGraw-Hill Companies, Inc./Gary He, photographer

Page 239: Pardon My Planet (I Need Help) © Vic Lee. King Features Syndicate

Page 250: Rob Melnychuk/Getty Images

Page 254: DILBERT © 2004 Scott Adams. Used By permission of UNIVERSAL UCLICK. All rights reserved.

Index

A

Abbreviations
    medical assistant's perspective, 94
    note-taking, 93
Absolute Beginner's Guide to Computer Basics (Miller), 167
Absolute words, 124
Academic honesty, 126
Achievable goals, 10
Acronym, 77, 78
Acrostic, 78
Action words, essays, 123t, 125
Active listening, 91
Advanced search, 159–160, 159f, 160f
Advance organizers, 64–65, 66, 67
    exercise, 65, 67
Affirming Diversity (Nieto), 236
Aga Khan, 226
AlltheWeb.com, 157
Alta Vista, 157
American Psychological Association (APA), 162, 175
Analogy, 201
Anger diffusion, 229–230, 232
Annotated page
    exercise, 75
    sample, 73
Apple Safari, 141
Arguments, 171
Article conclusions, 66
The Art of the Moment: Simple Ways to Get the Most Out of Life (Vienne and Lennard), 60
Ask.com, 157
Asking the Right Questions: A Guide to Critical Thinking (Prentice Hall, 2009), 212
Assignments, completion of, 41, 43, 55, 88
Assumptions, 207
    and cultural competence, 227
Attention deficit hyperactivity disorder (ADHD), 27–28
Attention span
    definition, 68
    exercise, 69
Auditory/verbal learning style, 18–19
Axelrod, Alan, 60

B

Baker, Murray, 266
Barnum effect, 205
Berger, Lisa, 85
Blackboard (computer software), 142
Blended courses, 145
Blogs, 143
Bluetunes, 141
Bodily kinesthetic intelligence, 26, 26t
Brainstorming
    definition, 217
    exercise, 218
Breaking Through: College Reading (Smith), 85
Breaks, 50, 70
Brown-bag lunches, 258
Browsers, Web, 141
Buckley, Peter, 141, 167
Budget
    balancing, 257–258, 257t
    definition, 253

    expenditures, 255, 256t
    income, 254–255, 255t
    preparation, 254–257
    reviewing, 258, 260
    saving money, 258, 259
Business professional's perspective, presentations, 182
Business reports, 176–177

C

Campus resources
    computer lab, 167
    decision making, 211
    discrimination, 236
    financial aid, 266
    libraries, 167
    mental health counsellors, 266
    note-taking, 107
    presenting, 189
    problem solving, 211
    reading and remembering, 84–85
    technology, 167
    test-taking, 116–117, 134
    time management, 59
    typical resources, 31–32
    writing, 189
Canada Yearbook, 236
Canadian Mental Health Association (CMHA), 241
Career Connections
    budgeting, 257
    job interview, 185
    note-taking, 105
    and P.O.W.E.R. Learning, 16
    prospects, 5, 197, 198t
    reading, 81
    test-taking, 127
    time management, 55
    web skills, 162
    workplace diversity, 226
Carlson, Richard, 247
Case analysis, 177–178
Cataclysmic events, 240
Catalogue, library, 155
Causality exercise, 208
Check off, to-do list, 54
Chicago Style Guide, 175
Child-care demands, 54
Chilton, David, 266
Chin, Beverley, 134
Circular reasoning, 204
Class notes, evaluating, 101
    See also Note-taking
Cloud computing, 141
Coin toss, decision making, 198
Collaboration *See* groups
College
    See also Post-secondary education
    choosing, 4f
Commitments, and stress management, 245
Common sense, 205, 207
Common Sense (Paine), 66
Communication, 4
    group, 220–221
    and stress management, 248
Community service, and cultural competence, 227

Companion websites, 143
Computer
    calendar and to-do system, 140–141, 140f
    desktop icons, organizing, 139, 139f
    folders, 140, 140f
Concept mapping, 96–97, 97f
Conflict resolution, 229–233
Connectivism, 153
Control, 12, 13
Conversational markers, 220–221
Cookie, 142
Coping
    definition, 241
    strategies, 241, 244–245, 247–249
Cornell method of note-taking, 96, 96f
Cortina, Joe, 85
Course Connections
    big picture, 11
    classroom diversity, 229
    critical thinking, 207
    math anxiety techniques, 119
    note-taking, 102
    PowerPoint presentations, 144
    presentations, 184
    staying alert, 252
    study time, 40
    textbooks, 71
Course-taking personal style, 146
Course websites, 142–143
Course work as test preparation, 112
Covey, Stephen, 60
Cramming, 118, 120
Credit
    counsellors, 263
    use of, 260–263
Credit cards, 260–261
Credit rating, 261
Critical thinking, 3
    avoidance of, 204–207
    in classroom, 207
    definition, 15, 192
    note-taking, 100–101, 103
    pitfalls, 204–207
    in problem solving, 199–204
    and reading, 80
Cultural competence, 224, 227–228
Culture
    definition, 222–224
    and ethnicity, personal, 228–229
    exercise, 223t

D

Daily hassles, 240, 240f
Daily to-do list, 43, 49f
    check off, 49f, 54
The Debt-Free Graduate (Baker), 266
Decision making
    alternatives, identification of, 193
    alternatives assessment, 193–195
    alternatives selection, 195–198
    career prospects, 197, 198t
    decision tree, 196f
    definition, 192
    in everyday life, 209
    framework, 192–199
    outcome consideration, 198–199
    pitfalls, 204–207

pros and cons list, 195f
reconsidering, 199
Decision tree, 196f
Delicious, 141
DePorter, Bobbi, 107
Desire2learn, 142
Dictionary, 73
Diet, and stress management, 248–249
Differences, acceptance, 227–228
Digital readers, 76
Discrimination, 225–227
Disposable income, 252
Distance learning
    definition, 145
    exercise, 148
Distractions
    listening, 221
    and reading, 70
    and time management, 49–51
Diversity, 4–5, 221–224
    acceptance, 224–225
    in classroom, 229
    exercise, 224
    generations, workplace
        characteristics, 223t
Diversity Wheel, 222f
Draft, for writing, 173–174
Dranitsaris, Anne, 21
Drawing, in problem solving, 201, 204
Drexler, Wendy, 153
Dry run, 180
Duarte, Nancy, 189
Durand, Alexandre, 238
Dyslexia, 27

E

Earnings, post-secondary vs. high school
    graduate, 3
*Eat That Frog! 21 Great Ways to Stop
    Procrastinating and Get More Done in Less
    Time* (Axelrod and Tracy), 60
E-books, 143
E-breaks, 50
ECollege, 142
E-distractions, 50
Editing, writing sample, 176
Editorial assistant, reading perspective, 80
Educated guessing, 124–125
Einstein, Albert, 28
Elder, Janet, 85
Elder-care demands, 55–56
Electronic catalogue, 155
Email, 151–152
    address, 150
    effective use of, 151–152
    netiquette, 152
Emerson, Ralph Waldo, 247
Emoticon, 150
Emotional intelligence (EQ)
    definition, 217
    and stress management, 241t
*Emotional Intelligence: Achieving Academic and
    Career Excellence* (Prentice Hall), 266
Employability Skills 2000+, 5, 6f
Encyclopedias, 155
Endnote, 163
End-of-chapter summaries, 64, 66
Ennis, Robert, 192
Essay tests, 114, 114t, 122–124
    action words, 123t
    exercise, 125
Ethnicity
    definition, 222–224
    personal, 228–229

Evaluate, P.O.W.E.R. Learning step
    decision making, 198–199
    described, 13–15
    distance learning, 149
    groups, 219
    money management, 258, 260
    note-taking, 100–101
    reading, 80–81
    test-taking, 126–128
    time management, 56
    writing, 174–175
Evaluation, 14
Exercise, and stress management, 249
Expenditures, 255, 256t
*The Extreme Searcher's Internet Handbook: A
    Guide for the Serious Searcher* (Hock), 167

F

Facebook, 143, 216
Fact vs. opinion, 205
    exercise, 206
Family demands, 54–56
Feedback, presentations, 184
    exercise, 185
Fences (computer software), 139
Fill-in question tests, 114, 114t, 124
    exercise, 130
Financial aid office, 266
Financial difficulties, 262–263, 263t
Flash cards, 104
Flextime, 54
Flickr, 141
Fogler, Janet, 85
Free applications, 142
Freedigitalphotos.net, 181
Freewriting
    definition, 193
    exercise, 194
Frontmatter, 66

G

Gardner, Howard, 25
Gender prejudice, 225
Generalities, 204–205
Generations, workplace characteristics, 223t
Gladwell, Malcolm, 32
Glossary, 104
Goals
    course, 88
    identifying instructor's, 88
    measurement, 8
    note-taking, 88–89
    setting, 8–10
    SMART approach, 8–10
Goleman, Daniel, 217
Google, 157, 159f, 160f
Google Calendar, 141, 140f
Google Chrome, 141
Google Docs, 141, 144
Gordon, Barry, 85
Gottesman, Greg, 159
Government documents, 155
Graduate's perspective on personal budget, 255
Groups
    adjourning stage, 219–220
    communication, 220–221
    forming stage, 218
    function, determination, 217–218
    norming stage, 219
    performing stage, 219
    selection of members, 216–217
    stages in a group's evolution, 217

storming stage, 219
team charter, 218–219
topic selection for group project, 217
working productively in, 216–220
Gut feeling, 196, 198

H

Hamlet (Shakespeare), 13
Handouts, 184
Hansom, Bell, 54
Health, and stress management, 247, 248–250
Hearing, 90–91
Hernacki, Mike, 107
Hicks, R.D., 57
Highlighting
    key points, 72
    while reading, 90
Hock, Randolph, 167
How to Ace Any Test (Chin), 134
How to Do Everything with Microsoft Outlook
    (Mann), 60
*How to Study: Use Your Personal Learning
    Style to Help You Succeed When It Counts*
    (Wood), 32
Hubble space telescope, 15
Human resources specialist's perspective on
    relationships, 230
Hybrid courses, 145

I

IGoogle, 161f
Imaginary Conversations (Landor), 72
Improving Your Memory (Fogler and Stern), 85
Impulse buying, 258
Income, 254–255, 255t
Information competency, development of,
    153–161
Information feeds, organizing, 161, 161f
Information storage, 79
Initial recording, memory, 79
Insider's Guide to Beating Test Anxiety, 134
Instructions, tests, 121, 124
Instructor style, and note-taking, 89, 98–99
Intelligence, multiple forms, 25–26
Intelligent Memory (Gordon and Berger), 85
Internet, 141, 148, 150
    See also web (World Wide Web, www)
Internet Explorer, Microsoft, 141
Interpersonal intelligence, 25, 26t
Interruptions
    manage, 70
    and reading, 70
    and time management, 37, 50
In-text review questions and tests, 81
Intrapersonal intelligence, 26, 26t
IPad, 76
"I" statements
    definition, 230
    exercise, 231

J

Job interviews, 185
Jumping to conclusions, 205

K

Kaiser, Henry J., 200
Keller, Helen, 89
Kesselman-Turkel, Judy, 107

Key ideas and words, lecture note-taking, 91–92, 95, 105
Keywords, 158–159
Khan, Melissa, 137
Kindle, 76
Knowles, Jeff, 62
Kobo, 76

L

Landor, Walter Savage, 72
Lao Tzu, 7
Laptop computer
 note-taking, 90
 study notes, 105
Law enforcement professional's perspective on technology, 157
Learning, lifelong habit, 5
Learning centre resources, 116
Learning disabilities, 27–28
Learning styles
 definition, 18
 described, 17–18, 19t
 exercise, 20–21
 key facts, 27
 reading attention span, 68
Learning to Think Things Through: A Guide to Critical Thinking Across the Curriculum (Nosich), 212
Lecture notes, 100f
 See also Note-taking
Lecture outlining, 95
Legal assistant's perspective, test-taking, 128
Lennard, Erica, 60
Less-absolute words, 124
Libraries
 basic collection, 154–156
 catalogue, 155
 library databases *vs.* web, 154t
Linguistic intelligence, 25, 26t
Linked In, 144, 216
Linnell, Jessica, 32
Lipson, Charles, 32
Listening, 220–221, 232
Listening style, 91
Live Mesh, 141
Lives and Opinions of Eminent Philosophers (Hicks), 57
Loan Repayment Calculator, 262
Locke, John, 82
Logical-mathematical intelligence, 25, 26t
Long-term goals
 definition, 8
 exercise, 9
Loose-leaf notebook, 90

M

Mann, Bill, 60
Mason, Douglas, 85
Master calendar, 43, 44f
Matching question tests, 114–115, 114t, 126
 exercise, 130
Math anxiety techniques, 119
Maxims (Napoleon I), 193
McLuhan, Marshall, 181
Measurable goals, 8
Medical assistant's perspective, abbreviations, 94
Meditation, 245
Meetings, note-taking, 105
Memory
 identification of key points for reading, 66–67
 note-taking, 102–103
 strategies, 76–80

The Memory Doctor (Mason and Smith), 85
Mental health counsellors, 266
Mental health self-assessment, 242–243
Mental movie, 196
Mental organization, 11
Meta-message, 91
Meta-search tools, 157
Microsoft Outlook, 141
Miller, Michael, 167
Mind mapping, 172, 172f
 exercise, 173
Minor irritants, and stress, 240
Mnemonics, 77
Modern Language Association (MLA), 162, 175
Money management, 250
 budget, preparation, 254–257
 dealing with difficulties, 262–263, 263t
 expenditures, 253–254, 255, 256t
 income, 254–255, 255t
 needs *vs.* wants, 252–253
 saving money, 258, 259
Motivation, 12
Mozilla, Firefox, 141
Multiculturalism, 2f
Multiple-choice tests, 114–115, 114t, 124
 exercise, 130
Multiple intelligence, 25–26, 26t, 27
Multiple senses, and remembering, 79
Multi-tasking, and stress management, 248
Musical intelligence, 26, 26t
Musical scores, 155
MySpace, 143

N

Napoleon I, 193
Naturalistic intelligence, 26, 26t
Needs *vs.* wants, 252–253
Nenshi, Naheed, 215
Netiquette
 described, 150–152
 exercise, 152
 in-person, 153
The Networked Student (Drexler), 153
New situations, 4
Nieto, Sonia, 236
Nonverbal signals, lecture note-taking, 92
Noodlebib, 163
Nosich, Gerald M., 212
Note-taking
 abbreviations, 93
 active listening, 91
 balance between too many and too few, 99–100
 in class, 93–98
 concept mapping, 96–97, 97f
 critical thinking, 100–101, 103
 effective, 100–102, 103
 evaluating, 100–101
 goals identification, 88–89
 instructor style, 89, 98–99
 integration text and study notes, 104
 meetings, 105
 memory, 102–103
 on non-writable material, 104–105
 outlining, 94–95, 94f
 phrases, 92
 PowerPoint handout, 97–98, 98f
 question asking, 99
 sharing notes, 100f
 skill practice, 103
 study notes, 103–104
 tools, 89–90
 while reading, 72
 on written material, 104

Note-Taking Made Easy (Kesselman-Turkel and Peterson), 107
Nursing assistant, learning styles, 19

O

Odes (Pindar), 129
Office Live, 137, 144
Off-peak periods, 45
Off to College: Now What? (Linnell), 32
Of the Conduct of the Understanding (Locke), 82
Online databases, 154–155
Online learning centres, 143, 145
Online review questions and tests, 81
Online Writer's Lab (OWL), 175
On-the-job time management, 55
Opening Doors: Understanding College Reading (Cortina and Elder), 85
Opinion *vs.* fact, 205
 exercise, 206
Organize, P.O.W.E.R. Learning step
 decision making, 193–195
 described, 10–11
 distance learning, 148
 groups, 217
 money management, 254–257
 note-taking, 89–90
 reading, 67–68
 test-taking, 120–121
 time management, 43–49
 writing, 173
Ortiz, Matt, 87
Outliers: The Story of Success (Gladwell), 32
Outlines
 advance organizer, 66, 67f
 definition, 173
 for note-taking, 94–95
 sample, 94f
 for writing, 173
Outlining, 96
Overlearning, 79–80

P

P.O.W.E.R. Learning
 framework, 5–7
 and work, 16
P.O.W.E.R. Plan
 decision making, 192
 distance learning, 147
 groups and teams, 216
 money management, 253
 reading, 64
 time management, 35
 writing, 172
Paine, Thomas, 66
Panic, test-taking, 121, 128
Paper-based periodicals, 154
Perfectionism, 17
Periodicals, library, 154
Personal cultural background, 228–229
Personal finance, knowledge of, 251
Personal identification, in reading, 65
Personality style *See* Striving Styles™ Personality Assessment
Personal stressors, 240
Personal style
 course-taking, 146
 saving, 259
 time management, 56–57
Peterson, Franklynn, 107
Peterson's Guide to Online Learning, 167
Pharmacy technician's perspective, asking questions, 203

Phrase writing, in note-taking, 92
Physical organization, 11
Picasa, 141
Pindar, 129
Plagiarism
    avoiding, 175
    definition, 126, 163
    detection programs, 164
    types of, 163–164
Podcasts, 143
Point of view, author's, 65
Positive thinking, 13
Post-secondary education
    See also College
    benefits of, 2–5
    reasons for attending, 3
PowerPoint
    effective presentations, 180–182
    instructors' presentation, 144
    and note-taking, 97–98, 98f
Pre-class warm-up, 89
Prejudice, 225–227
Prepare, P.O.W.E.R. Learning
    time management, 36–37
Prepare, P.O.W.E.R. Learning step
    decision making, 192–193
    described, 7–10
    distance learning, 147–148
    groups, 216–217
    money management, 253–254
    note-taking, 88–89
    reading, 64–67
    test-taking, 112–120
    writing, 172–173
Presentation anxiety
    definition, 178
    exercise, 179
Presentations, 178–186
    anxiety, overcoming, 178–179
    audience involvement, 183
    beginning, 182–183
    checklist, 184
    clothing choices, 182
    dry run, 180
    ending, 183–184
    environment, 182
    feedback, 184
    handouts, 184
    plan, 180
    slides, use of, 180–182
    switching it up, 183
    visuals, use of, 180–182
Print resources
    in general, 32
    time management, 60
Priorities
    competing, 37, 39–40
    definition, 37
    list, 40f
    setting, 39–41, 40f, 42f
    and stress management, 247
Prioritization, and reading, 80
Problem solving
    causality exercise, 208
    critical thinking, 199–204
    critical thinking, avoidance of, 204–207
    definition, 200
    in everyday life, 209
    exercise, 202
    fact *vs.* opinion, 205, 206
    identification of problem, 200
    pitfalls, 204–207
    reflection of process, 203–204
    solution assessment, 202–203
    strategies, 200–201

Procrastination, 51–53
Procrastination quotient, 53
Pros and cons list, 195f

Q

Quantum Notes (DePorter and Hernacki), 107
Questioning, 65, 93, 221
    See also SQ3R approach to reading

R

Reading
    author's point of view, 65
    digital, 76
    focusing, 70
    purpose of assignment, 65
    and reciting, 70–75
    and rereading, 76
    retention, 63–64
    strategies, 70–73, 76–80
    timing, 68
    tools, 67–68
    and writing, 70–75
Read/write learning style, 18
Realistic goals, 10
Real Simple Syndication (RSS), 160, 160f
Reflective feedback, 221
RefWorks, 163
Registrar's Office, 59
Rehearsal, 77
Relaxation, and stress management, 245
Remember the Milk, 141
Rephrase, while reading, 72
Reserve collections, 155–156
Responsibility
    for personal failure and success, 13
    prioritize, 247
Rethink, P.O.W.E.R. Learning step
    decision making, 199
    described, 15–17
    distance learning, 149–150
    groups, 219–220
    money management, 260
    note-taking, 102–103
    reading, 82
    test-taking, 128–129
    time management, 56–57
    writing, 175–176
Retrieval, memory, 79
Robinson, Francis, 64
Rogers, Carl, 221
Roosevelt, Theodore, 199
*The Rough Guide to Cloud Computing: 1
    00 websites that will change your life*
    (Buckley), 141–142, 167

S

Saving style, 259
Search engines
    advanced search, 159–160, 159f, 160f
    described, 156–157
    exercise, 157
    use of, 156f
Section objectives, advance organizer, 66
Seinfeld, Jerry, 178
The Seven Habits of Highly Successful People
    (Covey), 60
Shakespeare, William, 13
Short-answer tests, 114, 114t, 124
    exercise, 131

Short-term goals
    definition, 8
    exercise, 9
Silver lining coping strategy, 245, 246
Singh, Nandini, 1
Skills Assessment and Portfolio Building Tool
    (SCT), 5
Sleep, and stress management, 249–250
*Slide-ology: The Art and Science of Creating Great
    Presentations* (Duarte), 189
Sliderocket, 141
SMART approach to goal setting, 8–10
Smiley, 150
Smith, Brenda, 85
Smith, Spencer, 85
Social networking, time spent on, 52f
Social networking websites, 143–145
Social support, 245
Sony Reader, 76
Soriano, Bayani, 191
Spatial intelligence, 25, 26t
Specific goals, 8
Speed reading, 63–64
Spielberg, Steven, 18
SQ3R approach to reading, 64
Stages in a group's evolution, 217
Stereotypes, 225–227
Stern, Lynn, 85
Stevenson, Adlai, 253
Stress
    definition, 240
    and emotional intelligence (EQ), 241t
    and health, 247, 248–250
    managing, 241, 244–245, 247–249
    in perspective, 247
    physical reaction to, 240–241
    sources of, 239–240
Stressor, 240
Stress-related illness, 239
Striving style, definition, 21
Striving Styles™ Personality Assessment
    collaborating with others, 219
    decision making, 209
    described, 21, 25t
    exercise, 22–24
    key facts, 27
    presenting, 186
    problem solving, 209
    reading and remembering, 63
    test-taking, 121
    writing, 186
Student loans, 262
Student perspective of
    decision making, 196
    diversity, 225
    effective writing using technology, 177
    reading retention, 72
    stress, 247
    technology, 143
    time logs, 37, 37f
The Student's Guide to Exam Success (Tracy), 134
Study group
    definition, 115
    forming, 115–116, 117
    and reading comprehension, 81
Study group exercises
    book page annotation, 74
    decision making, freewriting, 194
    distance learning, 148
    essay tests, 131
    lecture outline, 95
    note-taking, 101
    personal finance, knowledge of, 251
    problem solving skills, 202
    procrastination, 53
    silver lining coping strategy, 246

Study group exercises
    study group, formation, 117
    success and failure, 14
    switch "you" to "I" statements, 231
    time log, 39
Study notes
    See also Note-taking
    definition, 104
    laptop, 105
Study time, 40
Succeeding as an International Student in the
    United States and Canada (Lipson), 32
Success and failure exercise, 14
Support groups, and stress management, 245
Surprises, and time management, 49–51
Surveying, 64
    See also SQ3R approach to reading
SWOT analysis, 177

T

Table of contents, 66
Tactile/kinesthetic learning style, 19
Taking charge, and stress management, 244
Talking out loud, in reading, 80
Tatum, Beverly, 224, 236
Team charter
    definition, 218
    sample, 219
Teams and teamwork *See* groups
Technology
    See also Internet
    advances, 4
    appropriate use, 150–151
    and course work, 142–143
    distance learning, 145–147
    and group work, 143–145
    and information competency, 153–161
    netiquette, 150–153
    and networking, 143–145
    as organizational tool, use of, 138–142
    time management, 51
10 Simple Solutions to Stress: How to Tame
    Tension and Start Enjoying Your Life (New
    Harbinger Publications), 266
Test anxiety, 117–120
Tests, 111–112
    learning from, 128–129
    machine-scored, 122
    questions, types of, 114–115, 114t
    types of, 113t
Test-taking
    answer specific questions, 122–126
    checking over, 126–127
    cramming, 118, 120
    exercise, 130–131
    practice, 115
    preparation, checklist, 116
    preparation, course work, 112
    preparation, test yourself, 115
    stopping, 127–128
    strategies, 114–117, 121–126
    style, 118
    tools, 120
Textbook
    companion websites, 143
    taking to class, 90
    writing in, 70–75
Textbook Online Learning Centres, 143
Texting (text messaging), 150, 151
Text messages, 150, 151
Thesis, 171

Time-bound goals, 10
Time log, 37, 37f, 38–39
Time management
    balance school, work and family demands,
      54–56
    balance school and work demands, 54
    career, 55
    control of environment, 50–51
    definition, 35
    effective, 35
    on-the-job, 55
    personal style, 56–57
    priorities, 37, 39–41
    and procrastination, 51–53
    and stress reduction, 247–248
    working parent perspective, 49
Time style, 36
Topic selection for group project, 217
Tracy, Brian, 60
Tracy, Eileen, 134
Travel, and cultural competence, 227
True-false tests, 114–115, 114t, 125–126
    exercise, 131
Trukese people, 17
Tufte, Edward, 181
Tutorial centre resources, 116–117
Twitter, 141

U

Underlining, 72

V

Vienne, Veronique, 60
Visual aids, while reading, 72–73
Visual/graphic learning style, 18
Visualization, 79, 79f
Vlogs, 143

W

The Wall Street Journal Guide to Information
    Graphics (Wong), 189
The Wealthy Barber (Chilton), 266
Web (World Wide Web, www)
    address, 150, 156, 158
    browsers, 141
    civility, on the, 150–151
    information evaluation, 160–161
    information location, 156–157
    skills, 162
    vs. library databases, 154t
WebCT, 142
Web resources
    conflict resolution, 236
    critical thinking, 212
    decision making, 212
    emotional intelligence, 236
    groups, 236
    health, 266–267
    learning, 32
    libraries, 167–168
    money management, 267
    note-taking, 108
    presenting, 189
    problem solving, 212
    reading and remembering, 85
    stress, 266–267
    student loans, 267

    technology, 167–168
    test-taking, 134
    time management, 60
    writing, 189
Website credibility, 157–158
Weekly timetable, 43, 46f, 47f
Why Are All the Black Kids Sitting Together in the
    Cafeteria? (Tatum), 224, 236
Wikipedia, 161
Windows Explorer, 139
Windows Live Calendar, 141
Win–win proposition, 230–233
Wong, Dona M., 189
Wong, Jen, 34
Wood, Gail, 32
Work, P.O.W.E.R. Learning step
    decision making, 195–198
    described, 12–13
    distance learning, 149
    groups, 217–218
    money management, 257–258
    note-taking, 90–93
    reading, 70–73
    test-taking, 121–126
    time management, 49–56
    writing, 173–174
Workback, 48–49
Work demands, 54
Working backward, 201
Working parent perspective, time management,
    49
Working with others, 52
Writer's block, 174
Writing
    business reports, 176–177
    case analysis, 177–178
    and distance learning, 146
    guidelines, 171–172
    initial draft, 173–174
    process of, 172–178
    rest, reread, revise, 174–175
    sample, before and after editing, 176
    in textbook, 70–75
Written material, note-taking, 104
www.canlearn.ca, 262
www.creditcounsellingcanada.ca, 263
www.equifax.ca, 261
www.listorious.com, 160
www.toodledo.com, 141
www.transunion.ca, 261
www.turnitin.com, 164

Y

Yahoo!, 156
YOU: The Owner's Manual, Updated and
    Expanded Edition: An Insider's Guide to the
    Body That Will Make You Healthier and
    Younger (Collins Living), 266

Z

Zeno of Citium, 221
Zero-sum game, 233
Zoho, 144
Zotero, 163

NOTES

NOTES

NOTES

NOTES

NOTES

NOTES